The Waite Group's
MS-DOS® Bible

HOWARD W. SAMS & COMPANY
HAYDEN BOOKS

Related Titles

**The Waite Group's
MS-DOS® Developer's Guide,
Revised Edition**
John Angermeyer and Kevin Jaeger

**The Waite Group's
Understanding MS-DOS®**
Kate O'Day and John Angermeyer

**The Waite Group's
Tricks of the MS-DOS®
Masters**
*John Angermeyer, Rich Fahringer,
Kevin Jaeger, and Dan Shafer*

**The Waite Group's
Discovering MS-DOS®**
Kate O'Day

**Hard Disk Management
Techniques for the IBM®**
Joseph-David Carrabis

**IBM® PC AT User's
Reference Manual**
Gilbert Held

**IBM® PC & PC XT User's
Reference Manual,
Second Edition**
Gilbert Held

**The Waite Group's
Desktop Publishing Bible**
*James Stockford, Editor,
The Waite Group*

**Personal Publishing with PC
PageMaker®**
Terry Ulick

Micro-Mainframe Connection
Thomas Wm. Madron

**The Waite Group's
Modem Connections Bible**
*Carolyn Curtis, Daniel Majhor,
The Waite Group*

**The Waite Group's
Printer Connections Bible**
*Kim G. House, Jeff Marble,
The Waite Group*

*For the retailer nearest you, or to order directly from the publisher,
call 800-428-SAMS. In Indiana, Alaska, and Hawaii call 317-298-5699.*

The Waite Group's
MS-DOS® Bible

Second Edition

Steven Simrin

HOWARD W. SAMS & COMPANY

A Division of Macmillan, Inc.
4300 West 62nd Street
Indianapolis, Indiana 46268 USA

International Standard Book Number: 0-672-22617-0
Library of Congress Catalog Card Number: 88-60064

From The Waite Group:
Developmental Editor: Mitchell Waite
Editorial Director: James Stockford
Technical Reviewer: Blair Hendrickson

From Howard W. Sams & Company:
Acquisitions Editor: James S. Hill
Manuscript Editor: Diana Francoeur
Cover Artist: Kevin Caddell
Chapter Opening Art: Bob Johnson
Illustrators: Ralph E. Lund, William D. Basham
Indexer: Ted Laux
Typographer: Shepard Poorman Communications, Indianapolis

Printed in the United States of America

Trademarks

To Benjamin, to the one to come, and to the memory of Jeb

Contents

Part 4   Appendixes

A   MS-DOS Interrupts and Function Calls

B   Some Undocumented Features of MS-DOS

C   Practical Batch Files

Preface
to the First Edition

This book is about MS-DOS, the powerful disk operating system developed by Microsoft for microcomputers. MS-DOS is the manager of your computer. It is responsible for supervising the flow of information into and out of your machine and for controlling the interaction of the various parts of your computer system. This book will show you how to master MS-DOS and take advantage of its enormous capabilities. It is an easy-to-use guide, written to provide you with a ready reference to both the fundamentals and the more-advanced aspects of MS-DOS.

When I first began using MS-DOS, I quickly realized that I was virtually on my own. While it was easy to find material on the basics of MS-DOS, most advanced sources of information were hard to find and often quite sketchy in their treatment. Many questions came up for which I could find no answer. I would spend hours pouring over user's manuals, magazine articles, and how-to books. Often my searches were fruitless, and I would end up sitting in front of my computer, trying to figure things out for myself. Of course, experimenting is half the fun of using a computer, but it can be frustrating when you are in a hurry or you simply aren't in the mood for experimenting. I determined to spare others some of these "laboratory experiments" and share the results of my research.

The result has been this book. *MS-DOS Bible* is for all users of MS-DOS, from beginners to computer professionals. It begins with starting up your system and creating, editing, and managing files. It moves on to data handling and customizing your keyboard. Then it covers such advanced topics as exploring with DEBUG, using LINK, and understanding the structure of MS-DOS.

This book features:

▶ Learn-by-doing approach
▶ Jump table for quick access of specific topics
▶ Step-by-step tutorials

- ► Coverage of the basics up through advanced programming information
- ► Special in-depth section on MS-DOS commands
- ► Appendixes listing error messages, function calls and interrupts, practical batch files, and ASCII codes

MS-DOS Bible assumes no prior knowledge on your part. Each topic is discussed in a logical fashion from beginning to end, without relying on computerese. Those of you who are interested in only an overview of a topic can skim for highlights. Those who are interested in details will find them here, presented thoroughly and clearly.

Acknowledgments to the First Edition

I am grateful to all who provided assistance during the writing of *MS-DOS Bible*. In particular, I would like to thank Mike Van Horn of The Waite Group, who initially suggested that I write this book. Many thanks to Mary Johnson, also of The Waite Group, who acted as my editor. Finally, special thanks to family members and friends who gave valuable encouragement and moral support throughout the project.

Preface
to the Second Edition

It has been three years since I wrote the first edition of *MS-DOS Bible*. At that time, IBM PCs and PC compatibles were starting to appear in businesses and homes worldwide. With each computer came a copy of the still young MS-DOS. Things were different back then. There was little talk of TSRs, PC networks, ATs, or 386 machines. Fixed disks were still somewhat of a luxury, and 640 Kbytes of memory seemed to be more than anyone could possibly ever use. Obviously a lot has happened in three years, and MS-DOS has had to grow to accommodate these changes.

MS-DOS is now the most widely used microcomputer operating system in the world. This is not surprising, given the incomparable marketing strength of IBM, but it is significant in understanding how MS-DOS has evolved over the years. Many new demands have been placed on MS-DOS. Many of these demands were not anticipated when the operating system was first designed. In most cases, ways have been found to satisfy the demands simply because the market for a solution was so strong.

The changes in this second edition of *MS-DOS Bible* mirror the changes that have occurred in MS-DOS. The primary objective of the book continues to be to provide the reader with an up-to-date, comprehensive, easy-to-understand guide. *MS-DOS Bible* is designed for all users of MS-DOS. No assumptions are made about a reader's computer expertise. A strong attempt has been made to make the book as self-contained as possible. Information needed to understand the more advanced topics is thoroughly presented in the earlier chapters and the appendixes.

The second edition represents a substantial rewriting of the first edition. The first four chapters have been revised to more thoroughly address the issues of fixed disk usage. Chapter 5 has additional, new batch files. Chapter 11 of the first edition has been expanded into two chapters. This change was due to the many developments that have occurred in the areas of disk media, disk formats, and memory configuration. Chapter 13, also new, has been added to cover terminate and stay resident programs.

Throughout the book, there is a stronger emphasis on programming.

New examples show how to use DEBUG to explore MS-DOS. Programs written in C, Pascal, and assembly language have been added. All of the programs are discussed thoroughly and well commented. In addition, the expanded appendixes now contain a primer on assembly language programming for those readers with little or no assembler experience.

Part 3, "MS-DOS Commands," has been revised and expanded to include all of the MS-DOS commands through version 3.3. Twenty new commands and examples have been added. Many of the examples used in the first edition have been revised or replaced.

Acknowledgments to the Second Edition

I would like to thank the members of The Waite Group for their help in the production of the second edition of *MS-DOS Bible*. In particular, thank you to Mitchell Waite for your ability to get the best out of the people with whom you work, and thank you to Jim Stockford for your creative and material input. Thanks also to Blair Hendrickson for helping with the TSR chapter, and to Jordan Breslow for the suggestion that led to **ADD2PATH.BAT**. Special thanks to Nadine, Andy, et al. for all that you have done. Finally, a very special thank you to my wife, Shelley, for your unwavering support through it all, and to my son, Benjamin, for your understanding each time I had to tell you that "Poppa's busy."

 **Steven Simrin** is a veterinarian living in Berkeley, California. He began working with microcomputers following graduation from veterinary school. Currently, he is involved in the design and implementation of "expert" computer systems as an aid in medical diagnostics.

Introduction

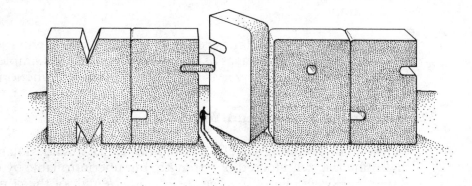

This book explains the MS-DOS operating system. Its primary goal is to provide a comprehensive, easy-to-understand guide to MS-DOS. The material is presented in order from fundamental to advanced. For those readers new to MS-DOS, topics such as booting the system, using the commands, and file organization are discussed in the early chapters. Advanced topics, such as TSR programming and device drivers, are discussed in the final chapters. The middle chapters cover the material needed to understand the advanced topics. Batch files, DEBUG, and the internal structure of MS-DOS are discussed fully, with programming examples provided.

This book is meant to be self-contained. No assumptions are made regarding the reader's level of computer expertise. Goals as diverse as maximizing your efficiency in using MS-DOS, to writing fully functional TSR programs are addressed.

All versions of MS-DOS and PC-DOS up to, and including, MS-DOS 3.3 and PC-DOS 3.3 are covered.

What Is MS-DOS?

MS-DOS stands for *Microsoft Disk Operating System*. An *operating system* is a computer program that coordinates the activities of a computer. The operating system is responsible for setting guidelines under which common computer tasks are carried out. A *disk* operating system is one that is used with disks (or diskettes). And Microsoft Corporation is the manufacturer of MS-DOS.

The three chief functions of an operating system are:

1. Transferring data between the computer and various peripheral devices (terminals, printers, floppy diskettes, hard disks, etc.). This transfer of data is called input/output, or I/O.
2. Managing computer files.
3. Loading computer programs into memory and initiating program execution.

MS-DOS handles all these duties admirably, as you will soon find out. In fact, one of the advantages of using MS-DOS is that it is simple to learn yet provides you with some very sophisticated, complex functions.

The Operating System and You

Without an operating system, a computer is like a wild, untamed beast—lightning fast, with incredible strength, but uncontrollable by humans. An operating system harnesses the speed and strength of the computer, converting its power into a useful tool.

How much you need to know about your computer's operating system depends largely on what tasks you wish to carry out. If you are primarily concerned with loading programs and copying files, you need understand only the most fundamental aspects of the operating system. On the other hand, if you are a systems programmer, you need to be familiar with the most intimate details of the operating system. Those of you who want to use the operating system to maximize the usefulness of your microcomputer are somewhere in-between.

Whichever category you fall into, the more familiar you are with your operating system, the better you can apply its capabilities to your own goals. The purpose of this book is to assist you in attaining those goals.

A Brief History of MS-DOS

The origin of MS-DOS can be traced to 1980, when Seattle Computer Products developed a microcomputer operating system for use as an in-house software development tool. Originally called QDOS, the system was renamed 86-DOS in late 1980 after it had been modified.

The rights to 86-DOS were purchased by Microsoft Corporation, which had contracted with IBM to produce an operating system for IBM's new line of personal computers. When the IBM PC hit the market in 1981, its operating system was a modified version of 86-DOS called PC-DOS version 1.0.

Shortly after the IBM PC was released, "PC-compatible" personal computers began to appear. These computers used an operating system called MS-DOS version 1.0. Microsoft had made available to the manufacturers of these machines an operating system that was a near replica of PC-DOS—the now famous MS-DOS.

The only significant difference between any of these operating systems was at the "systems level." Each operating system had to be customized for the particular machine on which it was to run. Generally speaking, these changes were apparent only to the systems programmer whose job was to "fit" the operating system to the machine. The users of the various operating systems were not aware of any significant differences.

Since the initial release of PC-DOS and MS-DOS, both operating systems have evolved along identical paths. Version 1.1 was released in 1982. The major change in 1.1 was double-sided disk drive capability. (Version 1.0 could be used only with single-sided disk drives.) Version 1.1 also allowed the user to redirect printer output to a serial port.

Version 2.0 was released in 1983. A major advancement over the earlier versions, it was designed to support a fixed (hard) disk and included a sophisticated hierarchical file directory, installable device drivers, and file handles.

MS-DOS 3.0 (released in 1984) provided improved support for fixed disks and microcomputers linked on a computer network. Subsequent versions through 3.3 (released in 1987) continued this trend.

Although this book is titled "*MS-DOS* Bible," the information presented in it applies equally to PC-DOS and MS-DOS. Unless otherwise noted, the names MS-DOS, PC-DOS, and DOS are interchangeable. Versions 1.0 and 1.1 will be referred to as MS-DOS 1 or 1.X. Versions 2.0, 2.10, and 2.11 will be referred to as MS-DOS 2 or 2.X. Versions 3.0, 3.1, 3.2, and 3.3 will be referred to as MS-DOS 3 or 3.X. PC-DOS 3.3 will be referred to as such.

Organization and Contents of This Book

This book is divided into four parts:

▶ An information jump table
▶ Tutorials on various MS-DOS topics
▶ Discussions of MS-DOS commands
▶ Appendixes covering functions and interrupts, undocumented features of MS-DOS, practical batch files, code pages, assembly language programming, ASCII codes, and hexadecimal arithmetic

Part 1—Information Jump Table is a quick guide to the tutorials and command discussions. Major topics are listed alphabetically, with specific tasks or commands listed by page number and frequency of use.

Part 2—MS-DOS Tutorials consists of 14 chapters, arranged in order from those most fundamental to the use of MS-DOS to those required by programmers. Tutorials within the chapters provide hands-on learning aids, guiding you through the concepts presented in the chapter.

Part 3—MS-DOS Commands explains 70 MS-DOS commands. Since MS-DOS is a "command-driven" system (it takes action in response to commands that you enter), this part emphasizes the purpose of each command and the procedure for using it.

Part 4—Appendixes contains supplemental material related to many of the topics covered in the book. Appendix A has a general introduction to the MS-DOS interrupts and function calls and then offers detailed discussions of each. Appendix B discusses some undocumented, but widely used, features of MS-DOS. Appendix C presents a simple menu-driven system that is constructed using batch files. Appendix D discusses code pages—what they are and how they are used. Appendix E is a primer on assembly language programming. It is provided so that readers with little or no assembly language experience may understand the assembly language programs presented in the book. Appendix F contains two ASCII cross-reference tables and explains hexadecimal to decimal conversion and vice-versa.

Chapter Summaries

Here is a brief summary of each of the 14 chapters covered in Part 2.

- ▶ **Chapter 1, Starting MS-DOS**: getting MS-DOS up and running, backing up the system diskette, and formatting a diskette.
- ▶ **Chapter 2, MS-DOS Files**: the fundamentals of data storage, naming and copying files.
- ▶ **Chapter 3, Directories, Paths, and Trees**: file management techniques, including creating directories and subdirectories and using the PATH command.
- ▶ **Chapter 4, Installing a Fixed Disk**: procedures for setting up a fixed disk by using the FDISK utility.
- ▶ **Chapter 5, MS-DOS Batch Files**: what batch files are and how to create them. How to use replaceable parameters and execute batch file commands.
- ▶ **Chapter 6, Redirection, Filters, and Pipes**: advanced data-handling features of MS-DOS.
- ▶ **Chapter 7, EDLIN, the MS-DOS Text Editor**: how to use EDLIN to create and modify files. Using EDLIN commands.

▶ **Chapter 8, Extended Keyboard and Display Control**: techniques for customizing your keyboard and display screen.

▶ **Chapter 9, DEBUG**: exploring the inner workings of your computer, examining and modifying computer programs, and using DEBUG commands.

▶ **Chapter 10, LINK**: modifying object code into relocatable modules, combining separate object modules into a single relocatable module, and using LINK switches.

▶ **Chapter 11, Disk Structure and Management**: how MS-DOS organizes and manages data stored on disk, including discussion of the file directory, the file allocation table, and the MS-DOS system files.

▶ **Chapter 12, Memory Structure and Management**: how MS-DOS organizes and manages memory, including explanation of program loading, the program segment prefix, the MS-DOS environment, and memory control blocks.

▶ **Chapter 13, Terminate and Stay Resident Programs**: what they are, how they function, and guidelines for "well-behaved" TSRs. A fully functional pop-up TSR is presented.

▶ **Chapter 14, MS-DOS Device Drivers**: what they are and how they function. A device driver skeleton that can be used to build a working device driver is presented.

How to Use This Book

This book can be used in several ways. It can be read in order, from start to finish, or it can be read in skip-around fashion, using the Information Jump Table to locate a particular topic of interest. Experienced users of MS-DOS will probably use this latter method. The generous use of cross references throughout the book will help hit-and-miss users fill in information gaps.

Before you begin your exploration of MS-DOS, you should be aware of some of the conventions used in this book.

Screen Output and User Input

Unless noted otherwise, text identical to that appearing on the computer screen is printed in a special typeface:

```
Current date is Tue 7-08-1987
Enter new date: _
```

Note that the underscore character (_) indicates the position of the cursor.

Text that you are to type (user input) is shown in an italicized version of the same special typeface:

```
Current date is Tue 7-08-1987
Enter new date: 6/01/1989
```

If you are entering information from a tutorial, be sure to type it exactly as shown, including blank spaces and punctuation marks.

Some characters cannot be printed in italic type. These are:

asterisk (*)

backward slash (\)

caret (^)

double quotation mark (")

forward slash (/)

greater than (>)

hyphen (-)

left bracket ([)

less than (<)

plus (+)

right bracket (])

single quote (')

vertical bar (¦)

When these special characters are used in MS-DOS commands and programs, they will be shown within an italicized command, such as

```
C>dir¦find "-88 "
```

The characters ¦, ", and - do not appear to be italicized, but regard them as if they were and enter them along with the rest of the command.

Note that in EDLIN, the MS-DOS text editor (chapter 7), the asterisk is used as a prompt; and in DEBUG, an MS-DOS utility (chapter 9), the hyphen is used as a prompt. For example, in the following EDLIN command

```
*2L
```

you would not enter the * because it is the EDLIN prompt; you would enter only 2L. The same is true for DEBUG commands:

```
-d
```

All you enter is d.

Commands

Special command keys are shown with an initial capital letter, like this: Esc, Del, Alt. The carriage return is indicated as Enter. Commands using control characters are shown as Ctrl-D, Ctrl-N. On screen, such commands are represented as ^d, ^n. This is the same as Ctrl-D and Ctrl-N in this book's notation. In either case, you press the Ctrl key and the letter simultaneously. You do not have to shift to capitalize the letter.

Entering commands into your computer is easy. When you see the MS-DOS prompt (A> or C>), simply type the command and press Enter to signal MS-DOS that you are finished. On some keyboards, the Enter key may appear as Return or ←. In any case, you must press the Enter key in order for the computer to respond.

Commands may be entered in uppercase letters, lowercase letters, or a combination. It makes no difference to MS-DOS. This book shows commands entered in lowercase, since that is the way most people will enter them. In typing your command, be sure to include all punctuation and blank spaces as shown. Always leave a space between the command and the drive indicator and between a command and a filename. If you don't, MS-DOS may become confused and not execute your command properly.

Do not type a lowercase "L" for the number 1, and do not use an uppercase "O" for a zero. MS-DOS does not recognize one for the other. If you have entered a command and it doesn't work, check your typing. You may have made a typing error or failed to enter the appropriate punctuation or spacing.

A Word about Disks and Diskettes

Throughout this book we will be discussing MS-DOS operations that utilize data stored on floppy diskettes and fixed (hard) disks. Unless otherwise noted, the word "disk" will refer to both floppy diskettes and fixed disks.

1

Information Jump Table

Information Jump Table

To use this table, first find the major topic you are interested in; then locate the specific task or command that you wish to perform. Major topics are listed alphabetically. Specific ones are listed by frequency of use.

Batch Files

Code Pages

Commands

Note: See the table of contents for a complete list of MS-DOS commands.

The Environment

Files

Fixed (Hard) Disk

Procedures

Programming under MS-DOS

Utility Programs

Wildcards

HOWARD W. SAMS & COMPANY

Bookmark

DEAR VALUED CUSTOMER:

Howard W. Sams & Company is dedicated to bringing you timely and authoritative books for your personal and professional library. Our goal is to provide you with excellent technical books written by the most qualified authors. You can assist us in this endeavor by checking the box next to your particular areas of interest.

We appreciate your comments and will use the information to provide you with a more comprehensive selection of titles.

Thank you,

Vice President, Book Publishing
Howard W. Sams & Company

COMPUTER TITLES:

Hardware
- ☐ Apple 140   ☐ Macintosh I01
- ☐ Commodore I10
- ☐ IBM & Compatibles I14

Business Applications
- ☐ Word Processing J01
- ☐ Data Base J04
- ☐ Spreadsheets J02

Operating Systems
- ☐ MS-DOS K05   ☐ OS/2 K10
- ☐ CP/M K01   ☐ UNIX K03

Programming Languages
- ☐ C L03   ☐ Pascal L05
- ☐ Prolog L12   ☐ Assembly L01
- ☐ BASIC LO2   ☐ HyperTalk L14

Troubleshooting & Repair
- ☐ Computers S05
- ☐ Peripherals S10

Other
- ☐ Communications/Networking M03
- ☐ AI/Expert Systems T18

ELECTRONICS TITLES:
- ☐ Amateur Radio T01
- ☐ Audio T03
- ☐ Basic Electronics T20
- ☐ Basic Electricity T21
- ☐ Electronics Design T12
- ☐ Electronics Projects T04
- ☐ Satellites T09

- ☐ Instrumentation T05
- ☐ Digital Electronics T11

Troubleshooting & Repair
- ☐ Audio S11   ☐ Television S04
- ☐ VCR S01   ☐ Compact Disc S02
- ☐ Automotive S06
- ☐ Microwave Oven S03

Other interests or comments: _____

_____

_____

Name_____

Title _____

Company _____

Address _____

City _____

State/Zip _____

Daytime Telephone No. _____

A Division of Macmillan, Inc.
4300 West 62nd Street   Indianapolis, Indiana 46268

22617

Bookmark

BUSINESS REPLY CARD

FIRST CLASS   PERMIT NO. 1076   INDIANAPOLIS, IND.

POSTAGE WILL BE PAID BY ADDRESSEE

HOWARD W. SAMS & CO.
ATTN: Public Relations Department
P.O. BOX 7092
Indianapolis, IN 46209-9921

NO POSTAGE
NECESSARY
IF MAILED
IN THE
UNITED STATES

HOWARD W. SAMS & COMPANY

HOWARD W. SAMS & COMPANY
HAYDEN BOOKS

The Waite Group's MS-DOS® Developer's Guide, Revised Edition
John Angermeyer and Kevin Jaeger
ISBN: 0-672-22630-8, $24.95

The Waite Group's Understanding MS-DOS®
Kate O'Day and John Angermeyer
ISBN: 0-672-27067-6, $17.95

The Waite Group's Tricks of the MS-DOS® Masters
John Angermeyer, Rich Fahringer, Kevin Jaeger, and Dan Shafer
ISBN: 0-672-22525-5, $24.95

The Waite Group's Discovering MS-DOS®
Kate O'Day
ISBN: 0-672-22407-0, $19.95

The Waite Group's MS-DOS® Papers
The Waite Group
ISBN: 0-672-22594-8, $26.95

Hard Disk Management Techniques for the IBM®
Joseph-David Carrabis
ISBN: 0-672-22580-8, $22.95

IBM® PC AT User's Reference Manual
Gilbert Held
ISBN: 0-8104-6394-6, $29.95

IBM® PC & PC XT User's Reference Manual, Second Edition
Gilbert Held
ISBN: 0-672-46427-6, $26.95

The Waite Group's Desktop Publishing Bible
James Stockford, Editor, The Waite Group
ISBN: 0-672-22524-7, $24.95

Personal Publishing with PC PageMaker®
Terry Ulick
ISBN: 0-672-22593-X, $18.95

Micro-Mainframe Connection
Thomas Wm. Madron
ISBN: 0-672-46583-3, $29.95

The Waite Group's Modem Connections Bible
Carolyn Curtis, Daniel Majhor, The Waite Group
ISBN: 0-672-22446-X, $16.95

The Waite Group's Printer Connections Bible
Kim G. House, Jeff Marble, The Waite Group
ISBN: 0-672-22406-2, $16.95

To order, return the card below, or call 1-800-428-SAMS. In Indiana call (317) 298-5699.

Please send me the books listed below.

Title	Quantity	ISBN #	Price

☐ Please add my name to your mailing list to receive more information on related titles.

Name (please print) _____

Company _____

City _____

State/Zip _____

Signature _____
    (required for credit card purchase)

Telephone # _____

Subtotal _____
Standard Postage and Handling __**$2.50**__
All States Add Appropriate Sales Tax _____
TOTAL _____

Enclosed is My Check or Money Order for $_____

Charge my Credit Card: ☐ VISA   ☐ MC   ☐ AE

Account No.   Expiration Date _____
☐☐☐☐ ☐☐☐☐ ☐☐☐☐ ☐☐☐☐

22617

Place
Postage
Here

HOWARD W. SAMS & COMPANY

Dept. DM
4300 West 62nd Street
Indianapolis, IN 46268–2520

P A R T

2

MS-DOS Tutorials

- ▶ Starting MS-DOS
- ▶ MS-DOS Files
- ▶ Directories, Paths, and Trees
- ▶ Installing a Fixed Disk
- ▶ MS-DOS Batch Files
- ▶ Redirection, Filters, and Pipes
- ▶ EDLIN, the MS-DOS Text Editor
- ▶ Extended Keyboard and Display Control
- ▶ DEBUG
- ▶ LINK
- ▶ Disk Structure and Management
- ▶ Memory Structure and Management
- ▶ Terminate and Stay Resident Programs
- ▶ MS-DOS Device Drivers

1

Starting MS-DOS

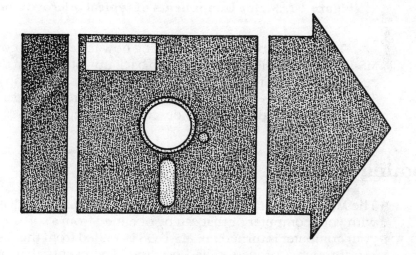

Booting MS-DOS
Backing Up the System Diskette
Formatting a Diskette
Changing Disk Drives

This chapter explains how to start MS-DOS. It contains a quick course on "booting the system," changing disk drives, backing up the system diskette, and formatting a disk. In short—everything you need to know to begin using MS-DOS. Along the way, you will learn some computer terms and concepts (figure 1-1). Subsequent chapters will build on this foundation, exploring the various functions and also the structure of MS-DOS.

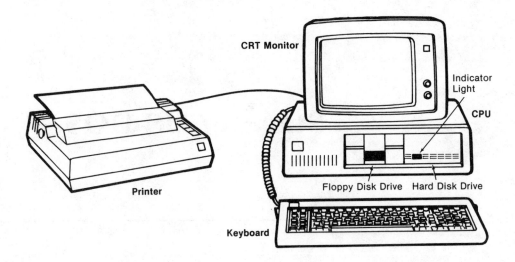

Figure 1-1. Major components of typical microcomputer system.

The chapter begins by explaining how to start your computer with the MS-DOS system diskette and how to back up your system diskette. The procedures given are for systems with either one or two floppy diskette drives. These procedures should be carried out before you install MS-DOS on a fixed disk. Fixed disk usage is described in chapter 4.

Booting MS-DOS

The MS-DOS operating system is supplied on a floppy diskette that comes with your computer or that can be obtained from a software vendor. When your computer is turned on, MS-DOS is loaded from the diskette into memory through a process called *booting*. The events that occur during the booting process are discussed in chapter 12. This chapter describes the steps that you need to take the first time you "boot-up" MS-DOS.

Before turning on your computer, place the original MS-DOS diskette in drive A. Refer to the manual supplied by your computer's manufacturer if you are uncertain about the location of drive A. With the diskette in drive A, close the drive door and turn on the computer (figure 1-2). For a time, it may appear as though nothing is happening. Actually, a series of checks is being run to verify that all is well inside your computer. Eventually, the *cursor*, the small flashing line that marks your place on the screen, will appear. You will hear some whirring and clicking coming from the drive, and the drive's indicator light will flash. The flashing light indicates that MS-DOS is being loaded from the diskette into computer memory.

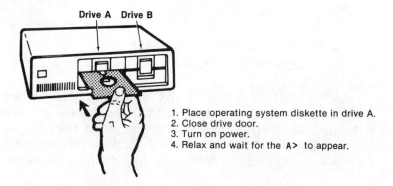

1. Place operating system diskette in drive A.
2. Close drive door.
3. Turn on power.
4. Relax and wait for the A> to appear.

Figure 1-2. Booting the system, using two floppy diskette drives.

Setting the Date

Now that MS-DOS has been loaded into memory, you are ready to set the date. Your display screen should look something like this:

```
Current date is Tue 7-08-1987
Enter new date: _
```

In the last line of the display, MS-DOS prompts you to enter a new date (today's date). The date that you enter will be used by MS-DOS as a *date stamp* to help identify all files stored on disk during the current work session. Having to enter a date may seem inconvenient to you, but that date might be important months from now when you are trying to locate a file.

Notice that the second to the last line of the display shows the "current date." This is the date that MS-DOS was manufactured and first stored on a disk. This date will be displayed each time that you boot MS-DOS.

To enter the new date, follow these steps:

1. Type the number of the current month; for example, 01=January, 02=February, etc. The leading zero in the number may be omitted (January, for example, may be entered as "1" or "01").

2. Type a dash (–) or a slash (/) to separate the month from the day.

3. Type the number of the day of the month. Again, a leading zero may be omitted.

4. Type a dash (–) or a slash (/) to separate the day from the year.

5. Type the year. MS-DOS will accept any year in the range 1980 through 2099. You do not have to type all four digits of the year, only the last two (1988 may be entered as either "1988" or "88").

6. Press the Enter key.

The new date should appear on the screen:

```
Current date is Tue 7-08-1987
Enter new date: 6/13/88      ←Enter
```

After you press Enter, MS-DOS checks to make sure that the date you have specified is valid (the screen will display the message `Invalid date` if it is not) and then stores the date in memory. The date is stored in memory only while your computer is turned on. When you switch off the power, the date is lost and must be reentered the next time you boot the system.

Setting the Time

Once you have entered a valid date, MS-DOS prompts you to enter the new time (the present time). The time that you enter will be used by MS-DOS as a *time stamp* to help identify all files stored on disk during the current work session. Like entering the date, entering the time may seem to be a nuisance, but you may be glad you did six months from now.

```
Current date is Tue 7-08-1987
Enter new date: 6/13/88
Current time is: 0:01:01.58
Enter new time: _
```

Notice that the "current time" is displayed in the second to the last line. This is the time of day that MS-DOS was manufactured and first stored on a disk. It will be displayed each time that you boot MS-DOS.

To enter the new time, follow these steps:

1. Type the hour of the day. Any number in the range 01 through 24 is valid. A leading zero may be omitted (01 and 1 are both valid).
2. Type a colon (:) to separate the hours from the minutes.
3. Type the minutes. A leading zero is optional.
4. (Optional) Type a colon followed by the seconds. After entering the seconds, you may specify hundredths of a second by typing a period (.) and the hundredths of the second.
5. Press the Enter key.

The new time should appear on the screen:

```
Current date is Tue 7-08-1987
Enter new date: 6/13/88
Current time is: 0:01:01.58
Enter new time: 9:40      ←Enter
```

After you have pressed Enter, MS-DOS checks to make sure that the time you have specified is valid (the screen will display the message `invalid time` if it is not) and then stores the time in memory. The time is updated several times a second by your computer's internal timer. The current time is stored in memory only while your computer is turned on. When you switch off the power, the time is lost.

The System Prompt

Once a valid date and time have been entered, MS-DOS displays its *system prompt* (**A>**). Notice that a blinking cursor follows the **A>** prompt. The prompt and the blinking cursor are your signal from MS-DOS that it is ready for use:

```
Current date is Tue 7-08-1987
Enter new date: 6/13/88
Current time is: 0:01:01.58
Enter new time: 9:40

The XYZ Personal Computer MS-DOS
Version 3.30 Copyright Microsoft Corp 1981, 1987

A> _
```

Date and Time Defaults

While entering the new date and time is a good work habit, there may be occasions when you decide not to enter the date and time. If so, simply press the Enter key. The date and time will be set to the *default values,* the preset values used by MS-DOS unless you specify otherwise. In this case, the default values are the "current" date and time that are displayed by MS-DOS each time you boot the system. There is no correlation between these values and the date and time that you are actually using the computer. If you choose the default values, the screen will leave a blank in place of the new time and date:

```
Current date is Tue 7-08-1987
Enter new date:      ←Enter
Current time is: 0:01:01.58
Enter new time:      ←Enter

The XYZ Personal Computer MS-DOS
Version 3.30 Copyright Microsoft Corp 1981, 1987

A> _
```

Time/Date Boards

If your computer has a time/date board and the corresponding software has been stored on the disk used to boot MS-DOS, the time and date will be automatically set whenever MS-DOS is booted. Refer to the information provided by the manufacturer of your board.

Date and Time Stamps

While MS-DOS is running, the computer's internal timer is used to update the present time, changing the value that is stored in memory several times a second. MS-DOS will also update the present date whenever the time reaches midnight (24:00:00.00).

When MS-DOS stores a file on a disk, the current date and time are stored on the disk along with other information about the file. These date and time stamps can be viewed by using the DIR command (more about DIR later). Date and time stamps can help you keep track of when a file was created or last modified but only if you entered the correct date and time when you booted MS-DOS.

Rebooting with Ctrl-Alt-Del

The procedure just described for booting MS-DOS is known as a *cold boot* because it began with the computer turned off. However, MS-DOS can also be started (or restarted) with the computer turned on. Naturally, this is known as a *warm boot*.

With the computer running, place your MS-DOS system diskette in drive A, close the drive door, and press the Ctrl-Alt-Del keys simultaneously. MS-DOS will be loaded (or reloaded) into memory. Just as it does for a cold boot, MS-DOS will prompt you to enter the current date and time.

Backing Up the System Diskette

If you are using MS-DOS for the first time, you should make a *backup copy,* or duplicate, of your system diskette before proceeding any further. The method used to make a backup depends on whether your system has two floppy disk drives or just one floppy disk drive. We will describe the method for two-drive systems first.

Note: If your system has a fixed disk, determine whether it has one or two floppy disk drives and then use the appropriate method. In fixed disk systems, it is especially important that you back up the system diskette before using the fixed disk, since you might inadvertently erase the system diskette when setting up the fixed disk.

Backing Up on Two-Drive Systems

If your computer has two floppy disk drives, place the *system diskette* in drive A and the diskette that will be the backup in drive B (see figure 1-2). Make sure that the diskette in drive B either is blank or does not contain any data that you want to save, since all existing data on the diskette will be lost in creating the backup. If you are using an old diskette in drive B and you want to see the names of the files that are on it before making it the backup, type the following:

```
A>dir b:/w
```

You have just given MS-DOS your first *command*. A command is an instruction to the operating system, usually in the form of an abbreviation or a short word. "DIR" is an abbreviation for DIRectory and tells MS-DOS to display information about the files on a specific diskette. (We will return to the subject of files in chapter 2.) The "b:" tells MS-DOS that you want to see the files on the diskette in drive B. The "/w" is an optional switch that can be used with the DIR command. A *switch* instructs MS-DOS to execute, or perform, a command in a certain way. In this case, the /w switch instructs MS-DOS to list the files in columns across the screen. Commands can be entered in either lowercase, uppercase, or a combination.

If, after viewing the files on the diskette in drive B, you want to save some of them, either use another diskette or copy the file(s) onto another diskette. Refer to chapter 2 for help in copying files.

Once you have reassured yourself that the diskette in drive B does not contain any essential data, recheck to make sure that the original system diskette is in drive A, take two deep breaths, and type the following MS-DOS command:

```
A>diskcopy a: b:
```

Press Enter and MS-DOS will respond with the message:

```
Insert source diskette in drive A
Insert target diskette in drive B
Strike any key when ready
```

The *source* diskette is the original diskette. In this case, the source is your system diskette in drive A. The *target* diskette is the diskette receiving the information; here, it is the backup diskette in drive B.

You have already placed the source and target diskettes in drives A and B, respectively, so go ahead and strike any key. Lights will flash, the drives will spin, and the system diskette will be backed up. After backing up the system diskette, MS-DOS will display:

```
Copy complete
Copy another (Y/N)? _
```

Type **N** or **n** (for "No") to terminate the DISKCOPY command, and the system prompt will be displayed.

If you wish, you can use the DISKCOMP command to verify that the diskette in drive B is a copy of the diskette in drive A. Refer to Part 3 for details on DISKCOMP.

Remove the original system diskette from drive A and store it in a safe place. Use the backup as your "working" diskette, reserving the original to make more backups as they are needed.

Backing Up on One-Drive Systems

If your computer has one floppy disk drive, place the diskette that is to be the backup diskette in drive A. Make sure that the diskette is blank or does not contain any data that you want to save, since all existing data will be destroyed in making the backup. If you are using an old diskette and you want to see the names of the files that are on it before making it the backup, type the following:

```
A>dir /w
```

You have just given MS-DOS your first *command,* or instruction. The DIR command instructs MS-DOS to display the names of all the files on the specified diskette. For an explanation of the DIR command and the /w switch, please refer to the discussion on two-drive systems. If, after viewing the files, you want to save any of them, either use another diskette or copy the file(s) to another diskette. See chapter 2 for help in copying files.

Now you are ready to remove the backup diskette from drive A and insert the system diskette. Enter the following command:

```
A>diskcopy a: b:
```

MS-DOS will respond with the message:

```
Insert source diskette in drive A
Strike any key when ready
```

The *source* (system) diskette is already in drive A, so go ahead and strike any key. MS-DOS will read some data from the system diskette and then display the message:

```
Insert target diskette in drive A
Strike any key when ready
```

In a one-drive system, MS-DOS treats drive A as if it were *two* drives, A and B. Try to think of each diskette as representing a different drive. When you switch diskettes, MS-DOS pretends to switch drives too, although actually it just switches drive labels. Remove the system diskette from drive A, insert the *target* (backup) diskette, and strike any key. Data will be written to the backup diskette, and MS-DOS will prompt:

```
Insert source diskette in drive A
Strike any key when ready
```

Remove the backup, insert the system diskette, and strike any key. When MS-DOS prompts you, swap the diskettes again. Continue to repeat this process until MS-DOS notifies you that the entire system diskette has been copied. The number of swaps is determined by the amount of read/ write memory (RAM) in your computer. The copy is complete when MS-DOS displays the message:

```
Copy complete
Copy another (Y/N)? _
```

Press **N** or **n** (for "No") to terminate the DISKCOPY command. The system prompt will be displayed.

If you wish, you can use the DISKCOMP command to verify that the backup diskette is an accurate copy of the system diskette. Refer to Part 3 for details on DISKCOMP.

Store the original system diskette in a safe place. Use the backup as your "working" diskette, reserving the original to make more backups as they are needed.

Formatting a Diskette

Before a diskette can store data that is usable by MS-DOS, it must be *formatted*. During formatting, the diskette is divided into parcels called *sectors*, which are readable by MS-DOS. Formatting also analyzes the diskette for defects and sets up a file directory. Most (but not all) versions of MS-DOS will automatically format a diskette, if necessary, when the DISKCOPY command is used to back up a diskette.

If you use an unformatted diskette for your system backup, and your version of MS-DOS does not automatically format with DISKCOPY, MS-DOS will display the following message:

```
Disk error reading drive A
Abort, Retry, Ignore?
```

Type **A** (or **a**), and the system prompt will be displayed. Insert your MS-DOS system diskette in drive A and type **format a:** to begin the formatting process. MS-DOS will prompt you as follows:

```
A>format a:     ←Enter
Insert new diskette for drive A:
and strike any key when ready
```

Remove the system diskette from drive A, and replace it with the diskette that is to be formatted. Formatting destroys all existing data on a diskette so make sure that the diskette does not contain any data that you will need later on. (If you want to abort the formatting process at this point, press Ctrl-C). Press any key to format the diskette in drive A. MS-DOS will tell you when formatting is complete:

```
Formatting...Format complete

 362496 bytes total disk space
 362496 bytes available on disk

Format another (Y/N)?n     ←you press "n"
A>
```

The formatted diskette can now be removed from drive A and may be used to store data. Refer to the previous section, "Backing Up the System Diskette," if you want to use the formatted diskette to create a backup copy of another diskette. Part 3 of this book contains further details on the use of the FORMAT command.

Changing Disk Drives

Most MS-DOS commands involve storing and/or retrieving data on a disk. You can specify which drive MS-DOS is to use by including the letter designator of the appropriate drive in the MS-DOS command. If you do not specify a drive in the command, MS-DOS assumes that the disk is in the *default drive*.

MS-DOS displays the letter of the *current* default drive in the system prompt. When you start MS-DOS from a diskette, the A drive is the default and MS-DOS displays the prompt **A>**.

To change the default drive, type the letter of the drive you wish to be the new default, type a colon, and then press Enter:

```
A>b:     ←Enter
B>
```

The colon tells MS-DOS that "b" refers to a disk drive. If you omit the colon, MS-DOS will assume that "b" is a command and will try to execute it. The default drive will come on for a second or two, and MS-DOS will search for command "b". When no command named "b" is found, MS-DOS will display an error message and then prompt you to enter another command:

```
A>b
Bad command or file name
A>
```

2

MS-DOS Files

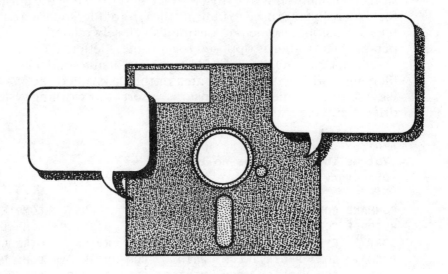

Filenames and Extensions
File Specifications
Copying a File
Wildcards

One of the chief responsibilities of an operating system is the management of computer files. A *computer file* is similar to any other type of file in that it is a collection of related information stored in one place. Unlike paper files, which are stored in filing cabinets or desk drawers, computer files are stored on disks. They are then loaded into the computer's memory when the information they contain is to be used. The operating system controls both the storing and the loading of computer files.

This chapter will explain how files are named and what information MS-DOS needs to know about files in order to work with them. The procedures for copying files and for using "wildcards" in files are also explained.

If your computer has a fixed disk, you may want to skim this chapter and the next one before installing MS-DOS on your fixed disk. Fixed disk installation is discussed in chapter 4.

Filenames and Extensions

Each MS-DOS file has a *filename* and an optional *filename extension*. MS-DOS uses these names to differentiate one file from another. Some filenames and extensions, such as those for the files on the operating system diskette, are preassigned; others are assigned by you. Filenames and extensions are usually chosen so that they are descriptive of the information in the file. Extensions are used to indicate the *type* of file, such as a data file or a text file. Extensions also help to distinguish closely related files; for example, a personal letters file as opposed to a business letters file.

When MS-DOS stores a file on a disk, it automatically stores the file's filename and extension in an area of the disk called the *file directory*. To view some filenames and extensions, insert your working system diskette in drive A and enter the command **dir/w**:

```
A>dir/w
 Volume in drive A has no label
 Directory of A:\

COMMAND COM   DEBUG    COM   EXE2BIN EXE   CHKDSK    COM   EDLIN    COM
RECOVER COM   SYS      COM   MORE     COM   DISKCOPY  COM   LINK     EXE
SORT    EXE   FIND     EXE   FC       EXE   HDISK     SYS   GRAPHICS COM
FORMAT  COM   PHDINIT  COM   PRINT    COM   DISKCOMP  COM   DISKTEST COM
MODE    COM   ASSIGN   COM   MEMTEST  COM   BACKUP    COM   RESTORE  COM
FDISK   COM   TREE     COM   DIRCOMP  COM   DMA       COM   GWBASIC  EXE
SAMPLE1 TXT   CONFIG   SYS   ANSI     SYS
       33 File(s)   84992 bytes free

A>
```

The command "dir/w" directs MS-DOS to display the filenames and extensions that are contained in the directory of the diskette in the default drive. In this example, the "A" drive is the default drive. (The display that you obtain on your system may differ somewhat from the display shown here.) Notice that the last line (the line just before the A prompt) says that this diskette contains 33 files and has 84,992 unused bytes.

The first filename displayed is "COMMAND COM", the second "DEBUG COM", the third "EXE2BIN EXE", and so on. As you can see, each name has two parts and the parts are listed in two columns. The first column contains the filename, and the second column contains the filename extension. Looking at the first file in the display, you can see that the filename is "COMMAND" and the filename extension is "COM".

MS-DOS has specific rules for naming files. Each filename in the same directory must be unique. In other words, the filename *and* its extension cannot be the same as another filename and extension already in use in that directory. For example, you cannot give the name "letters.per" to two files; MS-DOS becomes confused and does not know which "letters.per" file you are referring to. You can, however, use the same filename but different extensions. For example, you could name your file of business letters "letters.bus" and your file of personal letters "letters.per". A few filenames are reserved by MS-DOS for its exclusive use. These are the names of MS-DOS program files and commands and the abbreviations for devices (such as "PRN" for printer). Check your user's guide for a list of reserved names. Filenames must take the form:

filename.*extension*

The *filename* is one to eight characters in length. The *extension,* which is optional, is one to three characters in length. A period (.) is used to separate the filename from the extension. If you accidentally enter a filename with more than eight characters and you do not enter an extension, MS-DOS will automatically place a period after the eighth character, use the next three characters as the extension, and disregard the remaining characters. If you enter a filename with more than eight characters and you also enter an extension, MS-DOS signals an error. If your extension has more than three characters, MS-DOS ignores the extra characters.

MS-DOS allows only certain characters to be used in filenames and extensions. These are:

letters of the alphabet
numbers 0 through 9
special characters $ # & @ ! % ( ) - { } ' _ ' ^ ~

In addition, MS-DOS 1.X allows these special characters:

¦ < > \

These four characters cannot be used for filenames or extensions in MS-DOS 2.00 and later versions, however.

The following characters *cannot* be used in filenames or extensions with any version of MS-DOS:

* + = [ ] : ; " , . / ?
space, tab, and control characters

Certain programs can create files by using some of the characters in the preceding list, but these files are not usable by MS-DOS.

MS-DOS treats uppercase and lowercase letters alike, so you may use any combination of capital and lowercase letters in filenames and extensions. In this book, filenames discussed in the text will be lowercased and enclosed in quotation marks (the "letters.per" file).

File Specifications

In order for MS-DOS to work with a file, it must know the file's filename and filename extension. In addition, it must know which disk drive contains the file. A disk drive is specified by a letter, called a *drive designator*. The first disk drive is specified by a drive designator of "A:" and is called "drive A." The second drive has a drive designator of "B:" and is called "drive B." A fixed disk is usually specified as "C:" and is called "drive C."

The drive designator combines with the filename and the extension to form the *file specification*, or *filespec* for short. The filespec contains the drive designator followed by the filename and filename extension (if there is an extension). For example, if a file with the filename "instruct" and the extension "txt" were located on disk drive A, its complete filespec would be "A:instruct.txt" (or "a:instruct.txt").

Copying a File

One of the most frequently performed tasks of an operating system is the copying of computer files stored on floppy disks. An experienced user routinely copies all valuable computer files at regular intervals. That way, if one copy of the file is damaged or destroyed, a backup is available.

The procedures for copying a file differ slightly, depending on whether your system has one or two floppy disk drives. The following sections will first describe the procedure for copying a file with a two-drive system and then describe the procedure for a one-drive system.

In copying a file, the first drive is called the *source drive* and the second the *target drive*. As you may recall from chapter 1, the same terminology is used for disks. The disk containing the original file is the *source disk,* while the disk receiving the copy is the *target disk*.

Two-Drive Systems

To copy a file using a two-drive system, insert the source diskette (the diskette containing the file to be copied) in drive A. Place the formatted target diskette in drive B. (Refer to chapter 1 for help in formatting a diskette.)

In the example shown here, the file "instruct.txt" is on the diskette in drive A. To copy the file onto the diskette in drive B, type the word **copy**, then type the filespec of the file to be copied, and finally type the filespec of the copy:

```
A>copy a:instruct.txt b:instruct.txt
```

Press Enter. The copying process will start, and MS-DOS will display a message when the copying is completed.

```
    1 File(s) copied
A>
```

Fixed Drive Systems

When copying a file to a fixed drive, you need to use the drive letter of the fixed drive in the filespec of the copy. For example, to copy "instruct.txt" from drive A to a fixed disk with drive letter C, enter the following command

```
A>copy a:instruct.txt c:instruct.txt
```

One-Drive Systems

To copy a file using a one-drive system, insert the source diskette into the system drive. Type **copy**, then type the filespec of the file to be copied, and finally type the filespec of the copy:

```
A>copy a:instruct.txt b:instruct.txt
```

Press Enter. MS-DOS will store as much of the file in memory as possible. The following message will then be displayed:

```
Insert diskette for drive B: and strike
any key when ready
```

This is MS-DOS's way of telling you that the system drive is now *logical* drive B (see the DEVICE command in Part 3 for a discussion of physical and logical drives). It is also your cue to insert into the system drive the formatted target diskette (the diskette on which the file copy will be written). Refer to chapter 1 if you need help in formatting diskettes.

Note: The preceding message may be displayed before the red light on the disk drive goes off. If so, wait until the light goes off before you change diskettes.

Once the diskette for logical drive B is in place, press any key to continue the operation. MS-DOS will write to the disk that portion of the file previously stored in memory. If the memory is not large enough to hold the entire file, MS-DOS will display the following message:

```
Insert diskette for drive A: and strike
any key when ready
```

This message says that the system drive is now logical drive A. Remove the target diskette and insert the diskette containing the original file. Strike any key. Continue to follow MS-DOS's instructions. Remember that the original file is on the diskette "for drive A" and the copy is on the diskette "for drive B." MS-DOS will tell you when the copy procedure has been completed:

```
    1 File(s) copied
A>
```

Once the file has been copied, you may use the COMP command (see Part 3) to verify that an accurate copy of the file has been made.

Wildcards

Wildcards are special symbols (sometimes called *global characters*) that are used to stand for one or more specific characters in a filename or extension. MS-DOS provides two wildcard symbols that you may use to specify files in MS-DOS commands—the question mark and the asterisk.

The question mark (?) is used to represent a *single character* in a filename or extension, while the asterisk (*) is used to represent a *group of characters* in a filename or extension. You will find wildcards are very handy, especially in the DIR, COPY, ERASE, and RENAME commands, because these commands frequently refer to groups of files.

The "?" Wildcard

Imagine that you have a diskette containing several files, including these four:

last.txt

list.txt

lost.txt

lust.txt

Let's say that you wanted to copy each of these files. There are two ways you could accomplish this. You could use the COPY command four times, specifying a different file each time; or you could use COPY one time, using a wildcard character in the filespec. If you chose the second way, your command would look like this:

```
A>copy a:l?st.txt b:l?st.txt
```

The "?" in the second position of the filename indicates that the second character is wild. MS-DOS is instructed to execute the command on all files on the diskette in drive A that have an "l" as the first character in the filename, an "s" as the third character, a "t" as the fourth character, and a filename extension of ".txt". Any character in the second position is acceptable according to this command.

The "*" Wildcard

Using an "*" in a filename or filename extension tells MS-DOS that all characters in the position of the "*" are wild. In addition, all characters to the right of the "*" are wild. As an example, let's say that you want to refresh your memory regarding the files in the system diskette. In particular, you want to see which system files have a filename beginning with "f" and a filename extension of ".com". Insert your working system diskette in drive A and enter the following command (see Part 3 for a complete discussion of DIR):

```
A>dir f*.com/w
FORMAT   COM        FDISK        COM
        2 File(s)             84992 bytes free
```

MS-DOS interprets the filespec "f*.com" to mean any file that has a filename beginning with "f" and a filename extension of ".com". The "/w" simply directs MS-DOS to display only the filenames and directory names.

A filespec may contain more than one wildcard character. For example, "f*.com" is equivalent to f???????.com. In the following example, wildcards are used in the filespec to indicate that all the files on the diskette in drive A should be copied onto the diskette in drive B:

```
A>copy a:*.* b:*.*
```

Don't be afraid to experiment with wildcards in MS-DOS commands. They can be a tremendous timesaver once you are familiar with their use. A word of caution though: *Make sure that you have backup copies of any important files before you start playing with wildcards.* It's very easy for even an experienced MS-DOS user to inadvertently wipe out many hours of work with a misplaced wildcard.

3

Directories, Paths, and Trees

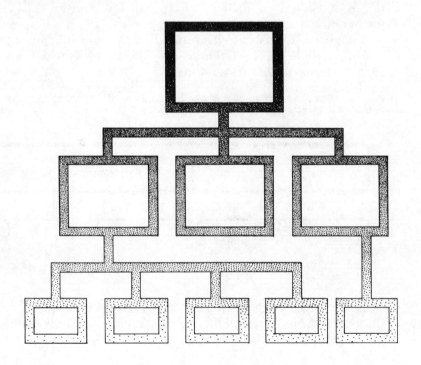

File Management
Setting Up a Hierarchical File System

Chapter 2 covered the basics of what a file is, how it is named, and the information that MS-DOS needs to know about a file in order to use it. Chapter 2 also explained some basic procedures for copying files. This chapter will discuss the way files are managed by MS-DOS.

If your computer uses a fixed disk, you may wish to skim this chapter and chapter 2 before installing MS-DOS on your fixed disk. Fixed disk installation is discussed in chapter 4.

File Management

The basis of file management is the *file directory*. The file directory is an area on the disk that is set aside during the formatting process. The file directory serves as a table of contents for the files stored on the disk. For each file stored, there is a corresponding entry in the file directory.

Each entry in the file directory stores a filename and a filename extension. The entry also contains the time and date that the file was created or last modified, the file's size in bytes, and other information that MS-DOS needs in using the file. The structure of file directories is covered in much more detail in chapter 11.

Figure 3-1 illustrates a simple directory and file system. All of the files are on a single level relative to the file directory. Such an arrangement is called *nonhierarchical*. Versions of MS-DOS prior to 2.0 use a nonhierarchical file system.

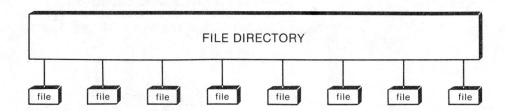

Figure 3-1. Nonhierarchical file management system.

The single biggest change implemented in MS-DOS 2.0 was the introduction of a *hierarchical* file system. Such a system is essential in managing the large number of files stored on fixed disks.

Hierarchical File Systems

It is not unusual for fixed disks to store hundreds or even thousands of files. Handling such a large number of files requires a more efficient storage and retrieval system than that used by nonhierarchical systems.

MS-DOS 2.0 and subsequent versions use a hierarchical file system (figure 3-2). In this type of system, files and groups of files are divided into a series of levels, beginning with the file directory at the uppermost level. The file directory is called the *root directory* because all the other levels branch

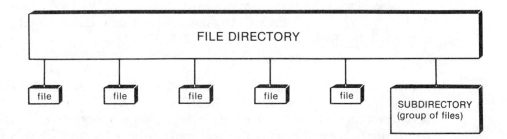

Figure 3-2. Single files and subdirectory.

out from it. The file directory can contain the names of single files as well as other directories. These directories are called *subdirectories* and can themselves contain the names of files or other subdirectories. By grouping related files into their own directory, the time necessary to search for a particular file on a disk is shortened. Each succeeding level within the hierarchy is referenced relative to the root directory (see figure 3-3).

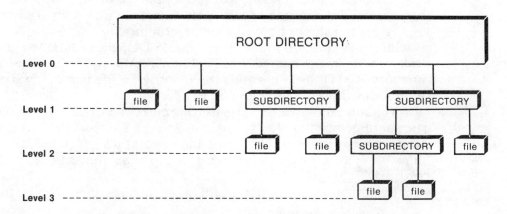

Figure 3-3. Hierarchical file management system.

When you use the DIR command to list the contents of the root directory, DOS will display both filenames and subdirectory names. For each file, the directory entry will show the filename and extension, the size of the file in bytes, and the time and date when the file was created or last modified. Files that are subdirectories are signified by the notation "<DIR>" for directory. MS-DOS will also show the total number of files (including subdirectories) and the number of free bytes remaining on the disk.

The number of entries that the root directory can hold is limited. On standard single-sided diskettes, the limit is 64 files and/or subdirectories. On standard double-sided diskettes, the limit is 112 files and/or subdirectories. On fixed disks, the limit depends on how the disk has been partitioned. (For information on fixed disks, see chapter 4.)

Note: From this point on, the word "directory" will refer to both a root directory and a subdirectory. Any comments that relate to one but not the other will be qualified.

Trees

The file arrangement used in MS-DOS 2.X and 3.X is described as *tree-structured*. In this case, however, the "tree" happens to be upside down, with the root (directory) at the top. Each branch coming out of the root corresponds to an entry, either a file or a subdirectory (a group of related files). Secondary branches arise from each subdirectory in level 1, tertiary branches arise from subdirectories in level 2, and so on.

This tree-structured arrangement allows each subdirectory and its entries to be treated as though there were no other data stored on the disk. This can make life much more tolerable when you are dealing with a hard disk containing several hundred files. Let's look at a typical example of the use of trees.

Suppose that you are using a word processing program to write a book. Each chapter in the book is stored as a file on a disk. Suppose that you also do some computer programming. On the same disk you store a program that you are writing. Finally, just to complicate things, suppose you also store on the disk a program and some data that you use in your business.

Figure 3-4 shows how you might structure these files. Notice that the root directory contains four entries: the MS-DOS file COMMAND.COM and three subdirectories named WRITE, PROGRAMS, and BUSINESS. The subdirectory WRITE itself contains three entries: a file named "wp.exe" and two subdirectories, LETTERS and BOOK.

The subdirectory LETTERS has one entry: a file named "hilburn.doc". The subdirectory BOOK also has one entry: a file named "start.doc". The subdirectory PROGRAMS contains two files: "gwbasic.exe" and "lifex.bas"; as does the subdirectory BUSINESS: "gwbasic.exe" and "records.bas".

By structuring your data in this way, the files are separated into func-

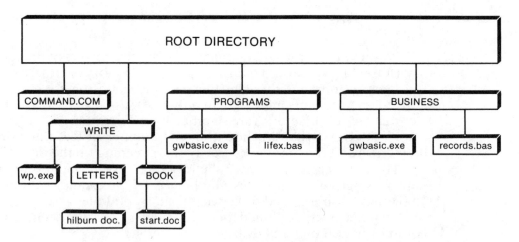

Figure 3-4. Tree-structured arrangement of files.

tional groups. For example, the subdirectory WRITE contains the word processing program ("wp.exe") and the documents that have been created by that program. These documents have been placed in separate subdirectories according to their subject matter. The subdirectory PROGRAMS contains the BASIC interpreter and one BASIC program. The subdirectory BUSINESS holds a second copy of the BASIC interpreter and a BASIC program used in business.

Setting Up a Hierarchical File System

This section will explain how the file structure shown in figure 3-4 was created. Along the way, it will discuss the commands used by MS-DOS to manage a hierarchical file system.

The examples presented show how to set up a file system on a fixed disk with drive letter C. It is assumed that the fixed disk has previously been partitioned and formatted (see chapter 4) for use by MS-DOS. The commands discussed here can also be used with floppy diskette files.

Paths

A *path* is the course that must be followed to get from one directory to another. For example, consider the subdirectory BOOK in figure 3-4. Suppose that you want to travel from the root directory to BOOK. What path would you take? Starting at the root directory, you would pass through the subdirectory WRITE and from there to the subdirectory BOOK.

In the same way, MS-DOS 2.X and 3.X find a file by taking a particular path to the directory containing that file. You tell MS-DOS which path to take by specifying the start of the path and the subdirectories to use. The path from the root directory to BOOK is:

ROOT DIRECTORY→WRITE→BOOK

This list of names is called a *path specifier*. When entering a path specifier in an MS-DOS command, use a backslash (\) to separate one directory from another. In entering the path specifier, do not enter "ROOT DIRECTORY". The root directory is represented by the first backslash. The path specifier from the root directory to BOOK is therefore:

\write\book

Creating a Subdirectory

With drive C as the default directory, enter the command **dir**. Your display screen will look something like this:

```
C>dir
```

```
Volume in drive C has no label
Directory of C:\

COMMAND  COM  25307   3-17-88   12:00p
       1 File(s)     10510200 bytes free
```

The line **Directory of C:** tells you that MS-DOS is displaying the names of the entries in the root directory (\) of the disk in drive C. In this case, the root directory contains only one entry, the MS-DOS file COMMAND.COM.

Now we will begin expanding the directory to include some subdirectories. The MS-DOS command MKDIR (MaKe DIRectory) is used to create a subdirectory. Let's use MKDIR to create the three subdirectories WRITE, PROGRAMS, and BUSINESS.

Before we do that though, let's go over the rules for naming subdirectories, just in case you want to make up your own subdirectory names. Subdirectory names can be up to eight characters long, with an optional extension of three characters. Each subdirectory must have a name that does not match the name of any file or subdirectory contained in the same directory. The valid characters used in the name are the same as those for filenames.

To create a subdirectory, type **mkdir** (or **md** for short) and then type the path specifier of the subdirectory being created. In entering your command, you may omit the path if the new subdirectory will be entered in the *current directory*. The current directory is the directory in which you are now working. (We will discuss the current directory in more detail later in this section.)

Now we are ready to create the subdirectory WRITE. Type **mkdir** (or **md**) followed by a backslash to indicate that the subdirectory will be an entry in the root directory; then type the name of the new subdirectory:

```
C>mkdir \write
```

When you press Enter, MS-DOS will create the new subdirectory. In a similar fashion, you can create the subdirectories PROGRAMS and BUSINESS:

```
C>mkdir \programs
C>mkdir \business
```

Now let's enter the DIR command to see what MS-DOS has done:

```
C>dir
 Volume in drive C has no label
 Directory of C:\

COMMAND  COM   25307  3-17-88   12:00p
```

```
WRITE         <DIR>      9-17-88   11:42a
PROGRAMS      <DIR>      9-17-88   11:43a
BUSINESS      <DIR>      9-17-88   11:44a
        4 File(s)    10505080 bytes   free
```

If you are following along on your computer, the size of your COM-MAND.COM file may not be 25,307 bytes. The date/time stamps on your disk will certainly differ from those shown here. The important points are that three subdirectories have been created and that they are entered in the root directory. The subdirectories are identified by the label <DIR>. Notice that creating three subdirectories used up 5,120 bytes of disk space. (Compare the number of free bytes before and after the subdirectories were created.)

Changing the Current Directory

A path tells MS-DOS the route to take to a particular directory. If an MS-DOS command does not specify a path, MS-DOS will attempt to execute the command in the current directory. At any given time, each drive on the system has a current directory.

The MS-DOS command CHDIR (CHange DIRectory) is used to change a drive's current directory. To use CHDIR, type **chdir** (or **cd** for short) followed by the path specifier of the desired directory.

In this tutorial, the current directory on drive C is the root directory. Entering the CHDIR command without any specifiers causes MS-DOS to display the path specifier of the current directory. Type **chdir**:

```
C>chdir
C:\
```

The backslash means that the root directory is the current directory on drive C.

We can make WRITE the current directory by including the path specifier to WRITE in the CHDIR command:

```
C>chdir \write
```

The first directory in a path specifier may be omitted if it is the current directory. Since the preceding command was invoked while the root directory was the current directory, the command could have been entered as:

```
C>chdir write
```

To verify that WRITE is now the current directory, type **chdir** without a path specifier. MS-DOS will display the path to the current directory:

```
C>chdir
C:\WRITE
```

A Word about Parents

All subdirectories are entries in another directory. WRITE, PROGRAMS, and BUSINESS are entries in the root directory. A directory is said to be the *parent directory* of the subdirectories that it contains as entries. The root directory is the parent directory of WRITE, PROGRAMS, and BUSINESS.

Putting Files into a Subdirectory

Now that WRITE is the current directory, let's put some files in it. We will start off by putting a copy of the file "wp.exe" in WRITE. This is done simply by making a copy of the file. Place a diskette with the file "wp.exe" in drive A and enter the following command:

```
C>copy a:wp.exe c:
```

A Directory for MS-DOS

Many users store the MS-DOS files in a single subdirectory. This reduces the clutter that can result if many files are kept in the root directory. The files CONFIG.SYS and COMMAND.COM (see chapters 8 and 11) must be stored in the root directory if they are to be used by MS-DOS.

This command instructs MS-DOS to copy the file "wp.exe" to drive C. Since no paths were included in the command, MS-DOS will look for "wp.exe" in the current directory on drive A (in this case the root directory) and copy it to the current directory on drive C. WRITE is the current directory on drive C, so "wp.exe" will be copied into WRITE.

The MKDIR command can be used to create a subdirectory in WRITE. Recall that to use this command you must type **mkdir** (or **md**) followed by the path to the new subdirectory.

The current directory is WRITE, so the path to the subdirectory LETTERS (see figure 3-4) is WRITE\LETTERS. But, remember that the first directory in a path may be omitted when it is the current directory. Therefore, to create LETTERS, enter the following command:

```
C>mkdir letters
```

The subdirectory BOOK is created in the same way:

```
C>mkdir book
```

Now that we have established our three subdirectories, let's place some files in them. Notice that the subdirectory LETTERS in figure 3-4 contains the file "hilburn.doc". However, before we enter "hilburn.doc" in LETTERS, let's make LETTERS the current directory:

```
C>cd letters
```

Now place a diskette with the file "hilburn.doc" in drive A and enter:

```
C>copy a:hilburn.doc c:
```

Next we will copy the file "start.doc" into the subdirectory BOOK. Let's begin by making BOOK the current directory. Recall that the current directory is LETTERS. The path from LETTERS is WRITE\BOOK. But entering the command "cd write\book" results in an "Invalid directory" message. The reason for this is that WRITE is the parent directory of LETTERS. The parent of a directory is represented in MS-DOS commands by two periods (..). The path specifier from LETTERS to BOOK is therefore "..\book". To make BOOK the current directory, enter the following command:

```
C>cd ..\book
```

Note that this command could also have been entered as "cd \write \book".

Now we can copy "start.doc" into BOOK by inserting a diskette with "start.doc" in drive A and entering:

```
C>copy a:start.doc c:
```

Before going any further, let's step back and see what we have accomplished. First, though, we will make WRITE the current directory. WRITE is the parent directory of the current directory (BOOK), so we can make WRITE the current directory by entering:

```
C>cd ..
```

Note that this command could also have been entered as "cd \write".

To make sure that WRITE is now the current directory, type **cd** without a path specifier. MS-DOS will display the path from the root directory to the current directory:

```
C>cd
C:\WRITE
```

Let's use the DIR command to display the contents of the current directory:

```
C>dir

Volume in drive C has no label
Directory of   C:\WRITE

.              <DIR>      9-17-88     11:42a
..             <DIR>      9-17-88     11:42a
WP      EXE    72960      6-20-85      5:02p

LETTERS        <DIR>      9-17-88      2:00p
BOOK           <DIR>      9-17-88      2:00p
        5 File(s)      10262392 bytes free
```

Notice that the first two lines contain periods rather than names. The single period (.) in line 1 designates the current directory. The two periods in line 2 represent the parent directory of the current directory. The next three lines show the file and subdirectories that have been entered in WRITE.

Completing the remainder of the file structure shown in figure 3-4 is simply a matter of repeating some of our previous steps. First, the root directory is made the current directory:

```
C>cd \
```

Then the subdirectories PROGRAMS and BUSINESS are created as entries in the root directory:

```
C>md programs
C>md business
```

Next the current directory is changed to PROGRAMS. A diskette with the files "gwbasic.exe" and "lifex.bas" is placed in drive A, and the files are copied into PROGRAMS:

```
C>cd programs
C>copy a:gwbasic.exe c:
C>copy a:lifex.bas c:
```

The current directory is then changed to BUSINESS. A disk containing the files "gwbasic.exe" and "records.bas" is placed in drive A, and the files are copied into BUSINESS:

```
C>cd \business
C>copy a:gwbasic.exe c:
C>copy a:records.bas c:
```

This completes the construction of the directory and file structure shown in figure 3-4.

Looking at the Tree

As the number of files and subdirectories on a disk increases, the organization of the disk becomes more and more complex. TREE is an MS-DOS command that is used to construct a map of a disk's tree structure. To demonstrate this command, place your working system diskette in drive A, making sure that the file TREE.COM is on the working system diskette. Enter the command a:tree c:/f. This command tells MS-DOS to display the tree of directories found on fixed disk C. The /f switch directs MS-DOS to list the files on the fixed disk as well.

```
C>a:tree c:/f

TREE: Full-disk sub-directory listing - Version 3.30
Copyright (C)1987 XYZ Data Systems, Inc.

C:\COMMAND.COM                              17664 bytes
C:\WRITE
C:      \WP.EXE                             72960 bytes
C:      \LETTERS
C:             \HILBURN.DOC                  4608 bytes
        1 file(s)
C:      \BOOK
C:             \STARTING.DOC                15360 bytes
   3 file(s)
C:\PROGRAMS
C:      \GWBASIC.EXE                        57344 bytes
C:      \LIFEX.BAS                           7808 bytes
   2 file(s)
C:\BUSINESS
C:      \GWBASIC.EXE                        57344 bytes
C:      \RECORDS.BAS                         9088 bytes
   2 file(s)
   4 file(s)
                        10109816 bytes free
                        10592256 bytes total
End of listing
```

Verify for yourself that this listing contains all the information in figure 3-4. Notice that it also contains the size of each file on the disk.

Removing a Subdirectory

The MS-DOS command RMDIR (ReMove DIRectory), RD for short, is used to remove a subdirectory from a disk. To use RMDIR, type **rmdir** (or **rd**) and then type the path to the subdirectory. However, before you can remove the subdirectory, you must empty it of any files and/or subdirectories that it contains.

Suppose that you want to remove the subdirectory BOOK from the fixed disk (figure 3-4). The first step is to erase all the files entered in BOOK. This can be accomplished by using the MS-DOS command ERASE and the wildcard *.* (see chapter 2). After you enter the following command, MS-DOS will ask if you are sure that you want to erase all the files in the specified subdirectory:

```
C>erase \write\book *.*
Are you sure? (Y/N) y
```

Since you responded "yes," MS-DOS erased the files in BOOK, and the subdirectory can now be removed by entering:

```
C>rmdir \write\book
```

The PATH Command

An *executable file* is a set of directions that the computer executes in order to perform a specific task. An executable file may be an application program (such as a word processing program), an external MS-DOS command (such as TREE), or a batch file (see chapter 5). When you enter the name of an executable file, MS-DOS looks for the file in the current directory. The PATH command is used to tell MS-DOS where to look for an executable file that is not in the current directory.

To use the command, type **path** followed by the path(s) that you want MS-DOS to follow in its search for the executable file. If you want to specify more than one path, separate the paths with semicolons. If you enter PATH without any parameters, MS-DOS will display the command paths that were set the last time the PATH command was used. If you enter PATH followed by just a semicolon, MS-DOS will cancel the command paths that were set by the previous PATH command.

Why the Bother?

This chapter has shown you how the hierarchical file structure of MS-DOS 2.X and 3.X can be used to manage files. For the sake of clarity, we have used very simple examples, with few files and few subdirectories. However, as we mentioned at the beginning of this chapter, MS-DOS 2.X and 3.X are designed to handle large numbers of files, such as those found on hard disks. This chapter will end with an example of how MS-DOS can organize several hundred files.

Pretend that you are using a word processing program to write several different types of documents. Let's say that you are writing a computer book, a novel, personal letters, business letters, save-the-whales letters, and miscellaneous letters. Let's also say that you are a very prolific writer. You have already written 30 chapters in both the computer book and the novel, and you have a total of 400 letters that are evenly divided among the personal, business, whale, and miscellaneous categories. Each of your chapters and each of your letters is saved as one file on your hard disk. That's a total of 460 files just for your word processor. How can you use MS-DOS to organize these files?

There is no single right way to organize any hard disk system. The best approach is to try something out, see if you like it, and change it if you don't. Here is one way you might organize your files. Create a separate subdirectory for each of the different categories of word processing documents. These subdirectories will be entered in the root directory of the hard disk. Into each subdirectory enter the corresponding documents. Finally, enter a copy of the file "wp.exe" (the word processing program) in the root directory. Figure 3-5 shows how the files might be structured on your imaginary hard disk.

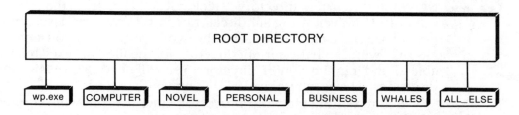

Figure 3-5. Organizing files by grouping them into subdirectories.

In a typical computer work session, you might sit down to do some work on your novel. You might want to quickly review some of the already completed chapters and then revise your latest chapter. For the time being, you aren't concerned about your 100 save-the-whales letters or anything else on the hard disk that is not part of your novel.

First, make NOVEL the current directory on drive C:

```
C>cd \novel
C>
```

Now, if you want a list of the chapters that you have written, all you have to do is type **dir/w**, the MS-DOS command for displaying a directory of filenames. Only the files in the NOVEL subdirectory will be displayed. (See Part 3 for a discussion of DIR.)

```
C>dir /w

Volume in drive C is HARD_DISK
```

```
Directory of C:\novel

 .             ..              CHAPT01.DOC CHAPT02.DOC CHAPT03.DOC
CHAPT04.DOC CHAPT05.DOC CHAPT06.DOC CHAPT07.DOC CHAPT08.DOC
CHAPT09.DOC CHAPT10.DOC CHAPT11.DOC CHAPT12.DOC CHAPT13.DOC
CHAPT14.DOC CHAPT15.DOC CHAPT16.DOC CHAPT17.DOC CHAPT18.DOC
CHAPT19.DOC CHAPT20.DOC CHAPT21.DOC CHAPT22.DOC CHAPT23.DOC
CHAPT24.DOC CHAPT25.DOC CHAPT26.DOC CHAPT27.DOC CHAPT28.DOC
CHAPT29.DOC CHAPT30.DOC
        32 File(s)  352224 bytes free


C>
```

If you want to copy all the chapters of your novel onto a diskette in drive B, simply type **copy *.doc b:**. Only the chapters of your novel will be copied; the other files on the disk will not.

The preceding example showed you how designating the subdirectory NOVEL as the current directory "shielded" MS-DOS from the other files on the disk. However, using subdirectories in this way can also cause some problems. For example, to start the word processor, you enter "wp". MS-DOS will search the current directory for the file "wp.exe" but won't be able to find it in the NOVEL directory. You will need to give MS-DOS some directions. This is where the PATH command comes in.

Before starting the word processor, enter the following command:

```
C>path c:\write
```

This command tells MS-DOS that if it can't find an executable file in the current directory, it should look in the directory `c:\write`. MS-DOS will now be able to load and execute the word processing program when you enter "wp".

The APPEND Command

PATH will direct MS-DOS only to executable files. Executable files have a filename extension of COM, EXE, or BAT. PATH will not direct application programs to data files. For example, many programs come with on-line help files. If the program is running and it needs to access a help file, the information provided by PATH is of no value since the help file is not executable.

The APPEND command, implemented in MS-DOS 3.3, is designed to eliminate this problem. APPEND is used just like PATH. For example, the following command is valid:

```
append c:\programs
```

This command tells MS-DOS to look in the directory PROGRAMS when searching for both executable and nonexecutable files.

APPEND is a very valuable command, and it is discussed more thoroughly in Part 3 of this book. Part 3 also discusses some annoying bugs in APPEND that you should know about before using this command.

C H A P T E R

4

Installing a Fixed Disk

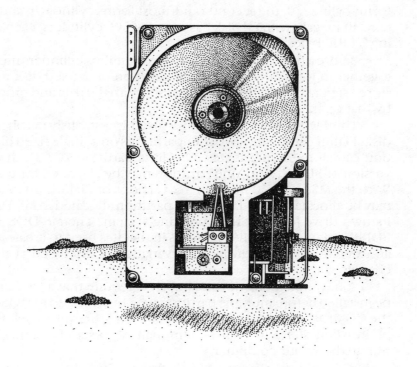

Disk Partitions and FDISK
MS-DOS 3.3 Enhancements

This chapter discusses the MS-DOS utility program FDISK. FDISK is used to initialize a fixed (hard) disk for use with MS-DOS. Before using a fixed disk, you should be familiar with the material presented in chapters 1 through 3 of this book. You should also know about the commands BACKUP and RE-STORE. BACKUP is used to create *archival* copies of files. Archival files are files used for storage and nothing else. RESTORE is used to convert archival files to normal files. These two commands are very useful in managing backup copies of the large number of files that can be stored on a fixed disk. Both commands are described fully in Part 3.

Disk Partitions and FDISK

A fixed disk consists of one or more platters. Each platter has two surfaces that are used to store data. Each platter surface is divided into a series of concentric circles called *tracks*. All tracks of equal diameter are grouped together to form a *cylinder*. The outermost group of tracks on each platter forms cylinder 0, the second-outermost forms cylinder 1, and so on. A standard 10-megabyte fixed disk has a total of 306 cylinders, each cylinder holding 34,816 bytes.

Before a fixed disk can be used, contiguous cylinders must be grouped together to form *partitions*. Each partition on a fixed disk may be used to store a separate operating system, along with the data and program files used by that operating system.

The FDISK utility program is used to establish partitions on a fixed disk. FDISK can create up to four partitions on a single fixed disk. Each partition can store 32 megabytes. On disks partitioned with the MS-DOS 2.X version of FDISK, only one partition may be allocated for use by MS-DOS. With the MS-DOS 3.0 through 3.2 versions of FDISK, up to four partitions may be allocated to MS-DOS. Each partition allocated to MS-DOS is assigned its own drive letter by the operating system. The MS-DOS 3.3 version of FDISK differs from earlier versions in that it is used to create a *primary* and an *extended* DOS partition. This variation is discussed at the end of this chapter.

Some implementations of MS-DOS require that a special device driver be installed before multiple partitions can be allocated to DOS. For example, the COMPAQ Computer release of MS-DOS 3.1 requires that ENHDISK.SYS be installed. Refer to your system manual to see if a similar procedure is required on your computer.

Starting FDISK

Before describing how FDISK is used, it should be noted that there is some variability among the different implementations of FDISK. The behavior and appearance of your version may differ somewhat from that presented in the following examples. However, the principles and the terminology will be the same.

```
A> fdisk

XYZ Data Systems
Fixed Disk Setup Program Version 3.30
(C)Copyright 1983, 1987 XYZ Data Systems, Inc.

FDISK Options


Choose one of the following:

    1.  Create DOS Partition
    2.  Change Active Partition
    3.  Delete DOS Partition
    4.  Display Partition Data

Enter choice: [1]

Press Esc to return to DOS
```

As you can see, FDISK presents you with several options. We are interested in option 1, **Create DOS Partition**, which is the first step in installing the fixed disk with MS-DOS. In the line **Enter choice:**, notice that MS-DOS has already entered a "1" for you. The "1" is the default answer. Whenever MS-DOS asks you to enter a response in the Fixed Disk Setup Program, it displays a default answer. If you wish to use the default answer, simply press Enter. If you do not want the default, type in your desired response and press Enter. Since "1" is the selection we want, you would press Enter.

Creating the MS-DOS Partition

When you select option 1, FDISK will display the **Create DOS Partition** screen. An error message will be displayed if you are using MS-DOS 2 and the disk already contains a DOS partition.

If you want to change the size of an existing DOS partition, you must return to the main menu (press Esc) and choose option 3. Then proceed to create a new partition of the desired size, using option 1.

FDISK checks to see if the fixed disk has previously been partitioned. If not, FDISK asks if you want to use the entire disk for the DOS partition. If you reply "Y", FDISK will proceed to create the DOS partition. Once created, the partition must still be activated and formatted (discussed later in this chapter).

If you will be storing other operating systems, or creating multiple DOS partitions, you will not want DOS to use the entire disk. Reply "N" to the above query. FDISK will display some information about the fixed disk. Your screen will look something like this:

```
XYZ Data Systems
Fixed Disk Setup Program Version 3.30
(C)Copyright 1983, 1987 XYZ Data Systems, Inc.

Create DOS Partition

No partition defined

Total fixed disk is 305 cylinders.
Maximum available space is 305
cylinders at cylinder 0.

Enter partition size .......:[ 305]

Press Esc to return to FDISK Options
```

FDISK asks you to enter the partition size. Enter the number of cylinders that you want the DOS partition to occupy. The default number will be the largest space available. To use the default size, just press Enter. Otherwise, type in the number of cylinders desired and press Enter:

```
Enter partition size .......:[ 200]      ←Enter
```

Next, FDISK will ask for the number of the starting cylinder in the DOS partition. The default will be the first cylinder of the largest contiguous space that is available. Type in a number or press Enter for the default:

```
Enter starting cylinder number ...:[   0]      ←Enter
```

At this point, your screen will look something like this:

```
XYZ Data Systems
Fixed Disk Setup Program Version 3.30
(C)Copyright 1983, 1987 XYZ Data Systems, Inc.

Create DOS Partition

Partition   Status   Type   Start   End    Size
        1      N      DOS        0   199    200

Total fixed disk is 305 cylinders

Press Esc to return to FDISK Options
```

The information near the middle of the screen shows you that the DOS partition has been created. FDISK has assigned it partition number 1. Its current status is N (not active). The DOS partition begins at cylinder number

0 and ends at cylinder number 199. The size of the DOS partition is 200 cylinders.

Before the DOS partition can be used it must be activated and formatted. These procedures will be discussed later in the chapter.

Adding DOS to a Previously Partitioned Disk

If a disk has previously been partitioned by another operating system, selecting option 1 (**Create DOS Partition**) on the main FDISK menu will display a screen similar to this:

```
XYZ Data Systems
Fixed Disk Setup Program Version 3.30
(C)Copyright 1983, 1987 XYZ Data Systems, Inc.


Create DOS Partition


Partition   Status   Type    Start   End    Size
      1        A    non-DOS   000    099    100


Total fixed disk is 305 cylinders
Max avail space is 205 cyls at cyl 100.


Enter partition size .......:[ 205]
Press Esc to return to FDISK Options
```

FDISK asks you to enter the partition size. You must enter the number of cylinders that you want the DOS partition to occupy. The default number will be the largest space available. Press Enter if you want the default; otherwise, type in the number of cylinders desired and press Enter:

```
Enter partition size .......:[ 150]      ←Enter
```

Next, FDISK asks you for the number of the starting cylinder in the DOS partition. The default will be the first cylinder of the largest contiguous space available. Type in a number or press Enter for the default:

```
Enter starting cylinder number ...:[ 100]      ←Enter
```

Your screen should look something like this:

```
XYZ Data Systems
Fixed Disk Setup Program Version 3.30
(C)Copyright 1983, 1987 XYZ Data Systems, Inc.


Create DOS Partition
```

```
Partition   Status   Type    Start   End    Size
    1         A      non-DOS   000    099    100
    2         N       DOS      100    249    150

Total fixed disk is 305 cylinders

Press Esc to return to FDISK Options
```

The information near the middle of the screen shows you that the DOS partition has been created. FDISK has assigned it partition number 2. Its current status is N (not active). The DOS partition begins at cylinder number 100 and ends at cylinder number 249. The size of the DOS partition is 150 cylinders.

Activating and Formatting a DOS Partition

Once a DOS partition has been created, it must be activated and formatted. To activate the DOS partition, you must return to the FDISK main menu and select option 2. Your display will look something like this:

```
XYZ Data Systems
Fixed Disk Setup Program Version 3.30
(C)Copyright 1983, 1987 XYZ Data Systems, Inc.

Change Active Partition

Partition   Status   Type    Start   End    Size
    1         A      non-DOS   000    099    100
    2         N       DOS      100    249    150

Total fixed disk is 305 cylinders
The current active partition is 1.

Enter the number of the partition you
want to make active...............: [ ]

Press Esc to return to FDISK Options
```

This screen says that partition 1, which contains a non-DOS operating system, is the active partition. Enter 2 to make the DOS partition the active one. The screen will be modified to show that the DOS partition is active. Press Esc one time to return to the main FDISK menu. Press Esc again to return to the MS-DOS system prompt.

The DOS partition is now activated, but it must still be formatted before it can store any data. *A partition is formatted only once.* Never format a partition that has already been formatted. ***Reformatting a partition will destroy all existing data on the partition.***

To format the DOS partition, place your working copy of the MS-DOS system diskette in drive A. Make sure that you are at the MS-DOS command level (the MS-DOS prompt is displayed). Enter the command **format c:/s/v**. The /s and /v switches are optional. Use the /s switch if you will be using the DOS partition to boot your system. Use the /v switch if you want to assign a volume label to the DOS partition. The fixed disk will have a drive designator of "C:" if it is the first fixed disk in the system. The second fixed disk will have a designator of "D:", and so on.

After you have entered the format command, MS-DOS will display the following prompt:

```
Press any key to begin formatting drive C:
```

Reread the preceding warning about reformatting a partition. If you now want to cancel the command, press Esc. Press any other key to execute the command. The light on your fixed disk will come on. Formatting the fixed disk will take several minutes. MS-DOS will display a message telling you when formatting has been completed. If you included the /s switch in the FORMAT command, it will tell you that the system files have been transferred to the fixed disk. You will be prompted to enter a volume label if you included the /v switch in the FORMAT command. MS-DOS will display some data about the fixed disk, and the system prompt will be displayed. Your fixed disk is now ready to be used by MS-DOS.

Booting with the Fixed Disk

Your fixed disk will be bootable if you have included a /s switch in the FORMAT command. However, before attempting to boot, make sure that drive A does not contain a bootable diskette because, if it does, the computer will attempt to boot from drive A rather than the fixed disk. Should your computer attempt to boot from drive A, remove the bootable diskette from drive A, and press Ctrl-Alt-Del. Your system should reboot from the fixed disk if all is in order.

Note: Some computers will not boot from the fixed disk even if the DOS partition contains a copy of the system files. These computers require a system diskette in drive A for booting to take place.

If a system contains more than one fixed disk, only the first drive in the system (drive C) will be bootable.

Deleting a DOS Partition

You cannot change the size of an existing DOS partition. You must delete the existing partition and then create a new partition. You may also want to delete the DOS partition if you need the storage area for another operating system. Make sure that you back up any important data before deleting. All data in a partition are lost when the partition is deleted.

To delete a DOS partition, place a diskette containing the file FDISK.COM in drive A and enter **fdisk**. Enter option 3 when the FDISK main menu is displayed. Your display screen will look something like this:

```
XYZ Data Systems
Fixed Disk Setup Program Version 3.30
(C)Copyright 1983, 1987 XYZ Data Systems, Inc.

Delete DOS Partition

Partition   Status   Type    Start   End   Size
        1        A    non-DOS   000   099   100
        2        N    DOS       100   249   150

Total fixed disk is 305 cylinders
The current active partition is 1.



Warning! All data in the DOS partition
will be DESTROYED. Do you wish to
continue.....................? [N]

Press Esc to return to FDISK Options
```

If you are sure that you have made backup copies of all important data, press Y and Enter; otherwise, press Esc or just Enter. ("N" is the default response.)

The DOS partition will be deleted, and the partition information on the screen will be adjusted accordingly if you press "Y" and Enter. You will have to insert an MS-DOS system diskette in drive A if you wish to continue running your computer under MS-DOS.

Displaying the Partition Data

FDISK can be used to display a fixed disk's partition data. Enter option 4 when the FDISK menu is displayed. Your display screen will look similar to this:

```
XYZ Data Systems
Fixed Disk Setup Program Version 3.30
(C)Copyright 1983, 1987 XYZ Data Systems, Inc.

Display Partition Information
```

```
Partition    Status   Type    Start   End    Size
    1          A      non-DOS  000     099    100
    2          N      DOS      100     249    150


Total fixed disk is 305 cylinders

Press Esc to return to FDISK Options
```

There are two partitions on the fixed disk in this example. Partition 1 contains a non-DOS operating system and is the partition currently active. Partition 2 is the DOS partition. The starting and ending cylinders of each partition are listed, as is the size of each partition. No modification of the system can be made from this screen. Press Esc one time to return to the main FDISK menu and a second time to return to the MS-DOS prompt.

Selecting the Next Fixed Disk Drive

If your system contains more than one fixed disk, each FDISK screen display will contain a line stating the current or active fixed disk. Systems with more than one fixed disk will also have a fifth option selectable from FDISK's main menu:

```
XYZ Data Systems
Fixed Disk Setup Program Version 3.30
(C)Copyright 1983, 1987 XYZ Data Systems, Inc.


FDISK Options


Current Fixed Disk Drive: 1



Choose one of the following:

    1.   Create DOS Partition
    2.   Change Active Partition
    3.   Delete DOS Partition
    4.   Display Partition Data
    5.   Select Next Fixed Disk Drive

Enter choice: [1]

Press Esc to return to DOS
```

Select option 5 to change the number of the current fixed disk drive.

MS-DOS 3.3 Enhancements

The MS-DOS 3.3 version of FDISK also allows up to four partitions on a single fixed disk. However, MS-DOS 3.3 has two types of DOS partitions: primary and extended. Only a single primary partition is required for DOS to boot off the fixed disk. Only one primary and one extended partition may be active at a time.

The primary partition is limited to 32 megabytes and is assigned a single drive letter. There is no specified limit to the size of the extended partition. The extended partition may be divided into multiple logical drives. Each logical drive is limited to 32 megabytes and is assigned its own drive letter.

The extended DOS partition eliminates the need for special device drivers for very high capacity disk drives. Access time on high capacity drives is also improved.

5

MS-DOS Batch Files

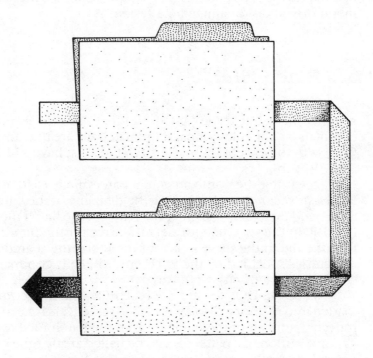

Computers are useful tools because they are capable of performing repetitive tasks without getting bored. Computers can maintain the same level of efficiency regardless of how many times they carry out the same task. Computer users, on the other hand, become bored rather easily when performing repetitive tasks, and a bored computer user tends to be inefficient and error-prone.

One repetitive task that computer users are often faced with is entering a series of commands over and over again. If you find yourself in this situation, don't despair because MS-DOS offers a way out. It allows you to take a series of commands and store them in a special kind of file called a *batch file*. This "batch" of MS-DOS commands can then be used over and over again, always producing the same result. This chapter will explain batch files and show you some MS-DOS features that can be used in conjunction with batch files. (See appendix C for examples of batch files used to implement a menu-driven disk maintenance system.)

What Is a Batch File?

A *batch file* is a text file (ASCII file) that contains a sequence of MS-DOS commands. The rules for naming a batch file are the same as those for other files, with the exception that a batch file must have a filename extension of .BAT (BATch).

Executing the commands in a batch file is easy. You simply give MS-DOS a *start command* by typing the filename of the batch file and pressing the Enter key. When you enter the name of the batch file, MS-DOS searches the disk in the specified (or default) drive for the file. If MS-DOS does not find the file in the drive's current directory, the search is extended to any directories specified by the PATH and APPEND commands. (Both of these commands are discussed in Part 3.)

When MS-DOS locates the batch file, the first command in the file is loaded into memory, displayed on the screen, and executed. This process is repeated until all of the commands in the batch file have been executed.

Execution of a batch file can be halted at any time by pressing the Ctrl-Break key combination. If you press Ctrl-Break, MS-DOS will ask you the following question:

```
Terminate batch job (Y/N)? _
```

If you enter "Y", execution of the batch file will be stopped and the MS-DOS prompt will be displayed. Entering "N" will stop only the command currently being executed. Execution will continue with the next command in the batch file.

Creating a Batch File

There are several ways to create a batch file. One way is to use a text editor, such as a word processing program or the MS-DOS program EDLIN (discussed in chapter 7). Another convenient way is to store the commands in a text file directly from the keyboard. This is done by directing MS-DOS to copy the input from the keyboard into a file and store it on a disk.

The MS-DOS device name for the keyboard is "CON" (CONsole). (MS-DOS device names are discussed in chapter 6.) To copy the input from the keyboard to a file, type **copy con:**, followed by the filename and filename extension of the file being created. For example, to create a batch file named "sample.bat", enter:

```
C>copy con: sample.bat
```

Then enter the MS-DOS commands that will make up the batch file. After entering the last command, press Ctrl-Z (or press the F6 function key) and then press Enter. The file will be stored on the disk in the default drive with the name "sample.bat". If there is an existing file named "sample.bat" in the current directory of the default drive, it will be replaced by the new file.

Batch files can be used to make automatic backup copies of important files. Imagine that you are using a word processing program to work on a file named "essay.doc". Let's say that this file is very important to you and that you want to make a backup copy of it at the end of each working session. A simple batch file will guarantee that a backup of "essay.doc" is made each time that you terminate execution of the word processing program. Such a batch file is very convenient because you do not have to enter the COPY command at the end of each word processing session. Assume for this example that the word-processing program file is named "wp.exe".

To create this batch file, enter:

```
C>copy con: backup.bat
wp.exe
copy essay.doc a:
^Z        ←you press Ctrl-Z and Enter
```

After you enter Ctrl-Z, the disk drive will turn on and the batch file "backup.bat" will be written to the disk in drive C. MS-DOS will display a message saying that one file has been copied and then will display the system prompt.

To execute the batch file, simply enter its filename:

```
C>backup
```

MS-DOS will display each command in a batch file before it is executed. Thus, after the filename has been entered, MS-DOS will display the first command:

```
C>WP.EXE
```

The word processing program will then start to run. When the word processor is terminated, control will be returned to MS-DOS. The system prompt and the next command in the batch file will automatically be displayed:

```
C>COPY ESSAY.DOC A:
```

"Essay.doc" will be copied to the disk in drive A, and execution of the batch file will be complete. The system prompt will then be displayed, and MS-DOS will wait for you to enter the next command.

Replaceable Parameters

Batch file commands may contain one or more *replaceable parameters*. A parameter is a command item that gives additional information to MS-DOS, such as the name of the file on which the command is to be performed. A *replaceable* parameter is a variable that is replaced with a string of characters (such as a filename). A batch file replaceable parameter is written as a percentage sign (%) followed by a single digit. Up to ten different replaceable parameters may be included in a batch file. You specify the character string that is to be substituted for each replaceable parameter when the batch file is called up in the batch file start command.

Substitution of character strings for the replaceable variables takes place according to the order in which the character strings are included in the start command. The first string is substituted for the replaceable variable %1, the second string is substituted for %2, and so on. MS-DOS automatically substitutes the file specification of the batch file for the replaceable variable %0.

Replaceable variables increase the flexibility of batch files. For example, suppose you find yourself in a situation similar to the one described in the first example of this tutorial. You want to set up a batch file that will automatically copy a file at the end of each work session. The batch file in the first example automatically made a copy of a particular file. You can use replaceable parameters to create a batch file that will automatically make a copy of any file. The file to be copied will be specified in the batch file start command.

To create this batch file, which we will call "copyall.bat", enter the following:

```
C>copy con: copyall.bat
wp.exe
copy %1 a:
^Z        ←you press Ctrl-Z and Enter
```

Pressing Enter will store the file on the disk in drive C.

To start execution of this batch file, enter the filename of the batch file, followed by the filename and filename extension of the file that is to be copied (in this example, "shoplist.doc"). Note that you must separate the parameters in the start command by using a space, a comma, or a semicolon:

```
C>copyall shoplist.doc

C>WP.EXE
```

MS-DOS begins execution of the batch file by loading and executing "wp.exe". When the word processor terminates, control is passed back to MS-DOS and the next command in the batch file is executed:

```
C>COPY SHOPLIST.DOC A:
        1 File(s) copied
```

Notice that MS-DOS automatically substitutes the name of the file to be copied for the replaceable variable in the batch file.

Let's carry this example one step further. Let's create a batch file called "difnam.bat" that will automatically make a copy of a specified file, and the name of the copy will be specified in the batch file start command:

```
C>copy con: difnam.bat
wp.exe
copy %1 a:%2
^Z
        1 File(s) copied
```

To start execution of this batch file, enter the batch filename, followed by the filename and filename extension of the file to be copied (in this example, "new.doc"), followed by the filename and filename extension to be given to the copy (in this example, "old.doc"):

```
C>difnam new.doc old.doc
```

The word processor is loaded and executed. When control is returned to MS-DOS, the batch file continues:

```
C>COPY NEW.DOC A:OLD.DOC
        1 File(s) copied
```

The first character string ("new.doc") in the batch file start command has been substituted for the replaceable variable %1. The second character string ("old.doc") has been substituted for the replaceable variable %2.

Wildcards and Replaceable Variables

The character strings included in a batch file start command can include the MS-DOS wildcards ? and *. When a string containing a wildcard is specified for a replaceable variable, the batch file command containing the variable is executed one time for each file that matches the string. Consider the following batch file:

```
C>copy con: display.bat
copy %1 con:
^Z

        1 File(s) copied
```

This batch file copies a file (represented by the replaceable parameter %1) to the display screen (CON). The file to be copied is specified in the start command. When the specified file is found, its contents are displayed on the screen.

Once "display.bat" has been created, the following command may be entered:

```
C>display *.txt
```

MS-DOS will search the default drive for each file that matches the wildcard (*.txt) and then will display its contents. (For more information on wildcards, see chapter 2.)

Occasionally, one of the filenames in a batch file will contain a percentage sign. To prevent MS-DOS from confusing the filename with a replaceable parameter, type the sign two times when listing the file. For example, if you want to include the file "hiho%.txt" in a batch file, it should be listed as "hiho%%.txt".

PAUSE

The PAUSE command can be used in a batch file when you want to temporarily suspend execution of the batch file. When MS-DOS encounters PAUSE, it ceases execution of the batch file and displays the following message:

```
Strike a key when ready...
```

Pressing any key, except the Ctrl-C combination, will resume execution of the batch file.

Pressing Ctrl-C causes MS-DOS to display the message:

```
Abort batch job (Y/N)? _
```

Entering "Y" terminates batch file execution. Entering "N" resumes execution of the batch file.

As you will see in the next example, the PAUSE command can be used to allow you time to change disks during batch file execution. The following batch file automatically makes two copies of a file. The original file, the first copy, and the second copy can each be assigned any valid filename and filename extension that you wish. The two copies will be on different disks. The batch file will pause after making the first copy so that a second disk can be put in drive A:

```
C>copy con: copytwo.bat
wp.exe
copy %1 a:%2
pause
copy %1 a:%3
^Z
        1 File(s) copied
```

To execute this batch file, type **copytwo**, followed in order by the filename and filename extension of the file to be copied, the filename and filename extension of the first copy, and the filename and filename extension of the second copy. Execution of the batch file begins when you press Enter:

```
C>copytwo new.doc old1.doc old2.doc

C>WP.EXE
```

This command loads and executes the word processor. When control is returned to MS-DOS, execution of the batch file continues:

```
C>COPY NEW.DOC A:OLD1.DOC
        1 File(s) copied

C>PAUSE
Strike any key when ready ...5

C>COPY NEW.DOC A:OLD2.DOC
        1 File(s) copied
```

Again, notice that the string characters in the start command replaced the variables in the batch file. After the first copy ("old1.doc") is made, the PAUSE command temporarily halts batch file execution. This allows you to put a new disk in the A drive. Batch file execution continues when a key (the "5" in this case) is pressed. The file is copied a second time ("old2.doc"), completing execution of the batch file.

The PAUSE command may also be used to display messages. When PAUSE is entered in a batch file, it can be followed by a character string. The string may be up to 121 characters long. The string will be displayed when the batch file is executed:

```
C>copy con: copytwo.bat
wp.exe
copy %1 a:%2
pause put disk number2 in drive a
copy %1 a:%3
^Z
        1 File(s) copied
```

The only difference between this batch file and the one in the previous example is that a message will be displayed when the PAUSE command is executed:

```
C>COPY NEW.DOC A:OLD1.DOC
        1 File(s) copied

C>PAUSE PUT DISK NUMBER 2 IN DRIVE A
Strike any key when ready ... 5

C>COPY NEW.DOC A:OLD2.DOC
        1 File(s) copied
```

REM

The REM (REMark) command can be used to display a message during the execution of a batch file. Enter **rem** in the batch file, followed by the message that will be displayed. The message can be up to 123 characters long. For example, enter the following:

```
C>copy con: copytwo.bat
wp.exe
rem making copy number 1
copy %1 a:%2
pause put disk number 2 in drive a
rem making copy number 2
```

```
copy %1 a:%3
^Z
        1 File(s) copied
```

The REM commands will help you follow the batch file's execution:

```
C>REM MAKING COPY NUMBER 1

C>COPY NEW.DOC A:OLD1.DOC
        1 File(s) copied

C>PAUSE PUT DISK NUMBER 2 IN DRIVE A
Strike any key when ready ...5

C>REM MAKING COPY NUMBER 2

C>COPY NEW.DOC A:OLD2.DOC
        1 File(s) copied
```

AUTOEXEC.BAT

A very useful batch file to know about is AUTOEXEC.BAT. When AUTOEXEC.BAT is stored in the root directory of the default drive, MS-DOS will automatically execute the commands in the file each time the system is booted. AUTOEXEC.BAT is a tremendous timesaver, since there is generally a sequence of commands to be executed each time the system is started. Typically, AUTOEXEC.BAT is used to set the directory search path, establish the current directories on each drive, and load an application program. AUTOEXEC.BAT will not prompt the user to enter the date and time unless the commands DATE and TIME are included in the batch file.

The following AUTOEXEC.BAT file is one used by the author during the writing of this book. The first command in the batch file (ECHO OFF) is discussed in the next section of this chapter.

```
echo off
rem
rem Set prompt to display working directory of default drive
prompt $p$g
rem
rem Set the search path and append path
path c:\dos;c:\misc;c:\kermit;c:\procom24;c:\utils;
append /e /x
append c:\mltmate;c:\vedit;c:\masm
rem
rem Set up environment variables
```

```
set comspec=c:\command.com
set procomm=c:\procom24\
rem
rem Establish default drive, working directories
cd c:\book\newchp
cd a:newchp
rem
rem Start text editor
vplus
rem
rem XCOPY all new or changed files
xcopy * a: /m
```

ECHO

As you have already seen, under normal circumstances MS-DOS displays the commands in a batch file on the screen immediately before it executes them. With the ECHO command, you can control whether or not the commands are displayed.

To use ECHO in a batch file, type **echo**, followed by either **on** or **off**. ECHO ON causes MS-DOS commands to be displayed in the normal fashion. ECHO OFF suppresses the display of all MS-DOS commands including REM commands. However, ECHO OFF does not suppress any messages that are produced while commands are being executed.

If there is no ECHO command in a file, the default state is ECHO ON. ECHO is automatically turned on when a batch file is terminated. Entering ECHO without any parameters causes MS-DOS to display the current ECHO state (ON or OFF). The following batch file demonstrates the use of ECHO:

```
C>copy con: example1.bat
rem this message will be displayed
rem since echo is on
echo off                              ←ECHO is turned off
rem this message will not be displayed
rem since echo is now off
echo                                  ←ECHO state is displayed
echo on                              ←ECHO is turned on
rem echo is back on
echo                                  ←ECHO state is displayed
^Z
        1 File(s) copied

C>example1

C>REM THIS MESSAGE WILL BE DISPLAYED
```

```
C>REM SINCE ECHO IS ON

C>ECHO OFF
ECHO is off

C>REM ECHO IS BACK ON

C>ECHO
ECHO is on
```

In the preceding example, the first two REM commands are displayed, since ECHO is initially in the default ON state. The third command in the batch file turns ECHO off, so the next two REM commands are not displayed. The sixth command (ECHO) verifies that the ECHO state is OFF. The seventh command then turns ECHO back ON, and the final REM command is displayed. The last command in the file (ECHO) verifies that ECHO is back ON.

If a message is entered in a batch file following ECHO, the message will be displayed regardless of the ECHO state:

```
C>copy con: example2.bat
echo off
rem this message will not be displayed
echo but this one will be
echo on
rem this will be displayed
echo so will this ... twice
^Z
        1 File(s) copied

C>example2

C>ECHO OFF
BUT THIS ONE WILL BE

C>REM THIS WILL BE DISPLAYED

C>ECHO SO WILL THIS ... TWICE
SO WILL THIS ... TWICE
```

The first command in this batch file turns ECHO OFF. With ECHO OFF, the first REM command is not displayed. The third command in the file is an ECHO command. Since ECHO is OFF, the command is not displayed, but the message within the ECHO command (**THIS WILL BE DISPLAYED**) *is* displayed. The fourth command in the file turns ECHO ON so that the following REM command is displayed. The final command in the file is an ECHO command. Since ECHO is ON, this command is displayed, and then the message within the command is displayed again.

Using ECHO to Send a Blank Line to the Screen

Often the text on a display screen is easier to read if it is occasionally interspersed with a blank line. With this in mind, it would be nice if ECHO could be used to send a blank line to the screen. Unfortunately, no simple way to do this exists for both the 2.X and 3.X versions of MS-DOS.

The command "ECHO " (ECHO followed by two spaces) will send a blank line to the screen under MS-DOS 2.X but not under 3.X. The command "ECHO." (ECHO followed by a period) will send a blank line to the screen under 3.X but not 2.X. You have to be tricky if you want something that works under both versions.

The command "ECHO ^H" (ECHO followed by a space and a Ctrl-H character) will send a blank line to the screen under 2.X and 3.X. Many word processors allow you to place control characters in a text file. If you do not have a word processor with this capability, use your word processor to enter "ECHO *". Then use DEBUG (chapter 9) to replace the * with a Ctrl-H character. Ctrl-H is the same as the backspace character (ASCII value 008).

Suppressing ECHO OFF

MS-DOS 3.3 allows you to suppress the display of a line in a batch file by preceding the line with an at character (@). One place where this is useful is in suppressing the display ECHO OFF at the start of a batch file. As an example, no display is generated from the following batch file:

```
@echo off
rem this is a test
```

Without the @, the ECHO OFF command will be displayed.

A trick can be employed to make it appear as though ECHO OFF is not displayed. This technique can be used in MS-DOS 2.X and 3.X. To begin, you must have ANSI.SYS installed as the keyboard device driver. (See chapter 8 for an explanation of how to do this.) Then, start your batch file with the following two lines:

```
echo off
echo ^[[s^[[1A^[[K^[[u
```

Note that each ^[is a single escape character, not two separate characters. Most word processors allow you to place escape characters in a text file. You can also use DEBUG (chapter 9) to replace dummy characters with escape characters (escape characters have ASCII value 1BH). If you refer to table 8-1, you will see that the second ECHO command is a sequence of instructions for ANSI.SYS. The screen device driver is instructed to:

^[[s   Save the current position of the cursor.

^[[1A	Move the cursor up one line.
^[K	Erase from the cursor to the end of the line.
^[[	Restore the cursor to its original position.

In this way, "echo off" is displayed on the screen but is erased before it can be read.

GOTO

The GOTO command is used to transfer control within a batch file. GOTO directs the batch file to jump to a labeled line within the batch file. A *line label* in a batch file consists of a colon (:) followed by up to eight characters. For example, enter the following:

```
C>copy con: example3.bat
rem this is the first line
rem this is the second line
goto four
rem this is the third line
:four
rem this is the fourth line
^Z
        1 File(s) copied

C>example3

C>REM THIS IS THE FIRST LINE
C>REM THIS IS THE SECOND LINE

C>GOTO FOUR

C>REM THIS IS THE FOURTH LINE
```

The first two commands in the batch file are executed. Execution then jumps to the ":four" label and continues with the final command in the batch file.

The label in a GOTO command can be a replaceable variable. This allows the execution of the batch file to jump to a line that is determined by a parameter included in the batch file start command. The following example shows how this works:

```
C>copy con: example3.bat
goto %1
:one
rem this is one
```

```
goto finish
:two
rem this is two
goto finish
:three
rem this is three
:finish
^Z
        1 File(s) copied

C>example3 three

C>GOTO THREE

C>REM THIS IS THREE
```

When this batch file is called up, the character string "three" is included in the start command. When the first command in the batch file is executed, "THREE" replaces the variable %1. Execution then jumps to the label ":three". The REM command ("this is three") is executed. The final line in the batch file is another line label. Line labels are not displayed during batch file execution.

IF

You can use the IF command to create commands in a batch file that will be executed if a specified condition is true. There are three types of conditions that IF can test: IF EXIST, IF String1==String2, and IF ERRORLEVEL.

IF EXIST

The first condition is called the EXIST condition. This conditional statement checks to see if a specified file exists. If the file exists, the condition has been met and the command will be executed. Consider the following command in a batch file:

```
if exist somefile.dat type somefile.dat
```

In executing this command, MS-DOS determines first if the file "somefile.dat" exists on the default drive. Then, if the file exists, MS-DOS executes the command to type the file. If "somefile.dat" does not exist, MS-DOS skips to the next batch command.

IF may be used to check for files on a drive other than the default. Simply precede the file specified in the IF command with the appropriate drive letter designator (such as A: or B:).

IF can check for files only in the current directory of a drive. To check a directory other than the current one, you must first make that directory the drive's current directory. Directories are discussed in chapter 3.

IF String1 = = String2

The second type of condition that may be tested by an IF statement is whether two character strings are identical. Consider the following batch file:

```
C>copy con: example4.bat
echo off
if %1==roses goto roses
if %1==candy goto candy
if %1==perfume goto perfume
echo you are in big trouble
goto finish
:roses
echo you sent roses. how thoughtful.
goto finish
:candy
echo you sent candy. how sweet.
goto finish
:perfume
echo you sent perfume. how romantic.
:finish
^Z
        1 File(s) copied

C>example4 perfume

C>ECHO OFF
YOU SENT PERFUME. HOW ROMANTIC.
```

Each of the IF statements compares a replaceable variable to a character string. Note that the IF statements use double equal signs (==). The string parameter that is included in the batch file start command replaces the variable in each IF statement. When the condition tested by an IF statement is true, the command contained in that statement is executed; in this case, execution branches to the PERFUME line label.

Notice that this batch file begins with the command ECHO OFF. This results in a screen display that is much less cluttered and easier to read.

IF ERRORLEVEL *n*

ERRORLEVEL is a system variable maintained by MS-DOS and used to monitor error conditions. Many of the MS-DOS commands (see table 5-1) set ERRORLEVEL if an error is encountered during execution of the command.

The type of error encountered determines the value to which ERRORLEVEL is set. Application programs can also use DOS service functions 31H and 4CH to set ERRORLEVEL (see appendix A). The statement

IF ERRORLEVEL *n command*

tells MS-DOS that if ERRORLEVEL is equal to or greater than *n*, execute *command*. Refer to the discussion of the individual MS-DOS commands for details on how they set ERRORLEVEL.

Table 5-1. MS-DOS Commands That Set ERRORLEVEL

MS-DOS 2.XX	MS-DOS 3.20	MS-DOS 3.30
BACKUP	BACKUP	BACKUP
RESTORE	RESTORE	RESTORE
	FORMAT	FORMAT
	REPLACE	REPLACE
		GRAFTABL
		KEYB

IF NOT

An IF NOT statement can also test to see if a condition is false. Consider the following statement:

```
if not exist somefile.bak copy somefile.txt somefile.bak
```

This statement tests for the nonexistence of a file. If the file does not exist, the MS-DOS command within the IF statement is executed. IF NOT may be used to test any condition that may be tested with IF.

FOR

The FOR command allows a batch file command to be executed repeatedly on a set of specified parameters. The syntax (or rules) of FOR is a little involved, so let's begin with an example:

```
for %%a IN (file1 file2 file3) DO del %%a
```

As you can see from the example, a FOR statement begins with the word "for", followed by a dummy variable. The dummy variable must be preceded by two percentage signs (%%). The variable is followed by the word "IN", which must be entered in uppercase. "IN" is followed by the set of parameters on which the command is to operate. The set of parameters is usually a list of files. In our example, three files are specified as parameters. The set of parameters is followed by "DO", which must also be entered in uppercase. "DO" is followed by the command that is to be executed. In the example, the command "del %%a" is executed three times, deleting sequentially the files "file1", "file2", and "file3".

A FOR statement is useful when you want to execute a command on a group of files that cannot be specified with wildcards. Suppose that three text files named "example1.bat", "program.txt", and "letter" existed on a disk and that you wanted a printed copy of each file. You could enter the command "copy example.bat prn", sit back and wait while the file is being printed, enter the same command for "program.txt", wait again, and then enter the command for "letter". If you do this, you will spend a lot of time sitting around, waiting for the computer to print each file.

The following command, included in a batch file, will perform the same task without all that wasted time:

```
for %%a IN (example.bat program.txt letter) DO copy %%a prn
```

The three text files will be printed, and you had to enter only one command.

FOR commands are not limited to use in batch files. They can be used as standard MS-DOS commands and will execute repeatedly on a set of parameters. When FOR commands are used in this fashion, the dummy variable is preceded by only one percentage sign.

Any file specified as a parameter in a FOR command must be located in the current directory of the specified or default disk drive. Current directories are discussed in chapter 3.

SHIFT

The SHIFT command allows you to specify more than ten parameters in a batch file start command. Recall that a batch file can normally contain up to ten replaceable variables. A list of character strings, included in the start command, sequentially replaces the variables as the batch file is executed. The first string specified replaces the variable %1, the second string replaces %2, and so on. The replaceable variable %0 is reserved for the file specification of the batch file.

The SHIFT command "shifts" the parameters one position to the left. The first parameter in the start command replaces %0, the second parameter replaces %1, and so on. Each time a SHIFT command is executed, the parameters shift one position to the left. The following batch file should help clarify the use of SHIFT:

```
C>copy con: example6.bat
echo off
echo %0 %1 %2 %3 %4 %5 %6 %7 %8 %9
shift
echo %0 %1 %2 %3 %4 %5 %6 %7 %8 %9
shift
echo %0 %1 %2 %3 %4 %5 %6 %7 %8 %9
shift
echo %0 %1 %2 %3 %4 %5 %6 %7 %8 %9
^Z
        1 File(s) copied

C>example6 00 01 02 03 04 05 06 07 08 09 10

C>ECHO OFF
EXAMPLE6 00 01 02 03 04 05 06 07 08
00 01 02 03 04 05 06 07 08 09
01 02 03 04 05 06 07 08 09 10
02 03 04 05 06 07 08 09 10
```

The batch file echoes the current values of the variables four times. The first time, %0 is "EXAMPLE6", %1 is "00", and so on. After one SHIFT, %0 is "00", %1 is "01", and so on. Notice that after the third SHIFT, only nine of the variables have a value. (For another, more practical, application of SHIFT, refer to the batch file presented at the end of this chapter.)

CALL

The concept of *modular programming* is widely accepted by computer programmers. Modular programming refers to the practice of dividing a computer program into small modules, each module being responsible for a single function (such as performing a calculation or copying a file). Programmers try to write modules that are reusable, meaning that a module written for one program can be reused in another program. This saves programmers from having to "reinvent the wheel" each time they write a program. The other big attraction of modular programming is that small modules are easy to debug, unlike large programs which can be very difficult to debug. Programmers use existing modules by issuing a "call." A *call* is a command to invoke a module.

Batch file programming lends itself well to the development of reusable batch file modules. Unfortunately, with versions of MS-DOS prior to 3.3, it is cumbersome to call a batch file module. To illustrate the problem, let's see what happens when the following two batch files are executed:

```
C>copy con one.bat
```

```
echo starting one
two
echo ending one
^Z
      1 File(s) copied

C>copy con two.bat
echo starting two
echo ending two
^Z
      1 File(s) copied
```

Now here is what happens when we call ONE.BAT:

```
C>one

C>echo starting one
starting one

C>two

C>echo starting two
starting two
C>echo ending two
ending two

C>
```

ONE.BAT echoes its starting message and then calls TWO.BAT. TWO.BAT displays its starting and ending messages, and its execution terminates. However, control is then passed to DOS (rather than back to ONE.BAT), and ONE.BAT's ending message does not get displayed. This failure to display ONE.BAT's ending message can be overcome with a small modification of ONE.BAT, namely, the use of the CALL command to execute TWO.BAT.

```
C>copy con one.bat
echo starting one
call two
echo ending one
^Z
      1 File(s) copied
```

Now we can see that control returns to ONE after TWO is executed:

```
C>one
```

```
C>echo starting one
starting one

C>call two

C>echo starting two
starting two

C>echo ending two
ending two

C>echo ending one
ending one
```

See the last section of this chapter, "Using Environment Variables," for another example using CALL.

Calling Batch File Modules without CALL

CALL is implemented in MS-DOS 3.3 only. Batch files running under earlier versions of MS-DOS can call other batch files by loading a *secondary command processor* and having the secondary command processor execute the second batch file. The following version of ONE.BAT works under versions 2.X and 3.X of MS-DOS. See the discussion of COMMAND in Part 3 for details on the use of a secondary command processor.

```
C>copy con one.bat
echo starting one
rem
rem The command "command /c two" invokes a secondary command processor
rem which loads two.bat. When two.bat terminates execution, control
rem is passed back to one.bat.
rem
command /c two
echo ending one
^Z
    1 File(s) copied
C>
```

Using Environment Variables

Batch files running under MS-DOS 3.X can access and modify the MS-DOS environment variables (the environment and environment variables are discussed in chapter 12). To reference an environment variable from within a batch file, use the variable's name preceded and followed by a percentage sign. Thus, if a batch file contains the command "ECHO %PATH%", the current directory search path is displayed.

The following batch file, ADD2PATH.BAT, can be used to append additional search paths to the current PATH variable. The batch file is called with a command having this format:

add2path newpath1;newpath2;newpath3 . . .

where each "newpath" is a search path (for example, a:\subdir2\subdir2). The batch file loops one time for each newpath entered on the command line. Each loop appends the replaceable variable "%1" to the end of PATH. The SHIFT command then moves the next newpath on the command line into variable "%1". The command that is after the loop label checks to see if the end of the command line has been reached. Notice the double quotes around %1.

```
echo off
echo ^[[s^[[1A^[[K^[[u
rem
rem                     ADD2PATH.BAT
rem
rem This batch file adds a search path to an existing PATH variable.
rem The syntax for using ADD2PATH is as follows:
rem
rem             ADD2PATH newpath1;newpath2 ...
rem
rem Each "newpath1", "newpath2", etc., specifies a new search
rem path, which is added to the existing PATH variable. The
rem "newpath's" may be separated by a semicolon, space, tab,
rem or equal sign.
rem
rem The batch file uses "%path%" to access the current PATH
rem variable and append the newpaths to it. The total number
rem of characters that may be added to the PATH variable is
rem limited by 2 factors: (1) Each time ADD2PATH is invoked,
rem there is a limit on the number of characters that can be
rem entered on the command line, and (2) there is a limit on
rem the number of characters that can be stored in the DOS
rem environment (see chapter 12 of MS-DOS Bible). DOS will display:
rem
rem             Out of environment space
rem
rem if the limit is reached.
rem
rem ADD2PATH "loops" one time for each new path specifier
rem entered, exiting after all have been processed.
rem The new PATH variable is displayed when execution
rem terminates.
rem
```

```
rem NOTE: The echo commands at the start of this batch file
rem require ANSI.SYS to work correctly. See chapter 8 of
rem MS-DOS Bible.
rem
:loop
rem exit if all parameters have been read
if "%1"=="" goto exit
rem append %1 to existing path
set path=%path%;%1
rem shift parameters one to left
shift
goto loop
:exit
echo PATH=%path%
echo.
```

ADD2PATH.BAT is useful if you want to add information to the end of PATH without having to enter the existing path string on the command line. If you want to modify PATH from the command line (using "SET PATH="), you are limited by the 149-character restriction imposed by MS-DOS's keyboard buffer. Therefore, you may not be able to set as long a PATH variable as you would like. Using ADD2PATH.BAT, you are limited only by the size of your DOS environment (the size of which can be adjusted, see chapter 12).

ADD2PATH.BAT is also useful for adding search paths that you do not ordinarily use but need for a particular application. The following batch file could be used to initialize MS-DOS to use such an application.

```
echo off
rem                 WP_INIT.BAT
rem
rem A batch file to initialize MS-DOS to use "WP"
rem
rem Append WP's directory to PATH
call add2path \wp
rem
rem Set up working directories
c:
cd \letters\aug_81
cd a:\letters\aug_81
rem
rem Load the word processor
wp
rem
rem copy any new or modified files upon exit
xcopy *.* a: /m
```

6

Redirection, Filters, and Pipes

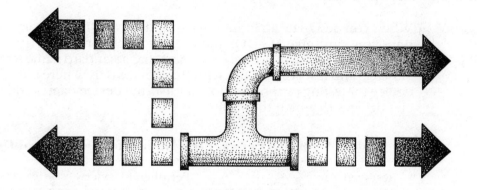

Standard Input and Standard Output Devices

Reserved Device Names

Redirecting an MS-DOS Command

Filters

Pipes

Redirection versus Piping

Input and *output* are the processes through which computers receive and send data. Versions 2.X and 3.X of MS-DOS allow you to modify these processes through the use of some sophisticated data management techniques known as *redirection, filtering,* and *piping.* You can use these techniques and their associated MS-DOS commands to build your own information pipeline. Like a plumber, you can redirect the flow of information from one place to another, have the information modified through a filter, and then pipe the output to a final destination. This chapter will explain how to use these special techniques with MS-DOS 2.X and 3.X.

Standard Input and Standard Output Devices

As you know from your own experience, most of the time you use the keyboard to enter data into your computer, and during most operations this data is sent to the display screen for your viewing. The keyboard is therefore the *standard input device,* and the display screen or monitor is the *standard output device.*

MS-DOS 2.X and 3.X allow you to specify a device, other than the standard input device, as the source of input data. Similarly, you can specify a device, other than the standard output device, as the destination of output data. These input and output devices are called *peripheral devices* because they are hardware that is external to the microcomputer.

Reserved Device Names

When you designate an input or output device different from the standard one, you must give MS-DOS the correct name for that peripheral device. Each device, such as a printer or modem, has a standard name recognized by MS-DOS and reserved for use with that device only. There is even a dummy device for testing purposes. Table 6-1 lists the device names and the peripheral devices to which they refer.

Table 6-1. MS-DOS Reserved Names for Peripheral Devices

Reserved Name	Peripheral Device
AUX	First asynchronous communications port
COM1, COM2, COM3, COM4	Asynchronous communications ports 1 through 4
CON	Keyboard and display screen (CONsole)
LPT1, LPT2, LPT3	First, second, and third parallel printers
NUL	Dummy device (for testing)
PRN	First parallel printer

Redirecting an MS-DOS Command

The output of an MS-DOS command can be redirected to a device, other than the standard output device, by entering an MS-DOS command, followed by " > " (the symbol for redirected output), followed by the name of the device that is to receive the output (see figure 6-1).

Let's look at an example using the MS-DOS command TYPE, which is used to display the contents of a file on the screen. When the command

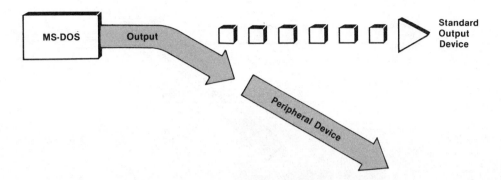

Figure 6-1. Redirection of output (>).

"type myfile" is entered, the contents of "myfile" can be viewed on the display screen. To "redirect" the display to the printer, enter the following command:

```
C>type myfile > prn
```

Because you used PRN—the reserved device name for the parallel printer—in your command, MS-DOS recognizes that the output of "type myfile" is to be redirected to the printer. No screen display results from this command.

In addition to the devices listed in table 6-1, MS-DOS also recognizes files as peripheral devices. This means that you can redirect output to an MS-DOS file. For example, the following command stores the output of the command DIR in a file named "dir.lst":

```
C>dir > dir.lst
```

If a file named "dir.lst" already exists on the disk in the default drive, it will be overwritten by this command. The data already in the file will be lost, replaced by the output of the command.

By using the symbol ">>", you can append output from a command to the end of an existing file. For example:

```
C>dir >> dir.lst
```

This command will add the output of the DIR command to the end of an existing file named "dir.lst". If there is no existing file with that name, a file will be created that contains the output of the DIR command.

So far we have been talking about redirected output. However, input can be redirected too (see figure 6-2). As you might expect, the symbol for redirection of input (<) is the opposite of the one for redirection of output. The next section will show you how redirection of input can be used with filters.

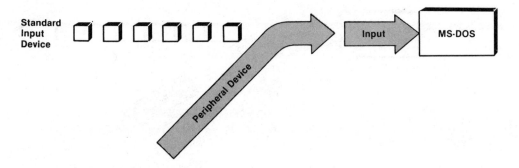

Figure 6-2. Redirection of input (<).

Filters

A *filter* is an MS-DOS command (or a computer program) that accepts data from an input device, rearranges or "filters" the data, and then outputs the filtered data to the designated output device. MS-DOS 2.X and 3.X contain three filter commands: SORT, FIND, and MORE. As we discuss these commands, we will also elaborate on the concept of redirection.

SORT

The SORT command reads data from an input device, sorts the data, and writes the data to an output device. Let's demonstrate the use of SORT by creating a short text file called "records.txt". You can create this file by entering **copy con:** (or use EDLIN). Do not use any tab characters when creating this text file because tabs can confuse SORT.

```
C>copy con: records.txt
springsteen     bruce     born to run              1975
floyd           pink      dark side of the moon    1973
stevens         cat       tea for the tillerman    1970
ronstadt        linda     heart like a wheel       1974
^Z        ←you press Ctrl-Z
         1 File(s) copied
```

Now that we have a text file, we can use it to demonstrate the SORT command. SORT is an external DOS command. This means that SORT is not stored in memory when DOS is booted. Thus, in order to use SORT, a disk containing the file SORT.EXE must be in the current directory of one of the system drives. (See chapter 3 for a discussion of current directories.) In the following example, SORT.EXE and our file "records.txt" are both in the root directory of the default drive.

The input redirection symbol (<) can be used to input data to SORT.

The following command inputs the data contained in "records.txt" to SORT. The data are sorted according to the ASCII characters (see appendix F) in the first column of each line. The sorted data are then output to the display screen, which is the standard output device.

```
C>sort < records.txt
```

```
FLOYD          PINK      DARK SIDE OF THE MOON    1973
RONSTADT       LINDA     HEART LIKE A WHEEL       1974
SPRINGSTEEN    BRUCE     BORN TO RUN              1975
STEVENS        CAT       TEA FOR THE TILLERMAN    1970
```

SORT can be used to sort according to the ASCII characters in any column. To sort according to the characters in column *n,* type **sort** /+*n*. The next example sorts "records.txt" according to the ASCII characters in the 17th column of each line. (In the examples that follow, an asterisk (*) has been placed above the column on which the sort was based.)

```
C>sort /+17 < records.txt
                         *
SPRINGSTEEN    BRUCE     BORN TO RUN              1975
STEVENS        CAT       TEA FOR THE TILLERMAN    1970
RONSTADT       LINDA     HEART LIKE A WHEEL       1974
FLOYD          PINK      DARK SIDE OF THE MOON    1973
```

SORT considers a tab to be a single character and will be confused if tabs are used to align columns of text. Let's see what would have happened if tabs had been used in the first two lines of the previous sort. The first letter in "BRUCE" is preceded by 16 characters: "SPRINGSTEEN" + 5 spaces. Similarly, the first letter in "CAT" is preceded by 16 characters: "STEVENS" + 9 spaces. If tabs had been used to align columns, "BRUCE" would have been preceded by 12 characters ("SPRINGSTEEN" + tab) and "CAT" would have been preceded by 8 characters ("STEVENS" + tab). So, if tabs had been used, SORT would not have recognized "BRUCE" or "CAT" as starting in column 17, and the results of the sort would have been different.

A file can be sorted in reverse order by entering "sort /r+*n*", where *n* is the column on which the sort will be based. If the command is entered as "sort /r", the sort will be based on the first column in each line.

In the following example, "records.txt" is sorted in reverse order. The sort is based on the 52nd character in each line:

```
C>sort /r+52 < records.txt
                                                  *
SPRINGSTEEN    BRUCE     BORN TO RUN              1975
RONSTADT       LINDA     HEART LIKE A WHEEL       1974
FLOYD          PINK      DARK SIDE OF THE MOON    1973
STEVENS        CAT       TEA FOR THE TILLERMAN    1970
```

The output from SORT can be redirected to a device other than the standard output device. In the next example, "records.txt" is sorted according to the ASCII characters in the 25th column of each line. The output is then redirected to the printer. PRN is the device name reserved by MS-DOS for parallel printer number 1.

```
C>sort /+25 < records.txt > prn
```

The following output is redirected to the printer:

```
                                 *
    SPRINGSTEEN    BRUCE    BORN TO RUN              1975
    FLOYD          PINK     DARK SIDE OF THE MOON    1973
    RONSTADT       LINDA    HEART LIKE A WHEEL       1974
    STEVENS        CAT      TEA FOR THE TILLERMAN    1970
```

This same output could also have been redirected to a file. The following command outputs the sorted data to the file "sorted.txt":

```
C>sort /+25 < records.txt > sorted.txt
```

Enter the command **type sorted.txt** to display "sorted.txt" on the screen.

FIND

The FIND command is an MS-DOS filter that searches the lines of a text file for a specified string. The output from FIND can be sent to the standard ouput device or redirected to another device. FIND is an external MS-DOS command. That means that FIND is not stored in memory when MS-DOS is booted. Thus, in order to use FIND, a disk containing the file FIND.EXE must be in the current directory of one of the system drives. In the following example, FIND.EXE and "records.txt" (refer to the discussion of SORT for the contents of "records.txt") are both in the root directory of the default drive.

To execute FIND, type **find**, followed by a string (enclosed in double quotation marks), followed by the path(s) and file specification(s) of the file(s) to be searched. In the example, FIND searches "records.txt" for the string "BRUCE". FIND will display any lines in the file containing "BRUCE".

```
C>find "bruce" records.txt

----------- RECORDS.TXT
SPRINGSTEEN    BRUCE    BORN TO RUN              1975
```

FIND offers three optional switches. The /v switch searches for and displays the lines in a text file that do not contain a specified string. In the next example, FIND searches "records.txt" for lines that do not contain the string "FLOYD":

```
C>find /v "floyd" records.txt

------------ RECORDS.TXT
SPRINGSTEEN    BRUCE    BORN TO RUN            1975
STEVENS        CAT      TEA FOR THE TILLERMAN  1970
RONSTADT       LINDA    HEART LIKE A WHEEL     1974
```

The /c switch displays a count of the lines in a text file containing a specified string. In the following example, FIND displays the number of lines in "records.txt" containing the string "LINDA":

```
C>find /c "linda" records.txt

---------- RECORDS.TXT: 1
```

The FIND /n option displays the lines within a text file that contain a specified string. The *line number* of the line is also displayed.

```
C>find /n "born" records.txt

------------ RECORDS.TXT
[1]SPRINGSTEEN    BRUCE    BORN TO RUN            1975
```

The output from FIND can be redirected to a device other than the standard output device. In the next example, FIND searches "records.txt" for any lines that contain the string "1975". Any lines containing the string are output to the file "1975.txt". The TYPE command is used to display the contents of the file:

```
C>find "1975" records.txt > 1975.txt
C>type 1975.txt
SPRINGSTEEN    BRUCE    BORN TO RUN            1975
```

MORE

The MS-DOS command MORE is a filter that displays 23 lines of data (one full screen) at a time. MORE is an external MS-DOS command. This means that MORE is not stored in memory when MS-DOS is booted. Therefore, in order to use MORE, a disk containing the file MORE.COM must be in the current directory of one of the system drives. In the following examples, MORE.COM and "sample.txt" are located in the current directory of drive C.

Data is input to MORE by redirection:

```
C>more < sample.txt
```

This command redirects the data in the file "sample.txt" as input to the filter MORE. MORE outputs the data, 23 lines at a time, to the standard output device. When the screen is filled, the prompt -- **MORE** -- is displayed. Pressing any key gives another filled screen of data. The process is repeated until the entire file has been displayed.

The output from MORE may be redirected to a device other than the standard output device. The following command sends 23 lines of "sample.txt" at a time to the printer:

```
C>more < sample.txt > prn
```

The prompt -- **More** -- will also be sent to the printer.

Pipes

Pipes are connections between two programs or two commands or a command and a program. Pipes allow data that is output from one program to be redirected as input to a second program (see figure 6-3).

**Figure 6-3. Piping a command's output as input
for a second command.**

The MS-DOS symbol for a pipe is a vertical bar (¦). To redirect the output from one command (or program) to another, type the first command, followed by a vertical bar, followed by the second command.

Consider the following command:

```
C>dir¦find "-85 "
```

This command directs MS-DOS to send the output of the DIR command (usually sent to the display screen) as input to the FIND filter. FIND searches each line of the input for the character string "-85 ". The result is that all the files in the current directory with a 1985 date stamp are displayed on the screen. (Date stamps are discussed in chapter 2.) Any files with a filename or filename extension containing "-85" would also be displayed.

A command may contain more than one pipe. In the preceding command, the output of the FIND filter is sent to the screen. The output can be redirected with another pipe:

```
C>dir¦find "-85 "¦sort /+14
```

Now, the output of the FIND command is piped to the SORT filter, which sorts the 1985 files according to their size (the 14th column of each line). The sorted output is sent to the display screen. Try this command with one of your own files. Remember that FIND and SORT are external MS-DOS commands; therefore, the files FIND.EXE and SORT.EXE must be in the current directory of the specified (or default) drive.

Redirection versus Piping

The difference between redirection and piping can be a little confusing. Redirection refers to the modification of input from, or output to, peripheral devices (see table 6-1 and figures 6-1 and 6-2). Piping refers to the conversion of the output from an MS-DOS command or computer program into the input for another command or program (figure 6-3).

We'll try to clarify this with one more example:

```
C>dir¦find "-85 "¦sort /+14 > prn
```

A pipe is used to convert the output from DIR into the input for FIND. A second pipe is used to send the output from FIND as input to SORT. Finally, the output from SORT is redirected to a peripheral device (the parallel printer).

7

EDLIN, the MS-DOS Text Editor

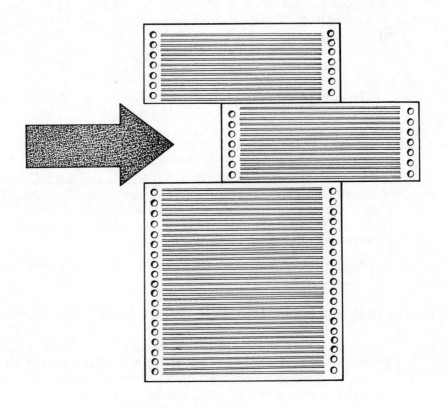

Creating a File with EDLIN
Modifying an Existing File with EDLIN
Ending EDLIN
EDLIN Commands

EDLIN is a line-oriented text editor that comes with MS-DOS. Given the current proliferation of high-powered processors, you may never need to use EDLIN. EDLIN is definitely not a word processor, or even close to it. If you are doing any sort of document preparation, use a word processor or other editing program, rather than EDLIN. However, if you want a handy tool to write batch files and CONFIG.SYS files, EDLIN is just what you need.

Creating a File with EDLIN

To create a new file with EDLIN, enter **edlin** and the filespec of the file that you are creating (filespecs are discussed in chapter 2). After you press Enter, DOS will load EDLIN into memory, and EDLIN will take control. EDLIN will search the specified or default drive for the filename that was entered in the start command. If it cannot find the file, EDLIN displays the message **New file** and then displays its prompt (`*`) to indicate that an EDLIN command may be entered:

```
C>edlin newfile.txt

New file
*
```

> The examples presented in this chapter assume that MS-DOS can locate the file EDLIN.COM. For this to occur, either EDLIN.COM must be stored in the current directory of drive C or the PATH command must specify the directory containing EDLIN.COM. Current directories and PATH are discussed in chapter 3.

Modifying an Existing File with EDLIN

To modify a file that already exists, the file EDLIN.COM must be in drive C. Enter the EDLIN start command by typing **edlin** and the filespec of the existing file. When you press Enter, MS-DOS will search the specified or default directory for the file. If it finds the file, the file will be loaded into memory until available memory is 75% full. If the entire file is loaded, EDLIN displays the message **End of input file** and then displays its prompt (`*`) to indicate that an EDLIN command may be entered:

```
C>edlin oldfile.txt
End of input file
*
```

If the entire file cannot be loaded into memory, EDLIN will load lines until memory is 75% full but will not display a message. The * prompt appears when EDLIN is ready to accept a command.

The B Option

If you use the method just described to load an existing file with EDLIN, the load will stop when EDLIN encounters the first Ctrl-Z character in a file's text. The Ctrl-Z character is an end-of-file marker, indicating the end of a text file. If you wish to edit a file containing embedded Ctrl-Z characters, add /b to the end of the EDLIN start command. For example:

```
C>edlin oldfile.txt/b
```

EDLIN will load the entire file regardless of any embedded end-of-file markers.

Ending EDLIN

When you have finished editing a file, you can exit from EDLIN by entering the END command e. The original file (if it existed) is renamed with the extension ".BAK" to indicate that it is a backup file, and the edited file is stored on the disk specified in the initial EDLIN start command. After the file has been saved, EDLIN terminates and the MS-DOS C> prompt is displayed.

If you decide not to save the file that you have been editing, enter the QUIT command q. EDLIN will display a prompt asking if you want to abort the editing session. If you enter "y" (or "Y"), the original file (if one existed) is saved with its original filename. No .BAK file is created, and control is returned to MS-DOS. If you enter "n" (or "N"), the editing session will continue. Both the END and QUIT commands will be covered in more detail later in the chapter.

The following section will discuss each of the EDLIN commands, beginning with the most frequently used ones. Table 7-1 provides an alphabetical summary of the commands.

EDLIN Commands

Before you start using the individual EDLIN commands, you need to know the conventions or rules used by EDLIN. EDLIN commands are invoked by typing a letter and pressing Enter. In addition, most EDLIN commands either allow or require that one or more numbers be included as command parameters. When a command contains more than one number, the numbers must be separated by a comma or a space. In certain instances, a comma is required. These instances will be pointed out in the discussion of the individual commands.

EDLIN does not differentiate between uppercase and lowercase letters. For example, you can invoke the QUIT command by entering "Q" or "q". It makes no difference to EDLIN.

EDLIN designates a particular line in the file being edited as the *current line*. The current line serves as a sort of bookmarker that allows EDLIN to keep track of where it is in a file. When EDLIN displays a portion of a file, the current line has an asterisk following the line number.

The pound sign (#) may be used to refer to the last line of a file that is in memory. This can be useful when you want to perform a task involving the last line of a file but you do not know the last line number. For example, the command "50,# d" will delete everything from line 50 to the end of the file.

It is possible to refer to line numbers relative to the current line. The minus sign (−) is used to indicate a line *before* the current line. The plus sign (+) is used to indicate a line *after* the current line. As an example, the command "−5,+5 L" will list the 5 lines before the current line, the current line, and the 5 lines after the current line.

More than one EDLIN command may be entered at a time. With some exceptions, which will be noted, one command can follow another without any special delimiting characters. For example, the command "1,10 d 1,10L" deletes the first ten lines of a file and then lists the new lines 1 through 10.

Control characters may be entered in a text file by typing "i" (for IN-SERT) and then pressing Ctrl-V and typing the desired control character in uppercase. For example, to enter Ctrl-Z, type "i", press Ctrl-V, and then type capital Z.

Table 7-1. Summary of EDLIN Commands

Command	Purpose	Format
(A)PPEND (page 113)	Adds a specified number of lines from disk to the file being edited in memory	[*number*] a [*number*]
(C)OPY (page 115)	Copies a range of lines to a specified location in a file	*,,line* c [*line1*],,*line* c [*line1*], [*line2*],*line* c [*line1*],[*line2*],*line, count* c
(D)ELETE (page 107)	Deletes a range of lines	d [*line1*] d ,[*line2*] d [*line1*],[*line2*] d
EDIT (page 105)	Edits a line of text	[*line*]
(E)ND (page 113)	Ends EDLIN and saves the edited file	e

Table 7-1. (cont.)

Command	Purpose	Format
(I)NSERT (page 100)	Inserts lines of text	i [*line*] i
(L)IST (page 102)	Lists lines of text	L [*line1*] L ,[*line2*] L [*line1*],[*line2*] L
(M)OVE (page 114)	Moves a range of lines to a specified location	,,*line* m [*line1*],,*line* m ,[*line2*],*line* m [*line1*],[*line2*],*line* m
(P)AGE (page 117)	Lists lines of text	p [*line1*] p ,[*line2*] p [*line1*],[*line2*] p
(Q)UIT (page 114)	Ends EDLIN and does not save the edited file	q
(R)EPLACE (page 111)	Replaces all occurrences of a string in a specified range with a second string	r [*line1*] r ,[*line2*] r [*line1*],[*line2*] r [*line1*],[*line2*] r [*string1*] F6 [*string2*] [*line1*],[*line2*] ? r [*string1*] Ctrl-Z [*string2*]
(S)EARCH (page 109)	Searches a specified range of lines in order to locate a string	s [*line1*] s ,[*line2*] s [*line1*],[*line2*] s [*line1*],[*line2*] s [*string*] [*line1*],[*line2*] ? s [*string*]
(T)RANSFER (page 118)	Merges the contents of a specified file with the file being edited	t [*filespec*] [*line*] t [*filespec*]
(W)RITE (page 112)	Writes a number of lines from memory to disk	w [*number*] w

Note: Italics indicate items that you must supply. Items in square brackets are optional.

INSERT

The INSERT command is used to insert lines of text into the file being edited. To invoke the command, enter **i** (or **I**) when you see the EDLIN prompt (*****). In the following example, INSERT is used to add text to a new file. Starting with the MS-DOS prompt (**C>**), type **edlin** followed by the name of the file that will be created ("demo1.txt"). EDLIN will display its prompt (*****) to indicate that it is ready to accept a command:

```
C>edlin demo1.txt
New file
*
```

The message **New file** tells you that no file named "demo1.txt" exists on the default disk. Following the ***** prompt, enter the letter "i" to begin the INSERT command. EDLIN will respond by displaying **1:***, which is the signal to enter the first line of text.

Each line of text may hold up to 253 characters. To terminate a line, press Enter. EDLIN will insert the ASCII characters for carriage return and line feed at the end of the line. These two characters do not appear on the display screen.

Each time you press Enter, EDLIN stores a line of text in memory and then displays the next line number. You may enter another line of text or end the INSERT command by pressing the Ctrl-Break key combination.

The following example shows how lines of text could be entered in "demo1.txt". If you decide to enter these lines on your computer, press Enter to end each line of text (lines 1 through 11).

```
C>edlin demo1.txt
New file
*i
  1:*This is how you would create a new text file with EDLIN.
  2:*Enter "i" in response to the EDLIN prompt. EDLIN displays
  3:*"1:*". This is your signal to enter the first line of text.
  4:*You may enter up to 253 characters in a line.
  5:*        ←to skip a line press Enter
  6:*To end a line, press Enter. EDLIN will store the line of
  7:*text in memory and display the next line number. You may
  8:*enter another line of text or terminate the INSERT command.
  9:*To terminate, press Ctrl-Break.
 10:*When a command is terminated, EDLIN displays its prompt
 11:*and waits for you to enter another command.
 12:*
 13:*^C       ←you press Ctrl-Break

   *            ←EDLIN displays its prompt and waits for your next command
```

Text is inserted before the *current line* when you enter "i" with no other parameters. The current line is the last line in the file that was modified. In the preceding example, line 13 is the current line. Enter "i" to insert text beginning at line 13:

```
*i
 13:*!!!!!!!!!!!!!!!!!!!!!!!!!!!!!!!!!!!!!!!!!!!!!!!!!!!!!
 14:*These 3 lines are being inserted at lines 13, 14, and 15.
 15:*!!!!!!!!!!!!!!!!!!!!!!!!!!!!!!!!!!!!!!!!!!!!!!!!!!!!!!
 16:*^C

*
```

You can use the LIST command (enter uppercase L) to display a portion of the file:

```
*L
  5:
  6:To end a line, press Enter. EDLIN will store the line of
  7:text in memory and display the next line number. You may
  8:enter another line of text or terminate the INSERT command.
  9:To terminate, press Ctrl-Break.
 10:When a command is terminated, EDLIN displays its prompt
 11:and waits for you to enter another command.
 12:
 13:!!!!!!!!!!!!!!!!!!!!!!!!!!!!!!!!!!!!!!!!!!!!!!!!!!!!!!
 14:These 3 lines are being inserted at lines 13, 14, and 15.
 15:!!!!!!!!!!!!!!!!!!!!!!!!!!!!!!!!!!!!!!!!!!!!!!!!!!!!!!

*
```

To suspend scrolling while using LIST, press Ctrl-NumLock. To resume scrolling, press any key. Press Ctrl-Break to terminate the listing. (For more about LIST, see the next section.)

You may specify the line at which text insertion is to begin by preceding the letter "i" with a line number. In this way, text can be inserted between existing lines in the file. Lines following the insertion will be renumbered. For example:

```
*11i
   11:*+++++++++++++++++++++++++++++++++++++++++++++++++++
   12:*These 3 lines are being inserted starting at line 11.
   13:*+++++++++++++++++++++++++++++++++++++++++++++++++++
   14:*^C

*
```

The command "5L" tells EDLIN to display the file beginning with line 5:

```
*5L

    5:
    6:To end a line, press Enter. EDLIN will store the line of
    7:text in memory and display the next line number. You may
    8:enter another line of text or terminate the INSERT command.
    9:To terminate, press Ctrl-Break.
   10:When a command is terminated, EDLIN displays its prompt
   11:++++++++++++++++++++++++++++++++++++++++++++++++++++++
   12:These 3 lines are being inserted starting at line 11.
   13:++++++++++++++++++++++++++++++++++++++++++++++++++++++
   14:and waits for you to enter another command.
   15:
   16:!!!!!!!!!!!!!!!!!!!!!!!!!!!!!!!!!!!!!!!!!!!!!!!!!!!!!!
   17:These 3 lines are being inserted at lines 13, 14, and 15.
   18:!!!!!!!!!!!!!!!!!!!!!!!!!!!!!!!!!!!!!!!!!!!!!!!!!!!!!!!

*
```

In the preceding example, three lines have been inserted beginning at line 11. Note that the line numbers following the insertion have been automatically renumbered.

If you precede the letter "i" with a number that is greater than the highest-existing line number in the file or if you specify "#" as the line number, the insertion begins following the last line of the file stored in memory.

LIST

The LIST command (enter uppercase L) is used to display a specific range of lines in a file. We will demonstrate this command by using EDLIN to work on the following file:

```
    1: This is line 1.
    2: This is line 2.
    3: This is line 3.
       .
       .
   14: This is line 14.
   15* This is line 15.
   16: This is line 16.
       .
       .
   24: This is line 24.
   25: This is line 25.
   26: This is line 26.
```

The current line (the last line modified by EDLIN) is denoted by an asterisk. In the preceding example, line 15 is the current line. Using the LIST command will not change the current line.

If you enter "L" without any line numbers, EDLIN will display the 11 lines before the current line, the current line, and the 11 lines after the current line, for a total of 23 lines—the maximum number that can be listed at any one time:

```
*L
   4: This is line 4.
   5: This is line 5.
   6: This is line 6.
   .
   .
   .
  14: This is line 14.
  15:*This is line 15.
  16: This is line 16.
   .
   .
   .
  24: This is line 24.
  25: This is line 25.
  26: This is line 26.


*
```

If there are fewer than 11 lines before the current line, extra lines are displayed after the current line so that a total of 23 lines is displayed.

To list a particular range of lines, specify the starting and ending line numbers of the range in your LIST command. The numbers must be separated by a comma or a space and must precede the letter "L". To list lines 1 through 4, enter:

```
*1,4L
   1: This is line 1.
   2: This is line 2.
   3: This is line 3.
   4: This is line 4.


*
```

If you precede the LIST command with only one number, the listing will begin at that line number. A total of 23 lines will be listed. In the following example, the 23 lines from lines 2 through 24 are listed:

```
*2L
   2: This is line 2.
```

```
    3:*This is line 3.
      .
      .
      .
   23: This is line 23.
   24: This is line 24.

*
```

If you precede the LIST command with a comma and a line number, the listing will begin 11 lines before the current line and end at the line number that is included in the command:

```
*,16L
    4: This is line 4.
    5: This is line 5.
      .
      .
      .
   14: This is line 14.
   15:*This is line 15.
   16: This is line 16.

*
```

If the line you specify is more than 11 lines before the current line, the display is the same as if you had entered only "L":

```
*,2L
    4: This is line 4.
      .
      .
      .
   15:*This is line 15.
      .
      .
      .
   26: This is line 26.

*
```

You can use the LIST command to obtain a printout of a portion or all of a text file. Try printing out one of the preceding examples. Turn on your printer and press the Ctrl-PrtSc key combination. Then enter the appropriate LIST command. The display that appears on your screen will be sent to the printer.

The display will start to scroll off the screen if you list more than 24 lines. To suspend the listing, press the Ctrl-NumLock key combination. The listing will continue when you press any key. To terminate the listing, press the Ctrl-Break combination.

EDIT

The EDIT command is used to edit a line of text. To specify the line to be edited, simply enter its line number. To specify the current line, enter a period (.). To specify the line following the current line, press Enter.

When you specify a line for editing, EDLIN displays the line number and the text of that line. The line number is then repeated on the line below. For example:

```
*6
    6:*The old gray mare, she ain't what she used to be.
    6:*
```

To edit a line, simply type the new text. The edited line is placed in the file and becomes the current line when you press Enter. If you decide to retain the original line without any changes, press Esc or Ctrl-Break instead of Enter. Pressing Enter with the cursor at the beginning of the line has the same effect as pressing Esc or Ctrl-Break.

If you include the EDIT command on a line with one or more other EDLIN commands, you must use semicolons to separate the commands on the line. For example, the command "22;1,5 d" will first edit line 22 and then delete lines 1 through 5.

When you specify a line for editing, the text of that line forms the *template*. The template is the current structure of the line that is stored by MS-DOS. As the line is edited, the template is modified to reflect the editing changes.

MS-DOS Editing Keys

The MS-DOS editing keys may be used to edit the template. These keys consist of the F1, F2, F3, F4, and F5 function keys, plus the Ins and Del keys.

The **F1 function key** displays one character in the template. By repeatedly pressing the F1 key (or the → key in some computers) you can cause all or part of the template to be displayed:

```
6:*The old gray mare, she ain't what she used to be.    ←template
6:*The old gray mare, she ain't what                     ←press F1 33 times
```

The last line will be placed in the file and will become the current line if Enter is pressed. If Esc is pressed, a backslash (\) will be displayed and the changes entered in the second line will be cancelled:

```
6:*The old gray mare, she ain't what she used to be.    ←template
6:*The old gray mare, she ain't what                     ←press F1 33 times;
                                                          press Esc
```

The **F3 function key** displays the template from the position of the cursor to the end of the line:

```
6:*The old gray mare, she ain't what she used to be.     ←template
6:*The old gray mare, she ain't what she used to be._    ←press F3 once
```

The **F2 function key** copies the template up to the first occurrence of a specified character. Nothing is copied if the character specified is not in the template. The last line in the following display is obtained by first pressing the F2 key and then pressing the comma (,) key. The template is copied up to, but not including, the first comma:

```
6:*The old gray mare, she ain't what she used to be.     ←template
6:*The old gray mare_                                    ←press F2 once;
                                                           enter comma
```

The **F4 function key** skips over a template until it encounters a specified character. No characters are skipped if the specified character is not present in the template. In the next example, the F4 key is pressed and then the "s" key is pressed. This deletes the characters in the template up to the first "s". The F4 key does not display any text. To display the new template, press the F3 key:

```
6:*The old gray mare, she ain't what she used to be.     ←template
6:*She ain't what she used to be._                       ←press F4, "s",
                                                           and F3
```

The **Ins key** can be used to insert text into the template. Pressing Ins one time turns the insert mode on. Pressing it a second time turns the insert mode off.

When the insert mode is on, any characters that you type are inserted into the template. These characters do not replace characters already in the template. When the insert mode is off, any characters that you type replace characters in the template.

In the following example, the F1 key is pressed three times. The Ins key is then pressed to turn on the insert mode. Five characters (4 letters and a blank) are inserted into the template. The remainder of the template is then copied with the F3 key:

```
6:*The old gray mare, she ain't what she used to be.          ←template
6:*The very old gray mare, she ain't what she used to be._    ←press F1, Ins,
                                                                "very", and
                                                                F3
```

The **Del key** can be used to skip over one character in the template at a time.

```
6:*The old gray mare, she ain't what she used to be.    ←template
6:*The old gray mare, he ain't what she used to be.     ←press F1 20 times;
                                                          press Del, F3
```

The **F5 function key** moves the line that is currently being displayed into the template without entering it in the file. An "@" character is displayed to indicate that the new line is now in the template. Once you have entered F5, you can proceed to edit the new template. Pressing Enter stores the new template in the file.

In the next example, a new line of text has been added. The F5 key is then pressed to store the new line as the template. The new template can be edited using the techniques described in this section. The original line of text remains in the file as the current line if Enter is pressed immediately after F5 is pressed:

```
6:*The old gray mare, she ain't what she used to be.    ←template
6:*And now for something completely different@          ←type new template;
                                                          press F5
```

Right now you are probably thinking that it is more trouble than it is worth to memorize the functions of the different editing keys. Typing in new lines of text seems to require less thought than remembering which key does what. However, if you spend some time working with the editing keys, you will find that EDLIN will become more productive for you.

DELETE

The DELETE command is used to delete a range of lines. The line following the deleted range becomes the current line. The current line and any subsequent lines are renumbered following a deletion.

To use DELETE, enter **d** (or **D**) in response to the EDLIN prompt. The current line will be deleted:

```
        1: This is line 1.
        2: This is line 2.
        3: This is line 3.
        4: This is line 4.
        5:*This is line 5.
        6: This is line 6.

*d
*L
        1: This is line 1.
        2: This is line 2.
        3: This is line 3.
        4: This is line 4.
```

```
    5:*This is line 6.
*
```

In the preceding example, the current line was initially line 5. When "d" was entered, the current line was deleted and the line after the deleted line became the current line. The line following the deleted line was renumbered.

You can specify a range of lines to be deleted by including the beginning and ending line numbers of the range in the DELETE command. The two numbers must be separated by a comma or a space. The line following the deleted range will become the current line:

```
    1: This is line 1.
    2: This is line 2.
    3: This is line 3.
    4: This is line 4.
    5:*This is line 6.

*2,4d
*L
    1: This is line 1.
    2:*This is line 6.
*
```

Lines 2 through 4 have been deleted, and what was originally line 6 is now the current line.

DELETE can be used to delete a range of lines from the current line through a specified line. The command starts with a comma followed by the last line in the range to be deleted. The first line following the deleted range becomes the current line:

```
    1: This is line 1.
    2: This is line 6.
    3: This is line 7.
    4:*This is line 8.
    5: This is line 9.
    6: This is line 10.

*,5d
*L
    1: This is line 1.
    2: This is line 6.

    3: This is line 7.
    4:*This is line 10.

*
```

The range of lines starting with the current line (line 4) and ending with line 5 has been deleted. The line following the deleted range has become the current line.

SEARCH

The SEARCH command (enter s or S) searches a range of lines for a specified character string. The first line found to contain the character string becomes the current line.

The SEARCH command can include the starting and ending line numbers of the range to be searched. Line numbers must be separated by a comma or a space. The command can also include the character string that is to be the object of the search. The string is specified with its first character in the position immediately following the "s". The string is terminated by pressing Enter.

In the following example, the SEARCH command searches the block of text beginning at line 2 and ending at line 6 for the character string "and". If the string is found within the block, EDLIN will display the first line on which it is located:

```
1: This is a demonstration file that will be used
2: to show how the SEARCH command operates. The
3: SEARCH command can be very handy. Imagine that
4: you are writing a paper and you realize that you
5: have been misspelling the word "gigolo." You could
6: use the SEARCH command to locate the gigolos in
7: your paper.

*2,6 sand
  2: to show how the SEARCH command operates. The


*
```

The search began at line 2. The string "and" was located in line 2 as part of the word "command." Line 2 is now the current line, since it was the first line found to contain the string.

Entering "s" by itself causes EDLIN to search for the last string that was specified with a SEARCH or REPLACE command. The search begins at the line following the current line and ends with the last line of the file that is stored in memory. We can illustrate this application of SEARCH by continuing with the previous example.

Line 2 is the current line, and the last string entered was "and". If we enter "s", EDLIN will begin searching at line 3 for "and":

```
*2,6 sand
  2: to show how the SEARCH command operates. The
```

```
*s
    3: SEARCH command can be very handy. Imagine that

*s
    4: you are writing a paper and you realize that you

*s
    6: use the SEARCH command to locate the gigolos in

*s
Not found

*
```

The command "s" was used three times to find the string "and". The string was found in lines 3, 4, and 6. None of the lines in the file beyond line 6 contained the string. Therefore, the fourth time that "s" was entered, EDLIN replied **Not found**.

Rather than reenter "s" each time to continue searching, you can enter a question mark immediately before the letter "s". EDLIN will display the prompt **O.K.?** when it finds a line containing the character string specified in the command. If you respond "y" or press Enter, the line found becomes the current line and the search ends. Pressing any other key continues the search. Once all of the lines within the range have been searched, the "Not found" message is displayed:

```
*2,6? sand
    2: to show how the SEARCH command operates. The
O.K.? n
    3: SEARCH command can be very handy. Imagine that
O.K.? n
    4: you are writing a paper and you realize that you
O.K.? y

*
```

The string was found in three lines. Each time, EDLIN asked if the search should be ended. The search was ended at line 4 when the response was "y".

Both the starting and ending line numbers of the range to be searched can be omitted from the SEARCH command. If the starting number line is omitted, the search begins at the line following the current line. If the ending line number is omitted, the search ends at the last line of the file that is in memory. The ending line number must be preceded by a comma if the starting line number is omitted and the ending line number is specified.

If the SEARCH command is entered on a line along with other EDLIN commands, the string in the command may be terminated by pressing Ctrl-Z rather than Enter.

REPLACE

The REPLACE command (enter **r** or **R**) is used to search a specified range of lines for a character string and replace that string with a second character string. The first string is replaced at each location that it occurs within the specified range. The last line changed by REPLACE becomes the current line.

The starting and ending line numbers of the range to be searched may be specified in the REPLACE command. Line numbers must be separated by a comma or a space. The character string to be replaced and the replacement character string may also be specified in the command. The two strings must be separated by Ctrl-Z.

In the next example, lines 2 through 4 are searched for the string "you". When the string is located within the range, it is replaced with "we":

```
1: This is a demo file to show how the REPLACE command
2: works. REPLACE can be very handy. Imagine that you
3: are writing a paper and you realize that you have
4: misspelled "gigolo" as "jiggloh." You could use the
5: REPLACE command to locate the jigglohs in your paper
6: and replace them with gigolos.

*2,4 ryou^Zwe
2: works. REPLACE can be very handy. Imagine that we
3: are writing a paper and we realize that you have
3: are writing a paper and we realize that we have
*
```

Notice that the two strings in the command are separated by "^Z". This character can be entered by pressing the F6 function key or by pressing the Ctrl-Z key combination. If you have modified your function keys (see chapter 8), you will have to use the Ctrl-Z combination.

Each time that "you" is located within the specified range, it is replaced with "we". Each time a line is changed, it is displayed. Notice that line 3 is displayed two times since "you" is replaced twice. Line 4 contains the string "You". However, "You" is *not* replaced because REPLACE differentiates between uppercase and lowercase letters.

As with the SEARCH command, you can use a question mark with RE-PLACE. The question mark is included immediately before the "r". EDLIN will display the prompt **O.K.?** each time that a line is modified. If you respond by pressing "y" or Enter, the suggested modification is made. The modification is discarded if you press any other key in response to the prompt. In either case, the search continues through the entire range specified in the command. The following example demonstrates this, beginning where the last example ended:

```
    2: works. REPLACE can be very handy. Imagine that we
    3: are writing a paper and we realize that you have
    3: are writing a paper and we realize that we have

*2,4? rwe^Zyou
    2: works. REPLACE can be very handy. Imagine that you
O.K.? y
    3: are writing a paper and you realize that we have
O.K.? y
    3: are writing a paper and you realize that you have
O.K.? y


*
```

You may omit from the command both the starting and ending line numbers of the range to be searched. The search begins with the line after the current line if you omit the starting line number. The search ends with the last line in memory if you omit the ending line number. If you specify only the ending line number in the command, the line number must be preceded by a comma.

One or both of the character strings may be omitted from the REPLACE command. If you omit the second string, EDLIN deletes all occurrences of the first string within the specified range. The first string must end with ^Z. If you omit both strings, EDLIN will reuse the search string of the most recent SEARCH or REPLACE command and the replace string of the last RE-PLACE command.

If you include the REPLACE command on a line with one or more other EDLIN commands, the replace string can be terminated by pressing Ctrl-Z rather than Enter.

WRITE

When EDLIN begins to work on an existing file, its first task is to load the file into computer memory. EDLIN will fill up to 75% of available memory with the file. EDLIN displays the message **End of input file** followed by the EDLIN prompt if memory is large enough to accommodate the entire file at one time. If the file is too large to be loaded into memory at one time, EDLIN loads a portion of the file and displays only the prompt.

If a file is larger than 75% of memory, the WRITE command (enter **w** or **W**) can be used to write a number of lines from memory to a disk. This frees a portion of memory so that additional lines in the file may be loaded into memory using the APPEND command. The WRITE command is meaningful only if the file you are editing is too large to fit in memory.

The WRITE command writes text to the disk beginning with line number 1. You can specify the number of lines to be written by preceding the letter "w" with a number. The next example writes the first 100 lines in memory to the disk that was specified in the EDLIN start command:

```
*100 w
*
```

If you do not specify the number of lines to be written (entering only "w"), EDLIN writes lines until 25% of available memory is occupied by the file. No action is taken if less than 25% of available memory is occupied by the file. After the lines are written, all lines remaining in memory are renumbered so that the first remaining line in memory becomes number 1.

APPEND

The APPEND command (enter **a** or **A**) is used to add a number of lines to the EDLIN file currently in memory. This command is used after a portion of memory is made available with the WRITE command. The APPEND command is meaningful only if the file being edited is too large to fit in memory. Refer to the previous discussion of the WRITE command for information on when to use the WRITE and APPEND commands.

The APPEND command adds lines of the file to memory starting at the end of the lines already in memory. You can specify how many lines are to be added to memory by preceding the letter "a" with a number. The following example adds 100 lines of a file to the portion of the file already in memory:

```
*100 a
*
```

If you do not specify the number of lines to be added, lines are added until available memory is 75% full. No action is taken if available memory is already 75% full. (If necessary, you can use the WRITE command to free a portion of memory.)

The message **End of input file** is displayed when the APPEND command has read the last line of the file into memory.

END

The END command (enter **e** or **E**) terminates EDLIN, saves the edited file, and returns control to MS-DOS. The edited file is saved by writing it to the disk and file specified in the EDLIN start command. As you may recall, the original unedited file is saved and given the extension "BAK". However, a .BAK file will not be created if you are creating a new file with EDLIN rather than modifying an existing file.

If the disk specified in the EDLIN start command does not have enough free space to save the entire edited file, only a portion of the file is saved. The saved portion is given a filename extension of "$$$", and the remainder of the edited file is lost. The original unedited file is stored with its original extension.

QUIT

The QUIT command (enter **q** or **Q**) is used to terminate EDLIN and return control to MS-DOS. The changes made during the editing session are not saved, and no .BAK file is created. QUIT is used only when you want to discard all of the changes made in an EDLIN session.

When you enter the command "q", EDLIN displays a prompt asking if you want to end the editing session and return to MS-DOS. A response of "y" terminates EDLIN and returns control to MS-DOS. All changes made during the EDLIN session are discarded. Only the original unedited file is saved. A response of "n" returns control to EDLIN, which displays its prompt and waits for you to enter another command.

MOVE

The MS-DOS 2.X and 3.X versions of EDLIN include a MOVE command. With MOVE, you can transfer a range of lines in a text file from one location to another. The first line moved becomes the current line. Lines are renumbered according to the direction of the move.

The starting and ending lines of the block to be moved may be specified in the MOVE command. The block is moved ahead of a third line, which must be specified in the command. All numbers in the command must be separated by commas.

In the next example, lines 2 through 5 are moved ahead of line 9. The first line moved (line 2) becomes the current line, and the lines are renumbered:

```
 1: This is line 1.
 2: This is line 2.
 3: This is line 3.
 4: This is line 4.
 5:*This is line 5.
 6: This is line 6.
 7: This is line 7.
 8: This is line 8.
 9: This is line 9.
10: This is line 10.

*2,5,9 m
*L
 1: This is line 1.
```

```
 2: This is line 6.
 3: This is line 7.
 4: This is line 8.
 5:*This is line 2.
 6: This is line 3.
 7: This is line 4.

 8: This is line 5.
 9: This is line 9.
10: This is line 10.


*
```

You may omit the first line in the block from the command. If you do this, the block will start at the current line. You can also omit the last line in the block. In this case, the block that is moved will end at the current line.

Consider the command ",,1 m". The starting line number has been omitted, so the block to be moved begins at the current line. The ending line number has also been omitted, so the block to be moved ends at the current line. In other words, the block to be moved consists of one line— the current line. The command instructs EDLIN to move the current line ahead of line number 1. The commas must be included in this command.

COPY

The COPY command (enter **c** or **C**) is included in the MS-DOS 2.X and 3.X versions of EDLIN. This command is used to duplicate a range of lines.

You may specify the beginning and ending lines of the range to be copied by including the beginning and ending line numbers in the COPY command. The command must include a line number to specify where the copy will be located. All line numbers must be separated by a comma or a space. The first line copied becomes the current line:

```
 1: This is line 1.
 2: This is line 2.
 3: This is line 3.
 4: This is line 4.
 5:*This is line 5.
 6: This is line 6.
 7: This is line 7.

*1,2,6 c
*L
 1: This is line 1.
 2: This is line 2.
 3: This is line 3.
```

```
  4: This is line 4.
  5: This is line 5.
  6:*This is line 1.
  7: This is line 2.
  8: This is line 6.
  9: This is line 7.
*
```

In the example, the range of lines beginning with line 1 and ending with line 2 is copied ahead of line 6.

A range of lines can be copied more than one time by including a *count* in the command. The *count* is inserted between the line number that specifies where the copy is to be located and the letter "c". For example, if you wanted to copy lines 1 and 2 twice, you would enter the command "1,2,6,2 c". Compare this to the command in the previous example, which copied the lines one time. As in the previous example, if no *count* is included in the command, the range of lines is copied one time.

The starting and/or ending line numbers of the range to be copied may be omitted from the COPY command. The command assumes the omitted line(s) to be the current line:

```
  1: This is line 1.
  2: This is line 2.
  3:*This is line 3.
  4: This is line 4.
  5: This is line 5.
  6: This is line 6.
  7: This is line 7.

*1,,6 c
*L
  1: This is line 1.
  2: This is line 2.
  3: This is line 3.
  4: This is line 4.
  5: This is line 5.
  6:*This is line 1.
  7: This is line 2.
  8: This is line 3.
  9: This is line 6.
 10: This is line 7.
*
```

In the example, the range of lines beginning with line 1 and ending with the current line is copied ahead of line 6. The first line copied becomes the current line.

PAGE

The PAGE (enter **p** or **P**) command is included in the MS-DOS 2.X and 3.X versions of EDLIN. The PAGE command lists lines of a file. Its actions are similar to those of the LIST command, with one important difference. The LIST command does not change the current line; the PAGE command does. The significance of this difference will be demonstrated in the next example.

The beginning and ending line numbers of the block of lines to be listed can be specified with the PAGE command:

```
*1,5 p
    1: This is line 1.
    2: This is line 2.
    3: This is line 3.
    4: This is line 4.
    5:*This is line 5.


    *
```

If you omit the first line number of the block to be listed, the command assumes that the first line is the current line plus one. The usefulness of the PAGE command stems from the fact that the last line listed becomes the current line.

Continuing with the previous example, we find that the current line is line 5. If we invoke the PAGE command without specifying a starting line, the listing will begin with line 6. If we do not specify an ending line number, 23 lines will be listed. The last line listed becomes the current line:

```
*p
    6: This is line 6.
    7: This is line 7.
    .
    .
    .
   27: This is line 27.
   28:*This is line 28.


    *
```

In this fashion, we could continue to enter the command "p", paging through the file 23 lines at a time. Try doing this with the LIST command. Repeatedly entering the letter "L" will repeatedly list the same 23 lines. The reason is that LIST does not change the current line.

TRANSFER

The TRANSFER command (enter **t** or **T**) is included in the MS-DOS 2.X and 3.X versions of EDLIN. The TRANSFER command merges the contents of a specified file with the file being edited.

You can specify the location at which the merged file is inserted into the file being edited by including a line number in the TRANSFER command. The merged file will be inserted ahead of the specified line. If you do not specify a line number, the merged file is inserted ahead of the current line. As an example, the command "100 t b:demo.txt" merges the file on drive B named "demo.txt" with the file being edited. "Demo.txt" is inserted ahead of line 100 in the file being edited.

The file being merged must be located in the current directory of the specified or default drive. The current directory cannot be changed while EDLIN is running. Refer to chapter 3 for a discussion of current directories.

8

Extended Keyboard and Display Control

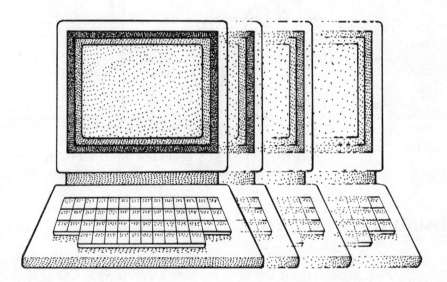

Installing ANSI.SYS	**Keyboard Reassignment**
Using ANSI.SYS	**Screen Control**

With MS-DOS 2.X and 3.X, you can modify input from the keyboard, and output to the display screen, through the use of *ANSI.SYS*. ANSI.SYS is a device driver contained on the MS-DOS system diskette.

A *device driver* is a computer program that acts as a connector between the operating system (MS-DOS) and a peripheral device such as a printer, disk drive, or console. (MS-DOS device drivers are discussed in chapter 14.) For the purposes of this chapter, ANSI.SYS can be thought of as a black box that modifies input from the keyboard and output to the display screen (figure 8-1). ANSI.SYS gives you a tremendous amount of control over the keyboard and the display screen, since you can customize MS-DOS to suit your own needs. This chapter will show you how to use ANSI.SYS to control the cursor position, erase all or part of the display screen, reassign character strings to individual keys on the keyboard, and set display modes and attributes.

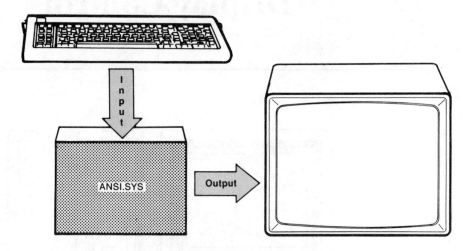

Figure 8-1. ANSI.SYS receives input from the keyboard and sends output to the display screen.

Installing ANSI.SYS

During booting, MS-DOS searches the root directory of the boot disk (the disk used to boot the system) for *CONFIG.SYS*. CONFIG.SYS is a text file containing the names of any device drivers that are to be installed (stored) in computer memory. The first step in installing ANSI.SYS is to create CONFIG.SYS (or modify an existing CONFIG.SYS file) so that ANSI.SYS is named as an installable device driver. Because CONFIG.SYS is a text file, it can be created with a text editor (such as EDLIN) or with the COPY command. EDLIN (or any other text editor) can also be used to modify an existing CONFIG.SYS file. In this tutorial, we will create CONFIG.SYS by using COPY in conjunction with the CON device name.

We begin by using the CHDIR (CHange DIRectory) command to place CONFIG.SYS in the root directory of the boot disk. CHDIR can be abbreviated "CD". In the following example, drive C is the default drive:

```
C>cd \
```

```
C>copy con: config.sys
device=ansi.sys
^Z        ←you press Ctrl-Z and Enter
     1 File(s) copied
```

The first command ("cd \") ensures that CONFIG.SYS will be located in the root directory. The remaining entries create CONFIG.SYS, a text file that contains one line ("device=ansi.sys").

Note: If you are using a text editor to modify a previously existing copy of CONFIG.SYS, simply add the line "device=ansi.sys" to the file. However, make sure that CONFIG.SYS is in the root directory of your boot disk.

A path specifier and/or a drive letter designator for ANSI.SYS may be included in CONFIG.SYS. For example, if ANSI.SYS is in the root directory of the disk in drive B, CONFIG.SYS would contain the statement "device=b:ansi.sys".

Once CONFIG.SYS has been created (or modified), MS-DOS must be rebooted in order for the device driver to be installed. With the boot disk in place, press the three-key combination Ctrl-Alt-Del. MS-DOS will reboot and install ANSI.SYS.

Using ANSI.SYS

Data entered from the keyboard are sent to the computer as a sequence of ASCII characters. When ANSI.SYS is installed, it processes all character sequences sent from the keyboard. ANSI.SYS recognizes certain character sequences as being *command sequences.* Command sequences direct ANSI.SYS to modify keyboard input or to modify display screen output. All ANSI.SYS command sequences begin with an *escape character* whose ASCII value is 27 (see appendix F for ASCII values). ANSI.SYS command sequences are not displayed on the screen.

ANSI.SYS can perform four types of commands: control cursor position, erase all or part of the display screen, reassign character strings to individual keys on the keyboard, and set display modes and attributes. Tables 8-1 through 8-5 give the individual commands, the corresponding command sequences, and a brief explanation of each command.

Table 8-1. ANSI.SYS Commands for Controlling Cursor Position

Command Name	Command Sequence	Description
Cursor position	ESC[#; #H	Moves the cursor to a specified position on the display screen. The position is specified by the # parameters. The first parameter

Table 8-1. (cont'd)

Command Name	Command Sequence	Description
		specifies the line number, and the second parameter specifies the column number of the cursor position. The cursor will move to the home position if no position is specified. The command sequence must end with an uppercase "H".
Cursor up	ESC[#A	Moves the cursor up a number of lines without changing columns. The value of **#** determines the number of lines moved. The default is one. The command sequence must end with an uppercase "A".
Cursor down	ESC[#B	Moves the cursor down a number of lines without changing columns. The value of **#** determines the number of lines moved. The default is one. The command sequence must end with an uppercase "B".
Cursor forward	ESC[#C	Moves the cursor forward without changing lines. The value of **#** determines the number of columns moved. The default is one. The command sequence must end with an uppercase "C".
Cursor backward	ESC[#D	Moves the cursor backward without changing lines. The value of **#** determines the number of columns moved. The default is one. The command sequence must end with an uppercase "D".
Horizontal/ vertical position	ESC[#; #f	Has function identical to cursor position command. Command sequence must end with a lowercase "f".
Save cursor position	ESC[s	Saves, in memory, the current position of the cursor. The position of the cursor can be restored with the restore cursor position command. The command sequence must end with a lowercase "s".

Table 8-1. (cont'd)

Command Name	Command Sequence	Description
Restore cursor position	ESC[u	Restores the cursor to the position it occupied when the previous save cursor position command was issued. The command sequence must end with a lowercase "u".
Device status report	ESC[6n	Requests that ANSI.SYS issue a cursor position report. The command sequence must end with a lowercase "n".
Cursor position report	ESC[#; #R	Reports the current position of the cursor. The first parameter is the current line. The second parameter is the current column. ANSI.SYS issues a cursor position report in response to a device status report.

**Table 8-2. ANSI.SYS Commands for
Erasing the Display Screen**

Command Name	Command Sequence	Description
Erase display	ESC[2J	Erases entire display and positions the cursor at the home position. The command sequence must end with an uppercase "J".
Erase line	ESC[K	Erases from the cursor to the end of the line. The command sequence must end with an uppercase "K".

**Table 8-3. ANSI.SYS Commands for
Controlling Display Screen Attributes**

Command Name	Command Sequence	Description
Set graphics rendition	ESC[#; . . . ;#m	Sets the screen display attributes. The command sequence may contain one or more of the parameters that are listed below. The command sequence must end with a lowercase "m".

Table 8-3. (cont'd)

Attribute Parameters	Meaning
0	All attributes off. Normal display.
1	High intensity display on.
4	Underscore on. Underscore will not work with a color display.
5	Blink on.
7	Reverse video on.
8	Concealed on. No display.
30	Black foreground.
31	Red foreground.
32	Green foreground.
33	Yellow foreground.
34	Blue foreground.
35	Magenta foreground.
36	Cyan foreground.
37	White foreground.
40	Black background.
41	Red background.
42	Green background.
43	Yellow background.
44	Blue background.
45	Magenta background.
46	Cyan background.
47	White background.

Table 8-4. ANSI.SYS Commands for Setting Display Mode

Command Name	Command Sequence	Description
Set mode	ESC[=#h	Sets display mode according to the parameter (#) specified. Command sequence must end with a lowercase "h". (See the section "Screen Control" later in this chapter for more information on the display mode.)
Reset mode	ESC[=#l	Resets display mode according to the parameter (#) specified. Equivalent to set mode except for parameter 7, which turns end-of-line wrap off. Command sequence must end with a lowercase "l".

Table 8-4. (cont'd)

Mode Parameters	Meaning
0	40x25 black and white.
1	40x25 color.
2	80x25 black and white.
3	80x25 color.
4	320x200 color.
5	320x200 black and white.
6	640x200 black and white.
7	End-of-line wrap turned on.

Table 8-5. ANSI.SYS Commands for Controlling Keyboard Reassignment

Command Name	Command Sequence	Description
Keyboard reassignment	ESC[#; # . . . ;# p or ESC[#;"string";p	Reassigns a character string to the key specified by the first ASCII code (#) in the sequence. The character string is determined by the remaining ASCII codes in the sequence. If the first ASCII code is a zero, the second ASCII code in the sequence determines which function key is assigned the character string. (See the section "Keyboard Reassignment" later in this chapter.)

An Example

The erase display command (table 8-2) is coded by the ASCII character sequence ESC [2 J. Note that "ESC" refers to the escape character—a single ASCII character—and not the three characters "E", "S", and "C". The display screen is erased when the sequence ESC [2 J is sent to ANSI.SYS. This sounds simple, and it is, except for one problem. All ANSI.SYS commands begin with an escape character, and sending an escape character to the display screen may require some special tactics.

Unless your system is one of those made by a few certain suppliers, you cannot use the Esc key to enter an escape character. In most machines, pressing Esc causes MS-DOS to cancel the current line being entered and skip to the next line. You can verify this by entering **copy con:** to try to create a text file containing the erase display command:

```
C>copy con: erase.txt
\          ←pressing Esc displays a "\" and causes MS-DOS to skip to the next line
[2J
^Z
        1 File(s) copied


C>type erase.txt
[2J
```

The TYPE command displays the file that was created. As you can see, the file did not begin with an ESC character. The TYPE command would have erased the display screen if the file had contained the complete sequence for the erase display command.

Consider yourself fortunate if your system allows you to enter the escape character from the keyboard; entering ANSI.SYS commands will be much easier for you. For example, a file that erases the display screen could be created as follows:

```
C>copy con: erase.txt
^[[2J      ←pressing Esc displays the ^[, which represents the ESC character
^Z
        1 File(s) copied
```

Getting ESC into a File

One way to insert an escape character into a file is to create the file with a dummy character in place of the escape character. Once the file is created, you could use the MS-DOS utility program DEBUG to replace the dummy character with an escape character (see chapter 9). However, there is an easier way.

You can use the MS-DOS command PROMPT to enter an escape character in a text file. PROMPT is used to change the MS-DOS system prompt. Simply enter **prompt**, followed by the new system prompt. For example, if you wanted to change the system prompt to "ROCK AND ROLL", you could do it by entering the following command:

```
C>prompt ROCK AND ROLL
ROCK AND ROLL _
```

ROCK AND ROLL is now the system prompt, and MS-DOS will display it whenever it is ready to accept a command.

The PROMPT command is discussed in Part 3. Of interest to us now is the fact that we can place an escape character in the system prompt by including "$e" in the PROMPT command. Suppose that the current system prompt is the default prompt (**C>**) and that the following command is entered:

```
C>prompt $e[2J
```

What happens? Remember that MS-DOS sends all screen output to the ANSI.SYS black box (figure 8-1). When MS-DOS is ready to display the prompt, it sends the system prompt, as output, to ANSI.SYS. Since this system prompt begins with ESC [, ANSI.SYS recognizes the output as a command sequence, and the specified command is executed. In this case, the screen is cleared. The system prompt (ESC [2 J) is not displayed, since ANSI.SYS does not display command sequences. The screen simply goes blank each time that MS-DOS calls for a system prompt. While a screen that constantly blanks out is of limited value, this example does show how the prompt command can be used to send an escape character to ANSI.SYS.

The examples in this chapter will use the PROMPT command to enter the escape character, since most suppliers of MS-DOS do not include direct keyboard entry of ESC. However, if you are one of the lucky ones, you do not have to resort to this rather awkward technique when using ANSI.SYS.

The remaining sections of this chapter will present some examples of how ANSI.SYS can be used for more practical modifications to MS-DOS.

Keyboard Reassignment

The ANSI.SYS device driver can be used to reassign values to individual keys on the computer keyboard (table 8-5). Like all ANSI.SYS command sequences, *reassignment sequences* begin with the ESC character followed by a left bracket ([ ). The left bracket is followed by the ASCII code (see appendix F) of the key that is to have a new value assigned to it. For example, if you wanted to assign a new value to the "a" key, the command sequence would begin with ESC [97.

The first ASCII code is followed by one or more additional ASCII codes. The key indicated by the first code takes on the values of the remaining ASCII codes in the command sequence. All ASCII codes are separated by semicolons. The command sequences for keyboard reassignment are terminated by a "p". You must use a lowercase "p".

Let's say that you want to reassign "apple" to the "a" key. When you press "a", you want "apple" to be displayed on the screen. The command sequence used is ESC [97 followed by the ASCII values for "a", "p" (twice), "l", and "e". The command sequence is terminated by a lowercase "p". The entire command sequence would be:

```
esc[97;97;112;112;108;101p
```

Now we will add the command "prompt $e" to generate the ESC character. Let's put everything together. Enter the following command to turn your "a" into an "apple":

```
C>prompt $e[97;97;112;112;108;101p
```

Does it work? Press the "a" key; you should get "apple". If you don't, you may not have installed ANSI.SYS. Refer to the beginning of this chapter if you need help in installing ANSI.SYS. The other point to remember is that a new value has been assigned to lowercase "a" only. Pressing the key for the uppercase letter will still give "A". If you try this example on your computer, you will notice that no system prompt is displayed. This is because the prompt is now an ANSI.SYS command sequence and command sequences are not displayed. To get the familiar **C>** back, enter:

```
prompt
C>
```

You can get your "a" back by sending the sequence ESC [97; 97p to ANSI.SYS:

```
C>prompt $e[97;97p     ←reassigns the letter a to the "a" key
prompt                 ←resets the prompt to C
C>
```

In the previous example, we entered a series of ASCII values to be assigned to the "a" key. However, a keyboard reassignment command sequence can also contain the actual character string that you want to assign to a key. Instead of entering the ASCII value for each letter in "apple", you can enter the string "apple". Begin the control sequence as before, but replace the series of ASCII values with the string "apple". The string must be enclosed in quotation marks. The following sequence turns "a" to apple":

```
esc[97;"apple"p
```

The two methods just discussed may be combined. The following sequence will also turn "a" to "apple":

```
esc[97;"appl";101p
```

Function Keys

ANSI.SYS will reassign a string to one of the function keys (F1–F10) when the first ASCII code in a reassignment sequence is zero. The second ASCII code in the command sequence determines which key is reassigned. The following sequence reassigns the string "dir" to the F1 function key:

```
esc[0;59;"dir"p
```

This sequence can be sent to ANSI.SYS with the following command:

```
C>prompt $e[0;59;"dir"p
prompt

C>
```

Appendix F has a complete list of the extended ASCII codes for the 40 function keys (unshifted, shifted, Ctrl-shifted, and Alt-shifted). The next section will give you more examples of how strings can be reassigned to function keys.

Some Useful Applications of Keyboard Reassignment

Keyboard reassignment can be used to assign frequently entered commands to individual keys. Commands so assigned could then be entered with a single keystroke. Up to 128 characters may be reassigned to a single key.

Let's say that you use your computer for word processing and BASIC programming. To load your word processor, you have to type "wp". To load your BASIC interpreter, you have to type "gwbasic". You could save yourself some typing by reassigning each of these commands to a function key.

We will illustrate by first reassigning "gwbasic" to the F2 function key. The F2 key has an extended ASCII code of 0,60 (see appendix F); therefore, the reassignment code sequence will begin with ESC [0,60. The character string reassigned to the function key can be specified in the command sequence:

```
esc[0;60;"gwbasic"
```

This command sequence tells ANSI.SYS to display "gwbasic" when the F2 key is pressed. A carriage return must be requested before MS-DOS will load "gwbasic". This can be accomplished by including the ASCII code for carriage return (13) in the command sequence. The complete command sequence for key reassignment is terminated with a lowercase "p":

```
esc[0;60;"gwbasic";13p
```

Again, we use the command "prompt $e" to send an ESC character to the ANSI.SYS device driver:

```
C>prompt $e[0;60;"gwbasic";13p     ←this sends the command sequence
prompt                             ←this resets the prompt to default

C>
```

The BASIC interpreter will now be loaded when you press the F2 key.

We can assign "wp" to the F3 function key (ASCII code 0,61) by entering the following command:

```
C>prompt $e[0;61;"wp";13p
prompt

C>
```

Let's also assign the MS-DOS command DIR and the /w switch to the F1 function key (ASCII code 0,59):

```
C>prompt $e[0;59;"dir/w";13p
prompt

C>
```

Let's put all of these reassignment commands into a single batch file. If the file is given the name AUTOEXEC.BAT, it will automatically execute when MS-DOS is booted. We will also include the TIME and DATE commands in the batch file so that the time and date will be set when MS-DOS boots.

```
C>copy con: autoexec.bat
date
time
rem
rem reassign f1
prompt $e[0;59;"dir/w";13p
rem
rem reassign f2
prompt $e[0;60;"gwbasic";13p
rem
rem reassign f3
prompt $e[0;61;"wp";13p
rem
rem return prompt to default (C>)
prompt
^Z
        1 File(s) copied

C>
```

This batch file will automatically execute if it is in the root directory of the boot disk. The reassignments we entered will take effect once the file has been executed.

Screen Control

You can use the ANSI.SYS device driver to control cursor position and set display mode and attributes. The command sequences for screen control are listed in tables 8-2 through 8-5.

This section will show you how ANSI.SYS can be used to control the display screen by modifying the batch file used in the preceding discussion of key reassignment. We will add a PROMPT command to the end of the file that will send a series of display command sequences to ANSI.SYS. These commands will modify the display screen. When the batch file terminates, the system prompt will consist of these display commands. The commands will be sent to ANSI.SYS each time that the prompt is displayed. The screen modifications will be displayed each time MS-DOS requests that the system prompt be displayed.

The commands placed in the batch file will instruct ANSI.SYS to perform the following tasks: move the cursor to the home position (first line, first column), clear any text in the first line, switch to the high-intensity display mode, display three messages on the first line, move the cursor to the first column of the 25th line, display a prompt, return to the normal display mode, and, finally, clear line 25 of any text to the right of the prompt. Sounds complicated, but it can all be accomplished with one PROMPT command.

The first task that we want to accomplish is move the cursor to the home position. Table 8-1 shows the ANSI.SYS command sequences that control the cursor. The cursor position command is ESC [#;# H. Remember that the # symbols represent parameters. The first parameter is the line number, and the second parameter is the column number of the screen location where the cursor is to be located. The cursor will be moved to the home position if no parameters are included in the command sequence. The cursor position command must be terminated by an uppercase "H". Therefore, the first screen control command sequence that we will send to ANSI.SYS is ESC [H (move cursor to home position).

Next, we want ANSI.SYS to erase the first line on the display screen. This is accomplished with the sequence ESC [K (table 8-2). The command sequence must end with an uppercase "K".

The next command sequence will switch the display mode to high intensity. This is accomplished with the command sequence ESC [1m (table 8-4). A lowercase "m" is required.

So far our command series consists of three command sequences:

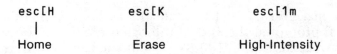

The ESC character will be sent to ANSI.SYS by using the "prompt $e" command; therefore, the three ANSI.SYS commands can be sent with the following command:

```
prompt $e[H $e[K $e[1m
```

After the cursor has been positioned, the line cleared, and the high-intensity mode set, we want ANSI.SYS to display a message. Since we will be using a PROMPT command to send the commands, we can simply include the message as part of the prompt:

```
prompt $e[H $e[K $e[1m directory-f1
```

Next, we want ANSI.SYS to advance the cursor eight spaces and then display another message. The cursor forward command advances the cursor. The command sequence is ESC [# C, where the # symbol represents the number of spaces forward that the cursor will be moved. The default value for # is one. The command sequence to move the cursor forward eight spaces is ESC [8C. The command must end with an uppercase "C":

```
prompt $e[H $e[K $e[1m directory-f1 $e[8C basic interpreter-f2
```

After displaying the second message, we want ANSI.SYS to advance the cursor eight more spaces and display a third message:

```
prompt $e[H $e[K $e[1m directory-f1 $e[8C basic interpreter-f2
$e[8C word processor-f3
```

After displaying the third message on the first line, we want ANSI.SYS to move the cursor to the first column in line 25. Again, we will use the cursor position command sequence (ESC [#;# H); this time we will specify some parameters:

```
prompt $e[H $e[K $e[1m directory-f1 $e[8C basic interpreter-f2
$e[8C word processor-f3 $e[25;1H
```

With the cursor at line 25, column 1, we will have ANSI.SYS display a prompt, return to the regular display mode, and clear line 25 of all text beyond the prompt:

```
prompt $e[H $e[K $e[1m directory-f1 $e[8C basic interpreter-f2
$e[8C word processor-f3 $e[25;1H ENTER COMMAND: $e[0m $e[K
```

If we make this PROMPT command the last command in a batch file, the system prompt at the end of the batch file execution will be the sequence of messages and ANSI.SYS commands and prompts that we have just discussed. Each time MS-DOS calls for a system prompt, ANSI.SYS will execute the commands and display the messages and prompts.

To get a better idea of what we are talking about, let's use EDLIN to modify this same batch file. (See the preceding section on keyboard reassignment for the original batch file, and see chapter 7 for a discussion of EDLIN commands.)

```
C>edlin autoexec.bat        ←edit file created in previous section
End of input file           ←EDLIN responds that the file has been loaded
*L                          ←enter "L"; EDLIN will display file

        1:*DATE
        2: TIME
        3: REM
        4: REM REASSIGN F1
        5: PROMPT $e[0;59;"DIR/W";13p
        6: REM
        7: REM REASSIGN F2
        8: PROMPT $e[0;60;"GWBASIC";13p
        9: REM
       10: REM REASSIGN F3
       11: PROMPT $e[0;61;"WP";13p
       12: REM
       13: REM RETURN PROMPT TO DEFAULT (C>)
       14: PROMPT
*                           ←EDLIN waits for the next command
```

The first step in modifying the batch file is to remove the lines that reset the system prompt to the default. This is accomplished by deleting the last three lines of the file:

```
*12,14d       ←delete lines 12–14
*1L           ←enter 1L to list file starting with line 1

        1:*DATE
        2: TIME
        3: REM
        4: REM REASSIGN F1
        5: PROMPT $e[0;59;"DIR/W";13p
        6: REM
        7: REM REASSIGN F2
        8: PROMPT $e[0;60;"GWBASIC";13p
        9: REM
       10: REM REASSIGN F3
       11: PROMPT $e[0;61;"WP";13p
*
```

Now we want to put into the file the PROMPT command that does all the wonderful things we have just described. We will also put some "rem" statements in the batch file to explain what is going on.

```
*12i              ←enter 12i to insert text beginning at line 12
   12:*rem        ←type a line of text and press Enter
   13:*rem the following prompt command instructs ansi.sys to
   14:*rem perform several functions:
   15:*rem move cursor to home, clear first line, set display mode to
   16:*rem hi intensity, print 3 messages at top of screen, move cursor
   17:*rem to line 25 column 1, print a prompt, reset display mode to
   18:*rem normal intensity, and clear right side of line 25.
   19:*rem
   20:*prompt $e[H $e[K $e[1m directory-f1 $e[8C basic interpreter-f2
$e[8C word processor-f3 $e[25;1H ENTER COMMAND: $e[0m $e[K
   21:*^Z          ←enter Ctrl-Z to terminate the INSERT command
*
```

The final line added to the batch file will be the MS-DOS command CLS. This command will clear the display screen:

```
*21i              ←enter 21i to insert text beginning at line 21
   21:*rem
   22:*rem the next command clears the screen. the batch file will
   23:*rem then terminate and return control to ms-dos.
   24:*cls
   25:*^Z          ←enter Ctrl-Z to terminate INSERT command
*1L               ←enter 1L to display file
    1: DATE
    2: TIME
    3: REM
    4: REM REASSIGN F1
    5: PROMPT $e[0;59;"DIR/W";13p
    6: REM
    7: REM REASSIGN F2
    8: PROMPT $e[0;60;"GWBASIC";13p
    9: REM
   10: REM REASSIGN F3
   11: PROMPT $e[0;61;"WP";13p
   12: rem
   13: rem THE FOLLOWING PROMPT COMMAND INSTRUCTS ANSI.SYS TO
   14: rem PERFORM SEVERAL FUNCTIONS:
   15: rem MOVE CURSOR TO HOME, CLEAR FIRST LINE, SET DISPLAY MODE TO
   16: rem HI INTENSITY, PRINT 3 MESSAGES AT TOP OF SCREEN, MOVE CURSOR
   17: rem TO LINE 25 COLUMN 1, PRINT A PROMPT, RESET DISPLAY MODE TO
   18: rem NORMAL INTENSITY, AND CLEAR RIGHT SIDE OF LINE 25.
   19: rem
   20: PROMPT $e[H $e[K $e[1m DIRECTORY-F1 $e[8C BASIC INTERPRETER-F2
$e[8C WORD PROCESSOR-F3 $e[25;1H ENTER COMMAND: $e[0m $e[K
   21: rem
   22: rem THE NEXT COMMAND CLEARS THE SCREEN. THE BATCH FILE WILL
   23: rem THEN TERMINATE AND RETURN CONTROL TO MS-DOS.
   24: CLS
*e                ←enter "e" to save the file and exit EDLIN
C>
```

The AUTOEXEC.BAT file is now stored in the root directory of the boot disk, and it will automatically execute when MS-DOS is booted. Let's try it out. Press the Ctrl-Alt-Del key combination to reboot the system. AUTOEXEC.BAT should begin execution, prompting you to enter the date and time. The first three PROMPT commands reassign character strings to the F1, F2, and F3 function keys. The fourth PROMPT command sets the screen control sequence. The CLS command clears the screen, and the batch file terminates, returning control to MS-DOS.

MS-DOS signals that it is ready to accept another command by displaying the system prompt. In this case, the system prompt is the screen control sequence that was the final PROMPT command in the batch file.

Figure 8-2 shows the appearance of the display screen upon conclusion of batch file execution. This display is the current system prompt. MS-DOS commands can be entered in the normal fashion. The commands "dir/w", "gwbasic", and "wp" may be entered simply by pressing function keys F1, F2, and F3. The screen control sequence will be executed each time that MS-DOS is ready to accept another command. The system prompt can be changed at any time by using the PROMPT command.

```
DIRECTORY-F1   BASIC INTERPRETER-F2   WORD PROCESSOR-F3




ENTER COMMAND:
ENTER COMMAND:
```

Figure 8-2. The appearance of the display screen after AUTOEXEC.BAT has been executed.

Note: MS-DOS displays the system prompt twice at the end of a batch file. Because of this, the bottom line in figure 8-2 (ENTER COMMAND:) will be displayed twice when the system first boots. Each subsequent display of the system prompt will display "ENTER COMMAND:" one time. You can avoid this minor annoyance by modifying the last PROMPT command in AUTOEXEC.BAT. The underscore indicates the modified portion.

```
prompt $e[H $e[K $e[1m directory-f1 $e[8C basic interpreter-f2 $e[8C word
processor-f3 $e[24;1H $e[K $e[25;1H ENTER COMMAND: $e[0m  $e[K
```

9

DEBUG

DEBUG Commands
Introductory DEBUG
Advanced DEBUG

DEBUG is an MS-DOS utility program used to examine and modify computer files and computer memory on a byte-by-byte basis. DEBUG also provides an environment under which computer programs can be executed step by step.

This chapter begins with an explanation of DEBUG commands and the rules for using them. Since many of DEBUG's features require some familiarity with 8086/8088 assembly language programming, the discussion of DEBUG itself is divided into two sections. The first section, "Introductory DEBUG," explains how to use DEBUG to examine the contents of computer memory. It is written as an introduction to DEBUG and is intended for all readers who are interested in gaining some familiarity with this powerful MS-DOS utility.

"Advanced DEBUG," the second section, explains how DEBUG can be used as a tool in examining and modifying computer programs. Some familiarity with assembly language programming is helpful, but not essential, in understanding the material presented in this section.

Here is a summary of the features provided by DEBUG:

▶ Loads program files and data files into computer memory.

▶ Displays the contents of a portion of computer memory in hexadecimal and ASCII formats.

▶ Changes the contents of a portion of memory.

▶ Moves blocks of data in memory to specified locations.

▶ Displays, creates, and modifies assembly language statements in memory.

▶ Follows, step by step, the execution of program instructions.

▶ Displays and modifies the contents of the CPU registers and flags.

▶ Stores the contents of a portion of computer memory on floppy and fixed disks.

▶ Performs hexadecimal addition and subtraction with a built-in calculator.

DEBUG Commands

DEBUG is a command-driven program, which means that you must enter a command before DEBUG will perform an operation. DEBUG displays a prompt to notify you when it is ready to accept a command. In MS-DOS 1, the DEBUG prompt is a greater than sign (>). In MS-DOS 2.X and 3.X, the DEBUG prompt is a hyphen (-). The examples in this chapter will use the hyphen as the DEBUG prompt.

Before we examine the DEBUG commands, we need to discuss the syntax, or rules, that must be followed when using DEBUG. All DEBUG commands begin with a letter. The letter may be entered in uppercase or lowercase. Most DEBUG commands include parameters other than the starting letter. When two consecutive parameters in a command are numbers, the numbers must be separated by a space or a comma. (All numbers used in DEBUG are hexadecimal.) In all other instances, parameters may be entered without separation.

To illustrate these rules, let's look at the following two commands, which are functionally equivalent. (Don't worry about the meaning of these commands for now.)

```
-D 100 L20
```

means the same as

```
-d100l20
```

Remember that any time consecutive parameters are hexadecimal numbers they must be separated by a comma or a space. The spaces in the following command are therefore necessary:

```
-SCS:0100 23 45 57
```

These rules will become second nature as you become familiar with the DEBUG commands. For the sake of clarity, we have inserted spaces between all parameters, though you need not use spaces except between consecutive hexadecimal numbers.

Table 9-1 is an alphabetical summary of the DEBUG commands. You can find a complete discussion of each command by referring to the page listed below each command's name.

Table 9-1. Summary of DEBUG Commands

Command	Purpose	Format
(A)SSEMBLE (page 160)	Assembles assembler statements into memory	a [start]
(C)OMPARE (page 165)	Compares contents of two blocks of memory	c [start1] [end] [start2] c [start1] L [length] [start2]
(D)UMP (page 142)	Displays memory contents	d d [start] [end] d [start] L [length]
(E)NTER (page 147)	Enters list of byte values and/or string characters into computer memory	e [start] [list]

Table 9-1. (cont.)

Command	Purpose	Format
	Displays and, if desired, changes memory contents	e [*start*]
(F)ILL (page 167)	Fills block of memory with list of byte values and/ or string characters	f [*start*] [*end*] [*list*] f [*start*] L [*length*] [*list*]
(G)O (page 155)	Begins program execution	g g=[*start*] g [*breakpoint(s)*] g=[*start*] [*breakpoint(s)*]
(H)EXADECIMAL Arithmetic (page 168)	Adds and subtracts two hexadecimal numbers	h [*number1*] [*number2*]
(I)NPUT (page 168)	Reads and displays byte from a port	i [*port*]
(L)OAD (page 162)	Loads a file into memory	L L [*start*]
	Loads sector(s) into memory	L [*drive*] [*sector*] [*number*] L [*start*] [*drive*] [*sector*] [*number*]
(M)OVE (page 166)	Moves block of data from one memory location to another	m[*start1*] [*end*] [*start2*] m [*start1*] L [*length*] [*start2*]
(N)AME (page 161)	Names a file	n [*filespec*]
	Names a parameter	n [*param*]
	Names two parameters	n [*param1*] [*param2*]
(O)UTPUT (page 168)	Sends byte value out a port	o [*port*] [*byte*]
(Q)UIT (page 142)	Ends DEBUG	q
(R)EGISTER (page 150)	Displays contents of registers and status flags	r
	Displays and	r [*register name*]

Table 9-1. (cont.)

Command	Purpose	Format
	changes contents of a register	
	Displays and changes status flags	rf
(S)EARCH (page 165)	Searches block of memory for list	s [*start*] [*end*] [*list*] s [*start*] L [*length*] [*list*]
(T)RACE (page 158)	Executes one machine instruction	t t=[*start*]
	Executes a number of machine instructions	t [*number*] t=[*start*] [*number*]
(U)NASSEMBLE (page 152)	Unassembles machine code	u u [*start*] [*end*] u [*start*] L [*length*]
(W)RITE (page 163)	Writes a file to disk	w w [*start*]
	Writes to sectors on disk	w [*drive*] [*sector*] [*number*] w [*start*] [*drive*] [*sector*] [*number*]

Note: Italics indicate items that you must supply. Items in square brackets are optional.

Introductory DEBUG

This section will explain how to start and end DEBUG, how to use DEBUG to display memory contents, and how to enter data with DEBUG. No knowledge of assembly language programming is necessary.

Starting DEBUG

To start DEBUG, enter the command **DEBUG**. MS-DOS will load DEBUG and display a prompt (–) when DEBUG is ready to receive your command. (All of the examples in this chapter assume that drive C contains a copy of the file DEBUG.COM.)

```
C>debug
–
```

In the DEBUG start command, you may specify the file to be debugged:

```
C>debug textpro.com
-
```

The DEBUG start command must include a drive letter designator and/or a path specifier if the file to be debugged is not located in the current directory of the default drive.

Ending DEBUG

To terminate DEBUG and return control to MS-DOS, enter **q** in response to the DEBUG prompt:

```
-q
C>
```

Displaying Memory Contents

Computer memory is an aggregate of individual memory *addresses*. Addresses are physical locations within memory that store one piece (a byte) of data. Computers that use MS-DOS divide memory into *segments*. Each segment consists of 64K contiguous bytes of memory. Individual memory addresses within a segment are referred to by their *offset*. The first byte in a segment is at offset 0 within the segment, the second byte is at offset 1 within the segment, and so on. Individual memory addresses are identifiable by stating their segment and offset addresses. With this background information, let's see how the DEBUG command DUMP is used to examine computer memory.

The DUMP command (enter **d** or **D**) is used to display the contents of a selected portion of computer memory. The "dump" is displayed in both hexadecimal and ASCII format. In the following example, DEBUG is started from MS-DOS:

```
C>debug
-
```

Recall that the hyphen is DEBUG's way of telling you that it is ready to accept a command. (On some systems, the DEBUG prompt is **>**.) Let's enter "d" and see what happens:

```
C>debug
-d
0958:0100  00 00 00 00 00 00 00 00-00 00 00 00 00 00 00 00   ................
0958:0110  00 00 00 00 00 00 00 00-00 00 00 00 00 00 00 00   ................
```

```
0958:0120  00 00 00 00 00 00 00 00-00 00 00 00 00 00 00 00   ................
0958:0130  00 00 00 00 00 00 00 00-00 00 00 00 00 00 00 00   ................
0958:0140  00 00 00 00 00 00 00 00-00 00 00 00 00 00 00 00   ................
0958:0150  00 00 00 00 00 00 00 00-00 00 00 00 00 00 00 00   ................
0958:0160  00 00 00 00 00 00 00 00-00 00 00 00 00 00 00 00   ................
0958:0170  00 00 00 00 00 00 00 00-00 00 00 00 00 00 00 00   ................
-
```

The first number in the upper left corner (0958:0100) of the display is the memory address where the dump begins. The address is read as "segment 0958H offset 0100H." The address displayed on your computer will probably be different from the address in the example.

The first 00 following 0958:0100 indicates that a byte value of 00H is stored at memory address 0958:0100. The next 00 in the top line means that a value of 00H is stored at the following address in computer memory (0959:0101). Proceeding across the top line, we see a total of 16 00's. This means that the 16 consecutive memory addresses beginning at 0958:0100 and continuing through 0958:010F all store a value of 00H.

The next seven lines (each preceded by a memory address) contain the remainder of the dump. We can see that this particular dump displays the contents of 128 consecutive memory addresses. The dump starts at address 0958:0101 and proceeds through address 0958:017F.

The dashes in the middle of each line serve as reference points. Eight of the 16 bytes on each line are to the left of the dash, and 8 are to the right. The 16 periods at the end of each line fill the space where memory contents are displayed in ASCII format. Unprintable characters are indicated by a period. We see nothing but periods, since there is no printable character with an ASCII value of 00H.

Let's try the DUMP command one more time and see what happens:

```
-d
0958:0180  00 00 00 00 00 00 00 00-00 00 00 00 00 00 00 00   ................
0958:0190  00 00 00 00 00 00 00 00-00 00 00 00 00 00 00 00   ................
0958:01A0  00 00 00 00 00 00 00 00-00 00 00 00 00 00 00 00   ................
0958:01B0  00 00 00 00 00 00 00 00-00 00 00 00 00 00 00 00   ................
0958:01C0  00 00 00 00 00 00 00 00-00 00 00 00 00 00 00 00   ................
0958:01D0  00 00 00 00 00 00 00 00-00 00 00 00 00 00 00 00   ................
0958:01E0  00 00 00 00 00 00 00 00-00 00 00 00 00 00 00 00   ................
0958:01F0  00 00 00 00 00 00 00 00-00 00 00 00 00 00 00 00   ................
-
```

Again, the screen displays all zeros and periods. But notice the memory addresses. This dump took off where the previous dump ended. What's happening?

If "d" is entered with no additional parameters, DEBUG displays (or "dumps") the contents stored in 128 consecutive memory addresses. The first byte displayed is located at the address immediately following the last byte displayed by the previous dump. If no previous DUMP command has been issued, the dump begins at the memory address used by DEBUG to load the file being debugged. (More on this in "Advanced DEBUG.")

We can tell DEBUG where to begin the dump by including an address in the command. The beginning address is specified by listing its segment and offset addresses. The two numbers are separated by a colon (:). The following command directs DEBUG to display 128 bytes of memory beginning at segment address 0958H, offset address 0000H:

```
-d 0958:0000
0958:0000   CD 20 00 20 00 9A EE FE-1D F0 34 02 68 06 62 02   M . ..n .p4.h.b.
0958:0010   68 06 E2 04 9C 05 9C 05-01 01 01 00 02 FF FF FF   h.b.............
0958:0020   FF FF FF FF FF FF FF FF-FF FF FF FF 65 06 BC 2A   ............e.<*
0958:0030   68 06 00 00 00 00 00 00-00 00 00 00 00 00 00 00   h...............
0958:0040   00 00 00 00 00 00 00 00-00 00 00 00 00 00 00 00   ................
0958:0050   CD 21 CB 00 00 00 00 00-00 00 00 00 00 20 20 20   M!K..........
0958:0060   20 20 20 20 20 20 20 20-00 00 00 00 00 20 20 20            .....
0958:0070   20 20 20 20 20 20 20 20-00 00 00 00 00 00 00 00        ........
-
```

Well, now we are getting somewhere. Notice that the dump started at the address specified in the DUMP command. Again, we have 128 consecutive bytes dumped. But this time we got something other than zeros and periods. The first byte dumped is located at memory address 0958:0000 and has a value of CDH.

Conventional ASCII values (see appendix F) fall in the range 00H to 7FH. DEBUG subtracts 80H from any byte with a value greater than 7FH and displays the character that corresponds to the resulting ASCII value. CDH minus 80H equals 4DH. 4DH is the ASCII value of the letter "M." Therefore, DEBUG displays an "M" as the first character in the ASCII portion of the dump.

The second memory location in the dump has a value of 20H. This is the ASCII value for a space, so DEBUG displays a space at the second position in the ASCII portion of the dump. The third address in the dump stores a value of 00H, which we know does not represent any printable ASCII character. DEBUG therefore prints a period at the third position of the ASCII dump.

This dump is not too exciting, as it consists of a few meaningless letters and a lot of periods. Let's try to find something more interesting to look at. We will briefly leave DEBUG and return to MS-DOS. To do this, simply enter q after the DEBUG prompt:

```
-q
C>
```

As you can tell from the MS-DOS prompt (C>), we have left DEBUG and have arrived back in MS-DOS. Before we return to DEBUG, we will use the MS-DOS text editor EDLIN to create a text file. (EDLIN is discussed in chapter 7.) If you are unfamiliar with EDLIN, just follow the instructions in the example.

The file to be created will take up about 250 bytes of disk space. In our example, the file will be stored on drive C, the default directory. Enter the following command:

```
C>edlin dbugpro.txt
```

This command tells MS-DOS to load EDLIN and instructs EDLIN to create a file named "dbugpro.txt". EDLIN will display the following message:

```
New file
*
```

EDLIN is now ready to accept a command. Type **Li** (or **li**). Then type the text that appears in each line. Press Enter at the end of lines 1–5 and Ctrl-Z at the end of line 6:

```
C>edlin dbugpro.txt
New file
*1i
        1:*+++++++++++++++++++++++++++++++++++++++++++++++++++++++++
        2:*This text file will be used to demonstrate DEBUG.
        3:*The file will be loaded into memory when DEBUG is started.
        4:*DEBUG is easy to use after some practice.
        5:*+++++++++++++++++++++++++++++++++++++++++++++++++++++++++
        6:*^Z
*e       ←type "e"
C>
```

The "e" command terminated EDLIN, and the **C>** prompt tells us that we have returned to MS-DOS. "Dbugpro.txt" has been created and stored on drive C. We can now return to DEBUG and examine the newly created file. With drive C as the default directory, enter the following command:

```
C>debug dbugpro.txt
-
```

As you can see, the DEBUG prompt tells us that we are back in DEBUG and that the file "dbugpro.txt" has been loaded into memory.

Enter **d** for a dump beginning at the memory address where "dbug-pro.txt" was loaded:

```
-d
0958:0100  2B 2B 2B 2B 2B 2B 2B 2B-2B 2B 2B 2B 2B 2B 2B 2B  ++++++++++++++++
0958:0110  2B 2B 2B 2B 2B 2B 2B 2B-2B 2B 2B 2B 2B 2B 2B 2B  ++++++++++++++++
0958:0120  2B 2B 2B 2B 2B 2B 2B 2B-2B 2B 2B 2B 2B 2B 2B 2B  ++++++++++++++++
0958:0130  2B 2B 2B 2B 2B 2B 2B-2B 0D 0A 54 68 69 73 20     +++++++++..This
0958:0140  74 65 78 74 20 66 69 6C-65 20 77 69 6C 6C 20 62  text file will b
0958:0150  65 20 75 73 65 64 20 74-6F 20 64 65 6D 6F 6E 73  e used to demons
0958:0160  74 72 61 74 65 20 44 45-42 55 47 2E 0D 0A 54 68  trate DEBUG...Th
```

```
0958:0170  65 20 66 69 6C 65 20 77-69 6C 6C 20 62 65 20 6C   e file will be l
-
```

Enter **d** again to continue the dump:

```
-d
0958:0180  6F 61 64 65 64 20 69 6E-74 6F 20 6D 65 6D 6F 72   oaded into memor
0958:0190  79 20 77 68 65 6E 20 44-45 42 55 47 20 69 73 20   y when DEBUG is
0958:01A0  73 74 61 72 74 65 64 2E-0D 0A 44 45 42 55 47 20   started...DEBUG
0958:01B0  69 73 20 65 61 73 79 20-74 6F 20 75 73 65 20 61   is easy to use a
0958:01C0  66 74 65 72 20 73 6F 6D-65 20 70 72 61 63 74 69   fter some practi
0958:01D0  63 65 2E 0D 0A 2B 2B 2B-2B 2B 2B 2B 2B 2B 2B 2B   ce...+++++++++++
0958:01E0  2B 2B 2B 2B 2B 2B 2B 2B-2B 2B 2B 2B 2B 2B 2B 2B   ++++++++++++++++
0958:01F0  2B 2B 2B 2B 2B 2B 2B 2B-2B 2B 2B 2B 2B 2B 2B 2B   ++++++++++++++++
-
```

In the preceding examples, each "d" command caused 128 bytes of memory to be displayed. The contents of "dbugpro.txt" were displayed in hexadecimal format at the center of the screen and in ASCII format to the right.

You may specify the start and stop addresses of a dump as follows:

```
-d 0958:01AA 01D2
0958:01AA  44 45 42 55 47 20                                 DEBUG
0958:01B0  69 73 20 65 61 73 79 20-74 6F 20 75 73 65 20 61   is easy to use a
0958:01C0  66 74 65 72 20 73 6F 6D-65 20 70 72 61 63 74 69   fter some practi
0958:01D0  63 65 2E                                          ce.
-
```

The preceding dump begins at address 0958:01AA and ends at 0958:01D2. The starting and ending addresses are specified in the DUMP command. Notice that the starting address is specified by segment (0958) and offset (01AA). Only the offset (01D2) is specified for the ending address.

Addresses stored in segment registers (see "Registers and Flags" in "Advanced DEBUG") may be specified in a dump by including the register's name in the command. The following command directs DEBUG to begin a dump at the memory location whose segment address is stored in the DS register and whose offset address is 01AAH. The ending offset address is specified as 01D2H.

```
-d DS:01AA 01D2
0958:01AA  44 45 42 55 47 20                                 DEBUG
0958:01B0  69 73 20 65 61 73 79 20-74 6F 20 75 73 65 20 61   is easy to use a
0958:01C0  66 74 65 72 20 73 6F 6D-65 20 70 72 61 63 74 69   fter some practi
0958:01D0  63 65 2E                                          ce.
-
```

We can leave out segment addresses altogether, entering only offset addresses. DEBUG will assume that the segment address is stored in the DS register:

```
-d DS:01AA 01D2
0958:01AA  44 45 42 55 47 20                                DEBUG
0958:01B0  69 73 20 65 61 73 79 20-74 6F 20 75 73 65 20 61  is easy to use a
0958:01C0  66 74 65 72 20 73 6F 6D-65 20 70 72 61 63 74 69  fter some practi
0958:01D0  63 65 2E                                         ce.
-
```

Finally, we can tell DEBUG the number of bytes to be dumped by following the start address with an "L" followed by the number of bytes to be dumped. The next command tells DEBUG to dump 41 (29H) bytes:

```
-d DS:01AA L29
0958:01AA  44 45 42 55 47 20                                DEBUG
0958:01B0  69 73 20 65 61 73 79 20-74 6F 20 75 73 65 20 61  is easy to use a
0958:01C0  66 74 65 72 20 73 6F 6D-65 20 70 72 61 63 74 69  fter some practi
0958:01D0  63 65 2E                                         ce.
-
```

Entering Data with DEBUG

The ENTER command (enter e or E) is used to place data into memory. This powerful command allows you to modify the contents of memory on a byte-by-byte basis. ENTER can be used in conjunction with the NAME and WRITE commands (see "Advanced DEBUG") to modify files and store the modified files on disk.

The command begins with the letter "e" followed by the address at which data entry will begin. DEBUG assumes that the segment address is stored in the DS register if you specify only an offset address.

Data to be entered are specified in the command as a sequence of hexadecimal numbers and/or character strings. You must separate hexadecimal numbers with a space or a comma. A string of characters must be enclosed in quotation marks. If a command contains a character string, the hexadecimal ASCII values for the characters in the string are stored in memory.

The following example demonstrates the ENTER command:

```
-e 0958:0000 20 2A 44 41 54 41 20 'IS' 20 48 45 52 45 2A 20
-
```

The preceding ENTER command instructed DEBUG to enter 16 bytes of data in memory. The data are stored at consecutive memory locations beginning at address 0958:0000. Fourteen of the bytes entered are listed in the command as hexadecimal numbers. Two of the bytes are listed as a character string ('IS').

We can use the DUMP command to display the data entered. The "L" option will tell DEBUG to dump 16 (10H) bytes of memory:

```
-d 0958:0000 L10
```

```
0958:0000  20 2A 44 41 54 41 20 49-53 20 48 45 52 45 2A 20  *DATA IS HERE*
-
```

Notice that memory addresses 0958:0007 and 0958:0008 store the hexadecimal ASCII values of the characters in the string "is". The ASCII representation of the data entered is displayed at the right.

The ENTER command can also be used to display, and optionally change, the byte value stored at an address. In this case, the command consists of the letter "e" followed by a memory address. No list of numbers or strings is included in the command. DEBUG responds by displaying the address specified and the byte value stored at that address:

```
-e 0958:0000
0958:0000  20.
```

Pressing the space bar displays the value at the next memory address:

```
-e 0958:0000
0958:0000  20. 2A.
```

The value stored at an address can be changed by entering a new hexadecimal value. Strings, however, cannot be entered when the command is used in this fashion:

```
-e 0958:0000
0958:0000  20. 2A.21
```

In the preceding example, memory address 0958:0001 originally contained a value of 2AH. The value stored at this address has been changed to 21H.

At each 8-byte boundary (an offset address ending in either 8 or 0), DEBUG displays the current address:

```
-e 0958:0000
0958:0000  20.   2A.21 44.   41.   54.   41.   20.   49.43
0958:0008  53.48 20.41 48.4E 45.47 52.45 45.44 2A.   20.
```

In the preceding example, the values stored at offset addresses 0001H and 0007H through 000DH have been changed. The values at the other addresses are unchanged.

The preceding memory address and the value stored at that address can be displayed by entering a hyphen (-). This value can be changed if desired:

```
-e 0958:0000
0958:0000  20.   2A.21 44.   41.   54.   41.   20.   49.43
0958:0008  53.48 20.41 48.4E 45.47 52.45 45.44 2A.   20.-
0958:000E  2A.
```

To terminate the command, press Enter. The reappearance of the DE-BUG prompt (–) signals that DEBUG is ready to receive your next command:

```
-e 0958:0000
0958:0000  20.   2A.21 44.  41.   54.   41.   20.   49.43
0958:0008  53.48 20.41 48.4E 45.47 52.45 45.44 2A.   20.-
0958:000E  2A.21       ←press Enter
-
```

The changes made can be examined with the DUMP command:

```
-d 0958:0000 L10
0958:0000  20 21 44 41 54 41 20 43-48 41 4E 47 45 44 20 21    !DATA CHANGED!
```

Advanced DEBUG

The following discussion of the remaining DEBUG commands is written to be as self-explanatory as possible. Although some knowledge of assembly language programming would be helpful, it is not essential. Let us begin with a few general concepts before we proceed with the commands.

Registers and Flags

The heart of a microcomputer is its *central processing unit* (CPU), the portion of the computer responsible for performing all arithmetic and logical operations and controlling the flow of information throughout the system. CPUs store data in structures called *registers.* Most computers that use MS-DOS have CPUs containing 13 registers. The registers are given the names AX, BX, CX, DX, SP, BP, SI, DI, CS, DS, SS, ES, and IP. The CS, DS, SS, and ES registers are called the *segment registers.*

In MS-DOS computers, the CPU also contains nine "flags." A *flag* is a structure that is either "set" or "cleared" by different computer operations. As we shall see, DEBUG can be used to examine and modify the registers and flags.

DEBUG Initialization

When you instruct MS-DOS to start DEBUG, the operating system places the file DEBUG.COM in memory at the lowest-available memory location. DE-BUG then takes control and constructs a *program segment prefix* (psp) at the lowest-available location in memory. The psp is a contiguous block of memory used by MS-DOS during program execution. The psp is 256 (100H) bytes in length. (For more on the psp, see chapter 11.)

Looking at Registers with DEBUG

The REGISTER command (enter **r** or **R**) is used by DEBUG to display and modify the contents of the CPU registers and status flags. This command also displays information about the next machine instruction scheduled for execution. Let's begin our discussion of REGISTER by starting DEBUG. With drive C as the default directory, enter the following command:

```
C>debug
-
```

DEBUG signals that it is ready to accept a command by displaying its prompt. Let's enter **r** and see what happens:

```
C>debug
-r
AX=0000  BX=0000  CX=0000  DX=0000  SP=FFEE  BP=0000  SI=0000 DI=0000
DS=0958  ES=0958  SS=0958  CS=0958  IP=0100     NV UP DI PL NZ NA PO NC
0958:0100  0000          ADD          [BX+SI],AL                    DS:0000=CD
-
```

The display shows the hexadecimal values stored in each of the 13 registers. The segment registers (DS, ES, SS, and CS) all store a value of 0958H. This number is the address of the lowest-available segment in the memory of the computer used in this example. If you are following along on your computer, the value stored in your segment registers may not equal 0958H.

The SP register has been initialized to a value of FFEEH. The IP register has been set to equal 0100H. The remaining registers have been set to equal zero.

The status of the eight flags is displayed on the right side of the second line. All flags are initially cleared by DEBUG. Table 9-2 lists the eight flags and the symbols used to indicate their status in the order that they are displayed by DEBUG.

A computer program is a sequence of *machine instructions* that the computer is to execute. Machine instructions are written in *machine code,* a series of bytes stored in memory. The machine code for the next instruction to be executed is stored in memory at the address pointed to by the CS and IP registers. In the previous example, this address is CS:IP=0958:0100.

The third line of each register display contains information about the instruction at CS:IP. The CS:IP address is displayed at the left of the third line. The next item displayed is the sequence of bytes that make up the machine instruction. In the previous example, the instruction sequence is 00H 00H (displayed as 0000). This sequence of machine code is represented by the assembly language *mnemonic* displayed in the middle of the third row— "ADD [BX+SI], AL". A mnemonic is a memory aid, such as an abbreviation or a code. Mnemonics are frequently used by programmers.

Table 9-2. Flags and Symbols in DEBUG

Flag Name	Set	Clear
Overflow (yes/no)	OV	NV
Direction (decrement/increment)	DN	UP
Interrupt (enable/disable)	EI	DI
Sign (negative/positive)	NG	PL
Zero (yes/no)	ZR	NZ
Auxiliary carry (yes/no)	AC	NA
Parity (even/odd)	PE	PO
Carry (yes/no)	CY	NC

In the preceding display, the instruction to be executed tells the computer to take the value stored in the AL register (the low-order byte in the AX register) and add that value to the value stored at memory address DS:0000. The resulting value is to be stored at DS:0000. The current value stored at DS:0000 is displayed at the right end of the third line.

You may alter the value stored in a register by entering "r" followed by the name of the register. The current value in the register will be displayed, and a new value can be entered. To retain the current value of the register, press Enter.

```
-r CX
CX 0000
:245D
-r
AX=0000  BX=0000  CX=245D  DX=0000  SP=FFEE  BP=0000  SI=0000 DI=0000
DS=0958  ES=0958  SS=0958  CS=0958  IP=0100    NV UP DI PL NZ NA PO NC
0958:0100 0000          ADD         [BX+SI],AL                  DS:0000=CD
-
```

Since CS:IP points to the next instruction, changing the CS and/or IP registers can have dramatic results:

```
-r IP
IP 0100
:0000
-r
AX=0000  BX=0000  CX=245D  DX=0000  SP=FFEE  BP=0000  SI=0000 DI=0000
DS=0958  ES=0958  SS=0958  CS=0958  IP=0000    NV UP DI PL NZ NA PO NC
0958:0000 CD20          INT     20
-
```

Now CS:IP points to memory address 0958:0000. The machine code sequence at this address is CD 20, which instructs the computer to execute interrupt 20.

DEBUG displays the status of the flags when the command "rf" is entered. Any or all of the flags can then be modified by entering one or more symbols (see table 9-2). The symbols may be entered in any order with or without spaces between them. In the following example, the overflow, sign, and carry flags are set:

```
-rf
NV UP DI PL NZ NA PO NC -OV NG CY
-r
AX=0000  BX=0000  CX=245D  DX=0000  SP=FFEE  BP=0000  SI=0000 DI=0000
DS=0958  ES=0958  SS=0958  CS=0958  IP=0000   OV UP DI NG NZ NA PO CY
0958:0000 CD20           INT    20
-
```

Unassembling with DEBUG

Recall that a computer program is a series of instructions stored in the computer as machine code. In machine code, each instruction to the computer consists of a sequence of one or more bytes. While machine code makes sense to a computer, it is very difficult for most people to make any sense out of it.

Because machine code is so cumbersome and difficult to work with, another low-level computer language called *assembly language* is often used instead. Assembly language programmers use symbolic instructions when writing programs. These symbols, called *mnemonics,* are easier for people to understand than machine code. For example, an assembly language programmer might used the statement "RD" for the instruction "read data." However, mnemonics don't mean a thing to computers; so before a program can be executed, the mnemonics must be converted to machine code. This conversion process is called *assembly* and is performed by a computer program called an *assembler.*

Often it is desirable to reverse the assembly process; that is, to take machine code and "unassemble" it back to the corresponding assembly language mnemonics. This process is performed by a computer program called, naturally, an *unassembler.*

The UNASSEMBLE command (enter u or U) is used to invoke DEBUG's unassembler. The command can be used to unassemble existing machine code and obtain what MS-DOS manuals term "assembler like" statements. This refers to the fact that assembly language programmers can use labels to reference specific memory locations. These labels are a tremendous help in understanding the logical flow of an assembly language program. The UNASSEMBLE command references memory locations by numerical addresses only; no labels are used. This difference can make an unassembled program listing much more difficult to follow than the original assembly language program. Nonetheless, an unassembler can be an extremely powerful aid in figuring out how a computer program works and how it can be modified.

To demonstrate DEBUG's unassembler, let's unassemble a portion of DEBUG.COM. We begin at the DOS level and instruct DEBUG to load the file DEBUG.COM. With drive C as the default directory, enter the command shown in the next example.

Note: If you follow this example on your computer and get markedly different results, you probably have a different version of DEBUG.COM. However, you can still use the concepts presented here to explore your version of DEBUG.COM.

```
C>debug debug.com
```

The appearance of the DEBUG prompt tells us that DEBUG is ready to accept a command. DEBUG has constructed a psp, at the end of which it has loaded the file DEBUG.COM. DEBUG has then stored the segment address of the psp in each of the four segment registers.

Let's begin our examination of the DEBUG.COM file by having DEBUG dump the first 80 bytes (50H) of the file. We will use the DUMP command, specifying an address at which to begin the dump. We know that DE-BUG.COM has been loaded at offset address 100H in the segment containing the psp. We do not know the value of that segment, but its value, whatever it is, has been stored in the four segment registers. Therefore, we can use any of the segment registers in the DUMP command:

```
-d CS:0100 L50
096C:0100  EB 09 56 65 72 73 20 32-2E 31 30 B4 30 CD 21 86   k.Vers 2.1040M!.
096C:0110  E0 3D 00 02 73 09 BA 69-2B B4 09 CD 21 CD 20 B4   '=..s.:i+4.M!M 4
096C:0120  51 CD 21 89 1E 4F 2B BC-D4 2A A2 D5 2C B4 52 CD   QM!..O+<T*"U.4RM
096C:0130  21 8C C8 8E D8 8E C0 E8-F1 00 B0 23 BA 62 02 CD   !.H.X.@hd.0#:b.M
096C:0140  21 8C CA B8 03 2F D1 E8-D1 E8 D1 E8 03 D0         !.J8./QhQhQhQh.P
-
```

This dump displays the first 80 bytes of the machine code making up the program file DEBUG.COM. On the computer used in this example, the CS register has been initialized to a value of 096CH. Do not be surprised if the value of the CS register on your computer is different. This would mean only that the lowest-available segment on your computer is located at a segment address other than 096CH.

The bytes in this dump mean a lot to the computer but not much to most people. We can use the unassemble command to obtain an assembly listing of the machine code. Unassembling begins at the same address as the dump:

```
-u CS:0100
096C:0100    EB09            JMP    010B
096C:0102    56              PUSH   SI
```

```
096C:0103      65                        DB       65
096C:0104      7273                      JB       0179
096C:0106      2032                      AND      [BP+SI],DH
096C:0108      2E                        CS:
096C:0109      3130                      XOR      [BX+SI],SI
096C:010B      B430                      MOV      AH,30
096C:010D      CD21                      INT      21
096C:010F      86E0                      XCHG     AL,AH
096C:0111      3D0002                    CMP      AX,0200
096C:0114      7309                      JNB      011F
096C:0116      BA692B                    MOV      DX,2B69
096C:0119      B409                      MOV      AH,09
096C:011B      CD21                      INT      21
096C:011D      CD20                      INT      20
096C:011F      B451                      MOV      AH,51
-
```

This is an unassembled listing of the first 33 bytes of DEBUG.COM. The first item (column 1) on each line is the starting segment and offset address of an instruction that the computer is to execute. The second item (column 2) in each line is the actual sequence of bytes that make up the machine code for the instruction. The third item (columns 3 and 4) on each line is the assembly language statement that corresponds to the machine-coded instruction.

In the first line, the instruction begins at address 096C:0100. The machine code for the instruction consists of the 2-byte sequence EBH, 09H (written as EB09). The corresponding assembly language statement is "JMP 010B". Even though the meaning of this assembly language statement is not entirely obvious, you can probably guess what it means. For someone experienced in assembly language programming, this unassembled listing is an essential aid in understanding the workings of a machine language program. By the way, "JMP 010B" is an instruction to the computer telling it to jump to offset address 010BH and continue program execution with the instruction that begins at that point.

The UNASSEMBLE command can be entered with or without a starting address. If you enter only an offset address, the command assumes that the segment address is stored in the CS register. If you do not enter an address, the command assumes that the starting address is the location following the last instruction that was unassembled. If you did not issue a previous UNASSEMBLE command, unassembling begins at address CS:0100.

A range of memory to be unassembled may be specified by entering a starting address and an ending address. The ending address must be an offset address. If the end address does not correspond to the last byte in an instruction, the complete instruction is still unassembled:

```
-u CS:0100 0104
096C:0100      EB09                      JMP      010B
```

```
096C:0102    56                      PUSH   SI
096C:0103    65                      DB     65
096C:0104    7273                    JB     0179
```

The number of bytes to be unassembled may be specified with the "L" option. The default value is 32. If the final byte specified does not correspond to the final byte in an instruction, the complete instruction is still unassembled:

```
-u CS:0106 L4
096C:0106    2032                    AND    [BP+SI],DH
096C:0108    2E                      CS:
096C:0109    3130                    XOR    [BX+SI],SI
```

One final word about the UNASSEMBLE command. If you specify a starting address for the command, be certain that the address is indeed the starting point of a machine instruction. If you specify a starting address that is in the middle of an instruction, or a memory address that contains data rather than program code, the resulting unassembled list may be meaningless.

To obtain a printout of an unassembly listing, press Ctrl-PrtSc before entering your UNASSEMBLE command.

Program Execution with DEBUG

The DEBUG command GO (enter **g** or **G**) is used to execute machine language programs in a controlled environment. We will demonstrate the GO command with a short computer program that will be written using DEBUG. To follow along, boot your system, using drive C as the default directory. After you see the prompt, start DEBUG:

```
C>debug
-
```

When the DEBUG prompt appears, carefully enter the following commands.

```
-e CS:0100 BO 01 BF 00 02 B9 1D 00 FC F2 AA BO 24
-e CS:010D AA 06 1F BA 00 02 B4 09 CD 21 CD 20
```

The preceding DEBUG commands place in memory a sequence of byte values that form a machine language computer program. When the program is executed, it will clear the display screen, print a row of happy face symbols on the screen, and then return control to DEBUG.

The UNASSEMBLE command can be used to examine the program before we execute it:

```
-u CS:100     117
0976:0100     B002                MOV       AL,01
0976:0102     BF0002              MOV       DI,0200
0976:0105     B91D00              MOV       CX,001D
0976:0108     FC                  CLD
0976:0109     F2                  REPNZ
0976:010A     AA                  STOSB
0976:010B     B024                MOV       AL,24
0976:010D     AA                  STOSB
0976:010E     06                  PUSH      ES
0976:010F     1F                  POP       DS
0976:0110     BA0002              MOV       DX,0200
0976:0113     B409                MOV       AH,09
0976:0115     CD21                INT       21
0976:0117     CD20                INT       20
-
```

The GO command may be entered without additional parameters. When this is done, execution begins at the instruction pointed to by CS:IP. Let's use the REGISTER command to check on the status of the registers:

```
-r
AX=0000  BX=0000  CX=0000  DX=0000  SP=FFEE  BP=0000  SI=0000 DI=0000
DS=0976  ES=0976  SS=0976  CS=0976  IP=0100   NV UP DI PL NZ NA PO NC
0976:0100 B001           MOV      AL,01
-
```

Since CS and IP are pointing to the first instruction of our program, enter **g** and see what happens:

```
-g
☺☺☺☺☺☺☺☺☺☺☺☺☺☺☺☺☺☺☺☺☺☺☺☺☺☺☺☺☺☺
```

You should see a row of 30 happy faces. DEBUG displays the following message:

```
Program terminated normally
-
```

The message **Program terminated normally** tells you that control has been passed from the program being executed back to DEBUG.

The GO command may be used to set *breakpoints*. Breakpoints are used to halt program execution at particular points in the machine code sequence. Breakpoints are set by specifying breakpoint addresses in the GO command. Up to ten breakpoints may be set in one command. DEBUG assumes that a breakpoint's segment address is stored in the CS register if you specify only an offset address in the GO command. Breakpoint addresses must be separated by a space or a comma.

When DEBUG encounters a breakpoint, program execution is halted and the contents of the registers and the status of the flags are displayed. Breakpoints can be very useful in following and/or debugging programs that contain branching logic. They can also be very useful in "sidestepping" portions of code that do not require the scrutiny of the TRACE command. (TRACE is discussed in the next section.)

The program we have written contains an instruction at offset address 0109 that is repeated 30 times during program execution. Single-stepping through this instruction eighty times with TRACE would be extremely monotonous and yield no new information about the workings of the program. Breakpoints allow us to rapidly execute the instruction, halting program execution at the instruction located at 010B.

Let's use TRACE to step through the first three instructions in the program. We will then use GO to rapidly execute the instructions at 0109. GO will set a breakpoint at address 010B.

```
-t
AX=0001  BX=0000  CX=0000  DX=0000  SP=FFEE  BP=0000  SI=0000 DI=0000
DS=0976  ES=0976  SS=0976  CS=0976  IP=0102   NV UP DI PL NZ NA PO NC
0976:0102 BF0002        MOV     DI,0200
-t

AX=0001  BX=0000  CX=0000  DX=0000  SP=FFEE  BP=0000  SI=0000 DI=0200
DS=0976  ES=0976  SS=0976  CS=0976  IP=0105   NV UP DI PL NZ NA PO NC
0976:0105 B91D00        MOV     CX,001D
-t

AX=0001  BX=0000  CX=001D  DX=0000  SP=FFEE  BP=0000  SI=0000 DI=0200
DS=0976  ES=0976  SS=0976  CS=0976  IP=0108   NV UP DI PL NZ NA PO NC
0976:0108 FC            CLD
-t

AX=0001  BX=0000  CX=001D  DX=0000  SP=FFEE  BP=0000  SI=0000 DI=0200
DS=0976  ES=0976  SS=0976  CS=0976  IP=0109   NV UP DI PL NZ NA PO NC
0976:0109 F2            REPNZ
0976:010A AA            STOSB
-g 010b

AX=0001  BX=0000  CX=001D  DX=0000  SP=FFEE  BP=0000  SI=0000 DI=0250
DS=0976  ES=0976  SS=0976  CS=0976  IP=010B   NV UP DI PL NZ NA PO NC
0976:010B B024          MOV     AL,24
-
```

The instructions at offset 0109 and 010A were actually repeated 30 times, but by setting the breakpoint we were able to zoom through them with GO.

You can use the GO command to specify the first instruction to be executed, thereby overriding the CS:IP pointer. After typing **g**, type an equal sign (=) followed by the address of what is to be the starting instruction. If you enter only an offset address, DEBUG assumes that the CS register contains the segment address.

If we were to continue the previous example by entering a "g", execution would commence with the instruction pointed to by CS:IP (0958: 010B). We can rerun the program from the start by including the starting address of the program in the GO command:

```
-g=100
```

██

A row of happy faces appears, and a message is displayed, telling us that program execution has terminated and control has been returned to DEBUG.

Single-Stepping through a Program

The TRACE command (enter t or T) is used to execute machine language programs in a single-step fashion. After each instruction is carried out, the contents of the registers and the status of the flags are displayed. Each display is identical to the display that results when the REGISTER command is used. The only difference is that each time a TRACE command is entered, one instruction is executed before the next display is put on the screen.

We will demonstrate TRACE with the same program that was used to demonstrate GO. If you no longer have the program in memory, start DEBUG and enter the following commands:

```
C>debug
-e CS:0100 B0 01 BF 00 00 B9 1D 00 FC F2 AA B0 24
-e CS:010D AA 06 1F BA 00 02 B4 09 CD 21 CD 20
```

Once the program is in memory, we can begin. Let's start with a REGISTER command to see where we are:

```
-r
AX=0001  BX=0000  CX=0000  DX=0000  SP=FFEE  BP=0000  SI=0000 DI=0250
DS=0976  ES=0976  SS=0976  CS=0976  IP=0100   NV UP DI PL NZ NA PO NC
0976:0100 B001          MOV     AL,02
-
```

Entering a "t" executes the instruction located at CS:IP. After the instruction is executed, the registers and flags are displayed:

```
-t
AX=0001  BX=0000  CX=0000  DX=0000  SP=FFEE  BP=0000  SI=0000 DI=0250
DS=0976  ES=0976  SS=0976  CS=0976  IP=0102   NV UP DI PL NZ NA PO NC
0976:0102 BF0002        MOV     DI,0200
-t
```

```
AX=0001  BX=0000  CX=0000  DX=0000  SP=FFEE  BP=0000 SI=0000 DI=0200
DS=0976  ES=0976  SS=0976  CS=0976  IP=0105     NV UP DI PL NZ NA PO NC
0976:0105 B91D00        MOV     CX,001D
-
```

You can use the TRACE command to specify which instruction will be executed by including the address of the instruction in the command. To specify an instruction, enter "t", followed by an equal sign (=), followed by the address of the instruction to be executed. DEBUG assumes that the instruction's segment address is stored in the CS register if you specify only an offset address in the TRACE command:

```
-t=0100
AX=0001  BX=0000  CX=0000  DX=0000  SP=FFEE  BP=0000 SI=0000 DI=0200
DS=0976  ES=0976  SS=0976  CS=0976  IP=0102     NV UP DI PL NZ NA PO NC
0976:0102 BF0002        MOV     DI,0200
-
```

The preceding trace executed the instruction at offset 0100H. CS:IP is now pointing to the instruction at offset 0102H.

TRACE can also be used to execute more than one instruction. You simply enter the number of instructions that are to be executed. After each instruction is executed, the registers and flags are displayed. If several instructions are executed, the display will scroll off the screen. You can suspend the scrolling by pressing the Ctrl-NumLock keys. To continue scrolling, press any key.

Pressing the Ctrl-C keys stops the trace, and the DEBUG prompt is displayed:

```
-t6
AX=0001  BX=0000  CX=0000  DX=0000  SP=FFEE  BP=0000 SI=0000 DI=0200
DS=0976  ES=0976  SS=0976  CS=0976  IP=0105     NV UP DI PL NZ NA PO NC
0976:0105 B91D00        MOV     CX,001D

AX=0001  BX=0000  CX=001D  DX=0000  SP=FFEE  BP=0000 SI=0000 DI=0200
DS=0976  ES=0976  SS=0976  CS=0976  IP=0108     NV UP DI PL NZ NA PO NC
0976:0108 FC            CLD

AX=0001  BX=0000  CX=001D  DX=0000  SP=FFEE  BP=0000 SI=0000 DI=0200
DS=0976  ES=0976  SS=0976  CS=0976  IP=0109     NV UP DI PL NZ NA PO NC
0976:0109 F2            REPNZ
0976:010A AA            STOSB

AX=0001  BX=0000  CX=001C  DX=0000  SP=FFEE  BP=0000 SI=0000 DI=0201
DS=0976  ES=0976  SS=0976  CS=0976  IP=0109     NV UP DI PL NZ NA PO NC
0976:0109 F2            REPNZ
0976:010A AA            STOSB

AX=0001  BX=0000  CX=001B  DX=0000  SP=FFEE  BP=0000 SI=0000 DI=0202
```

159

```
DS=0976  ES=0976  SS=0976  CS=0976  IP=0109    NV UP DI PL NZ NA PO NC
0976:0109 F2            REPNZ
0976:010A AA           STOSB

AX=0001  BX=0000  CX=001A  DX=0000  SP=FFEE  BP=0000  SI=0000 DI=0203
DS=0976  EX=0976  SS=0976  CS=0976  IP=0109    NV UP DI PL NZ NA PO NC
0976:0109 F2            REPNZ
0976:010A AA           STOSB
-
```

Four different instructions have been executed, but one of them was executed four times. Each time that the "REPNZ STOSB" instruction was executed, the CX register was decremented by one. The computer will execute this instruction 30 (001DH) times before it moves on to the next instruction in the program. To trace through all of that would have required a lot of time, so we stopped the trace.

Even if we entered the command "t 001D", it would take a while for all of the displays to scroll up the screen. Refer to the earlier discussion of GO breakpoints to see how you can speed up the execution of instructions that are repeated many times.

Assembling with DEBUG

The MS-DOS 2.X and 3.X versions of DEBUG can be used to enter 8088/8086/8087 assembly language statements directly into memory. (DEBUG in MS-DOS 1.X does not have this capability.) The ASSEMBLE command is useful in composing short assembly language programs and in modifying existing assembly language programs. This command allows you to enter assembly language mnemonics and operands. Labels cannot be entered with the command. The advantage of using the ASSEMBLE command is that the machine code for each instruction is entered directly into memory, eliminating the need to go through an assembly process.

To use the ASSEMBLE command, enter a followed by the memory address of the first machine instruction to be entered. DEBUG assumes that the segment address of the instruction is stored in the CS register if you specify only an offset address. When the command is entered, DEBUG displays the start address and waits for you to enter an assembly language statement. DEBUG displays the next address in memory if the instruction entered is valid. If the instruction is not valid, DEBUG indicates the location of the error. Pressing Enter without an instruction terminates the assembly command.

We will demonstrate the ASSEMBLE command by writing a short assembly language program that may look familiar to you. If you follow the next example on your own computer, the segment addresses may not match those in the text.

```
C>debug
```

```
-a100
0976:0100 MOV AL,01
0976:0102 MOV DI,0200
0976:0105 MOV CX,001D
0976:0108 CLD
0976:0109 REPNZ STOSB
0976:010B MOV AL,24
0976:010D STOSB
0976:010E PUSH ES
0976:010F POP DS
0976:0110 MOV DX,0200
0976:0113 MOV AH,09
0976:0115 INT 21
0976:0117 INT 20
0976:0119      ←press Enter
-
```

You may have recognized this program as being the same one used earlier to demonstrate the GO and TRACE commands. Previously we created that program by entering the machine code directly into memory. This time we used DEBUG's mini-assembler to create the same program with assembly language mnemonics.

Naming a File with DEBUG

The NAME command (enter n or N) is used to specify the name of a file to DEBUG. The named file can be loaded into memory with the LOAD command or saved on a disk with the WRITE command. (LOAD and WRITE are discussed later in this chapter.)

To name a file, type n followed by the desired file specification. DEBUG will store the length of the file specification at offset address 0080H in the program segment prefix. The file spec itself is then stored beginning at offset 0081H. The file specification is "parsed," and the product is entered by MS-DOS at offset address 005CH in the psp.

In the following example, the NAME command is used to specify a file as "mytest1.pro". Then the DUMP command is used to see how this information is stored in memory:

```
-n mytest1.pro
-d 0050 L40
0958:0050  CD 21 CB 00 00 00 00 00-00 00 00 00 00 4D 59 54   M!K.........MYT
0958:0060  45 53 54 31 20 50 52 4F-00 00 00 00 00 20 20 20   EST1 PRO.....
0958:0070  20 20 20 20 20 20 20 20-00 00 00 00 00 00 00 00            ........
0958:0080  0B 4D 59 54 45 53 54 31-2E 50 52 4F 0D 00 00 00   .MYTEST1.PRO....
-
```

This dump begins at offset 50H in the psp. The length of the filename specified by the NAME command is stored at offset address 0080H. The file specification begins at offset 0081H. The parsed form of the file specification is stored beginning at offset 005CH. The 00H at offset 005CH indicates that any subsequent read or write of this file will be done at the default drive.

The NAME command is also used to pass filename parameters. As an example, let's say that the program "mytest1.pro" performs some operation on two data files that we will call "file1.dat" and "file2.dat". The names of these data files must somehow be passed to "mytest1.pro". If we were starting "mytest1.pro" in MS-DOS, we could pass the parameter information by entering the filenames in the start command:

```
C>mytest1.pro file1.dat file2.dat
```

If we are executing "mytest1.pro" under DEBUG, the parameters are passed using the NAME command. One or two parameters can be passed with the command. Parameters must be separated by a space or a comma:

```
-n file1.dat file2.dat
-d 0050 L50
0958:0050  CD 21 CB 00 00 00 00 00-00 00 00 00 00 4D 59 54   M!K..........FIL
0958:0060  45 31 20 20 20 44 41 54-00 00 00 00 00 46 49 4C   E1   DAT.....FIL
0958:0070  45 32 20 20 20 44 41 54-00 00 00 00 00 00 00 00   E2   DAT........
0958:0080  14 20 46 49 4C 45 31 2E-44 41 54 20 46 49 4C 45   . FILE1.DAT FILE
0958:0090  32 2E 44 41 54 0D 00 00-00 00 00 00 00 00 00 00   2.DAT..........
-
```

The information in the command is again stored starting at offset 0081H. The two parameters are parsed, and one is stored at offset 005CH and the other at 006CH. "Mytest1.pro" will look at these two addresses to find the names of the files on which it is to operate.

You will find more information on the NAME command in the following discussions of the DEBUG commands LOAD and WRITE.

Loading a File with DEBUG

The LOAD command (enter L or l) is used to load files into computer memory. The specification for the file to be loaded must be stored at offset 005CH in the program segment prefix. This is accomplished either by including the specification in the DEBUG start command or by using the NAME command.

Once the appropriate information is stored at offset 005CH, the file can be loaded by entering "L". You may enter the memory address at which loading is to begin. If you enter only an offset address, the command assumes that the segment address is stored in the CS register. If you do not enter an address, the file will be loaded at address CS:0100. Files with the extension ".COM" and ".EXE" are always loaded at CS:0100. Any address that is specified when these files are loaded is ignored.

After a file is loaded, DEBUG sets the BX and CX registers to the number of bytes loaded into memory. For ".EXE" and ".HEX" files, this number will be smaller than the size of the file. The following example loads the file "dbugpro.txt" into memory at the default address of CS: 0100:

```
C>debug
-n dbugpro.txt
-L
-r
AX=0000  BX=0000  CX=00CF  DX=0000  SP=FFEE  BP=0000  SI=0000  DI=0000
DS=0958  ES=0958  SS=0958  CS=0958  IP=0100   NV UP DI PL NZ NA PO NC
0958:0100 2A2A        SUB    CH,[BP+SI]                        SS:0000=CD
-
```

The BX and CX registers show that 207 (000000CFH) bytes have been read into memory. We could have achieved these same results by including the file specification in the DEBUG start command ("debug dbugpro.txt"). The only difference is that when the file is loaded with the LOAD command, the memory location of the load may be specified.

It is important to recognize that the LOAD command loads the file specified at offset 005CH and that this information changes each time the NAME command is used. For this reason, it is advisable to use the NAME command immediately before loading a file with the LOAD command.

LOAD can also be used to load consecutive sectors of a disk into memory. (Sectors are discussed in chapter 11.) To specify the address at which the load is to take place, use the same procedure as you did in loading a file. Then enter the number designation of the disk to be read (0=default, 1=A, 2=B, 3=C, etc.). Enter the relative number of the first sector loaded into memory and the number of sectors to be loaded. A maximum of 80H sectors can be loaded:

```
-L 0500 0 00 02
-
```

This command loads consecutive sectors of data into memory, beginning at memory address CS:0500. The sectors are loaded from the default drive. The first sector loaded is relative sector 00 (the first sector on the disk). Two (02) consecutive sectors are loaded.

Storing Data with DEBUG

The WRITE command (enter **w** or **W**) is used to store data on a disk. A valid file specification must be located at offset address 005CH into the program segment prefix before WRITE can be used. To accomplish this, either include the file specification in the DEBUG start command or use the NAME command.

Before a file can be stored, the size of the file must be specified in the

BX and CX registers (a 4-byte hexadecimal number). It is good practice to check the values of the BX and CX registers (use the REGISTER command) before storing a file with the WRITE command.

You can specify the starting address in memory of the data to be written. If you specify only an offset address, DEBUG assumes that the segment address is stored in the CS register. If you do not specify an address, writing commences with the data at address CS:0100.

When a file is written, it is given the name specified at offset 005CH in the psp. If the disk already contains a file with that name, the existing file is overwritten. In order to avoid overwriting the wrong file, it is good practice to use the NAME command immediately before storing a file with the WRITE command. Files with the extension ".EXE" or ".HEX" cannot be written to disk using the WRITE command.

In the next example, the BX and CX registers are set to a value of 256 (00000100H). The NAME command is then used to set the file specification at offset address 005CH. The WRITE command writes to disk the 256 bytes starting at address CS:0100. The file is given the name "dbugtxt.pro". DEBUG then displays a message telling how many bytes have been stored:

```
-r BX
BX 0000
:0000
-r CX
CX 0000
:0100
-n dbugtxt.pro
-w
Writing 0100 bytes
-
```

You can use the WRITE command to write data to specific disk sectors. To specify the starting address of the data to be written, use the same procedure as you did earlier in writing a file. Then specify the number designation of the drive to be written to (0=A, 1=B, 2=C). Next, enter the relative disk sector at which writing is to begin. Finally, enter the number of consecutive sectors that will be written. A maximum of 80H sectors can be written.

In the following example, the data starting at address CS:0700 are written to the disk in drive B (1). The write begins at relative sector 50H (absolute sector 51H) and fills 20H consecutive sectors on the disk:

```
-w 0700 1 50 20
-
```

Writing to absolute sectors can be extremely powerful in modifying disk contents. It can also be extremely destructive if not used with caution. Double-check that all parameters are correct before you perform a sector write. Carelessness here can be very painful.

Comparing Blocks of Memory

The COMPARE command (enter **c** or **C**) is used to compare the contents of two blocks of memory. If unequal bytes are found, their addresses and the values at those addresses are displayed.

The command begins with the starting address of the first block of memory. If you enter only an offset address, DEBUG assumes that the segment address is stored in the DS register. To set the size of the blocks to be compared, enter the letter "L" followed by the number of bytes in each block. Then enter the starting address of the second block of memory. Again, entering only an offset address causes DEBUG to assume that the segment address is in the DS register.

In the next example, two 16-byte blocks of memory are compared. The first block begins at address CS:0000. The second block begins at CS:0030. The DUMP command is used two times to display each block. The COMPARE command is then used to display the addresses at which the blocks have unequal values:

```
-d CS:0000 L10
0958:0000  CD 20 00 20 00 9A EE FE-1D F0 34 02 68 06 62 02   M . ..N .p4.h.b.
-d CS:0030 L10
0958:0030  68 06 00 00 00 00 00 00-00 00 00 00 00 00 00 00   h...............
-c CS:0000 L10 CS:0030
0958:0000  CD  68  0958:0030
0958:0001  20  06  0958:0031
0958:0003  20  00  0958:0033
0958:0005  9A  00  0958:0035
0958:0006  EE  00  0958:0036
0958:0007  FE  00  0958:0037
0958:0008  1D  00  0958:0038
0958:0009  F0  00  0958:0039
0958:000A  34  00  0958:003A
0958:000B  02  00  0958:003B
0958:000C  68  00  0958:003C
0958:000D  06  00  0958:003D
0958:000E  62  00  0958:003E
0958:000F  02  00  0958:003F
```

The size of the blocks to be compared can also be set by including an ending offset address of the first block in the command. This offset will determine the ending address of the second block, since the blocks must be equal in size. Using this method, the preceding COMPARE command could be written as "c CS:0000 000F 0030". If no differences are found, the DEBUG prompt is displayed and another command can be entered.

Searching Memory

The SEARCH command (enter **s** or **S**) is used to search a block of memory for a list of byte values. The address at which the search is to start is included in the command. If you specify only an offset address as the start, DEBUG assumes that the segment address is stored in the DS register.

The address at which the search is to end is set in one of two ways. You can include in the command the ending address, which must be an offset address. Or you can specify the number of bytes to be searched by including in the command the letter "L", followed by the number of bytes to be searched.

Your command must include a list of byte values to be searched. The list may contain hexadecimal numbers and/or string characters. You must separate hexadecimal numbers by a space or a comma. String characters must be enclosed in quotation marks. Any string characters in the list will result in a search for the hexadecimal ASCII values of those characters.

Each time a match to the list is found, the address of the first byte of the match is displayed. If no matches are found, the DEBUG prompt is displayed and another command may be entered:

```
-s CS:0000 015F 44 4F 53 20 33 2E 33
0958:0004

-
```

This command searches the block of memory beginning at CS:0000 and ending at CS:015F for a match to the list of seven hexadecimal numbers included in the command. A match has been found starting at address CS:0004. The same command could have been entered as: **s CS:0000 L160 'DOS 3.3'**.

Moving Data in Memory

The MOVE command (enter **m** or **M**) moves a block of data from one memory location to another. The move overwrites any previously existing data at the destination. The command is executed in such a way that no data are lost if there is some overlap between the source and the destination. The source data are unaltered by the command unless it is overwritten.

The MOVE command must contain the starting address of the source data. If you enter only an offset address for the starting address, DEBUG assumes that the segment address is stored in the DS register.

The end address of the source data can be set in two ways. You can state in the command the end address, which must be an offset address. Or you can specify the length of the block to be moved by including in the command the letter "L", followed by a hexadecimal number.

In the following example, a dump displays a block of memory. The MOVE command is then used to move that block to another location. Another dump shows that the move was successful:

```
-d DS:0500 L20
0958:0500  CD 20 CB 00 00 00 00 00-00 00 00 00 00 00 00 00   M!K.............
```

```
0958:0510  4C 53 20 20 20 41 53 53-00 00 00 00 00 20 20 20  LS  ASS.....
-m DS:0500 051F DS:2000
-d DS:2000 L20
0958:2000  CD 20 CB 00 00 00 00 00-00 00 00 00 00 00 00 00  M!K.............
0958:2010  4C 53 20 20 20 41 53 53-00 00 00 00 00 20 20 20  LS  ASS.....
-
```

The MOVE command told DEBUG to take the block of data that starts at address DS:0500 and extends to DS:051F and move it to fill the block of memory that begins at address DS:2000. The move is actually a copy, since the original data was not altered. The same command could have been written as: m 0050 L20 2000.

Filling Memory

The FILL command (enter f or F) is used to fill a block of memory with a list of values. The command must include the starting address of the fill. If you do not state a segment address, this value is assumed to be stored in the DS register.

The address at which the fill is to end can be set in two ways. You can include in the command the end address, which must be an offset address. Or you can set the length of the block to be filled by entering in the command the letter "L", followed by a hexadecimal number.

The FILL command includes a list that will fill the memory block. The list can consist of hexadecimal numbers and/or string characters. You must separate hexadecimal numbers by a space or a comma. String characters must be enclosed in quotation marks. Hexadecimal ASCII values of string characters are stored in memory.

If the list is shorter than the block of memory to be filled, the list is repeated until the block is filled. If the list is longer than the block of memory, the list is copied until the block is filled, and the remaining characters in the list are ignored.

In this example, a portion of memory is filled with a list of values. A dump then displays that portion of memory:

```
-f DS:0100 017F 21 23 24 25
-d DS:0100 L80
0958:0100  21 23 24 25 21 23 24 25-21 23 24 25 21 23 24 25  !#$%!#$%!#$%!#$%
0958:0110  21 23 24 25 21 23 24 25-21 23 24 25 21 23 24 25  !#$%!#$%!#$%!#$%
0958:0120  21 23 24 25 21 23 24 25-21 23 24 25 21 23 24 25  !#$%!#$%!#$%!#$%
0958:0130  21 23 24 25 21 23 24 25-21 23 24 25 21 23 24 25  !#$%!#$%!#$%!#$%
0958:0140  21 23 24 25 21 23 24 25-21 23 24 25 21 23 24 25  !#$%!#$%!#$%!#$%
0958:0150  21 23 24 25 21 23 24 25-21 23 24 25 21 23 24 25  !#$%!#$%!#$%!#$%
0958:0160  21 23 24 25 21 23 24 25-21 23 24 25 21 23 24 25  !#$%!#$%!#$%!#$%
0958:0170  21 23 24 25 21 23 24 25-21 23 24 25 21 23 24 25  !#$%!#$%!#$%!#$%
```

The FILL command fills the block of memory starting at DS:0100 and ending at DS:017F with the hexadecimal numbers 21H, 23H, 24H, and 25H. The same command could have been written as

```
f 0100 L80 '!#$%'
```

Sending Data to a Port

The microprocessor inside your computer communicates with the outside world through the use of ports. The keyboard is connected to one port, the display screen to another, the printer to another, and so on. Each port is identified by its address, just as memory locations are identified by their addresses. Port addresses are very specific for each computer. Refer to the information supplied by your computer's manufacturer for port addresses.

The microprocessor reads data from a peripheral device (such as the keyboard) by reading the data sent in from the device's port. Similarly, the microprocessor sends data to a peripheral device (such as the printer) by sending out data from the device's port.

The OUTPUT command (enter o or O) is DEBUG's way of sending a byte value to an output port. The command must include the address of the output port and the byte value to be sent. The two parameters must be separated by a space or a comma. In the following example, the byte value 3CH is sent to output port 62H:

```
-o 62 3C
-
```

Reading Data from a Port

The INPUT command (enter i or I) is used to obtain and display 1 byte of input from a specified port. The command includes the address of the port. DEBUG then reads 1 byte from that port and displays its value on the screen. In the next example, 1 byte is read from port 62H. The value at that port (03H) is then displayed:

```
-i 62
03
-
```

Hexadecimal Arithmetic with DEBUG

The HEXADECIMAL Arithmetic command (enter h or H) is used to perform hexadecimal addition and subtraction on two numbers. The numbers can be one to four hexadecimal digits in length and must be separated in the command by a space or a comma. DEBUG adds the numbers and displays the result. DEBUG also subtracts the second number from the first and displays the result.

In the following example, 05CDH is added to 320FH, yielding a sum of 37DCH. Then 05CDH is subtracted from 320FH, yielding a difference of 2C42H:

```
-h 320F 05CD
37DC  2C42
-
```

If the second number entered is larger than the first, the difference is displayed in two's complement representation. (Refer to a text on assembly language programming for a discussion of two's complement representation.)

10

LINK

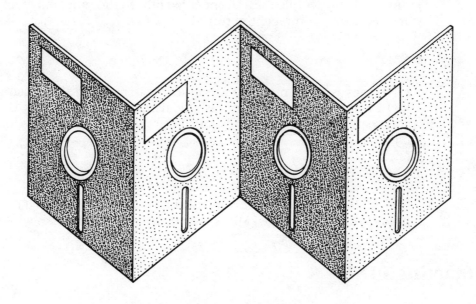

Overview of LINK
Starting LINK
LINK Switches

This chapter describes the use of the MS-DOS utility program called LINK. LINK is used in compiling or assembling computer programs. LINK is not supplied with all implementations of DOS. However, LINK is generally provided with the assemblers and compilers whose use requires LINK. The material in this chapter is applicable to all versions of LINK.

Overview of LINK

Compilers and assemblers produce *object code,* a code that can be executed by a computer without undergoing further simplification. LINK is an MS-DOS utility program used to modify a collection or module of object code so that the module is relocatable. A *relocatable module* is a computer program or a computer program subroutine that will execute successfully regardless of where it is stored in computer memory.

LINK is also used to combine separately produced object modules into a single relocatable module. LINK produces a single relocatable module, called a *run file,* by combining and modifying user-specified object modules. LINK searches for the specified object modules on the specified or default disk drive. A message is displayed, directing the user to change diskettes and press Enter if LINK cannot locate a module. At the user's option, LINK will produce a list file containing information about the code in the run file. LINK will also search specified libraries for any object modules that are needed to complete the run file.

VM.TMP

LINK uses as much memory as is available in creating a relocatable module. LINK will create a temporary disk file named VM.TMP on the default drive and display the following message if the system does not have enough free memory:

```
VM.TMP has been created
```

LINK will erase any existing file named VM.TMP when it creates a temporary storage file. VM.TMP is erased when LINK ends.

Starting LINK

There are three methods for starting LINK. In each case, one of the system drives must contain the MS-DOS file LINK.EXE. In the following examples, LINK.EXE is on the default drive.

Starting LINK involves entering one or more filenames in response to LINK's prompts. You have the option of preceding each filename with a drive designator and/or a path specifier.

Method 1

In the first method, LINK is started by typing **link** and pressing Enter. Begin the command with the letter designator of the drive containing LINK.EXE if LINK.EXE is not on the default drive:

```
C> link
```

MS-DOS will load LINK and display a copyright message followed by the prompt:

```
Object Modules [ .OBJ]:
```

This is a prompt to enter the object module(s) that LINK will use to produce the run file (the relocatable module). Individual modules must be separated by a space or a plus (+) sign. LINK assumes that each object module has an extension of ".OBJ". Any other extension must be specified.

To illustrate, let's suppose that you have used a compiler or an assembler to create the object modules "example1.obj" and "example2.obj". To combine them into a single relocatable module, you would enter their filenames in response to the initial LINK prompt:

```
Object Modules [ .OBJ]: example1+example2
```

Since no extensions are specified, LINK assumes that the modules have an extension of ".OBJ".

LINK next prompts you to enter the name to be given to the run file:

```
Run File [EXAMPLE1.EXE]:
```

If you do not enter a filename, LINK will default to the filename of the first object module listed in the previous command. A run file must have an extension of ".EXE". Any other extension will be ignored.

When you press Enter, LINK will display the following prompt:

```
List File [NUL.MAP]:
```

Enter a filename if you want LINK to create a *list file*. The list file contains the name and size of the segments within the relocatable module. The list file will also contain any errors that are detected by LINK. (Later in the chapter, we will discuss list files again and present an example.) LINK gives the list file an extension of ".MAP" if an extension is not specified. Press Enter if you do not want a list file created.

LINK's final prompt asks you for the names of any library files to be searched for unresolved references:

```
Libraries [.LIB]:
```

Some compilers contain a default library that LINK will search if you press Enter. LINK will look for the compiler library on the default drive. If the library is not on the default drive, LINK will look for it on the drive specified by the compiler.

You may specify up to eight library files to be searched. LINK assumes an extension of ".LIB" if an extension is not specified. Individual filenames must be separated by a space or a plus sign (+). If your response to the prompt includes a drive designator, LINK will look for the listed library file(s) on the specified drive. LINK will search the drive specified by the compiler (or the default drive) if no drive designator is included.

```
Libraries [.LIB]: c:mylib+yourlib+a:hislib+c:
```

The preceding response directs LINK to search the files "mylib.lib" and "yourlib.lib" on the C drive, "hislib.lib" on the A drive, and the default library (if one exists) on the C drive.

LINK will search the library files in the order that they are listed. If there is a default library, it will be searched last. When LINK finds the module that contains the symbol it is looking for, that module is processed in the normal fashion. LINK displays a message telling you to enter a new drive designator letter when it cannot find a specified library file.

You can use a comma to end a response to a LINK prompt. When you use a comma, you can type your response to the next prompt without waiting for the prompt to be displayed:

```
Object Modules [.OBJ]: example1,
List File [NUL.MAP]: example1
Libraries [.LIB]:
```

The first command tells LINK the name of the object module. The comma following the object module tells LINK that the response to the next prompt (run file) is also entered on the first line. In this case, no name is entered for the run file, so LINK assigns the default filename to the run file. Notice that the prompt for the run file is not displayed. The last two commands tell LINK to create a list file named "example1.map" and to search the default library file.

The first two commands in the previous example could have been combined as follows:

```
Object Modules [.OBJ]: example1,,example1
Libraries [.LIB]:
```

In this example, the first command ends with two commas, followed by the name that LINK will assign to the list file. Notice that the prompt for the list file is not displayed.

If you end any of the responses to a LINK prompt with a semicolon, the remaining responses will be assigned their defaults. No further prompts will be displayed:

```
Object Modules [.OBJ]: example1;
```

This command tells LINK that "example1" is the object module. Since the command ends in a semicolon, the remaining prompts are not displayed and are assigned their defaults.

Method 2

In the second method for starting LINK, the responses to the LINK prompts can be included in the LINK start command. The responses must be listed in the order in which LINK displays the prompts (Object Modules, Run File, List File, Libraries). You must separate the responses with a comma.

LINK will prompt for any responses that were not included in the start command:

```
C>link example1,,example1

Microsoft Object Linker V2.00
(C) Copyright 1982 by Microsoft Inc.

Libraries [.LIB]:
```

The start command tells MS-DOS to load LINK. The start command also tells LINK to search for the module "example1.obj," assign the run file its default filename, and create a list file named "example1.map". Notice that the prompts for these responses are not displayed.

If you include responses to LINK prompts in the start command and if you end the command with a semicolon, any subsequent prompts will not be displayed and they will be assigned their defaults:

```
C>link example1;

Microsoft Object Linker V2.00
(C) Copyright 1982 by Microsoft Inc.
```

This start command loads LINK and tells LINK to search for "example1.obj". The three remaining prompts are not displayed and are assigned their defaults.

Method 3

The third method for starting LINK requires that a set of LINK responses be stored in a text file. These responses must be stored in the order that the LINK prompts are displayed. LINK can then be started by including the name of the text file in the LINK start command. This method is convenient when you are entering a long list of object modules. A long response to the object module or library prompt may be stored on several lines by using a plus sign (+) to continue a response onto the next line.

A text file containing a sequence of responses can be created from your keyboard. Starting at the MS-DOS command level (the DOS prompt is displayed), type **copy con:** and then type the filename of the text file that you will be creating. The filename may be preceded by a drive designator letter and/or a pathname.

In the following example, a text file named "sample1.txt" is created.

```
C>copy con: sample1.txt                    ←Enter
example1+example2+example3,,;              ←Enter
^Z                                         ←you press Ctrl-Z and Enter
        1 File(s) copied
```

To start LINK with a text file, type **link**, followed by a blank space and the symbol @, followed by the filename and extension of the text file. LINK will assume that the first character in the filename is a blank if you include a space between the "@" and the filename of the text file:

```
C>link @sample1.txt

Microsoft Object Linker V2.00
(C) Copyright 1982 by Microsoft Inc.

Object Modules [.OBJ]: example1+example2+example3
Run File [EXAMPLE1.EXE]:
List File [EXAMPLE1.MAP]:
```

The responses to the prompts have been extracted from the file "sample1.txt". LINK automatically searches for the object modules "example1", "example2", and "example3". LINK then assigns the default filename to the run file and creates a list file named "example1.map". The library prompt is not displayed because of the semicolon at the end of the response line. LINK assigns the default response to the library prompt.

LINK Switches

LINK provides seven optional switches that you can specify when starting LINK. Each switch directs LINK to perform certain tasks when constructing a relocatable module. To specify a switch, type a forward slash (/) followed by the first letter of the switch name at the end of a response line. You may include a switch when using any of the three methods for starting LINK. Switches may be specified on any response line. Each letter specifying a switch must be preceded by a forward slash.

The /High Switch

Within each relocatable module, LINK stores information that tells MS-DOS where to load the module in computer memory. Normally, this information instructs MS-DOS to load the module at the lowest-available address in memory. The **/high switch** tells LINK to construct a module that MS-DOS will load at the highest-available memory address.

The next command directs LINK to combine the object modules "example1" and "example2" into a relocatable module. LINK will produce a run file named "example1.exe" (the default) and a list file named "example.map". The default library file will be searched. The LINK switch /high (entered as /h) directs LINK to produce a run file that MS-DOS will load at as high a memory location as possible. Enter the following command:

```
C>link example1+example2,,example1;/h
```

The /high switch should not be used when linking Pascal or FORTRAN object modules.

The /Dsallocate Switch

The /dsallocate switch (entered as /d) directs LINK to create a run file that loads all data at the high end of the data segment. If this switch is not used, LINK will create a run file that loads data at the low end of the data segment. The /dsallocate switch is required when linking Pascal or FORTRAN object modules.

The /Linenumber Switch

LINK will generate a list file when it is instructed to do so. The list file contains a list of the segments in the run file as well as each segment's relative start and stop addresses. A *segment* is a contiguous portion of the run file, which may be up to 64K bytes in length. Segments are generally used to partition a run file into functional components. Each segment within an object module is assigned to a class by the programmer. LINK combines the segments of the specified object modules according to each segment's class.

A segment's *relative start address* is the location of the first byte in a segment relative to the first byte in the run file. For example, if the first byte of a segment is the first byte of the run file, the segment's relative start address is 0. A segment's *relative stop address* is the location of the last byte in a segment relative to the first byte in the run file. For example, if the last byte of a segment is the 100th byte of the run file, the segment's relative stop address is 99 (99 bytes from the first byte in the run file).

The **/linenumber switch** (entered as /l) tells LINK to include in the list file the line numbers and relative addresses of the *source statements* in each object module. Source statements are the statements in a computer program in the form that they are entered by the programmer. The /linenumber switch only works with object modules produced by a compiler that numbers each source statement (such as the BASIC compiler).

The /Map Switch

Symbols (such as variable names) that are shared by two or more object modules are called *public symbols.* Symbols are designated as being "public" by the compiler or assembler used to create the modules. The /**map switch** (entered as /**m**) directs LINK to include in the list file all public symbols that are defined in the specified object modules.

The next set of commands directs LINK to create a list file named "example.map". The MS-DOS command TYPE is then used to display "example.map". Enter the following:

```
C>link example1,,example1/m

Microsoft Object Linker V2.00
(C) Copyright 1982 by Microsoft Inc.

Libraries [.LIB]:


C>type example.map


Start    Stop     Length   Name        Class
00000H   000C7H   00C8H    STACKSG     STACK
000D0H   000D5H   0006H    DATASG      DATA
000E0H   000F2H   0013H    CODESG      CODE

Origin     Group


Address              Publics by Name

000D:0004            AAA
000D:0002            PRICE
000D:0000            QTY


Address              Publics by Value

000D:0000            QTY
000D:0002            PRICE
000D:0004            AAA


Program entry point at 000E:0000
```

The first portion of the list file contains the name, class, length, and start and stop addresses of each segment in the run file.

The second section in the list file is headed "Origin Group". A *group* consists of one or more segments contained in the specified object modules that are to be combined into a single segment in the run file. Groups are defined by the programmer during program assembly or compiling. Any groups defined by the compiler or assembler are listed here, along with their relative starting addresses (origin) within the relocatable module. The module in this example does not contain any groups.

The third section of the list file is an alphabetical listing of the public symbols contained in the object modules. The relative addresses of each symbol within the relocatable module are also listed.

The fourth section of the list file is a listing of the public symbols contained in the object modules ordered by their relative addesses within the module.

The final line in the list file gives the relative address of the run file's *entry point*. The entry point is the location of the first executable computer instruction contained in the run file.

The /Pause Switch

The **/pause switch** (entered as **/p**) is used to suspend LINK execution before the run file is written to disk. This allows you to swap disks. To demonstrate the use of the /pause switch, enter the following:

```
C>link example1,,example1/p

Microsoft Object Linker V2.00
(C) Copyright 1982 by Microsoft Inc.

Libraries [.LIB]:
About to generate .EXE file
Change disks      ←press Enter when ready
```

It is important not to remove a disk if the VM.TMP file or the list file is to be stored on it.

The /Stack:[*Number*] Switch

The *stack* is a segment within the run file that is used to store data during program execution. Compilers and assemblers provide information in the object modules that allows LINK to compute the required size of the stack. The **/stack:[***number***] switch** can be used to override the stack size that is indicated in the object modules.

Any hexadecimal number from 0001H to FFFFH may be specified for the size of the stack in bytes. LINK will create a stack with 0200H bytes if you specify a number less than 0200H (decimal 512). Enter the following command to create a run file with a stack that contains 0300H bytes:

```
C>link example1,,example1/s:300
```

The /No Switch

The **/no switch** (entered as **/n**) directs LINK not to search the default library file for unresolved external references. For example, if you are linking modules that were created with a Pascal compiler, you could enter "/n" at the end of a response to a LINK prompt and LINK would not search "pascal.lib" for any unresolved external references.

Disk Structure
and Management

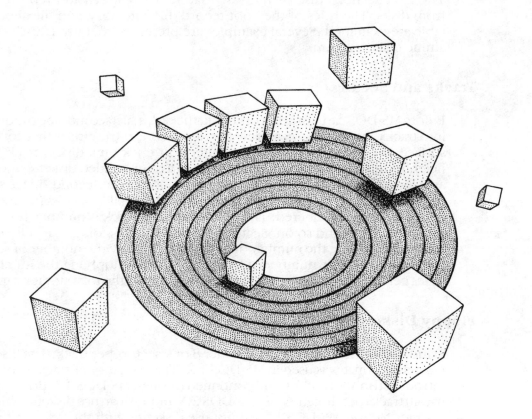

Structure of MS-DOS Disks

Formatting

Examining the File Directory
and the FAT

Exploring with DEBUG

MS-DOS File Management

In this chapter we will look at the internal structure of disks used by MS-DOS. We will also discuss how the operating system keeps track of files on a disk as well as how the contents of a file are accessed. Throughout this chapter, the word "disk" refers to both fixed disks and floppy diskettes unless specified otherwise.

This chapter does not contain any material needed for the routine use of MS-DOS. The material presented is intended for those readers who want a more thorough understanding of the operating system. Some familiarity with hexadecimal arithmetic and assembly language programming will be helpful but is not essential.

Structure of MS-DOS Disks

The next sections discuss the way that MS-DOS stores and retrieves data from disks. The roles of the boot record, file directory, and file allocation table are examined. Several examples are presented that use DEBUG to examine disk structure.

Tracks and Sectors

Before MS-DOS can store data on a disk, the disk's surface must be subdivided into tracks and sectors. *Tracks* are a series of concentric circles that cover the surface of a disk (figure 11-1). The outermost track on a disk is track 0, the neighboring track is track 1, and so on. On a double-sided diskette, the sides are also assigned numbers. The first side is side 0; the second side is side 1.

Each track is divided into a series of wedges called *sectors* (figure 11-2). Sectors are also numbered. The first sector on a track is number 1; the second, number 2; and so on. Sectors typically have a storage capacity of 512 bytes. Multiplying the number of bytes per sector by the number of sectors per track yields the number of bytes per track. Multiplying the number of bytes per track by the total number of tracks yields the total storage capacity.

Floppy Diskettes

Standard 5¼-inch diskettes have either 8 or 9 sectors per track. The 8-sector-per-track format was used in MS-DOS 1.X. The 9-sector-per-track format was introduced in MS-DOS 2.0 and continued through MS-DOS 3.3. Both formats use 40 tracks per diskette side. MS-DOS 2.X and 3.X can use diskettes with the 8-sector format. MS-DOS 1.X cannot use diskettes with the 9-sector format.

Quad-density 5¼-inch diskettes have 15 sectors per track and 80 tracks per side. Quad-density diskettes require quad-density drives and are supported by MS-DOS 3.X only.

In addition to the standard and high-density 5¼-inch diskettes, MS-DOS 3 also supports 3½-inch diskettes with 80 tracks per side and either 9

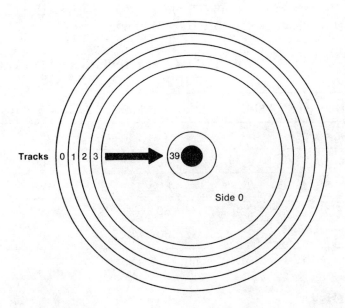

Figure 11-1. Each disk surface is divided into a series of concentric circles called *tracks*.

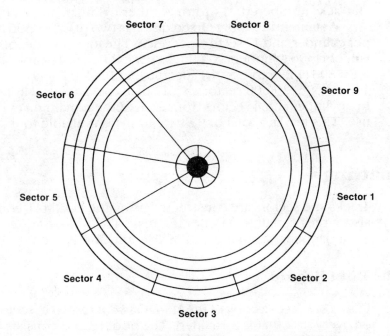

Figure 11-2. Each track is divided into *sectors* (8 sectors per track for MS-DOS 1.X, 9 for MS-DOS 2.X and 3.X).

or 18 sectors per track. Table 11-1 summarizes the characteristics of the floppy diskettes supported by MS-DOS.

**Table 11-1. Characteristics of Diskettes
Supported by MS-DOS**

Diameter	Sides	Tracks per Side	Sectors per Track	Capacity
5¼″	1	40	8/9	160K/180K
5¼″	2	40	8/9	320K/360K
5¼″	2	80	15	1.2M*
3½″	2	80	9	720K*
3½″	2	80	18	1.44M*

*Supported by MS-DOS 3 only.

Fixed Disks

Fixed disks consist of one or more *platters*. Each platter has two surfaces on which data are stored. MS-DOS divides the surface of each platter into tracks, and the tracks are subdivided into sectors. All tracks that have the same radius form a *cylinder*. Thus, all tracks numbered "0" form a cylinder, all tracks numbered "1" form another cylinder, and so on.

A standard 10-Mbyte fixed disk has two platters, 306 cylinders, 4 tracks per cylinder, and 17 sectors per track. The total number of tracks on the disk is 1,224 (306 cylinders × 4 tracks per cylinder). The total number of sectors is 20,808 (1,224 tracks × 17 sectors per track). The total number of bytes is 10,653,696 (20,808 sectors × 512 bytes per sector). MS-DOS reserves 1 entire cylinder and 4 sectors from each of the remaining cylinders for its own use. This leaves a total of 9,994,240 bytes available for storage.

Formatting

Tracks and sectors are constructed using the FORMAT command. FORMAT also writes certain data onto the disk. The following sections will discuss what happens when the FORMAT command is used.

The Boot Record

FORMAT places a copy of the MS-DOS *boot record* in sector 1, track 0, side 0 on every disk that is formatted. The boot record consists of (1) a table containing information about the disk and (2) machine language code that loads IO.SYS and MSDOS.SYS (discussed under "System Files") into memory. The first 4 bytes in the boot record contain a machine language instruction telling the computer to jump to a certain offset in the boot record to find loading code. The table containing the disk-specific information is stored between the jump instruction and the loading code.

File Allocation Table and File Directory

FORMAT also constructs the *file allocation table* (FAT) and the *file directory*. As we will see shortly, both of these structures are intimately involved in accessing files stored on the disk. MS-DOS maintains two copies of the FAT on each disk, ostensibly because the FAT is so important that a second copy is available should the first be damaged. However, MS-DOS never uses the second copy of the FAT.

Standard 8-sector-per-track diskettes have a 1-sector FAT. Standard 9-sector-per-track diskettes have a 2-sector FAT. Quad-density diskettes have a 7-sector FAT. Ten-megabyte fixed drives have an 8-sector FAT.

Standard single-sided diskettes have a 4-sector file directory. Standard double-sided diskettes have a 7-sector file directory. Double-sided quad-density diskettes have a 14-sector file directory. Ten-megabyte fixed drives have a 32-sector file directory.

Table 11-2 lists the physical locations of the boot records, FATs, and file directories of standard 5¼-inch diskettes. Figure 11-3 illustrates the arrangement of these structures on a standard 5¼-inch, 9-sector-per-track, single-sided diskette.

Table 11-2. Location of Boot Record, FAT, and File Directory on Standard 5¼″ Diskettes

	8 Sectors/Track Diskettes		9 Sectors/Track Diskettes	
	Single-Sided Diskette	*Double-Sided Diskette*	*Single-Sided Diskette*	*Double-Sided Diskette*
Boot Record	Sector 1 Track 0	Sector 1 Track 0 Side 0	Sector 1 Track 0	Sector 1 Track 0 Side 0
FAT, 1st copy	Sector 2 Track 0	Sector 2 Track 0 Side 0	Sectors 2–3 Track 0	Sectors 2–3 Track 0 Side 0
FAT, 2nd copy	Sector 3 Track 0	Sector 3 Track 0 Side 0	Sectors 4–5 Track 0	Sectors 4–5 Track 0 Side 0
File Directory	Sectors 4–7 Track 0	Sectors 4–7 Track 0 Side 0	Sectors 6–9 Track 0	Sectors 6–9 Track 0 Side 0
	Sectors 1–3 Track 0	Sectors 1–3 Track 0 Side 1		Sectors 1–3 Track 0 Side 1

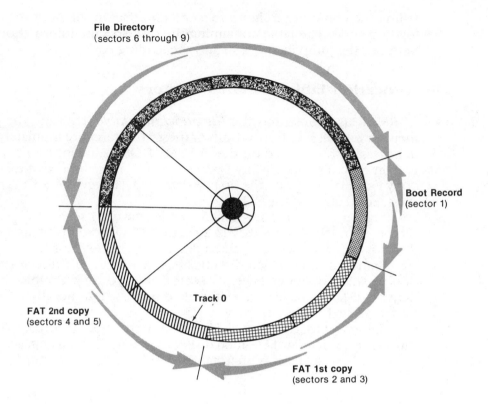

File Directory
(sectors 6 through 9)

Boot Record
(sector 1)

Track 0

FAT 2nd copy
(sectors 4 and 5)

FAT 1st copy
(sectors 2 and 3)

Figure 11-3. Layout for track 0 of boot record, FAT, and file directory on standard 5¼-inch, single-sided, 9-sector/track diskette.

System Files

The /s switch directs FORMAT to place a copy of the *system files* on the disk being formatted. The three MS-DOS system files are IO.SYS, MSDOS.SYS, and COMMAND.COM. In PC-DOS, IO.SYS is called IBMBIO.COM and MSDOS.SYS is called IBMDOS.COM. The system files must be stored on any disk that will be used to boot the system. FORMAT places these files in a particular physical location on the disk in a particular order.

IO.SYS is stored on the disk immediately after the last sector of the file directory. IO.SYS consists of the operating system's default *device drivers*. A device driver is a computer program that serves as the interface between the operating system and a peripheral device (device drivers are discussed in chapter 14). Since IO.SYS interacts directly with the hardware, it is highly system-specific and is generally implemented by the computer's manufacturer.

MSDOS.SYS is stored on the disk immediately after the last sector of IO.SYS. MSDOS.SYS forms the kernel of MS-DOS. MSDOS.SYS receives all requests for service functions (such as opening and reading a file) and channels the requests to IO.SYS. The protocol for communication between

MSDOS.SYS and IO.SYS is identical from system to system. Therefore, MSDOS.SYS is said to be *hardware independent.*

COMMAND.COM is the MS-DOS *command interpreter.* The command interpreter serves as the interface between the operating system and the user. COMMAND.COM displays the system prompt, accepts commands from the keyboard and processes the commands so that they can be executed. COMMAND.COM consists of three components: a resident component, a transient component, and an initialization component. The role of the three components is discussed in chapter 12.

Interchangeability of System Files

Generally, any implementation of DOS that is designed to run on a specific computer brand will run on any compatible computer. For example, PC-DOS will run on any truly compatible machine, as will COMPAQ's version of MS-DOS, as will Cordata's version. The only area where the various implementations are significantly different is the IO.SYS file. Recall that IO.SYS is a hardware-specific file, implemented independently by each of the computer manufacturers. However, the hardware used by the different manufacturers is similar enough that IO.SYS is usually compatible across brand lines.

Due to this compatibility, users can generally switch from one implementation of DOS to another without tremendous difficulty. However, anyone planning a switch must bear in mind that the size of the system file (particularly IO.SYS) varies from one implementation to another. Problems may arise if the physical location used to store one implementation of the system files is not large enough to store another implementation of the system files. In addition, some programs with automatic installation procedures assume a specific size for the system files. The installation procedures may fail if these assumptions are not correct.

Examining the File Directory and the FAT

The first part of this section takes a detailed look at the structure and use of the file directory and file allocation table. The second part of this section contains a description of how to use DEBUG to load the contents of the file directory and FAT into memory so that they might be examined.

File Directory

The *file directory* serves as the table of contents for a disk. For every file on the disk, there is a corresponding entry in the disk's file directory. Figure 11-4 illustrates the structure of a file directory entry. Each entry is composed of 32 bytes. The 32 bytes are partitioned into eight fields, each field containing information used by MS-DOS in file management. Table 11-3 lists the fields in a file directory entry and describes the information stored in each field.

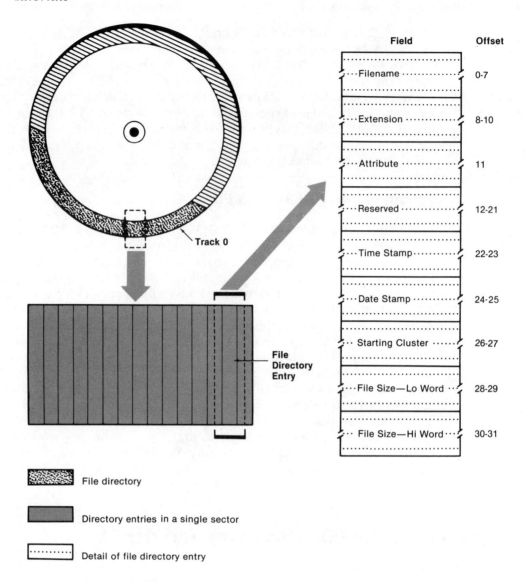

Figure 11-4. Structure of entry in file directory.

Table 11-3. Breakdown of Bytes in a File Directory Entry

Byte(s)	Purpose
0–7	**Filename.** The filename is padded with blank characters if it has fewer than 8 characters. The following values have special significance if they are the first byte in the filename field:
	00H The file directory entry has never been used. When MS-DOS sees 00H in this field, it skips over the entire entry. This can speed up performance.

Table 11-3. (cont'd)

Byte(s)	Purpose
	E5H The file that corresponds to this entry has been "erased." The file is not actually erased, however. The only change in this first byte is the filename field of the directory. Programs that recover "erased" files take advantage of this fact. On MS-DOS 1 disks, E5H may also indicate that the directory entry has not been used.
	2EH The file corresponding to this directory entry is another directory (or a subdirectory). If the second entry in this field is also 2EH, bytes 26–27 will contain the cluster of the directory's parent. The parent is the root directory if bytes 26 and 27 equal zero. (Clusters are discussed later in this chapter.)
8–10	***Filename extension.*** The field is padded with blank characters if the extension has fewer than three characters.
11	***File attribute.*** The file attribute is determined by the bit pattern of byte 11. The file has the attribute associated with a bit if that bit is set to equal 1. The file does not have the attribute if the bit equals 0.

Bit	File Attribute If Bit Set (Equals 1)
1	Hidden file. The file will not be listed when a DIR command is issued. (See the following box, "Modifying the Hidden File Attribute.")
2	System file. System files are used by MS-DOS during booting.
	The following bit settings are not valid for MS-DOS 1 disks:
0	Read only file. Any attempt to write to the file will generate an error message.
3	Volume label. Setting this bit tells MS-DOS that the characters in the filename and filename extension fields of this directory entry form the volume label for the disk. All other fields in this directory entry are irrelevant. This entry must be located in the root directory, and there can be only one such entry per disk.
4	Subdirectory. The directory entry corresponds to a subdirectory if this bit is set.
5	Archive. This bit is set if the file has been revised but not copied by the BACKUP command. Backing up a file clears the archive bit.

Byte(s)	Purpose
12–21	***Reserved.*** These bytes are reserved by MS-DOS. Look for them to be used in later versions of MS-DOS.

Table 11-3. (cont'd)

Byte(s)	Purpose
22–23	**Time stamp.** The time that the file was created or last modified. Byte 23 contains bits 8–15. Byte 22 contains bits 0–7. Bits 11–15 are the binary representation of the hour of the day (0–23). Bits 5–10 are the binary representation of the minutes (0–59). Bits 0–4 are the binary representation of the number of 2-second increments.
24–25	**Date stamp.** The date that the file was created or last modified. Byte 25 contains bits 8–15. Byte 24 contains bits 0–7. Bits 9–15 are the binary representation of the year less 1980 (1980 = 0). Bits 5–8 are the binary representation of the month (1–12). Bits 0–4 are the binary representation of the day of the month (0–31).
26–27	**Starting cluster.** The starting cluster tells MS-DOS where to look on the disk for the start of the file. Clusters are discussed in the following section of this chapter.
28–31	**File size.** The first word (bytes 28 and 29) contains the low-order portion of the file size. The second word (bytes 30–31) contains the high-order portion. Both words store the least-significant byte first.

Later in this chapter we will use DEBUG to see what an actual file directory looks like.

Modifying the Hidden File Attribute

The MS-DOS command ATTRIB (see Part 3) allows you to modify a file's read-only and archive attributes. However, ATTRIB does not provide for modification of the hidden file attribute. In listing 11-1, which follows, DEBUG is used to write two assembly language programs. HIDE.COM will allow you to set the hidden file attribute. UNHIDE.COM will allow you to clear the hidden file attribute. Enter **hide** [*filename.ext*] to set the hidden file attribute. Enter **unhide** [*filename.ext*] to clear the attribute. Note that files with the system attribute set will remain hidden after clearing the hidden attribute. You will need to clear both the hidden and system attributes to unhide these files. To create the programs in listing 11-1, enter the commands printed in italic type.

Listing 11-1. HIDE.COM and UNHIDE.COM, Two Assembly Language Programs for Setting and Clearing the Hidden File Attribute (see table 11-3)

```
C>debug
-a
68D8:100 mov cx,[0080]                 ;length of command tail
68D8:104 xor ch,ch                     ;clear high byte
68D8:106 dec cx                        ;ignore space in command tail
68D8:107 mov si,0082                   ;point to 1st letter in filename
68D8:10A mov di,0159                   ;point to buffer
68D8:10D repnz movsb                   ;move command tail to buffer
68D8:10F mov byte ptr [di],00          ;append 00 to filename in buffer
68D8:112 mov dx,0159                   ;point to 1st letter in buffer
68D8:115 mov ax,4300                   ;get file attribute function
68D8:118 int 21                        ;call MS-DOS
68D8:11A jc 012c                       ;jump if error
68D8:11C or cx,0002                    ;set hidden file bit
68D8:120 mov ax,4301                   ;set file attribute function
68D8:123 int 21                        ;call MS-DOS
68D8:125 jc 012c                       ;jump if error
68D8:127 mov dx,0135                   ;point to success message
68D8:12A jmp 012f
68D8:12C mov dx,0143                   ;point to error message
68D8:12F mov ah,09                     ;display string function
68D8:131 int 21                        ;call MS-DOS
68D8:133 int 20                        ;program terminate
68D8:135          ←press Enter
-e 135 'File hidden' 0d 0a '$' 'Unable to hide file' 0d 0a '$'
-f 159 L40 00                          ;start of buffer
-n hide.com
-rcx
CX 0000
:60
-w 100
Writing 0060 bytes
-a 10a
68D8:10A mov di,0174
68D8:10D          ←press Enter
-a 112
68D8:112 mov dx,0174
68D8:115          ←press Enter
-a 11c
68D8:11C and cx,fffd                   ;change fffd to fff9 for system files
68D8:120          ←press Enter
-a 12c
68D8:12C mov dx,0150
4f68D8:12F        ←press Enter
-e 135 'Hidden attribute removed' 0d 0a '$'
-e 150 'Unable to remove hidden attribute' 0d 0a '$'
```

```
-f 174 L40 00
-n unhide.com
-rcx
CX 0060
:1b4
-w 100
Writing 01B4 bytes
-q

C>
```

File Allocation Table

While the file directory serves as a disk's table of contents, the *file allocation table* (FAT) serves as a roadmap around the disk. For each file on the disk, there is a series of entries in the FAT telling MS-DOS where the file's contents are physically located.

MS-DOS divides a file's contents into *clusters*. Table 11-4 lists the number of adjoining sectors that form a cluster on the most commonly used types of disks. The cluster size on a fixed disk depends on how the disk was partitioned.

Table 11-4. Sectors per Cluster for Various Disk Types

Disk Type	Sectors per Cluster
Standard Single-sided	1
Standard Double-sided	2
Quad-density	1
10-Mbyte fixed (1 partition)	8

Clusters are numbered according to their physical location on the disk. The first cluster starts with the sector immediately following the last sector of the file directory. The second cluster follows the first and so on.

On single-sided diskettes, cluster numbers increase going from one sector to the next along a track. When the final sector on a track is reached, the next cluster is the first sector on the following track (see figure 11-5).

On double-sided diskettes, clusters increase along a track on side 0, continue on the same track on side 1, and then continue on the following track on side 0 (see figure 11-6).

MS-DOS uses two techniques for reading the FAT's contents. The first, generally used on disks with storage capacity of less than 20 Mbytes, is the more complicated. The second, generally used on large-capacity storage devices, will be easy to understand after you've read an explanation of the first technique.

Figures 11-5 and 11-6 show that standard diskettes contain over 300 clusters. Each entry in the FAT must point to one of these clusters, so each FAT entry must be able to take on at least 300 values. A single byte can take on only 256 values (00H–FFH), so a single byte is not adequate as a FAT entry. A 2-byte number can take on up to 65,536 values (0000H–FFFFH). Since this quantity is much more than is needed, the designers of MS-DOS decided that they could save some disk space by making each FAT entry 1.5 bytes in length (000H–FFFH). A little odd, but it works well in the computer and is really not too difficult to understand. In addition, the 4,096 values that are possible with 1.5 bytes are adequate for the FATs of quad-density diskettes (2,371 clusters) and 10-Mbyte fixed disks (2,587 clusters).

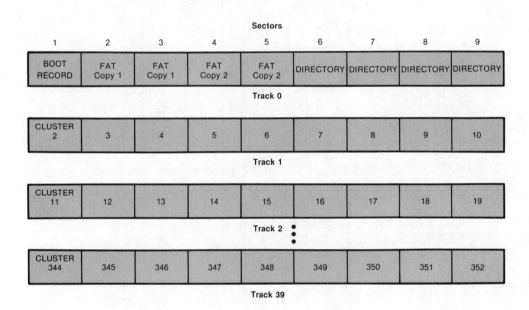

Figure 11-5. Layout of boot record, FAT, file directory, and clusters on a 9-sector, *single-sided* diskette.

The first step MS-DOS takes in using the FAT is to obtain the file's first cluster number stored in bytes 26 and 27 of the file's directory entry (figure 11-7A). To find the file's second cluster number, MS-DOS takes the first cluster number and multiplies it by 1.5. The integer portion of the resulting product is then taken as an offset into the FAT (figure 11-7B).

The word (2 bytes) at the calculated offset is then modified as follows: If the first cluster number was odd, the three high-order hexadecimal digits are taken as the next cluster number. If the first cluster number was even, the three low-order hexadecimal digits are taken as the next cluster number (figure 11-7C).

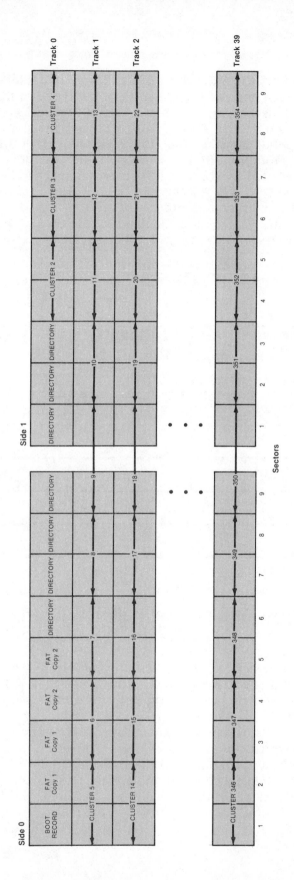

Figure 11-6. Layout of boot record, FAT, file directory, and clusters on a 9-sector, *double-sided* diskette.

File Directory

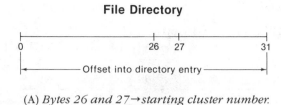

(A) *Bytes 26 and 27→starting cluster number.*

File Allocation Table

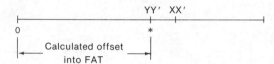

(B) *Starting cluster number × 1.5 = product. Integer portion of product = offset into FAT of 2nd cluster number (*).*

Word at Calculated Offset into FAT = XX'YY'

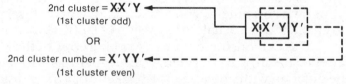

(C) *Word at calculated offset is modified.*

Figure 11-7. The steps taken by MS-DOS in using the FAT.

To find the file's next cluster, MS-DOS multiplies the second cluster number by 1.5. It takes the integer portion of the product as an offset into the FAT and then takes the word at the calculated offset. The high-order digit is discarded if the second cluster number was even. If the second cluster number was odd, the low-order digit is discarded. The resulting three-digit hexadecimal number is the next cluster number.

This process is repeated until the resulting three-digit hexadecimal number is in the range FF8–FFF. A number in this range indicates that the end of the file has been reached. Don't get discouraged if this process seems somewhat confusing. The example in the following section should help to clarify it.

The procedure used on large storage devices is similar but more straightforward. On these large devices, there are more than 4,096 clusters, so a 1.5-byte number is not adequate. FAT entries on these devices are 2 bytes. The first cluster number is read from the directory. Now the cluster number is multiplied by 2 and the product taken as an offset into the FAT. The 2-byte word stored at this location is the next cluster number. The low-order byte is stored first, the high-order byte second.

Table 11-5 summarizes how the values stored in the FAT are interpreted.

Table 11-5. Interpretation of Values for 1.5-Byte (XXX) and 2-Byte (XXXX) FAT Entries

Value	Meaning
(0)000	Cluster available
(F)FF0–(F)FF6	Reserved cluster
(F)FF7	Bad cluster
(F)FF8–(F)FFF	Last cluster of file
(X)XXX	Cluster belongs to a chain

Exploring with DEBUG

In this section, we will use the MS-DOS utility DEBUG to examine the file directory and FAT of a typical MS-DOS diskette. You can follow along on your own computer if you wish. Before you do that, you may want to refer to chapter 9 for a detailed discussion of DEBUG and the DEBUG commands.

This demonstration uses a working copy of the MS-DOS 2 system diskette (a standard double-sided, 9-sector-per-track diskette). The results would be different with a quad-density diskette or a fixed disk, but the concepts are identical.

Looking at the File Directory

Boot your system if you have not already done so. When the system prompt appears, type **debug** and press Enter. MS-DOS will load DEBUG, and DEBUG will take control. The DEBUG prompt (a hyphen on most systems) tells you that DEBUG is loaded and ready to go:

```
A>debug
-
```

We will begin by loading the first sector of the file directory into memory. The diskette that we are using is double-sided with 9 sectors. If you look at figure 11-6 again, you will see that the first sector of the file directory is at side 0, track 0, sector 6.

MS-DOS uses the term *relative sector* to describe a sector relative to side 0, track 0, sector 1, which is relative sector 0. Side 0, track 0, sector 2 is relative sector 1, and so on up to side 0, track 0, sector 9, which is relative sector 8. In MS-DOS 2.X and 3.X, the next relative sector on a double-sided diskette is at side 1, track 0, sector 1. MS-DOS 1 uses a different scheme, where the relative sectors proceed from side 0, track 0, sector 1 straight across side 0 through track 39 and then go to side 1, track 0, sector 1.

The point of all this is that DEBUG can load specific sectors of a disk into memory by using the relative sector scheme. The following command tells DEBUG to load into memory location CS:100 the fifth relative sector (side 0, track 0, sector 6) of the diskette in drive A. Substitute "03" for "05" in the command if you are using an MS-DOS 1 system diskette:

```
-L CS:100 0 05 01
-
```

Entering this command loads the first sector of the file directory into memory.

The following DEBUG command will display the first 48 bytes of the sector that was just loaded into memory. The initial portion of the dump, the portion that we will examine, is the first entry in the disk's file directory. If you want a printout of the display, press the Ctrl-PrtSc before entering the command (make sure that your printer is turned on).

```
-d CS:100 L30
0976:0100  49 4F 20 20 20 20 20 20-53 59 53 27 00 00 00 00   IO      SYS'....
0976:0110  00 00 00 00 00 00 43 4E-65 08 02 00 E4 13 00 00   ......CNs...d...
0976:0120  4D 53 44 4F 53 20 20 20-53 59 53 27 00 00 00 00   MSDOS   SYS'....
```

The numbers to the far left are memory addresses that may differ from system to system. The middle portion of the display is called a *memory dump*. The contents of memory are displayed in hexadecimal numbers.

Let's examine the dump closely:

Filename and extension (offset 0–7 and 8–10). The underlined portion of the display on the left side comprises the first 8 bytes of the dump. These 8 bytes make up the *filename* field of the first entry in the file directory. Notice that the 8-character filename field has been padded with blanks. The ASCII representation of the dump is the underlined portion on the right side of the screen. We can see that the filename is "IO".

The 3 bytes following the filename field (53 59 53) make up the *filename extension* field. In the right-hand column, we can see that the extension is "SYS".

Attribute (offset 11). Following the filename extension field is the *attribute* field. The attribute field is interpreted according to its bit pattern.

```
-d CS:100 L30
0976:0100  49 4F 20 20 20 20 20 20-53 59 53 27 00 00 00 00   IO      SYS'....
0976:0110  00 00 00 00 00 00 43 4E-65 08 02 00 E4 13 00 00   ......CNs...d...
0976:0120  4D 53 44 4F 53 20 20 20-53 59 53 27 00 00 00 00   MSDOS   SYS'....
```

In the preceding example, the field contains a value of 27H, which translates to the following bit pattern:

```
Bit:     7 6 5 4   3 2 1 0
Value:   0 0 1 0   0 1 1 1
```

Bits 0, 1, 2, and 5 have been set to equal 1. This tells us that the file IO.SYS has the attributes read only, hidden, system, and archive (see table 11-3).

    Reserved (offset 12–21). The 10 bytes (all 00H) that follow the attribute field form the *reserved* field of the file directory entry. This field has been reserved by the makers of MS-DOS.

    Time (offset 22–23). The next 2 bytes (43 4E) form the *time stamp* field. The time that the file was created or last modified is stored as the bit pattern of these two bytes.

```
-d CS:100 L30
0976:0100  49 4F 20 20 20 20 20 20-53 59 53 27 00 00 00 00   IO      SYS'....
0976:0110  00 00 00 00 00 00 43 4E-65 08 02 00 E4 13 00 00   ......CNs...d...
0976:0120  4D 53 44 4F 53 20 20 20-53 59 53 27 00 00 00 00   MSDOS   SYS'....
```

MS-DOS stores the 2 bytes of the preceding example in reverse order; thus, the bit pattern of the hexadecimal word (2 bytes) is 4E 43. The bit pattern is as follows:

```
        1  1  0  0    1  1 1 0    0 1 0 0    0 0 1 1
Bit    15 14 13 12   11 10 9 8    7 6 5 4    3 2 1 0
       |——— Hour ———→| |——— Minute ———→| |— Seconds —→|
```

Bits 11–15 store the binary representation of the hour of the day. These 5 bits store a value of $1+8$, or 9. Bits 5–10 store the minutes in binary. In this example, the minutes value is $2+16+32=50$. Bits 0–4 hold the seconds in 2-second intervals. In this case, the number of 2-second intervals is $1+2=3$.

    Putting all of this information together, we can tell that the file was created or last modified at 9:50:06 in the morning (to the closest 2 seconds).

    Date (offset 24–25). The bit pattern of the *date stamp* field stores the date that the file was created or last modified.

```
-d CS:100 L30
0976:0100  49 4F 20 20 20 20 20 20-53 59 53 27 00 00 00 00   IO      SYS'....
0976:0110  00 00 00 00 00 00 43 4E-65 08 02 00 E4 13 00 00   ......CNs...d...
0976:0120  4D 53 44 4F 53 20 20 20-53 59 53 27 00 00 00 00   MSDOS   SYS'....
```

Again, the bytes are stored in reverse order, so in this example we want the bit pattern of the hexadecimal word 08 65.

```
        0  0  0  0    1  0 0 0    0 1 1 0    0 1 0 1
Bit    15 14 13 12   11 10 9 8    7 6 5 4    3 2 1 0
       |——— Year ———→| |— Month —→| |— Day ——→|
```

Bits 9–15 store the year (less 1980). In this case, the year stored is 4, which means that IO.SYS was created or last modified in 4+1980=1984. Bits 5–8 store the month in binary. Here, the month is 1+2=3. The day is stored in bits 0–4. The day is 1+4=5. Thus, the date stamp is March 5, 1984. Putting this information together with the time information, we know that IO.SYS was created or modified on March 5, 1984 at approximately 9:50:06 in the morning.

   Starting cluster (offset 26–27). The hexadecimal word at offset 26–27 holds the starting cluster number of IO.SYS. Again, the word is stored in reverse order, so the starting cluster number is 00 02. We will see how MS-DOS uses this number shortly.

```
-d CS:100 L30
0976:0100   49 4F 20 20 20 20 20 20-53 59 53 27 00 00 00 00   IO      SYS'....
0976:0110   00 00 00 00 00 00 43 4E-65 08 02 00 E4 13 00 00   ......CNs...d...
0976:0120   4D 53 44 4F 53 20 20 20-53 59 53 27 00 00 00 00   MSDOS   SYS'....
```

   File size (offset 28–31). This field contains the file size stored as a 4-byte hexadecimal number. MS-DOS stores the bytes in reverse order, with the low-order byte stored first and the high-order byte stored last. The size of IO.SYS is 00 00 13 E4 (hex), or decimal 5,092 bytes.

```
-d CS:100 L30
0976:0100   49 4F 20 20 20 20 20 20-53 59 53 27 00 00 00 00   IO      SYS'....
0976:0110   00 00 00 00 00 00 43 4E-65 08 02 00 E4 13 00 00   ......CNs...d...
0976:0120   4D 53 44 4F 53 20 20 20-53 59 53 27 00 00 00 00   MSDOS   SYS'....
```

   This concludes our examination of an MS-DOS file directory. Next, we will use DEBUG to examine the FAT and see how MS-DOS uses the FAT, along with the starting cluster number, to keep track of a file.

Loading the FAT

Returning to figure 11-6, we can see that on a double-sided, 9-sector diskette the first sector of the first FAT copy is stored at side 0, track 0, sector 1. This is relative sector 1 and can be loaded into memory location CS:300 with the DEBUG command "L CS:300 0 01 01". To follow along with this tutorial, you should have DEBUG running and your backup system diskette in drive A. Refer to the discussion of the file directory if you need some help getting started. Enter the following command:

```
-L CS:300 0 01 01
```

When the disk drive turns off, enter:

```
-d CS:300 L20
```

DEBUG will display:

```
0976:0300  FD FF FF 03 40 00 05 60-00 FF 8F 00 09 A0 00 0B  }...a..'......
0976:0310  C0 00 0D E0 00 0F 00 01-11 20 01 13 40 01 15 60  a..'.......a..'
```

This is a dump of the first 32 bytes of the FAT. The first byte in the FAT is set according to the type of disk media on which the FAT is stored (table 11-6). In this case, the medium is a double-sided, 9-sector diskette. Thus, the first byte in the FAT is the hexadecimal number FD; the second and third bytes in the FAT are always FFH.

Table 11-6. Value of First Byte in FAT
According to Type of Storage Media

First Byte in FAT	Type of Media
FF	Double-sided, 8 sectors/track diskette
FE	Single-sided, 8 sectors/track diskette
FD	Double-sided, 9 sectors/track diskette
FC	Single-sided, 9 sectors/track diskette
F9	Double-sided, 15 sectors/track diskette
F8	Fixed disk

Looking at the FAT

In the previous section, we saw that the starting cluster number for the file IO.SYS was hexadecimal 02 (02H). Here is how MS-DOS uses the FAT to determine the second cluster number of IO.SYS. MS-DOS starts by taking the first cluster number (02) and multiplying it by 1.5. It uses the product (3) as a pointer into the FAT. Then, MS-DOS examines the 2-byte word located at the calculated offset:

```
-d CS:300 L20
0976:0300  FD FF FF 03 40 00 05 60-00 FF 8F 00 09 A0 00 0B  }...a..'.... ..
0976:0310  C0 00 0D E0 00 0F 00 01-11 20 01 13 40 01 15 60  a..'.... ..a..'
```

In this example, the bytes 03 40 are at offset 3 in the FAT. Since MS-DOS stores bytes in reverse order, the 2 bytes are interpreted as 4003H. MS-DOS uses 1.5 bytes for each FAT entry, so 1.5 bytes must be extracted from this 2-byte number. The extraction is performed as follows: If the previous cluster number (2 in this case) was even, MS-DOS discards the high-order digit of the 2-byte number. If the previous cluster number was odd, MS-DOS discards the low-order digit of the 2-byte number.

In our example, the previous (first) cluster number was 2, which is even. Thus, we discard the high-order digit of 4003 to yield 003. This is the second cluster number. MS-DOS computes the third cluster number of IO.SYS by multiplying 3—the previous (second) cluster number—times 1.5.

The product is 4.5. MS-DOS throws away the .5 and uses 4 as an offset into the FAT:

```
-d CS:300 L20
0976:0300  FD FF FF 03 40 00 05 60-00 FF 8F 00 09 A0 00 0B  }...a..'.... ..
0976:0310  C0 00 0D E0 00 0F 00 01-11 20 01 13 40 01 15 60  a..'.... ..a..'
```

The 2 bytes at offset 4 in the FAT are 40 00. MS-DOS reads them as the 2-byte number 0040H. Since the previous (second) cluster number—3—was odd, MS-DOS discards the low-order digit of 0040 to yield 004, which is the third cluster number of IO.SYS.

In a similar fashion, MS-DOS will compute the fourth cluster number of IO.SYS as 5 and the fifth cluster number as 6. Let's see what happens when MS-DOS computes the sixth cluster number. The previous (fifth) cluster number was 6. Multiplying 6 times 1.5 equals 9. The 2 bytes at offset 9 in the FAT are FF and 8F:

```
-d CS:300 L20
0976:0300  FD FF FF 03 40 00 05 60-00 FF 8F 00 09 A0 00 0B  }...a..'.... ..
0976:0310  C0 00 0D E0 00 0F 00 01-11 20 01 13 40 01 15 60  a..'.... ..a..'
```

MS-DOS forms the 4-byte number 8FFFH from these 2 bytes. The previous cluster number (6) was even, so MS-DOS throws out the high-order digit (8) to give the 1.5-byte number FFFH. MS-DOS reads any value in the range FF8–FFF as an end-of-file marker; therefore, FFFH tells MS-DOS that the last cluster of IO.SYS has been reached.

Without the FAT, MS-DOS would find itself adrift in a sea of clusters, unable to access any files. In fact, the FAT is so important to the operation of MS-DOS that each disk contains two copies of the FAT. Ostensibly, this second copy serves as a backup if the first is damaged. However, for reasons known only to the designers of MS-DOS, the second copy of the FAT is never used.

MS-DOS File Management

MS-DOS employs two techniques in managing files. The first technique, using data structures called *file control blocks* (FCBs), was implemented in MS-DOS 1. When MS-DOS was first developed, CP/M was the predominant operating system being used on microcomputers. FCBs were implemented specifically to provide some compatibility with CP/M files. When a hierarchical file structure was introduced in MS-DOS 2, a new technique for managing files was implemented. This technique utilizes a *file handle* and does not require the use of FCBs. File handles are patterned after the file management technique used by the UNIX operating system. This section discusses FCBs and file handles.

Structure of the File Control Block

The *file control* block is a 36-byte block of computer memory. The FCB, which is required for file management in MS-DOS 1, contains ten individual fields. Table 11-7 shows the ten fields and the purpose of each.

Table 11-7. Breakdown of File Control Block

Offset (Hex)	Purpose
00	***Disk drive number.*** Set by the programmer. **0** default drive **1** drive A **2** drive B **3** drive C etc.
01–08	***Filename of file to be created, written, or read.*** Set by the programmer. The field must be padded with blanks if the filename has fewer than 8 characters. The field may contain a valid device name (excluding the optional colon).
09–0B	***Filename extension.*** Set by the programmer. The field must be padded with blanks if the extension has fewer than 3 characters.
0C–0D	***Current block number.*** A block consists of 128 records. The size of a record is determined by bytes 0EH and 0FH of the FCB. A block is numbered according to its position relative to the start of the file. The current block number is set to zero by MS-DOS when a file is opened. Sequential read and write operations use the current block number and the current record number (FCB byte 20H) to locate a particular record.
0E–0F	***Logical record size.*** An "open file" operation assigns a value of 80H to this field.
10–13	***File size in bytes.*** When MS-DOS opens a file, it extracts the file's size from the file directory and stores the value in this field. The low-order word is stored in bytes 10H and 11H; the high-order word in 12H and 13H. This value should **not** be modified by the programmer.
14–15	***Date file was created or last modified.*** Also extracted from directory during an "open." This value should **not** be modified by the programmer.

```
Byte  |————— 15H —————|  |————— 14H —————|
Bit   15 14 13 12 11 10  9  8  7  6  5  4  3  2  1  0
      |— Year less 1980 —|  |-Month-|  |——— Day ———|
```

Table 11-7. (cont'd)

Offset (Hex)	Purpose
16–1F	***Reserved for use by MS-DOS.*** This value should **not** be modified by the programmer.
20	***Current relative record number.*** This field contains the relative record number (0–127) within the current block (FCB bytes 0CH–0DH). This field is not initialized by an "open" operation.
21–24	***Random record number.*** This field is used for "random" reading and writing of files. Records are numbered according to their position relative to the first record in the file. The first record is random number 0.

The *extended FCB* is used by MS-DOS to create files with a particular attribute or to search the file directory for such files. As table 11-8 shows, the extended FCB consists of a standard FCB with a 7-byte *header.* The bytes of the header are referenced by negative offsets relative to byte 00 of the standard FCB.

Table 11-8. Breakdown of Extended FCB Header

Offset (Hex)	Purpose
−07	***A flag byte set to FFH,*** indicating the beginning of an extended FCB header.
−06 to −02	***Reserved by MS-DOS.***
−01	***Attribute of file to be created or searched for:*** **02H** Hidden file **04H** System file **00H** Other file

Using an FCB

MS-DOS 1 requires you to set up an FCB for a file before any operations can be performed on that file. Once the FCB is set up in memory, you must place the FCB's segment address in the DS register and the FCB's offset address in the DX register. The DS and DX registers then act as a pointer directing MS-DOS to the FCB.

With DS:DX pointing to the FCB, you must place the value of the desired service function (see appendix A) in the AH register, initialize any other registers required by that particular service function, and then direct MS-DOS to execute an interrupt type 21 (hex). Interrupt 21 is the MS-DOS *func-*

tion dispatcher that tells MS-DOS to execute the service specified by the value in the AH register. The MS-DOS service functions are used to perform the nuts and bolts operations in a computer program.

When a computer program issues a call for interrupt 21, control will pass from the computer program to MS-DOS. The service function will operate on the file specified by the FCB and then return control to the calling program. Execution of the program will then continue in the normal fashion.

As we have seen, a big drawback in using the MS-DOS 1 file management functions is the requirement that a valid FCB be established for each file read or written. MS-DOS 2 effectively removed this annoyance with the implementation of file handles.

File Handles

MS-DOS versions 2.X and 3.X provide a group of file management service functions that do not require the use of FCBs. Before a file is opened or created, a character string is placed in memory that specifies the drive, path, filename, and extension of the file. The DS and DX registers are then used to point to this string and the *create* (DOS function 3CH) or the *open* (DOS function 3DH) function is called. The function returns a 16-bit file handle in the AX register. The file handle is then used for any subsequent access to the file; no FCB is used. MS-DOS takes care of the messy details. The programmer simply keeps track of which file handle belongs to which file.

MS-DOS versions 2.X and 3.X provide support for FCBs; therefore, programs written to execute under MS-DOS 1.X will run under versions 2.X and 3.X. Programs that utilize file handles will not run under MS-DOS 1.X.

Memory Structure
and Management

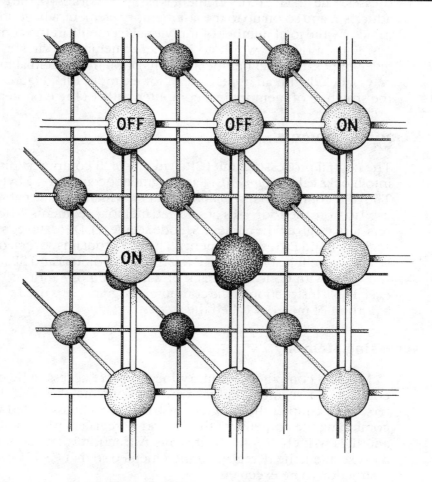

The purpose of the next two chapters is to give you a thorough understanding of how memory is organized and controlled in MS-DOS computers. This chapter is an overview, discussing structure and process in general terms. Chapter 13 then applies this information to terminate and stay resident computer programs.

Computer Memory

Computer memory consists of a large number of individual memory elements, each of which stores 1 byte of data. Each element is assigned a unique numerical address, and the elements are ordered according to these addresses. The first memory element is assigned address 0, the next is assigned address 1, and so on up to the last memory element whose address is determined by the total number of individual elements in the computer's memory. For reasons we won't go into here, memory addresses are generally given in hexadecimal numbers. In this book, hexadecimal numbers are always labeled with an uppercase *H*, for example 10H. Figure 12-1 illustrates the structure of memory in a computer with 1 Mbyte of memory.

Memory Segments

The central processing unit (CPU) in MS-DOS computers divides memory into blocks called *segments*. Each segment occupies 64 Kbytes of memory. The CPU contains four *segment registers*, which are internal storage devices used to store the addresses of selected memory segments. The four segment registers are given the names CS (code segment), DS (data segment), SS (stack segment), and ES (extra segment). The CPU contains several other registers. For now, we'll just mention IP (instruction pointer) and SP (stack pointer). IP is used with CS to keep track of which memory address stores the next executable instruction of the computer program. SP is used with SS to access a portion of memory called the *stack*.

Accessing Memory

In MS-DOS computers, memory locations are accessed by combining the contents of a segment register with the contents of one of the other registers. For example, the program instruction to be executed is accessed by combining the contents of the CS and IP registers (the combination of CS and IP is written "CS:IP"). After the instruction is retrieved from memory and executed, the IP register is incremented so that CS:IP points to the next instruction to be executed.

The manner in which register contents are combined places an upper limit on the amount of memory that is addressable by the computer hardware. MS-DOS was originally designed to run on computers with an Intel 8088 CPU. Each 8088 register stores a 16-bit number. The 8088 combines

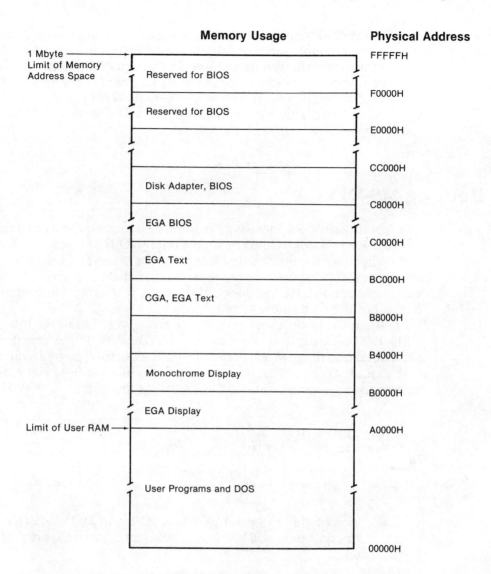

**Figure 12-1. Memory map for a computer with
1 megabyte of memory.**

the 16-bit number from a segment register (such as CS) with the 16-bit number from another register (such as IP) to produce a 20-bit memory address. This limits the amount of memory addressable by the 8088 to 2^{20} bytes, or 1 Mbyte.

Since the birth of MS-DOS, 8088 computers have been succeeded by 80286 and 80386 computers. These computers are capable of addressing more than 1 Mbyte of memory. However, the 1-Mbyte limitation is still (at least through version 3.3) built into MS-DOS. This limitation is one of the major restrictions of the operating system.

The memory diagram shown in figure 12-1 illustrates an additional restriction on usable memory. Memory addresses starting at A0000H are reserved for use by the system's video display and ROM (read only memory). This memory is not available for use by programs. Therefore, user programs are restricted to the 640-Kbyte range 00000H–9FFFFH. At the end of this chapter, we will discuss how this constraint has been overcome through the implementation of *expanded memory*.

Booting MS-DOS

The booting process consists of reading into memory the boot record and the files IO.SYS, MSDOS.SYS, and COMMAND.COM (see chapter 11).

When the computer is first turned on (or restarted), control is passed to an address in ROM (read only memory) that checks to see if the disk has a valid boot record. If a valid record is found, it is loaded into memory, and control of the computer is passed to it.

When the boot record receives control, it checks to see if IO.SYS and MSDOS.SYS are the first two files stored on the disk. If they are, the two files are loaded into the low end of memory, and control is passed to an initialization module contained in IO.SYS. If the two files are not on the disk in the appropriate physical location, the following message is displayed:

```
Non system disk
Replace and press any key
```

> In versions of MS-DOS prior to 3.3, IO.SYS and MSDOS.SYS must be stored in contiguous disk sectors. This restriction does not apply to version 3.3.

The initialization module passes control to MSDOS.SYS, which initializes a disk buffer and a file control block area that are used in executing service routines. MSDOS.SYS also determines the computer's equipment status and performs any necessary hardware initialization. MSDOS.SYS then passes control back to the IO.SYS initialization module.

The initialization module checks to see if there is a CONFIG.SYS file (discussed in chapter 8) in the root directory of the boot disk. If there is, and if it contains any instructions about installable device drivers, the specified drivers are installed in memory.

Next, the initialization module issues a call to DOS function 4BH, which invokes the DOS program loader. The loader, also called EXEC, is responsible for loading a program into memory and passing control to the program. In this case, the initialization module directs EXEC to load COMMAND.COM. EXEC can be directed to load a different command interpreter through the use of the SHELL command (see Part 3).

Recall from chapter 11 that COMMAND.COM consists of three parts: an initialization portion, a resident portion, and a transient portion. The resident portion is loaded by EXEC and is responsible for loading the transient portion. The resident portion also contains the routines that handle input and output errors, as well as routines that handle int 22H (terminate address), int 23H (Ctrl-Break), and int 24H (critical error).

The initialization portion of COMMAND.COM is loaded into memory immediately above the resident portion. This portion of the command interpreter processes AUTOEXEC.BAT files (see chapter 5). The initialization portion also prompts you for time and date. It is then discarded.

The transient portion of COMMAND.COM is loaded into the high end of memory. This portion of the command interpreter displays the system prompt, contains the internal system commands, and loads and executes external commands and executable files. As its name implies, the transient portion may be overwritten during the execution of a program. When a program terminates, the resident portion of COMMAND.COM determines if the transient portion has been overwritten and reloads it if necessary.

Once the transient portion of COMMAND.COM has been installed, the system prompt is displayed, indicating that the booting process has been completed and that MS-DOS is ready to accept a command. Figure 12-2 illustrates the structure of computer memory at the completion of the booting process.

Program Segment Prefix

Before loading any program (including COMMAND.COM), EXEC locates the lowest available segment in memory. This segment is designated the program segment. Beginning at offset 00 in the program segment, EXEC constructs a *program segment prefix* (psp). This program segment prefix is a 256-byte (100H) block of memory that serves as an area of communication between MS-DOS and the executing program. Once the psp is constructed, EXEC loads the program beginning at offset 100H in the program segment.

Table 12-1 describes the fields of the psp. Note that several of the fields described are not officially documented by either IBM or Microsoft. However, these fields seem to have served the same function from MS-DOS 2.0 through MS-DOS 3.3, and the descriptions presented in table 12-1 are widely accepted by DOS program developers.

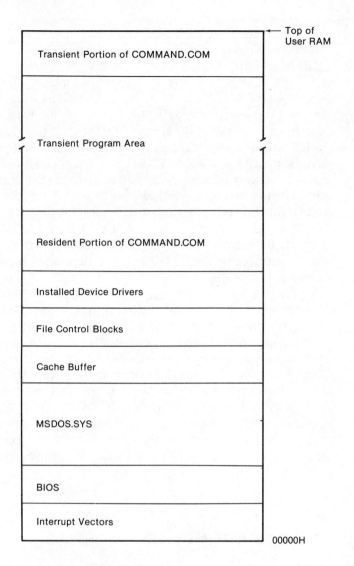

← Top of User RAM

Transient Portion of COMMAND.COM

Transient Program Area

Resident Portion of COMMAND.COM

Installed Device Drivers

File Control Blocks

Cache Buffer

MSDOS.SYS

BIOS

Interrupt Vectors

00000H

Figure 12-2. Configuration of computer memory immediately after MS-DOS is booted (exact memory addresses vary according to system configuration).

Table 12-1. Breakdown of Program Segment Prefix

Offset (hex)	Purpose
00–01	***Program terminate.*** The first two bytes of the psp are always CD and 20. These two hexadecimal numbers code for the MS-DOS interrupt "program terminate" (INT 20H). See appendix B for a discussion of MS-DOS interrupts.
02–03	***Top of memory.*** These 2 bytes store, in reverse order,

Table 12-1. (cont'd)

Offset (hex)	Purpose
	the starting segment address of any memory that MS-DOS has not allocated to the executable file. Since MS-DOS generally allocates all available memory to an executable file, these 2 bytes normally contain the address of the "top of memory."
04	**Byte of 00.** Although officially documented as "reserved," this field is not currently in use.
05–09	**Function dispatcher.** A long call to the MS-DOS function dispatcher. This field is implemented to provide compatibility with CP/M programs. New programs should not use this field to call the function dispatcher. The first byte in this field is the op-code for a long call. The second and third bytes store, in reverse order, the offset of the function dispatcher. This number also represents the number of bytes that are available in the program's code segment. The fourth and fifth bytes of the field store, in reverse order, the segment address of the function dispatcher. The function dispatcher is discussed in appendix A.
0A–0D	**Terminate address.** These 4 bytes store, in reverse order, the default address that receives control when a program terminates execution. The value stored here preserves the default so that it can be restored, if necessary, when the program terminates.
0E–11	**Ctrl-Break exit.** These 4 bytes store, in reverse order, the default address that receives control when Ctrl-Break is pressed. The value stored here preserves the default so that it can be restored, if necessary, when the program terminates.
12–15	**Critical error exit.** These 4 bytes store, in reverse order, the default address that receives control when a critical error is encountered. The value stored here preserves the default so that it can be restored, if necessary, when the program terminates. See appendix A for a discussion of critical errors.
16–17	**psp of parent.** This field stores in reverse order, the segment address of the parent's psp. For example, if COMMAND.COM uses EXEC to load an application program, then this field of the application's psp will contain the segment address of COMMAND.COM's psp. THE COMMAND.COM shell that was loaded during

Table 12-1. (cont'd)

Offset (hex)	Purpose
	booting has no viable parent. Therefore, this field in COMMAND.COM's psp stores its own segment address.
	The use of this field is undocumented by Microsoft and IBM. Officially the field is "reserved."
18–2B	***File handle alias table***. These 20 bytes are used to store the file handles that belong to this process. The byte at a given entry contains FFH if the corresponding handle is not in use by the process. A value other than FFH represents an offset into DOS's master file table, which contains the file-specific information. The size of this master table is set with the FILES=*nnn* command.
	The first 5 bytes in this field are reserved for the standard input, standard output, standard error, standard auxiliary, and standard printer devices. If any of these devices are redirected, the corresponding entry in this table will be changed by MS-DOS.
	The size of this table limits a process to 20 file handles. However, it is possible to create a table with more than 20 bytes and use it as a handle alias table. This can be accomplished by: (1) storing the size of the new table at offset 32H in the psp, (2) storing the offset and segment addresses of the table at offset 34H of the psp, and (3) copying the contents of the old alias table into the new alias table.
	The use of this field is not documented by Microsoft or IBM. Officially the field is "reserved."
2C–2D	***Environment address.*** These bytes store the segment address, in reverse order, of the program's environment. Refer to this chapter's discussion of the environment.
2E–31	***Reserved by MS-DOS.***
32–33	***Size of file handle alias table***. This 2-byte word stores the size of the process's file alias table. Current implementations of MS-DOS set the value of this field to 20. See the description of psp offset field 18H–2BH.
	The use of this field is undocumented by Microsoft and IBM. Officially this field is "reserved".
34–37	***Address of file handle alias table.*** The first 2 bytes of this field store, in reverse order, the offset address of the file handle alias table. The second 2 bytes of this field

Table 12-1. (cont'd)

Offset (hex)	Purpose
	store, in reverse order, the alias table's segment address. Current implementations of MS-DOS store the alias table at PSP:0018H. See the description of psp offset field 18H–2BH.
	The use of this field is undocumented by Microsoft and IBM. Officially the field is "reserved."
37–4F	***Reserved by MS-DOS.***
50–52	***Function dispatcher, return.*** This field contains the bytes CD 21 CB—the machine code for a call to the function dispatcher followed by a FAR return.
53–5B	***Reserved by MS-DOS.***
5C–6B	***File control block.*** This default file control block is used if the first command line parameter following the program name is a filename.
6C–7B	***File control block.*** This default file control block is used if the second command line parameter following the program name is a filename.
7C–7F	***Reserved by MS-DOS.***
80–FF	***Command tail, DTA.*** The first byte stores the length of the command line's parameter string. The parameter string (command tail) is stored beginning at byte 2 of this field. The entire field also serves as a default disk transfer area. This field is used if the program requires but does not establish a DTA. When the field is used in this fashion, the command tail is overwritten.

The segment address of the psp is sometimes referred to as the *process identifier*, or *PID*. Each program running on a computer is called a process and is identified by a unique PID. On MS-DOS computers, the PID and the psp segment address are identical. When MS-DOS was first implemented, it was used on relatively small personal computers that were never running more than one program (process) at a time. The current MS-DOS computers are quite different in this respect: it is not unusual for them to have one or more resident programs (such as Sidekick) while running the user's application program. In the environment, the concept of processes is very important, as is an understanding of the location, structure, and function of the psp. Processes and PIDs are discussed later in this chapter under "Memory Allocation."

MS-DOS 3.0 (and subsequent versions) implement DOS function 62H.

This function can be called by a program to obtain the segment address of its psp. Appendix A contains a Turbo Pascal program that demonstrates the use of function 62H.

For the 2.X versions of DOS, there is an undocumented DOS function that can be used to obtain the psp's segment address. Function 51H (which is also implemented in 3.X) returns the address in the BX register. Listing 12-1 is a Turbo Pascal program that demonstrates the use of function 51H. See appendix A for a general discussion on the use of the DOS functions.

DOS function 50H is available to set the current psp. This function is implemented in MS-DOS 2.X and 3.X, but its use is not officially documented. Despite this lack of sanction by IBM and Microsoft, function 50H is widely used in resident programs. When a resident program receives control (as when a "hot" key is pressed), DOS keeps the psp of the application program as the current psp. Function 50H may be used to tell DOS that the resident's psp is the current psp. Similarly, when the resident passes control back to the application program, function 50H may be used to reset the application's psp as current.

Listing 12-1. PsPeep, a Turbo Pascal Program Demonstrating the Use of Function 51H

```
program PsPeep;

{This program displays information about its psp using
MS-DOS function 51H. 51H is an undocumented function that is
identical to the MS-DOS 3.X function 62H. The difference is
that 51H is also implemented in MS-DOS 2.X.}

type
    registers = record
                ax,bx,cx,dx,bp,si,di,ds,es,flags: integer;
                end;
    HexString = string[4];
var
    dosreg : registers;
    psp_seg : integer;

function hex (i : integer) : HexString;
{Converts decimal to hex string}
const
    h : array[0..15] of char = '0123456789ABCDEF';
var
    low,high : byte;
begin
    low  := Lo(i);
    high := Hi(i);
    hex  := h[high shr 4]+h[high and $F]+h[low shr 4]+h[low and $F];
end;
```

```
function VerNum : integer;
{This function returns the version of DOS being used.}
begin
      dosreg.ax:= $3000;            {Set AH to 30H.}
      MsDos(dosreg);                {Call DOS}
      VerNum:= Lo(dosreg.ax);       {Major number in AL}
end;

procedure GetPsp;
{Uses DOS service function 51H to obtain the segment address
of the program's psp}
begin
      dosreg.ax := $5100;
      MsDos(dosreg);
      psp_ := dosreg.bx;
      writeln('PSP: ',hex(psp_seg));
end;

procedure TermAddr;
{Displays segment:offset address of termination handler}
begin
      write('Termination address: ');
      write(hex(MemW[psp_seg:$0c]));
      writeln(':',hex(MemW[psp_seg:$0a]));
end;

procedure ParentPsp;
{Displays psp of this program's parent. The purpose of offset
is not officially documented}
begin
      writeln('Parent PSP: ',hex(MemW[psp_seg:$16]));
end;

procedure EnvSeg;
begin
      write('Environment begins at: ');
      writeln(hex(MemW[psp_seg:$2c]),':0000');
end;

procedure FileHandles;
{Displays information about the file handle alias table. The format
for alias table is not officially documented.}
var
      AliasSeg,AliasOff,FileCnt,
      i,j                           : integer;

begin
      AliasSeg := MemW[psp_seg:$36];
      AliasOff := MemW[psp_seg:$34];
      write('Handle alias address: ');
      writeln(hex(AliasSeg),':',hex(AliasOff));
```

```
        write('Size of alias table: ');
        writeln(MemW[psp_seg:$32],' bytes');

        FileCnt := 0;
        for i := 0 to (MemW[psp_seg:$32] - 1) do
        begin
            j := Mem[psp_seg:$18 + i];
            if not (j in [$FF, 0..2]) then
                FileCnt := FileCnt + 1;
        end;
        writeln('Number of open file handles: ',FileCnt);

end;

procedure GoPeep;
begin
        TermAddr;
        ParentPsp;
        EnvSeg;
        FileHandles;
end;

{Program starts here.}
begin
        if VerNum < 2 then
            writeln('DOS 2.0 or later required.')
        else begin
            GetPsp;
            GoPeep;
        end;
end.
```

Executable Files

All programs written to run under MS-DOS go through a process called *linking* (see chapter 10). The linker evaluates the program and determines where in memory the different parts of the program are to be located relative to one another. The linker then stores this information in a header located at the front of the program file. All files produced by the linker have a filename extension of ".EXE" and are called EXE files.

EXE files that meet three requirements may be converted to COM files. The requirements for a COM file are: (1) the program and all of its data must occupy less than 64 Kbytes; (2) the program's code, data, and stack must all reside in the same memory segment; and (3) the first executable instruction of the program must be at offset 100H within the file. If an EXE file meets all of these requirements, it can be converted to a COM file by using the MS-DOS utility EXE2BIN. COM files do not contain a header.

MS-DOS always loads COM files beginning at offset 100H in the program segment, immediately following the psp. The starting address of the program segment is placed in all four segment registers, and a value of 100H is placed in the IP register. The SP register is set to point to the top of the program segment. MS-DOS then places 2 bytes of 00H at the top of the stack and passes control to the instruction at CS:100.

When an EXE file is loaded, the file's header is placed in memory beginning at offset 100H in the program segment. The remainder of the file is then relocated in memory according to the information contained in the header. The CS, IP, SS, and SP registers are initialized according to information in the header. The DS and ES registers are set to point to the start of the psp, control is passed to the instruction pointed to by CS:IP, and program execution commences.

The Environment

Any program running under MS-DOS may use EXEC to load and run another program. When this occurs, the program calling EXEC is referred to as the *parent* and the program loaded by EXEC is referred to as the *child*. The child inherits many items from its parent, including a block of memory called the *environment*.

The environment consists of a series of statements having the form

environment variable=some string of characters

An environment statement serves to communicate information to both MS-DOS and application programs. For example, the statement "PATH=*search path*" tells MS-DOS which directories to search for files; the statement "COMSPEC=*d*:[*path*]" tells MS-DOS where to locate the transient portion of COMMAND.COM; and the statement "LIB=[*path*]" tells the compiler where to look to locate library files used in compiling programs.

The statements within the environment are separated from each other by a byte of value 00H. The final statement in the environment is followed by 2 bytes storing 00H. In MS-DOS 3, the 2 bytes of 00H are followed by a word count and by the drive, path, filename, and filename extension of the program that owns the environment. As we discussed earlier in this chapter, offset 2CH in the program's psp stores the segment address of the program's environment.

Environment Size

The environment may be up to 32 Kbytes long. As part of the standard booting process, COMMAND.COM receives an environment that is 160 bytes long. An environment of this size can fill up quickly, in which case MS-DOS will display the message: **Out of environment space**.

Users of MS-DOS 3.1 through 3.3 can increase the size of the environment passed to COMMAND.COM by including the following command in their CONFIG.SYS file:

shell=[*d*:][*path*]command.com /p /e:*xxxx*

Refer to the discussion of SHELL in Part 3 for details on the use of this command.

Users of MS-DOS 2.X and 3.0 can also change the size of the environment, but it is necessary to use DEBUG to modify the contents of COMMAND.COM (DEBUG is thoroughly discussed in chapter 9). Place your working system diskette in drive A and enter the following command:

```
A>debug a:command.com
```

This command instructs MS-DOS to load DEBUG and tells DEBUG to load COMMAND.COM. You will want to use DEBUG to search for the portion of code within COMMAND.COM that sets the default size of the environment. When you see the DEBUG prompt (−), enter the following command:

```
-s 100 L 4500 BB 0A 00 B4 48 CD 21
```

DEBUG will search COMMAND.COM until it finds the appropriate sequence of machine code. When the code is found, DEBUG will display the address at which it is located. You should see something like this:

```
39D3:0ECE
-
```

The precise address on your machine will probably differ from the one in this example. The next step is to unassemble the machine code. Enter the following command (again, the address you use will probably differ from the one used in the example):

```
-u 39d3:0ece
39D3:0ECE BB0A00        MOV     BX,000A
39D3:0ED1 B448          MOV     AH,48
39D3:0ED3 CD21          INT     21
39D3:0ED5 E890F7        CALL    0668
39D3:0ED8 E8DCF7        CALL    06B7
39D3:0EDB 89166909      MOV     [0969],DX
39D3:0EDF A16709        MOV     AX,[0967]
39D3:0EE2 2D5900        SUB     AX,0059
39D3:0EE5 90            NOP
39D3:0EE6 A3B10B        MOV     [0BB1],AX
```

```
39D3:0EE9 E861F3        CALL    024D
39D3:0EEC 8916B70B      MOV     [0BB7],DX
-
```

The instruction "MOV BX,000A" sets the number of paragraphs (16-byte blocks) given to the environment. As you can see, the default is 10 (000AH) paragraphs. The following command changes the code so that 64 (0040H) paragraphs are set aside for the environment. Feel free to choose a smaller or larger number for your environment size. Remember that you are limited to 32 Kbytes and that DEBUG operates with hexadecimal numbers. By the way, 32 Kbytes is actually 32,768 bytes, or 2048 paragraphs.

```
-a 39d3:0ece
39D3:0ECE mov bx,0040
39d3:0ED1      ←press Enter
-
```

Since we are changing the contents of COMMAND.COM, it is a good idea to unassemble the changed code just to check our work.

```
-u 39d3:0ece
39D3:0ECE BB4000        MOV     BX,0040
39D3:0ED1 B448          MOV     AH,48
39D3:0ED3 CD21          INT     21
39D3:0ED5 E890F7        CALL    0668
39D3:0ED8 E8DCF7        CALL    06B7
39D3:0EDB 89166909      MOV     [0969],DX
39D3:0EDF A16709        MOV     AX,[0967]
39D3:0EE2 2D5900        SUB     AX,0059
39D3:0EE5 90            NOP
39D3:0EE6 A3B10B        MOV     [0BB1],AX
39D3:0EE9 E861F3        CALL    024D
39D3:0EEC 8916B70B      MOV     [0BB7],DX
-
```

Now enter **w** to write the modified file back to the disk. Then enter **q** to leave DEBUG. Test to see if COMMAND.COM has been successfully patched by using the diskette in drive A to reboot your system. If your system boots, copy COMMAND.COM into the root directory of the boot drive.

Passing an Environment to a Child

Before calling EXEC, the parent must set up a *pointer* to the environment block that the child will inherit. A pointer is a variable that stores an address in memory. In this case, the pointer stores the address of the first byte in the environment. The parent can create an environment of any size (up to 32

Kbytes) using the memory allocation function (see the following discussion). However, when control passes from the child back to the parent, the parent's environment will be unchanged from what it was originally. Therefore, the parent cannot use this mechanism to change the size of its own environment.

The parent can pass to the child an exact duplicate of its own environment by setting the pointer to equal zero. Any modifications that the child performs on its environment are strictly local: they have no effect on the parent's environment.

It is possible for a child to modify its parent's environment. One way is to have the child locate its parent's psp from offset 16H in its own psp. Once the parent's psp is located, the parent's environment address can be read from offset 2CH.

The parent's environment can also be accessed by using the memory control blocks discussed in the next section.

Memory Allocation

One of the most critical jobs of any operating system is managing computer memory. The operating system must constantly be aware of which portions of memory are being used and which portions are available. There are three fundamental requests that an operating system must be able to service in performing memory management: (1) requests for allocations of blocks of memory, (2) requests to modify the size of previously allocated blocks of memory, and (3) requests to release (deallocate) previously allocated blocks of memory.

MS-DOS carries out these tasks using functions 48H (allocate memory), 49H (release memory), and 4AH (modify memory allocation). If you refer back to the previous section where COMMAND.COM was patched to modify the environment size, you will see that function 48H was used to allocate a block of memory for the environment.

The first paragraph in each allocated memory block is set aside for the *memory control block* (mcb). The first byte of a memory control block is either 4DH or 5AH. If the first byte is 4DH, then the mcb is an internal member of the chain that links all of the mcb's. If the first byte of the mcb is 5AH, the mcb is the final mcb in the chain.

The second and third bytes of the memory control block store, in reverse order, the process identifier (PID) of the program that owns the memory block. Recall from the psp discussion that the PID is identical to the segment address of the program's psp.

The fourth and fifth bytes in the mcb store, in reverse order, the number of paragraphs in the allocated block of memory. Adding this number to the address of the current mcb gives the address of the next mcb in the chain.

As we mentioned earlier, MS-DOS supplies three functions to use in accessing mcb's. Direct manipulation of the mcb's is strongly discouraged by Microsoft and IBM. There is no way that programs can coexist unless programmers leave the mcb's alone and let DOS worry about them. Having said that, there is no reason why a programmer should not be able to look at the mcb's and use the information they contain.

Unfortunately, there is no documented way of accessing the mcb's. Even the mcb structure just described is not officially documented. Fortunately, there is a way (undocumented) to get at the mcb's: DOS function 52H. This function returns a pointer to the first mcb in the allocated chain. Once the first link is found, it is possible to traverse the entire chain.

Let's use DEBUG to see how the previous information can be used. Start DEBUG (**debug**) and wait for the prompt (−). When the prompt appears, invoke DEBUG's assembler by entering **a 100**. You should see something like this:

```
-a 100

1259:0100      ←press Enter
```

Now enter the following assembly language commands:

```
1259:0100 mov ah,52

1259:0102 int 21

1259:0104      ←press Enter


-
```

Next, enter **g 104**. This tells DEBUG to execute the assembly language commands entered and to stop at offset 104H.

```
-g 104

AX=5200 BX=0026 CX=0000 DX=0000 SP=FFEE BP=0000 SI=0000 DI=0000
DS=1259 ES=022B SS=1259 CS=1259 IP=0104  NV UP EI PL NZ NA PO NC
1259:0104 6F        DB      6F
```

DEBUG just called DOS function 52H. Function 52H returned the memory address in ES and BX. The 2-byte word at ES:BX −2 is the segment address of the first mcb in the allocation chain. The next DEBUG command displays the word at ES:BX −2:

```
-d es:0024 L2

022B:0020           73 09                         s.
```

This dump tells us that the first mcb is stored at address 0973:0000. Remember that mcb's always start at offset 0000 in a segment. We can now look at the first mcb:

```
-d 973:0 l10

0973:0000 4D 08 00 EF 02 07 03 00-36 C6 06 08 03 00 36 C7   M.......6.....6.
```

The first byte in the preceding dump is reassuring, since the first byte in each mcb must be either 4DH or 5AH. The second and third bytes store, in reverse order, the PID (psp segment address) of the process that owns this block of memory. MS-DOS always assigns PID 0008 to the block containing the CONFIG.SYS device drivers.

To find the next mcb, add the 2-byte word formed by the fourth and fifth bytes to the segment address of this mcb. DEBUG's hexadecimal calculator is useful for this:

```
-h 973 2ef

 0C62 0684
```

The first number is the sum; the second number is the difference.

The next mcb is at the paragraph following 0C62:0000:

```
-d c63:0 L10

0C63:0000 4D 64 0C D3 00 EA 75 07-3B FD 73 19 AA EB F3 4E   Md....u.;.s....N
```

The preceding display is the mcb for the second block of memory in the chain. This is the memory block used by COMMAND.COM. The second and third bytes tell us that COMMAND.COM's psp starts at address 0C64:0000. Let's take a look at the psp's contents.

```
-d c64:0

0C64:0000 CD 20 00 80 00 9A F0 FE-1D F0 B2 02 64 0C 3C 01   . . . . . . . . . . .d.<.
0C64:0010 64 0C 56 05 64 0C 64 0C-01 03 01 00 02 FF FF FF   d.V.d.d.........
0C64:0020 FF FF FF FF FF FF FF FF-FF FF FF FF 3C 0D 1D 08   ............<...
0C64:0030 64 0C 14 00 18 00 64 0C-FF FF FF FF 00 00 00 00   d.....d.........
0C64:0040 00 00 00 00 00 00 00 00-00 00 00 00 00 00 00 00   ...............
0C64:0050 CD 21 CB 00 00 00 00 00-00 00 00 00 00 20 20 20   .!...........
0C64:0060 20 20 20 20 20 20 20 20-00 00 00 00 00 20 20 20   .....
0C64:0070 20 20 20 20 20 20 20 20-00 00 00 00 00 00 00 00   ........
```

This is the beginning of COMMAND.COM's psp. We can use it to obtain the segment address of COMMAND.COM's environment block (offset 2CH). Thus, knowing how to get at the mcb's and traverse them allows us access to COMMAND.COM's environment. Any changes in this environment block will be passed on to all programs loaded by COMMAND.COM.

Expanded Memory

Recall from the beginning of this chapter that MS-DOS is constrained to operate with 640 Kbytes of memory. When IBM PCs and PC clones first appeared on the market, 640 Kbytes seemed to be an adequate amount of memory. However, with the rapid expansion of application programs, the 640-Kbyte limitation has become a serious issue.

This limitation has been overcome with the use of *expanded memory* plug-in boards. Expanded memory uses a technique called *bank switching* that allows MS-DOS to reach beyond 640 Kbytes. Expanded memory can provide up to 8 Mbytes of random access memory. All of expanded memory is divided into 16-Kbyte portions called *pages*. At any given time, particular pages can be mapped to 16-Kbyte *page frames* within the standard 640 Kbytes accessible by MS-DOS. By issuing the appropriate control command, the bank of pages mapped to the page frames can be switched, hence the term bank switching.

The first expanded memory model was implemented as a joint effort by Lotus, Intel, and Microsoft. This model, sometimes referred to as EMS or LIM, supports four page frames. Thus, 64 Kbytes of expanded memory may be mapped to regular memory at any given time.

A second expanded memory model was implemented as a joint venture by AST, Quadram, and Ashton-Tate. This model is referred to as AQA or EEMS (for enhanced expanded memory). AQA supports the use of up to 64 page frames (1 Mbyte) at a time. Of course, the use of 64 page frames at any time is impossible because of the overhead required by MS-DOS and the hardware.

Figure 12-3 illustrates the memory addresses that can be used as page frames with EMS and EEMS. As can be seen, EEMS supports all of the addresses usable under EMS. Because of this, software written to run on EMS should be able to run on EEMS.

EMS 4.0

Computer users and software developers have been reluctant to invest heavily in either of the expanded memory formats. The reason for this reluctance is that neither format has emerged as a standard. An investment in one format may turn out to be a decision regretted later on. Fortunately, a new expanded memory specification has emerged that appears to be the standard the industry has been looking for.

Lotus, Intel, and Microsoft have announced a version of expanded memory that they are calling Expanded Memory Specification 4.0. The EMS 4.0 standard is being supported by many software manufacturers, including

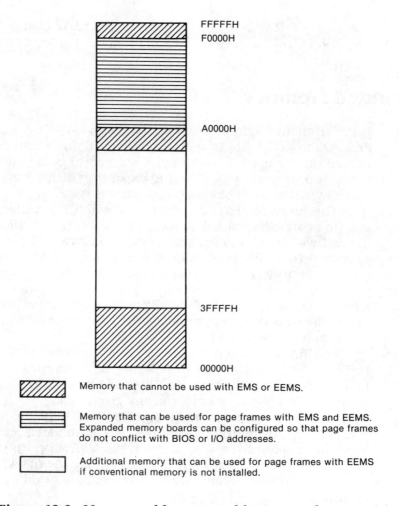

FFFFFH
F0000H

A0000H

3FFFFH

00000H

Memory that cannot be used with EMS or EEMS.

Memory that can be used for page frames with EMS and EEMS.
Expanded memory boards can be configured so that page frames
do not conflict with BIOS or I/O addresses.

Additional memory that can be used for page frames with EEMS
if conventional memory is not installed.

**Figure 12-3. Memory addresses usable as page frames with
EMS and EEMS.**

AST, Ashton-Tate, and Borland. EMS 4.0 supports multitasking (as does
EEMS), and the use of up to 32 megabytes of memory. Terminate and stay
resident programs, device drivers, and interrupt handlers are also well supported by EMS 4.0. In addition, programs written according to EMS 4.0
specifications will run on existing EMS and EEMS boards if the manufacturers of those boards supply new device drivers designed for EMS 4.0. Finally,
EMS 4.0 supports *dynamic linking*, an exciting feature that allows software
developers to write families of programs that can share modules of data and
program code.

The primary attraction of EMS 4.0 is that software developers and computer users should now be confident that an industry-wide solution to the
640-Kbyte constraint is in place. Software developers know that a market
exists for EMS 4.0 software, and users know that the widest selection of

software will be written according to EMS 4.0 specifications. It is hoped that EMS 4.0 will provide a focus for the microcomputer industry similar to that provided by MS-DOS and the IBM PC.

A Note on Extended Memory

Expanded memory must be differentiated from *extended memory*. Extended memory is memory that exists at physical addresses above 1 Mbyte and is directly accessible by 80286 and 80386 computers running in *protected mode*. MS-DOS does not run in protected mode, so extended memory is not available to programs under MS-DOS. However, 80286/80386 computers do allow access to extended memory through their ROM BIOS. Many RAM disk programs running on these machines are able to utilize this feature.

13

Terminate and Stay Resident Programs

TSRs—An Overview

TSRs—Guidelines for a Peaceful Coexistence

POPCLOCK—An Example of a TSR

Programs that remain loaded in memory after their execution terminates are called *terminate and stay resident* (TSRs). There are many types of TSRs, ranging from MS-DOS utilities such as PRINT.COM and APPEND.EXE to the popular "pop-up" utilities such as Sidekick. This chapter discusses the way in which TSRs are constructed. The first section describes, in a very general way, fundamental techniques for keeping a program resident after execution and subsequently accessing the program so that it can be reexecuted. The second section discusses in some detail the important issues that must be addressed when writing a well-behaved TSR. Finally, a working TSR program, "POPCLOCK" (see page 245), is presented and discussed in the third section of the chapter.

The material presented requires an understanding of interrupts and the MS-DOS function calls. Appendix A contains an introductory discussion on interrupts. The MS-DOS interrupts and function calls that are used extensively in this chapter are also discussed in appendix A.

The TSR presented at the end of this chapter is written in assembly language. Some familiarity with assembly language programming will be useful in getting the most out of the program discussion. Those readers with little or no experience with assembly language are referred to the assembly language primer in appendix E.

TSRs—An Overview

TSR programs generally consist of two components. The first component initializes the TSR and instructs MS-DOS on how to reexecute the TSR. This portion of the TSR is executed one time when the program is loaded into memory. The second component of a TSR is the part of the program that is run each time the TSR executes. It is this portion of the TSR that must remain accessible to MS-DOS. The relation between these two components is the topic of the following discussion.

Loading a TSR

When MS-DOS loads a program for execution, the operating system allocates all available memory to the program. Most programs keep all of the memory they are allocated until it is time to terminate execution. These programs then terminate by issuing a call to interrupt 20H or DOS function 4CH, either of which directs MS-DOS to deallocate all of the program's memory and make it available for use by other programs (see figure 13-1).

Just like other programs, TSRs are loaded into memory and allocated all available memory. However, TSRs terminate by issuing a call to DOS function 31H rather than interrupt 20H or DOS function 4CH. Function 31H is used because it allows the TSR to specify an amount of memory that is to remain allocated to the TSR. Prior to calling function 31H, the TSR places in the DX register the size of the memory block it wishes to retain. The size is specified in paragraphs, one paragraph being 16 bytes long. The block retained by the TSR always begins at the start of the program's psp (see figure 13-2).

As an example, let us say that a programmer has written a TSR that is 3200 bytes long. The program needs to keep 200 paragraphs of memory for

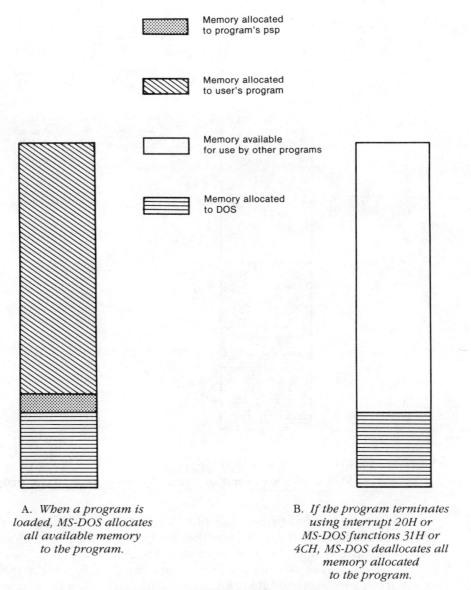

Memory allocated
to program's psp

Memory allocated
to user's program

Memory available
for use by other programs

Memory allocated
to DOS

A. *When a program is
loaded, MS-DOS allocates
all available memory
to the program.*

B. *If the program terminates
using interrupt 20H or
MS-DOS functions 31H or
4CH, MS-DOS deallocates all
memory allocated
to the program.*

**Figure 13-1. The operating system is responsible for allocating and
deallocating memory.**

itself, plus 16 paragraphs for its psp. Therefore, prior to calling function
31H, the program must store a value of 216 in DX. The following code shows
how this is carried out:

```
mov     ah,31h      ;terminate, stay resident function
mov     dx,216      ;paragraphs to remain allocated
int     21h         ;call MS-DOS
```

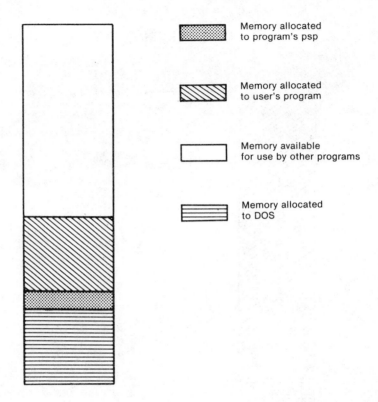

Memory allocated
to program's psp

Memory allocated
to user's program

Memory available
for use by other programs

Memory allocated
to DOS

**Figure 13-2. When a program terminates using MS-DOS function
31H, a block of memory remains allocated to the program.**

The program terminates, but now MS-DOS leaves 216 paragraphs of memory allocated to the TSR. No other programs will use this block of memory as long as it remains allocated to the TSR.

The point in writing a TSR is that once the program is resident in memory, it can be reexecuted repeatedly without having to be reloaded. Therefore, when the TSR is loaded, some type of initialization must occur so that the TSR can subsequently be reexecuted. This initialization typically involves a modification of the interrupt vector table.

Modifying the Interrupt Vector Table

Associated with each interrupt is an *interrupt vector* and an *interrupt handler*. The interrupt handler is program code that is responsible for processing the interrupt request. The handler may be supplied by the operating system, the ROM BIOS, or (as will be described) an application program.

The interrupt vector is a pointer to the interrupt handler. Each interrupt vector is stored in the operating system's *interrupt vector table*. Each entry in the interrupt vector table consists of the segment and offset address of the corresponding interrupt handler.

MS-DOS function 35H is used to obtain an interrupt vector. For example, if a programmer wishes to determine the memory address of the handler for interrupt 9, he or she would use MS-DOS function 35H. Prior to calling the function, an interrupt number is placed in the AL register. On return, ES:BX contains the interrupt vector. The following listing uses DEBUG to demonstrate the use of DOS function 35H:

```
C>debug

-a                           ;start DEBUG assembler
1226:0100 mov ah,35          ;request function 35h
1226:0102 mov al,9           ;return vector for int 9
1226:0104 int 21             ;call MS-DOS
1226:0106      ←press Enter

-g 106                       ;execute, stop at offset 106
AX=3509 BX=E987 CX=0000 DX=0000 SP=FFEE BP=0000 SI=0000 DI=0000
DS=1226 ES=F000 SS=1226 CS=1226 IP=0106  NV UP EI PL NZ NA PO NC

1226:0106 6D       DB        6D
-q

C>
```

On return from the function call, ES:BX contains the vector for interrupt 9.

The interrupt vector table is modified by using MS-DOS function 25H. This function is used by a programmer who writes an interrupt handler to replace the one provided by the operating system or the ROM BIOS. Prior to calling the function, the segment:offset address of the new handler is placed in DS:DX and the corresponding interrupt number is placed in AL. The following code modifies the interrupt table so that the vector for interrupt 9 will point to address 1010:2234:

```
mov ah,25h       ;request function 25h
mov al,9         ;modify vector for int 9
mov ds,1010h     ;segment of new handler
mov dx,2234h     ;offset of new handler
int 21h          ;call MS-DOS
```

During initialization, a TSR uses functions 25H and 35H to establish the conditions under which the TSR is reexecuted. For example, a pop-up TSR may be designed to execute each time that a particular key combination is pressed. The programmer might decide to modify the interrupt vector table so that the entry for interrupt 9 pointed to the TSR. Then each time a key was pressed, the TSR would begin to execute. The TSR would check to see which key combination had been pressed. If the appropriate combination had been pressed, the TSR would pop up. However, if any other key combination were detected, the TSR would pass control to the old interrupt 9 handler and that handler would process the keyboard input in the standard fashion. The following pseudocode shows how this would be carried out:

Initialization:

⋮

—get int 9 vector using function 35H
—save segment address of old handler
—save offset address of old handler
—reset int 9 vector with function 25H
  —on call, DS has segment of new handler
  —on call, DX has offset of new handler
—terminate and stay resident

New Handler:

⋮

—determine key(s) pressed
—if "hotkey" pressed, pop up
—call old handler, using save addresses

⋮

That, in a general sense, is how TSRs operate. Unfortunately, writing a working TSR is much more complicated. Several factors must be considered so that TSRs can peacefully coexist with MS-DOS, with the application program currently being run, and with any other TSRs that might be in memory at the same time. These considerations are discussed next.

TSRs—Guidelines for a Peaceful Coexistence

Writing a TSR is an exercise in circumventing DOS. There are two reasons why this is true. First, MS-DOS was designed to be a *unitasking* operating system. This means that MS-DOS is meant to run one program, throw it away, run another, throw it away, and so on. Asking MS-DOS to supervise more than one program at a time is beyond the operating system's capabilities. The programmer must circumvent this deficiency to get a working TSR.

The second reason why TSRs require a circumvention of MS-DOS is that TSR programmers must utilize features of MS-DOS that are not officially documented by Microsoft or IBM. Utilization of undocumented features is always a risky proposition, but for the time being TSR programmers have no other choice. They must rely on their own wits, as well as the wits of their fellow programmers, in unraveling the features of MS-DOS needed to write properly behaved TSRs. Recently, however, Microsoft, for the first time, published a set of guidelines for TSRs, including official documentation of many of the features presented in this chapter.

Some of the features of MS-DOS presented here remain undocumented, but all are well known and used by most programmers writing TSRs. Therefore, they can be considered reliable until proved otherwise. Unfortunately, it must be added that all undocumented features must be used cautiously and at the programmer's own risk. Since there is no official documentation of what the features do, programmers have nothing to fall back on if the features behave in an unexpected fashion. Programmers must also bear in mind that Microsoft and IBM have repeatedly stated that any or all of the undocumented features of MS-DOS may not be supported in future versions.

With that disclaimer out of the way, let us continue with the discussion of TSRs. There are three areas of consideration that must be addressed by TSR programmers. The first area relates to the manner in which the interrupt vector table is modified. Any modification of the table must utilize a technique called *chaining*. Chaining preserves the integrity of the system that existed prior to modification of the interrupt table.

The second area of consideration for the TSR programmer centers around the problem of *reentry*. Problems with reentry result from MS-DOS's deficiency in preserving its current state when an interrupt occurs. Getting around the reentry problem requires heavy reliance on undocumented MS-DOS features.

The third area of consideration for the TSR programmer involves TSRs' access to files. As will be discussed, TSRs must make special adjustments if they will be accessing files through the use of file handles.

Chaining

Whenever a TSR modifies the interrupt vector table, it is essential that the program "chains" onto the old interrupt handler. *Chaining* is the process by which the new interrupt handler always issues a call to the old interrupt handler. The new handler accomplishes this by using a pointer to the old handler. The pointer is usually saved during initialization of the TSR. Chaining is illustrated in figure 13-3.

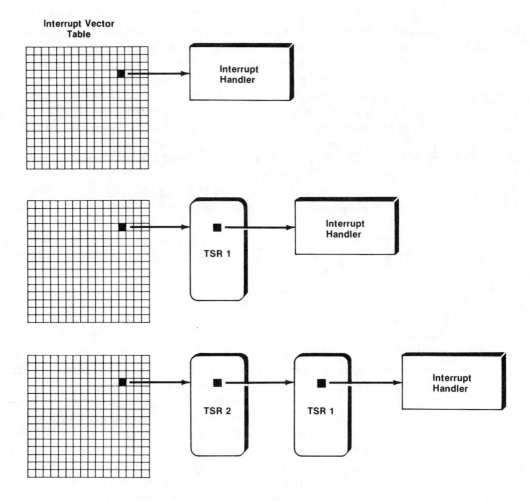

Figure 13-3. Chaining ensures that all handlers are serviced.

Chaining is necessary if TSRs are to coexist with each other. To understand why, consider what would happen if two TSRs were loaded into memory. If both of the TSRs modified the same interrupt vector, then the vector would end up pointing to whichever TSR was loaded into memory last. If this TSR did not chain to the first TSR, the first TSR would never execute. Chaining must be implemented so that TSRs can execute regardless of the loading order.

The Problem of Reentry

Whenever a program issues a DOS function call, the operating system is said to be *entered*. If an interrupt occurs while MS-DOS is entered, and the interrupt handler issues a function call, MS-DOS is said to be *reentered*. Reentry can cause MS-DOS to crash flat on its face. Therefore, precautions must be taken to see that reentry occurs only under certain circumstances. To understand further what reentry is and how it can be controlled, we need to discuss MS-DOS's internal stacks.

The Internal MS-DOS Stacks

MS-DOS maintains three internal stacks that it uses to process function calls. Stack number 1 is used to process requests for DOS function 00H and all DOS functions above and including function 0DH. Stack number 1 is also used to process requests for interrupt 25H (absolute disk read), interrupt 26H (absolute disk write), and interrupt 28H (discussed in the following section).

Stack number 2 is used to process requests for MS-DOS functions 01H through 0CH. In MS-DOS 2.X, stack number 2 is also used by DOS functions 50H (set process id) and 51H (get process id). As you will see later in this chapter, this causes problems for programs running under 2.X.

Stack number 3 is used by MS-DOS while it determines which of the other stacks to use in processing a function request. Stack number 3 is also used to process requests for function 59H (get extended error information). Finally, stack number 3 is used in place of stack number 2 if MS-DOS is called from a critical error handler (more on this later).

MS-DOS has no mechanism for preserving the contents of its internal stacks. Therefore, when MS-DOS is reentered, all three of the internal stacks are vulnerable. If the reentry call utilizes an internal stack that contains information MS-DOS still needs, the operating system will probably crash.

There are two undocumented features that are utilized in dealing with the reentry problem. The first involves reading a counter that is incremented when MS-DOS is entered, and decremented when it is exited. The second undocumented feature is an interrupt that is generated by MS-DOS when it is safe to use two of the internal DOS stacks.

The INDOS Flag

MS-DOS maintains an internal counter that the operating system increments each time MS-DOS is entered, and decrements each time it is exited. This counter has been given many names, but, since the counter is not documented, none of them are official. Most commonly, the counter is called the "INDOS FLAG," even though it is not really a flag (which is either set or clear) but is a counter (which can have any nonnegative value).

TSR programs locate the INDOS flag using (undocumented) DOS function 34H. On return from this call, the ES register contains the flag's segment address, and the BX register contains the flag's offset address. Function 34H should be executed when the TSR is initialized and the flag's address stored in variables local to the TSR. Then, when the TSR is reexecuted, the status of the flag can be determined directly, without using function 34H. This is important because calling function 34H can result in reentry and system failure.

There is some confusion as to the true significance of the INDOS flag. Before we get into the details of using the flag, it is important to recognize its major limitation. Whenever the MS-DOS prompt is displayed, the INDOS flag is nonzero. Therefore, if a TSR program executes only when INDOS equals zero, the program will not function when the MS-DOS prompt is displayed. Some additional way is needed to activate a TSR. The way most commonly used is interrupt 28H.

Interrupt 28H

If the INDOS flag is set, and MS-DOS is processing a call for any of functions 01H through 0CH, interrupt 28H is generated by MS-DOS at a rate of 18.2 times per second. Since functions 01H through 0CH all use DOS stack number 2, interrupt 28H is a signal that it is safe to use stacks 1 and 3.

When a TSR is accessed via interrupt 28H, MS-DOS functions 01H through 0CH cannot be called, since interrupt 28H ensures only that stacks 1 and 3 are safe. In fact, interrupt 28H ensures that stack 2 is not safe, so calling functions 01H through 0CH almost guarantees a crash if the TSR was activated by interrupt 28H.

The problem with using only interrupt 28H for access to the TSR is that many application programs do not issue calls for DOS functions 01H through 0CH. Therefore, interrupt 28H is not generated when these applications are running. Another interrupt must be used to activate the TSR from these applications. The handler for this interrupt must check INDOS before executing the TSR, since nothing is known about the status of the MS-DOS stacks when the interrupt is invoked.

The author's experience with TSRs indicates that any MS-DOS function can be called from a TSR if the INDOS flag equals zero. However, if the TSR is activated by interrupt 28H, the INDOS flag will not equal zero, and the system will probably crash if functions 01H through 0CH are used. Since functions 01H through 0CH can be replaced by ROM BIOS calls, the simplest solution is not to use functions 01H through 0CH in a TSR.

Critical Error

A *critical error* occurs when a peripheral device is needed by MS-DOS but the device is not available. Typical situations causing critical error are open drive doors or printers that are off-line.

When a critical error occurs, MS-DOS sets a *critical error flag* and invokes interrupt 24H. Interrupt 24H is a call to the critical error handler that is responsible for recovering from the critical error. Most users of MS-DOS are familiar with the "Abort, Retry, Fail?" message, which is displayed by the critical error handler when a drive door is left open.

Executing a TSR while a critical error is being processed can cause the system to crash. Therefore, prior to executing a TSR, the status of the critical error flag should be checked. If the flag is clear, then execution can proceed. The address of the critical error flag is obtained by using (undocumented) DOS function 5DH, subfunction 6. On return from the call, ES contains the flag's segment address, and BX contains its offset. This function is demonstrated as part of the program presented at the end of this chapter.

Programmers must also consider how their TSR will handle critical errors. The simplest course is to make no provisions for critical error. In that case, the TSR will rely on the critical error handler for the program that was interrupted by the TSR. Such an arrangement will suffice if a TSR does not perform disk i/o. However, if you are writing a TSR that performs disk i/o, you should consider writing a critical error handler for the TSR. Each time the TSR is activated, change the interrupt 24H vector to point to the new handler. Each time the TSR terminates, change the vector so that it points to the old handler.

File Handles and TSRs

Whenever MS-DOS loads a program into memory, it assigns the program a *process id*. In all cases, the process id is nothing more than the segment address of the program's psp. The current process id is the id of the program currently running. MS-DOS stores this id internally and uses it when a program accesses a file through the use of file handles. Recall from chapter 12 that each program stores a list of file handles in its psp. When MS-DOS receives a request to access a file, the operating system sees which process id is current and looks in the corresponding psp to locate the file handle.

Unfortunately, when a TSR executes, MS-DOS does not change the current process id. The operating system considers the application that was running to be the current one. It is the responsibility of the programmer to make the TSR current. The TSR is made current as follows:

1. MS-DOS function 51H is used to obtain the current id. This is the id of the program that was running when the TSR was invoked. The function returns the id in BX. The id is saved for later use.

   Function 51H is not documented but is implemented in MS-DOS 2.X and 3.X. It is identical to the documented function 62H that is implemented in MS-DOS 3.X.

2. MS-DOS function 50H is used to set the current id equal to the TSR's psp address. Function 50H is another undocumented DOS function. Prior to calling the function, BX is set to equal the psp address. This can be accomplished by pushing CS to the stack and popping BX.

   Once the TSR is made current, it can use the file handles that are stored in its psp.

3. Prior to returning to the application, the TSR uses function 50H to restore the current id to the value it had before executing the TSR.

As we mentioned earlier, functions 50H and 51H use DOS stack number 2 under MS-DOS 2.X. This causes a serious problem, as it groups these two functions with functions 01H through 0CH. If we stick by the guidelines discussed previously, functions 50H and 51H should be avoided in TSRs running under MS-DOS 2.X. Fortunately, there is a way to fool MS-DOS and get around this problem.

When the critical error flag is set, MS-DOS thinks a critical error is being processed. Under these conditions MS-DOS uses stack number 3 in place of stack number 2. Thus, a TSR running under MS-DOS 2.X can set the critical error flag, use functions 50H and 51H, and then clear the critical error flag.

POPCLOCK—An Example of a TSR

POPCLOCK.ASM (listing 13-1) is a TSR program that implements a pop-up clock. Once the program is loaded, the clock will pop up whenever the left and right shift keys are simultaneously depressed. POPCLOCK runs under MS-DOS 2.0 and later versions. POPCLOCK works with monochrome, CGA, and EGA adapters, although the clock will not pop up if the display is in graphics mode.

POPCLOCK is presented to illustrate the points about TSRs that are discussed in this chapter. As you can see from the length of listing 13-1, even simple TSRs such as POPCLOCK tend to be long programs. It is important to recognize, however, that a lot of the code in POPCLOCK is generic, in the sense that it can be used again in other programs. Therefore, once you have the code for one TSR, much of the work for subsequent TSRs is already done.

To make our discussion more manageable, we will divide POP-CLOCK.ASM into four parts and discuss each separately. The four parts are: lines 22–72, lines 73–202, lines 203–483, and lines 484–589.

Lines 22–72 of the listing declare the variables used by the program. These variables will be explained as they are used.

Lines 73–202 make up the new interrupt handlers used by POP-CLOCK. The program uses new handlers for the following interrupts:

Interrupt	Function
8H	Timer
9H	Keyboard hardware
10H	ROM BIOS video service
13H	ROM BIOS disk service
28H	MS-DOS scheduler

Lines 203–483 form the main portion of the TSR. This is the code that is executed each time the clock pops up.

Lines 484–589 make up the initialization portion of POPCLOCK. This section of code executed once at load time and then discarded.

We will discuss the initialization portion of the program first, followed by the handlers, and then the main portion of the TSR.

Initialization

POPCLOCK is executed as a COM file; therefore, the first executable instruction in the program must be at offset 100H. The directive `org 100h` ensures that this is the case. The first instruction (line 20 of the listing) is a jump to `init`. Initialization begins (lines 495–498) by using MS-DOS function 34H to obtain the segment and offset address of the INDOS flag. The address is stored using two variables local to the program.

Next, the address of the critical error flag is obtained using DOS function 5DH, subfunction 6. The offset is saved in local variable `errflag_off`. Notice that it is necessary to restore DS on return from the call. This is because the segment address of the error flag is returned in DS. Saving the segment address is not required, since the critical error flag and the INDOS flag are always located in the same segment (in fact, the critical error flag is sometimes called INDOS2).

Lines 529–574 reset the interrupt vector table. For each of the interrupt vectors modified (8H, 9H, 10H, 13H, and 28H), function 35H is used to retrieve the original vector value, each original value is saved as two variables, and function 25H is then used to reset the vector so that it points to the new handler. Let's walk through the first one to clarify this.

In line 531, a value of 35H is placed in AH and a value of 08H is placed in AL. This indicates a request for MS-DOS function 35H (get interrupt vector) and specifies the vector for interrupt 8H. The segment address contained in the vector is returned in ES, the offset in BX. These values are saved as local variables in lines 533 and 534.

In line 536, a value of 25H is placed in AH and a value of 08H placed in AL. This indicates a request for DOS function 25H (set interrupt vector) and specifies the vector for interrupt 8H. Prior to the call, the offset value for the new vector is placed in DX and the segment value in DS. The procedure `new8_hndlr` (line 76) is the new handler for interrupt 8H. Therefore, we want DX to store the offset of `new8_hndlr` and DS to store the segment. Notice that it is not necessary to place the segment address in DS, since DS already points to the correct segment. On return from the call, `new8_hndlr` is the new handler for interrupt 8H.

The process just described is repeated for the other interrupts used by the TSR. The program then displays a message stating that POPCLOCK is installed (lines 578–580). Notice that in the initialization portion of the program there is no concern about using MS-DOS functions 01H through 0CH. This is because during initialization the TSR owns the show. MS-DOS treats it like any other program. It is only when the TSR reexecutes by way of the modified interrupt table that issues of reentry must be considered.

Once the loaded message is displayed, initialization is complete and the program is ready to terminate but remain resident (lines 582–587). As we mentioned earlier in the chapter, DOS function 31H requires that the amount of memory that is to remain allocated to the program be specified in DX. In order to determine how much memory is required, a dummy variable (line 482) is placed at the end of the portion of the program that is to remain resident. The number of bytes to save is simply the difference between the dummy variable's offset minus the offset of the start of the program. Adding 15 bytes rounds the block up to the next highest paragraph. In line 585, the block size is divided by 16 to give the number of paragraphs to keep. Finally, the AX register is set to request function 31H, and MS-DOS is called. The call now returns control back to MS-DOS, and POPCLOCK is resident in memory. Notice that the initialization portion of the code loses its memory allocation. The program is written this way because the initialization code is not needed after the program is loaded.

The Interrupt Handlers

Once initialization is completed, all of the new interrupt handlers are active. We will now discuss them one at a time, starting with the simplest and working our way up.

Interrupt 10H

The new handler for interrupt 10H is listed in lines 146–152. Recall that int 10H is the ROM BIOS video service. The purpose of the new handler is to set a flag each time int 10H is called. The flag will ensure that the clock does not pop up while a call to the video service is in progress. Such an event, if allowed to occur, could make a mess of the screen.

The new handler also chains to the old handler. This has to be done or the video service requests would not be processed. Before calling the old int 10H handler, the new handler must push the flags register to the stack (line 147). This is necessary because the original int 10H handler thinks it is being called by way of an interrupt rather than a procedure call. Therefore, the final instruction in the original handler is an `iret` rather than a `ret`. Recall that an `iret` instruction pops the segment address, the offset address, and the flags from the stack. If the flags were not pushed, something else would be popped, the stack would be out of sync, and some sort of system failure would no doubt ensue.

After pushing the flags, the handler increments the `video_flag` and then chains to the original handler. On return, the `video_flag` is decremented. The new handler then terminates with an `iret` instruction.

Interrupt 13H

The new handler (lines 157–165) for interrupt 13H (ROM BIOS disk service) is almost identical to the new handler for interrupt 10H. In this case, `disk_flag` is set each time the handler is called. This will ensure that no pop-ups occur while the disk is being accessed. Such an event could confuse the system, and data might be lost in the process.

There are some differences in `new13_hndlr` that should be explained. The original 13H handler sets the flag register according to the outcome of the service request. The new handler is written so that this information can be transmitted back to the original caller. First, notice that the flags are pushed in line 161. This is necessary because the decrement in the next line may affect the flags. After the decrement, the flags are popped and a ret 2 is issued. This instruction tells MS-DOS to return to the caller and discard 2 bytes from the stack. But notice that new13_hndlr is declared as a far procedure. This means that when the ret is issued, MS-DOS pops a segment and offset address from the stack. The 2 bytes thrown away are the flags register, which was pushed when the new int 13H handler was originally called.

Interrupt 9H

Interrupt 9H is an interrupt generated by the hardware each time that a key is pressed or released. The new handler (lines 122–141) chains to the old handler, then uses function 2 of interrupt 16H to determine if the right and left shift keys are depressed. This function reads the byte at address 0000:0417H and stores the value in AL. This byte is set as follows:

If This Key Is Depressed	This Bit Is Set
Insert	7
Caps Lock	6
Num Lock	5
Scroll Lock	4
Alt	3
Ctrl	2
Left Shift	1
Right Shift	0

On return from the call to interrupt 16H, the handler executes and al, 0fh (line 130). This clears all the bits in AH and leaves AL unchanged. The next line compares the value in AL to 3. AL will equal 3 if the right and left shift keys are depressed. This is the signal to pop the clock. If the compare is false, the hot keys have not been pressed, so the handler jumps to the exit (line 133).

If the compare was true, the handler must continue. In line 135 the handler checks the value of running_flag. This flag is set by the main portion of the TSR each time that the clock is popped. The flag is cleared when the TSR exits. Therefore, if running_flag is set (not equal to zero), the clock is already popped and the handler exits. If running_flag is equal to zero, the clock is not currently popped. In this case, the handler sets hotkey equal to 18. The handler then exits (line 140) by an iret. The variable hotkey signals the handlers for interrupts 8H and 28H that the hot key combination has been pressed. The reasons for setting hotkey equal to 18 are discussed next.

Interrupt 8H

Interrupt 8H is the hardware timer interrupt. It is generated by the system's timer chip 18.2 times a second. Once POPCLOCK is loaded into memory, the new handler for interrupt 8H (lines 76–117) is called 18.2 times a second.

The first thing the new handler does is chain to the old handler (lines 77–78). The new handler then checks to see if **hotkey** equals zero. If it does, the handler exits.

If **hotkey** is nonzero, the new handler checks to see if **video_flag** or **disk_flag** are nonzero. Recall that these flags are set and cleared in the new handlers for interrupts 10H and 13H. If either of these flags is nonzero, we do not want to pop the clock. Accordingly, the program will jump to **dec_hkey** (line 114), and **hotkey** is decremented. Therefore, since the handler is called approximately 18 times a second, **hotkey** will remain nonzero for approximately a second if either **video_flag** or **disk_flag** is nonzero.

If both **video_flag** and **disk_flag** equal zero, the handler proceeds to the next step (line 88). The DI and ES register contents are saved, and ES:DI is set to point to the **indos** flag. If **indos** is nonzero, DI and ES are popped, **hotkey** is decremented, and the handler exited.

If **indos** equals zero, the handler proceeds. The next step is to check the critical error flag (lines 100–101). If the flag is nonzero, we do not want to pop the clock. ES and DI are popped, **hotkey** is decremented, and the handler exited.

If the critical error flag equals zero, all is clear to pop the clock. First, ES and DI are popped from the stack (lines 104–105), **hotkey** is set to zero, and **do_it** (the main portion of the TSR) is called.

Interrupt 28H

Interrupt 28H provides the other "hook" into POPCLOCK. The new handler (lines 170–201) is very similar to the new handler for interrupt 8H. The only difference is that this handler does not need to check the **indos** flag. Recall that int 28H is called only when **indos** is set. However, int 28H also indicates that it is safe to use MS-DOS as long as certain precautions are followed (i.e., stay away from DOS functions 01H–0CH).

As should ALWAYS be done, the new int 28 handler chains to the old handler. The flags **hotkey**, **video_flag**, and **disk_flag** are checked as in the int 8H handler. If these flags check out correctly, the critical error flag is checked. If the flag equals zero, all is clear to pop the clock. The **hotkey** flag is set to zero, and **do_it** is called (line 197).

Popping the Clock

The portion of the program that actually displays the clock is the procedure **do_it** (lines 206–480). It is important to bear in mind that when **do_it** gets control, the only registers whose status is known are CS and IP. The other registers, particularly the other segment registers, have the values that were being used when the hot keys were pressed. Before **do_it** can use DS, SS, or ES, the registers must be set appropriately.

The first thing **do_it** does is set **running_flag**. This prevents the int 9H handler from setting **hotkey** while the clock is popped (refer back to lines 135–136).

Next, **do_it** sets up a local stack (lines 211–217). This is necessary to avoid disturbing the MS-DOS stack. The first step in setting up a local stack is disabling the interrupts (line 211). This is important because if an interrupt occurs before both SS and SP have been reset, the system could crash. Once the interrupts are disabled, the values in SS and SP are saved in local variables, SS is set to equal CS (the local segment), and SP is set to point at the top of the local stack. Once the local stack is established, interrupts are enabled (line 217).

The contents of the MS-DOS registers are saved on the local stack (lines 219–227). Next, the ROM BIOS service is used to see if the display is in graphics mode (lines 231–236). If graphics are enabled, the program jumps to line 240, the stack is popped, the MS-DOS stack is reactivated, and the program issues a **ret** which sends control back to either the new int 8H handler or the new int 28H handler. The handlers then issue an **iret** (line 110 or 200), and POPCLOCK is exited.

If the display is not in graphics mode, it is time to display the clock. Lines 259 through 263 save the cursor's position and size so that they can be restored when POPCLOCK exits.

The ROM BIOS Video Services

Since TSRs should avoid DOS functions 01H–0CH, they must rely on the ROM BIOS video services for output to the screen. The ROM BIOS video services are accessed via interrupt 10H. Prior to the call, a function number is placed in AH. This determines which service is provided. The ROM BIOS video services used by POPCLOCK are described here. Appendix A contains additional information on the use of the ROM BIOS interrupts.

Int 10H

AH Value on Call	Function
01H	*Set cursor type*. On the call, the first 4 bits in CH store the cursor's starting line and the first 4 bits in CL store the cursor's ending line.
02H	*Set cursor position*. On the call, BH contains the page number, DH contains the *y* coordinate of the cursor, and DL contains the *x* coordinate of the cursor.

Int 10H (cont'd)

AH Value on Call	Function
03H	***Get cursor position***. On the call, BH contains the page number. On return, CH contains the starting line of the cursor, CL contains the ending line of the cursor, DH contains the cursor's *y* coordinate, and DL contains the cursor's *x* coordinate. Note that the starting and ending line determine the cursor's size, not its position.
07H	***Scroll window down***. On the call, AL contains the number of lines to scroll, BH contains the attribute used for the blanked area, CH contains the upper left *y* coordinate of the window, CL contains the upper left *x* coordinate of the window, DH contains the lower right *y* coordinate of the window, and DL contains the lower right *x* coordinate of the window. If AL equals zero on the call, the entire window is blanked.
08H	***Read attribute and character at cursor***. On the call, BH contains the page number. On return, AH contains the attribute byte and AL contains the ASCII character byte.
09H	***Write character and attribute***. On the call, AL contains the ASCII character byte, BH contains the page number, BL contains the attribute byte, and CX contains the number of times the character is to be written. The character is written at the current position of the cursor. This function does not advance the cursor.
0AH	***Write character only***. On the call, AL contains the ASCII character byte, BH the page number, BL the color byte (if in graphics mode), and CX the number of times the character is to be written.
0FH	***Get display mode***. On return, AH contains the number of character columns on the screen, AL contains the display (0–3 and 7 are text), and BH contains the active page number.

Lines 276–295 use a nested loop to save the contents of the screen that will be covered by the clock. The inner loop is traversed once for each character saved. The outer loop is traversed once for each line saved.

Lines 299–316 create the window. Interrupt 10H, function 07H is called twice to create a window with a border around it. Lines 320–366 display the text contained in lines 62–63 of the listing.

Line 371 calls the procedure **gettime** (lines 449–480), which uses DOS function 2CH to get the current time. DOS function 2CH can be used safely, since it is not in the forbidden range of 01H–0CH.

Lines 368–396 display the time (finally!!), which is stored in the variables listed in lines 64–71.

Lines 394–395 call the keyboard BIOS service to check on the keyboard's status. If no key is pressed, the service returns with the zero flag set. If this is the case, the test at line 396 is true and the time display loop is traversed again. If a key is pressed, the BIOS function returns with the zero flag clear, the test at line 396 is false, and the loop is exited. On exiting from the loop, the character input by the user is discarded so that it will not interfere with whatever program is continued when POPCLOCK terminates.

Lines 401–433 restore the screen in a manner similar to that used in saving the screen's contents. Lines 435–443 restore the cursor to the position and size it had when the clock was popped.

Finally, the jump at line 445 sends execution back to line 240. The MS-DOS registers are restored, and the MS-DOS stack is reestablished. The **ret** at line 255 sends things back to either the int 8H handler or the int 28H. In either case, the handler issues an **iret** and the program continues where it left off when the hot keys were pressed.

Listing 13-1. Pop-up Clock TSR Program

```
 1   ;****************************************************************
 2   ;                    POPCLOCK.ASM
 3   ;
 4   ; A memory-resident program that provides a pop-up clock.
 5   ; DOS 2.0 or later version required.
 6   ; To create an executable version of this program, enter
 7   ; the following commands:
 8   ;        C>masm popclock ;;;
 9   ;        C>link popclock ;;;;
10   ;        C>exe2bin popclock popclock.com
11   ;        C>popclock
12   ;****************************************************************
13
14   cseg     segment          para public 'code'
15
16   assume   cs:cseg
17       org  100h  ;required for COM programs
18
19   begin:
20       jmp  init
21
22   ;****************************************************************
23   ;Declare program variables
24   ;****************************************************************
25   old8_hndlr     label dword      ;old int 8h handler
```

```
26    old8_off       dw           ?
27    old8_seg       dw           ?
28    old9_hndlr     label dword      ;old int 9h handler
29    old9_off       dw           ?
30    old9_seg       dw           ?
31    old10_hndlr    label dword      ;old int 10h handler
32    old10_off      dw           ?
33    old10_seg      dw           ?
34    old13_hndlr    label dword      ;old int 13h handler
35    old13_off      dw           ?
36    old13_seg      dw           ?
37    old28_hndlr    label dword      ;old int 28h handler
38    old28_off      dw           ?
39    old28_seg      dw           ?
40
41    hotkey         db           0    ;greater than 0 if hotkey pressed
42    video_flag     db           0    ;int 10h flag
43    disk_flag      db           0    ;int 13h flag
44    running_flag   db           0    ;equals 1 if program running
45
46
47    indos_off      dw           ?    ;offset of indos flag
48    indos_seg      dw           ?    ;segment of indos flag
49    errflag_off    dw           ?    ;offset of critical error flag
50
51    cur_pos        dw           ?    ;saves cursor's position
52    cur_size       dw           ?    ;saves cursor's size
53    sp_save        dw           ?    ;stores MS-DOS stack pointer
54    ss_save        dw           ?    ;stores MS-DOS SS register
55    screen_buf     dw 174 dup(?)     ;buffer to save screen contents
56
57                   db 255 dup ("#") ;local stack
58    stk_top        db           ("#") ;top of local stack
59
60    load_msg       db "POPCLOCK Installed",0dh,0ah
61                   db "Right & left shift to activate",0dh,0ah,"$"
62    brk_msg        db "Any key to continue"
63    time_msg       db "Current time is "
64    hour10         db           ?      ;store time of day
65    hour           db           ?
66                   db           ":"
67    min10          db           ?
68    min            db           ?
69                   db           ":"
70    sec10          db           ?
71    sec            db           ?
72    dos1_msg       db           "DOS 2.X or 3.X required",0dh,0ah,"$"
73    ;************************************************************
74    ;New handler for int 8h (timer)
75    ;************************************************************
76    new8_hndlr     proc         near
```

```
77          pushf                       ;simulate INT
78          call old8_hndlr             ;chain to old handler
79
80          cmp  hotkey,0               ;hotkey pressed?
81          je   hkey0                  ;if no, exit
82
83          cmp  video_flag,0           ;int 10h busy?
84          jne  dec_hkey               ;if yes, dec. hotkey flag
85          cmp  disk_flag,0            ;int 13h busy?
86          jne  dec_hkey               ;if yes, dec. hotkey flag
87
88          push di                     ;save registers
89          push es
90
91          ;check value of indos flag
92          ;
93          mov  di,indos_off           ;offset of flag
94          mov  es,indos_seg           ;segment of flag
95          cmp  byte ptr es:[di],0
96          jne  pop_stk                ;exit if DOS busy
97
98          ;check critical error flag
99          ;
100         mov  di,errflag_off         ;offset of flag
101         cmp  byte ptr es:[di],0
102         jne  pop_stk                ;exit if flag set
103
104         pop  es                     ;restore registers
105         pop  di
106         mov  hotkey,0               ;clear hotkey flag
107         call do_it                  ;run program
108
109  hkey0:
110         iret
111  pop_stk:
112         pop  es
113         pop  di
114  dec_hkey:
115         dec  hotkey
116         iret                        ;return to MS-DOS
117  new8_hndlr      endp
118
119  ;***************************************************************
120  ;New handler for int 9h (keyboard hardware interrupt)
121  ;***************************************************************
122  new9_hndlr      proc      near
123         sti                         ;enable interrupts
124         pushf                       ;simulate INT
125         call old9_hndlr
126
127         push ax                     ;save ax
```

```
128        mov   ah,2               ;get shift key status
129        int   16h                ;call BIOS keyboard routine
130        and   al,0Fh
131        cmp   al,3                ;right and left shift pressed?
132        pop   ax
133        jne   exit_9             ;if no, exit
134
135        cmp   running_flag,0     ;program already running?
136        jne   exit_9             ;if yes, exit
137
138        mov   hotkey,18          ;hotkey active
139    exit_9:
140        iret                     ;return to MS-DOS
141    new9_hndlr     endp
142
143    ;****************************************************************
144    ;New handler for int 10h (ROM BIOS video service)
145    ;****************************************************************
146    new10_hndlr    proc      near
147        pushf                    ;simulate INT
148        inc   video_flag
149        call  old10_hndlr
150        dec   video_flag
151        iret
152    new10_hndlr    endp
153
154    ;****************************************************************
155    ;New handler for int 13h (ROM BIOS disk service)
156    ;****************************************************************
157    new13_hndlr    proc      far
158        pushf                    ;simulate INT
159        inc   disk_flag
160        call  old13_hndlr
161        pushf                    ;protect flags
162        dec   disk_flag
163        popf                     ;restore flags
164        ret   2                  ;return to MS-DOS; discard 2 bytes
165    new13_hndlr    endp
166
167    ;****************************************************************
168    ;New handler for int 28h (DOS scheduler)
169    ;****************************************************************
170    new28_hndlr    proc      near
171        pushf                    ;simulate INT
172        call old28_hndlr         ;chain to old handler
173
174
175        cmp   hotkey,0           ;hotkey pressed?
176        je    exit28             ;if no, exit
177
178        cmp   video_flag,0       ;int 10h busy?
```

```
179        jne   exit28              ;if yes, exit
180        cmp   disk_flag,0         ;int 13h busy?
181        jne   exit28              ;if yes, exit
182
183        push di                   ;save registers
184        push es
185
186
187        ;check critical error flag
188        ;
189        mov   es,indos_seg
190        mov   di,errflag_off       ;offset of flag
191        cmp   byte ptr es:[di],0
192        pop   es                   ;restore registers
193        pop   di
194        jne   exit28
195
196        mov   hotkey,0             ;clear hotkey flag
197        call  do_it                ;run program
198
199   exit28:
200        iret                       ;return to MS-DOS
201   new28_hndlr      endp
202
203   ;****************************************************************
204   ;DO_IT -- Main portion of POPCLOCK
205   ;****************************************************************
206   do_it   proc  near
207        mov   running_flag,1        ;set running flag
208
209      ;Set up local stack and save DOS registers
210          ;
211          cli                       ;disable interrupts
212          mov   sp_save,sp          ;save MS-DOS stack pointer
213          mov   ss_save,ss          ;save MS-DOS SS register
214          push cs
215          pop   ss                  ;local stack segment
216          mov   sp,offset stk_top   ;top of local stack
217          sti                       ;enable interrupts
218
219          push ax                   ;save MS-DOS registers
220          push bx                   ;on local stack
221          push cx
222          push dx
223          push si
224          push di
225          push ds
226          push es
227          push bp
228
229      ;Check display mode, exit if in graphics mode
```

```
230        ;
231            mov   ah,0Fh              ;get display mode function
232            int   10h                 ;call BIOS video service
233            cmp   al,3
234            jbe   get_cursor
235            cmp   al,7
236            je    get_cursor
237
238        ;Restore DOS stack and return to caller
239        ;
240   exit: pop   bp
241            pop   es
242            pop   ds
243            pop   di
244            pop   si
245            pop   dx
246            pop   cx
247            pop   bx
248            pop   ax
249
250            cli
251            mov   ss,ss_save
252            mov   sp,sp_save
253            sti
254            mov   running_flag,0       ;clear flag
255            ret                        ;return to caller
256
257        ;In text mode so continue
258        ;
259   get_cursor:
260            mov   ah,03                ;get cursor position, BH has page
261            int   10h                  ;call BIOS
262            mov   cur_pos,dx            ;save cursor's position
263            mov   cur_size,cx          ;save cursor's size
264
265        ;Save contents of window
266        ;
267            mov   ah,02                ;set cursor position
268            mov   dl,17                ;upper left of window
269            mov   dh,6
270            int   10h
271
272            push  cs
273            pop   es                   ;make es local
274            mov   di,offset screen_buf
275            mov   cx,6                  ;save 6 rows
276   loop1:
277            push  cx
278            mov   cx,29                 ;save 29 columns
279   loop2:
280            cld                         ;clear direction flag
```

```
281         mov   ah,8              ;read attribute and character
282         int   10h
283         stosw                   ;store in buffer
284
285         inc   dl                ;move cursor to next column
286         mov   ah,02
287         int   10h
288         loop  loop2             ;save next character
289
290         mov   dl,17             ;move cursor to start
291         inc   dh                ;of next row
292         mov   ah,02
293         int   10h
294         pop   cx
295         loop  loop1             ;save next row
296
297     ;make window border
298         ;
299         push  bx                ;save page number
300         mov   ax,0700h          ;blank a window
301         mov   bh,70h            ;reverse attribute
302         mov   ch,6              ;upper left y coordinate
303         mov   cl,17             ;upper left x coordinate
304         mov   dh,10             ;lower right y coordinate
305         mov   dl,45             ;lower right x coordinate
306         int   10h               ;call ROM video service
307
308     ;clear window interior
309         ;
310         mov   ax,0700h          ;blank a window
311         mov   bh,07h            ;normal attribute
312         mov   ch,7              ;upper left y coordinate
313         mov   cl,18             ;upper left x coordinate
314         mov   dh,9              ;lower right y coordinate
315         mov   dl,44             ;lower right x coordinate
316         int   10h               ;call ROM video service
317
318
319     ;display window contents
320         ;
321         pop   bx                ;restore page number
322         mov   ah,02             ;position cursor
323         mov   dh,10
324         mov   dl,21
325         int   10h
326
327         mov   ah,01h            ;turn cursor off
328         mov   cx,1000h
329         int   10h
330
331         push  cs
```

```
332        pop   ds                    ;make ds local
333        mov   si,offset brk_msg     ;quit prompt
334        mov   cx,19                 ;display 19 characters
335        cld                         ;forward direction
336    winloop1:
337        lodsb                       ;byte to AL
338        mov   ah,0ah                ;write character only
339        push  cx                    ;save loop counter
340        mov   cx,1                  ;output 1 time
341        int   10h
342
343        pop   cx                    ;restore loop counter
344        inc   dl
345        mov   ah,02                 ;advance cursor
346        int   10h
347        loop  winloop1              ;display another character
348
349        mov   ah,02                 ;position cursor
350        mov   dh,8
351        mov   dl,19
352        int   10h
353
354        mov   cx,16                 ;display 16 characters
355    winloop2:
356        lodsb                       ;byte to AL
357        mov   ah,0ah                ;write character only
358        push  cx                    ;save loop counter
359        mov   cx,1                  ;output 1 time
360        int   10h
361
362        pop   cx                    ;restore loop counter
363        inc   dl
364        mov   ah,02                 ;advance cursor
365        int   10h
366        loop  winloop2              ;display another character
367
368    ;display time until key pressed
369        ;
370    timeloop1:
371        call  gettime               ;get current time
372
373        mov   ah,02                 ;position cursor
374        mov   dh,8
375        mov   dl,35
376        int   10h
377
378        mov   si,offset hour10
379        mov   cx,8                  ;8 characters to display
380
381    timeloop2:
382        lodsb                       ;byte to AL
```

```
383         mov   ah,0ah                ;write character only
384         push  cx                    ;save loop counter
385         mov   cx,1                  ;output 1 time
386         int   10h
387
388         pop   cx                    ;restore loop counter
389         inc   dl
390         mov   ah,02                 ;advance cursor
391         int   10h
392         loop  timeloop2
393
394         mov   ah,01                 ;check input status
395         int   16h
396         jz    timeloop1             ;loop if no key pressed
397
398         mov   ah,00
399         int   16h                   ;throw away input
400
401    ;restore screen and exit
402         ;
403         mov   ah,02                 ;set cursor position
404         mov   dl,17                 ;upper left of window
405         mov   dh,6
406         int   10h
407
408         mov   si,offset screen_buf  ;start of stored display
409         mov   cx,6                  ;restore 6 rows
410    loop11:
411         push  cx                    ;save outer loop counter
412         mov   cx,29                 ;restore 29 columns
413    loop12:
414         cld                         ;clear direction flag
415         lodsw                       ;get character/attribute
416         mov   bl,ah                 ;attribute byte
417         mov   ah,9                  ;write character and attribute
418         push  cx                    ;save inner loop counter
419         mov   cx,1                  ;write one time
420         int   10h                   ;call BIOS
421         pop   cx                    ;restore inner loop counter
422
423         inc   dl                    ;move cursor to next column
424         mov   ah,02
425         int   10h
426         loop  loop12                ;save next character
427
428         mov   dl,17                 ;move cursor to start
429         inc   dh                    ;of next row
430         mov   ah,02
431         int   10h
432         pop   cx                    ;restore outer loop counter
433         loop  loop11                ;save next row
```

\

```
434
435      ;restore cursor to its size and position prior to call
436          ;
437          mov   ah,1                  ;restore size
438          mov   cx,cur_size
439          int   10h
440
441          mov   ah,2                  ;restore position
442          mov   dx,cur_pos
443          int   10h
444
445          jmp   exit
446
447      do_it    endp                   ;end of main procedure
448
449      gettime  proc  near
450
451          mov   ah,2ch                ;get time function
452          int   21h                   ;call MS-DOS
453
454      ;hours returned in ch, minutes in cl, and seconds in dh
455      ;convert these to ascii values and store
456          ;
457          mov   bl,10
458
459          xor   ah,ah
460          mov   al,ch                  ;hours
461          div   bl
462          or    ax,3030h
463          mov   hour10,al
464          mov   hour,ah
465
466          xor   ah,ah                  ;minutes
467          mov   al,cl
468          div   bl
469          or    ax,3030h
470          mov   min10,al
471          mov   min,ah
472
473          xor   ah,ah                  ;seconds
474          mov   al,dh
475          div   bl
476          or    ax,3030h
477          mov   sec10,al
478          mov   sec,ah
479          ret
480      gettime  endp
481
482      last_byte     db      "$"
483
484      ;****************************************************************
```

```
485     ;INITIALIZE -- Initializes POPCLOCK
486     ;************************************************************
487     initialize      proc      near
488     assume   ds:cseg                ;variables in this segment
489
490
491
492
493     ;locate indos flag
494         ;
495     init:   mov   ah,34h
496         int   21h
497         mov   indos_off,bx          ;offset address of flag
498         mov   indos_seg,es          ;segment address of flag
499
500
501     ;locate critical error flag
502         ;
503         mov   ah,30h                ;get MS-DOS version
504         int   21h
505         cmp   al,2
506         jg    call5d                ;function 5dh implemented in 3.X
507         je    calc                  ;MS-DOS 2.X, so calculate address
508     ;exit if DOS 1.X running
509         ;
510         mov   dx,offset dos1_msg
511         mov   ah,9
512         int   21h
513         int   20h                   ;return to MS-DOS
514     ;must be running 2.X so compute error flag's address
515         ;
516     calc:   mov   si,bx             ;bx has indos flag
517         inc   si
518         jmp   save_it
519     ;locate error flag using 3.X function 5dh
520         ;
521     call5d:  mov   ah,5dh           ;MS-DOS error function
522         mov   al,6                  ;return flag address
523         int   21h                   ;call MS-DOS
524     save_it: push  cs
525         pop   ds                    ;reset ds
526         mov   errflag_off,si
527
528
529     ;Insert new handlers into interrupt chains
530         ;
531         mov   ax,3508h              ;get int 8h vector
532         int   21h
533         mov   old8_off,bx           ;save it
534         mov   old8_seg,es
535
```

```
536        mov   ax,2508h             ;set vector function
537        mov   dx,offset new8_hndlr
538        int   21h
539
540        mov   ax,3509h             ;get int 09h vector
541        int   21h
542        mov   old9_off,bx          ;save it
543        mov   old9_seg,es
544
545        mov   ax,2509h             ;set vector function
546        mov   dx,offset new9_hndlr
547        int   21h
548
549        mov   ax,3510h             ;get int 10h vector
550        int   21h
551        mov   old10_off,bx         ;save it
552        mov   old10_seg,es
553
554        mov   ax,2510h             ;set vector function
555        mov   dx,offset new10_hndlr
556        int   21h
557
558        mov   ax,3513h             ;get int 13h vector
559        int   21h
560        mov   old13_off,bx         ;save it
561        mov   old13_seg,es
562
563        mov   ax,2513h             ;set vector function
564        mov   dx,offset new13_hndlr
565        int   21h
566
567        mov   ax,3528h             ;get int 28h vector
568        int   21h
569        mov   old28_off,bx         ;save it
570        mov   old28_seg,es
571
572        mov   ax,2528h             ;set vector function
573        mov   dx,offset new28_hndlr
574        int   21h
575
576   ;Display message then terminate but stay resident
577        ;
578        mov   dx,offset load_msg
579        mov   ah,09h
580        int   21h
581
582        ;amount of memory to retain in dx
583        mov   dx,(offset last_byte - offset cseg + 15)
584        mov   cl,4
585        shr   dx,cl                ;convert to paragraphs
586        mov   ax,3100h             ;TSR function
```

```
587          int  21h                    ;call MS-DOS
588
589   initialize      endp
590   ;
591   cseg    ends
592        end  begin                     ;end of program
```

14

MS-DOS Device Drivers

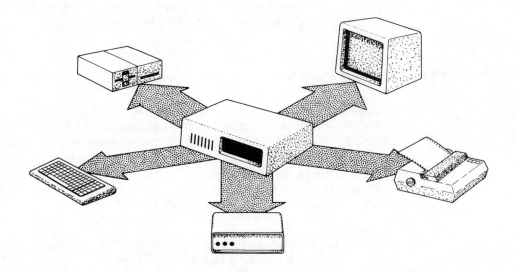

Using Device Drivers   **Function of Device Drivers**
Structure of Device Drivers   **Device Commands**

The two essential hardware elements of a computer are the central processing unit (CPU) and computer memory. All the other hardware components
(disk drives, keyboards, video displays, printers, modems, etc.) are considered external to the computer. These external components are called *peripheral devices,* or simply *devices.*

Communication between a peripheral device and the computer must
be carried out according to strict guidelines determined by the computer
and the particular peripheral device. For each peripheral device in a system,

there is a computer program responsible for regulating the communication between that device and the computer. These computer programs are called *device drivers* (figure 14-1). This chapter will discuss MS-DOS device drivers. The major portion of the discussion will center around *installable device drivers*.

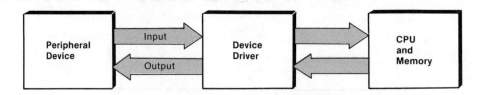

Figure 14-1. The device driver controls communication between the peripheral device and the computer.

Using Device Drivers

One of the primary roles of an operating system is to provide a set of device drivers that can be utilized by computer programs. MS-DOS provides device drivers that can be used by any program written to execute under MS-DOS. When a program running under MS-DOS needs to communicate with a peripheral device, the program tells MS-DOS which device it wants to communicate with and MS-DOS locates the proper device driver. Table 14-1 lists the standard device drivers provided with MS-DOS.

Table 14-1. Standard Peripheral Devices Supported by MS-DOS Device Drivers

Peripheral Device	Device Type*	Device Name
Console (keyboard/screen)	C	CON:
First asynchronous communications port	C	AUX: or COM1:
Second asynchronous communications port	C	COM2:
First parallel printer	C	PRN: or LPT1:
Second parallel printer	C	LPT2:
Dummy device	C	NUL:
Floppy diskette drive	B	—
Fixed disk drive	B	—

*C = character device   B = block device

Character and Block Devices

Character devices send and receive data in a serial fashion, one character at a time. Character devices include the serial and parallel ports, the keyboard, and the display screen. Every character device is assigned a *device name*. MS-DOS reserves particular names for certain character devices. These reserved names are listed in the right-hand column of table 14-1. Each character device driver controls one peripheral device.

Block devices send and receive data in blocks. Generally each block consists of 512 bytes. Block devices include floppy diskette drives, fixed disk drives, and other mass storage devices. Block devices do not have specific names, rather they are referenced by drive designator letters (A, B, C, etc.). A single block device driver may control more than one peripheral device.

Adding a New Device

Prior to MS-DOS 2.0, there was no standardized way of adding a new device driver to the operating system. Manufacturers of peripheral devices were forced to modify the PC's BIOS (basic input output system) in order to incorporate their drivers. The problem with this approach was that modifications were often not compatible with each other. MS-DOS 2.0 changed all that with the introduction of installable device drivers.

Installable device drivers are stored as files. The drivers are installed in memory through the use of a text file named CONFIG.SYS. CONFIG.SYS is created by the user and stored in the root directory of the disk used to boot the system. Device drivers are installed by placing the following type of statement in CONFIG.SYS:

device=[*d:*][*path*]*filename*

During booting, MS-DOS checks to see if there is a CONFIG.SYS file. If there is, MS-DOS installs the specified device driver(s).

Chapter 8 discusses the installation and use of ANSI.SYS, an installable console device driver that provides enhanced capabilities for the keyboard and display screen. In the remainder of this chapter, we will take a detailed look at the structure and function of device drivers. The material presented is not required for users of MS-DOS. Some familiarity with assembly language programming will be useful in following the text.

Structure of Device Drivers

MS-DOS *device drivers* are computer programs that are generally written in assembly language. Device drivers consist of three parts: a *device header*, a *strategy routine*, and an *interrupt routine*.

Device Header

The device header (figure 14-2) is an 18-byte-long data structure located at the beginning of each device driver. The device header is made up of five fields: the next header pointer, the device attribute field, the strategy routine, the interrupt routine, and the device name.

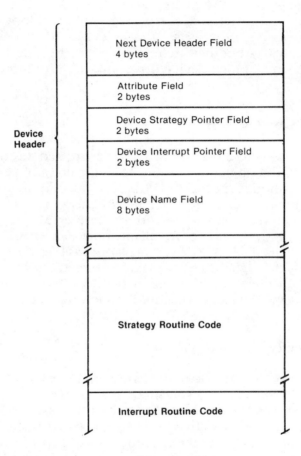

Figure 14-2. Structure of MS-DOS device driver.

Next Header Pointer

The first field of the device header consists of 4 bytes that store the segment and offset addresses of the *next device header*. As we will describe, MS-DOS creates a linked list of the drivers configured into the system. This first field serves as a pointer to the device header of the next driver in the linked list (figure 14-3). The programmer sets the value of this field to −1 (4 bytes of FFH), and MS-DOS inserts the appropriate pointer values as it constructs the

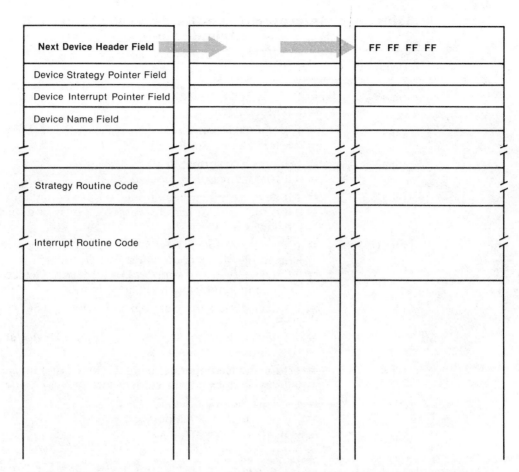

**Figure 14-3. MS-DOS sets the next device header field to contain
the segment and offset addresses of the next device header.**

linked list. The field retains a value of −1 in the header of the last driver in
the linked list.

Device Attribute Field

The second field in the device header consists of 2 bytes that store the *device
attribute* field. The bit pattern of this field is set by the programmer to contain
descriptive information about the device controlled by the driver (table 14-2).
The commands mentioned in table 14-2 are discussed later in this chapter.

Strategy Routine

The third field in the device header stores a 2-byte pointer to the driver's
strategy routine. The value in this field is set by the programmer according
to the strategy routine's location within the driver. The strategy routine is
discussed later in this chapter.

Table 14-2. Interpretation of Bit Patterns of Device Header Attribute Field

Bit Number	Meaning
bit 15	= 1 if character device = 0 if block device
bit 14	= 1 if IOCTL is supported = 0 if IOCTL not supported
bit 13	= 1 if non-IBM format disk = 0 if IBM format disk (block devices)
bit 12	= 1 if device can handle Output Til Busy command = 0 if device cannot handle Output Til Busy command (character devices)
bit 11	= 1 if device supports Device Open, Device Close, and Removable Media commands = 0 if device does not support Device Open, Device Close, and Removable Media commands
bit 6	= 1 if device supports Get Logical Device and Set Logical Device commands = 0 if device does not support Get Logical Device and Set Logical Device commands
bit 4	= 1 if the device implements int 29H for fast console i/o = 0 if device does not implement int 29H
bit 3	= 1 if current clock device = 0 if not current clock device
bit 2	= 1 if current NUL device = 0 if not current NUL device
bit 1	= 1 if current standard output device = 0 if not current standard output device
bit 0	= 1 if current standard input device = 0 if not current standard input device

Interrupt Routine

The fourth field in the device header stores a 2-byte pointer to the driver's *interrupt routine*. The value in this field is set by the programmer according to the interrupt routine's location within the driver. The interrupt routine is discussed later in this chapter.

Device Name

The fifth field in the device header is the *device name* field. In character device drivers, this field stores the name assigned by the programmer to the device. The field is padded with blanks if the name is less than 8 characters long. A name cannot be used as both a device name and a filename. In block device drivers (which do not have device names), this field is set by the programmer to specify the number of units controlled by the driver.

Function of Device Drivers

The following paragraphs cover the installation, location, and calling of device drivers. The fields of the *request header*—a data structure serving MS-DOS and the device driver—are explained. The section ends with an assembly language program that can be expanded to form a functional device driver.

Installation

As part of the booting process, MS-DOS installs the standard (resident) device drivers, which are stored in the IO.SYS system file. Recall that MS-DOS connects the drivers via a linked list. The driver for the NUL device (the "bit-bucket") is always the first driver on the list (figure 14-4). After the resident drivers are installed, MS-DOS places in memory any installable device drivers. The installable drivers are inserted into the linked list immediately after the NUL driver (figure 14-5). All of the resident drivers remain in the linked list, downstream from the installable drivers.

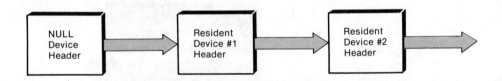

Figure 14-4. Driver chain with resident drivers only.

Locating a Driver

When a computer program requests the use of a peripheral device, the program issues a call to the appropriate MS-DOS function. MS-DOS searches the linked list of drivers, starting with the NUL driver, until it locates a driver with a name field corresponding to the one supplied by the program. MS-DOS always stops at the first match. Therefore, if the linked list contains more than one driver for a particular device, MS-DOS uses the one located closest to the front of the linked list.

Once MS-DOS locates the appropriate driver, the driver must be informed of the type of service required (read, write, status check, etc.). This information is sent to the driver in the form of a *driver command*. There are

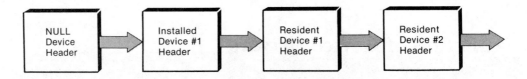

Figure 14-5. Driver chain with one installed driver.

20 valid driver commands, each of which is assigned a unique 1-byte command code. The driver commands are discussed at the end of this chapter.

Request Header

In response to the request issued by the program, MS-DOS places a command code in a data structure called the *request header*. The request header (figure 14-6) serves as the communication area between MS-DOS and the device driver.

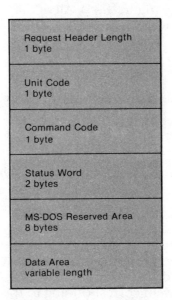

Figure 14-6. Structure of MS-DOS request header.

The first field in the request header is a single byte that stores the length of the request header. As we will discuss, the length of the request header is determined by the command code issued by MS-DOS.

The second field of the request header is a single byte that stores the *unit code.* The unit code is valid for block devices only and identifies the particular device requested. For example, if the system has two disk drives controlled by the same driver, the unit code is used to determine which drive is accessed.

The third field of the request header stores the 1-byte command code.

The fourth field of the request header stores a 2-byte *status word.* The bit pattern of this field is set by the driver to communicate information back to MS-DOS. Bit 15 of the status word is set if the driver encounters an error. Bit 9 is set to indicate a response of "busy" to a status request (command code 6). Bit 8 is set by the driver if processing required for the command code has been completed. The low-order byte (bits 0 through 7) is set to indicate the nature of any error (table 14-3).

Table 14-3. Error Codes Returned in the Low-Order Byte of Status Word

Error Code	Meaning
00	Write-protect violation
01	Unknown unit
02	Device not ready
03	Unknown command
04	CRC error
05	Bad drive request structure length
06	Seek error
07	Unknown media
08	Sector not found
09	Printer out of paper
0A	Write fault
0B	Read fault
0C	General fault
0F	Invalid disk change (MS-DOS 3.X only)

The fifth field in the request header is an 8-byte block that is reserved by MS-DOS and not available for use.

The sixth field of the request header is called the *data area.* The format and the length of the data area are dependent on the command code. As we will see, each command code has a specific set of parameters that must be set by the driver. When control passes from the driver back to MS-DOS, MS-DOS expects to find these parameters at specific locations within the request header's data area.

It is important to understand that identification of the appropriate device, selection of the command code, and initialization of the request header is performed by MS-DOS in response to a function request. The programmer of the device driver need not be concerned with how MS-DOS performs these tasks. Once MS-DOS actually calls the driver, the driver is in control, and the programmer's code goes into action.

Calling the Driver

Once a request header has been properly initialized by MS-DOS, the operating system sets the ES and BX registers to point to the segment and offset addresses of the request header (segment and offset addressing is discussed in chapter 9). MS-DOS then issues a call to the driver's strategy routine.

The only function of the strategy routine is to save the segment and offset addresses of the request header in two local variables. It is the programmer's responsibility to define these variables within the driver and see that they are initialized when the driver is called. The strategy routine then passes control back to MS-DOS, which immediately calls the driver's interrupt routine.

The interrupt routine is the heart of the device driver. The first portion of the interrupt routine consists of a look-up table, constructed by the programmer, which tells the routine where to jump, according to the command code passed in the request header.

In responding to the MS-DOS request, the interrupt routine reads the command code, performs the table look-up, and passes control to the procedure that processes the particular command code. The procedure then processes the command using the fields of the request header to store information regarding the outcome of the request.

When the interrupt routine completes its work, control is returned to MS-DOS. MS-DOS determines the results of the request by inspecting the contents of the request header. MS-DOS, in turn, passes these results back to the program that initially requested access to the peripheral device.

Listing 14-1 contains an assembly language skeleton of an MS-DOS device driver. The listing can be expanded to form a functional device driver.

Listing 14-1. Skeleton for an MS-DOS Device Driver

```
;                    Device Driver Skeleton
;
code_seg          segment  para     public  'code'
skeleton          proc     far
                  assume   cs:code_seg,es:code_seg,ds:code_seg
;
begin:
;
;Device Header
next_dev          dd       -1                ;segment:offset of next header
```

```
attrib_field    dw      8000h           ;character device
strat_ptr       dw      strategy        ;offset of strategy routine
int_ptr         dw      interrupt       ;offset of interrupt routine
name            db      'DEMO    '       ;name of driver
;
;
;Variable size area for use by driver. Store address of request
;header here.
rheader_off     dw      ?
rheader_seg     dw      ?
;
;This area can be used for other purposes as is necessary.
;
;Strategy routine                       ;called first by MS-DOS
strategy:
        mov     cs:rheader_off,bx       ;save address of request
                                        ;header
        mov     cs:rheader_seg,es
        ret                             ;return to MS-DOS
;
;
;Interrupt routine
interrupt:
        push    ds                      ;save MS-DOS registers
        push    es
        push    ax
        push    bx
        push    cx
        push    dx
        push    si
        push    di
;retrieve command code from request header
        mov     al,es:[bx+2]
;
;On the basis of the command code, which is now in al,
;branch to the appropriate routine and process the command.
;This area forms the meat, not the skeleton, of the driver. It
;can be coded as the programmer sees fit, as long as the
;requirements for each command code are met.
;
;
;After command is processed, exit the driver
        mov     es:word ptr [bx+3],0100h    ;set done bit in

                                            ;request header's
```

```
                                                     ;status word

          pop       di                    ;restore MS-DOS stack
          pop       si
          pop       dx
          pop       cx
          pop       bx
          pop       ax
          pop       es
          pop       ds
          ret;                            ;return to MS-DOS
;
;end of device driver
skeleton          endp
code_seg          ends
                  end       begin
```

Device Commands

There are twenty command codes that a device driver may be called upon to process. This section discusses each command and lists the specific tasks to be executed for that command. Also listed are the fields of the request header's data area that must be read by the driver (on the call from MS-DOS) and set by the driver (on the return to MS-DOS).

Note: For all commands, the driver reads the request header length, the unit code (block devices only), and the command code. Also, for all commands, the driver sets the status word. Refer back to figure 14-6.

INIT (Command Code 0)

This command is invoked only at boot time when MS-DOS installs the driver. INIT performs any initialization of the device that is necessary. Of all the driver commands, only INIT may call the MS-DOS functions. INIT may use functions 01H through 0CH and function 30H only.

The driver must perform the following tasks:

1. Set the number of units controlled by the driver. This task is required for block device drivers only. This number overrides the first byte in the device name field of the device header.

2. Determine the break address. This address marks the end of the portion of the driver that remains resident in memory following execution of INIT. Since INIT is used only one time, many programmers place the code for INIT at the end of the driver. Then the portion of memory storing INIT can be released to MS-DOS following device initialization.

3. Set up a pointer to the BIOS parameter block (BPB) table. For each block device, INIT must set up in memory a BPB (see command code

2) for each type of media that can be used with the device. The BPB table contains pointers to the BPBs for a particular device. INIT returns the segment:offset pointer to the BPB table in the request header's data area.

4. Set the status word in the request header.

The driver may read the following fields in the data area:

Request Header Offset	Description
18–21	Offset and segment addresses of first character after "=" in CONFIG.SYS statement that loaded the driver. The remainder of the command string may be read by the driver.
22	First available drive (0 = A, etc., MS-DOS 3+ only).

The driver must set the following fields in the data area:

Request Header Offset	Description
13	Number of units controlled by driver.
14–15	Offset address of break.
16–17	Segment address of break.
18–19	Offset address of BPB table.
20–21	Segment address of BPB table.

MEDIA CHECK (Command Code 1)

This command is valid for block devices only. Character drivers should set only bit 8 ("done") in the request header's status word. The command is issued to determine if the disk media on a drive has been changed. MS-DOS issues this command before performing any disk read or write. The driver must return one of three values:

−1 Media changed.
 0 Don't know if media changed.
 1 Media not changed.

For hard disks and RAM disks, the media cannot be changed, so the driver can be written to always return a "Media not changed" signal. This signal allows MS-DOS to access the disk without reading the file allocation table (since the FAT is in memory from the previous disk access).

Since there is no foolproof way to determine if a floppy disk has been changed, it is reasonable for drivers of devices having removable media to always return a "Don't know" signal. The manner in which MS-DOS handles a "Don't know" signal depends on the state of the drive's file buffers. If the buffers contain data that need to be written out ("dirty" data), MS-DOS will assume that no disk change occurred and will write the data. This action risks damaging the file structure of a new disk if there has been a disk swap. If the buffers do not contain dirty data, MS-DOS assumes that the media has been changed. In this case, MS-DOS invalidates the contents of any buffers associated with the drive, issues a BUILD BPB command (driver command code 2) to the driver, and reads the disk's FAT and file directory.

The driver must perform the following tasks:

1. Report the results of the media check.
2. Set the status word in the request header.

The driver may read the following fields in the data area:

Request Header Offset	Description
13	Media descriptor byte from disk's boot sector (the boot record is discussed in chapter 12).

The driver must set the following fields in the data area:

Request Header Offset	Description
14	Results of the media status check.
15–16	Offset address of the disk's volume label (MS-DOS 3+).
17–18	Segment address of disk's volume label (MS-DOS 3+).

BUILD BPB (Command Code 2)

This command is valid for block devices only. Character drivers only need set bit 8 ("done") of the request header's status word. BUILD BPB is called when MEDIA CHECK (driver command code 1) returns a "media changed" or "don't know" signal. The driver is responsible for locating the disk's boot sector, reading into memory the BIOS parameter block (BPB, see table 14-4), and returning to MS-DOS a pointer to the BPB. Under MS-DOS 3+, the driver should also store the disk's volume id label in memory.

The driver must perform the following tasks:

1. Read the new BPB into memory.
2. Return to MS-DOS a pointer to the new BPB.
3. Read the disk's volume id label into memory (MS-DOS 3+).
4. Set the status word in the request header.

**Table 14-4. Parameters Defined in the BPB, Their Lengths
and Offset Locations in the Boot Sector of the Device Media**

Parameter	Length	Offset
Bytes per sector	Word	11–12
Sectors per allocation unit	Byte	13
Reserved sectors	Word	14–15
Number of FATs	Byte	16
Number of root directory entries	Word	17–18
Total sectors on media	Word	19–20
Media descriptor	Byte	21
Number of sectors occupied by a single FAT	Word	22–23

The driver may read the following fields in the data area:

Request Header Offset	Description
13	Media descriptor byte.
14–17	If the non-IBM format bit (bit 13) of the device header attribute field is 0, these 4 bytes store the offset and segment addresses of a buffer that holds the first sector of the disk's file allocation table (the first byte of which is the disk's media descriptor). If bit 13 of the attribute field is 1, the buffer may be used as a work area by the driver.

The driver must set the following fields in the data area:

Request Header Offset	Description
18–19	Offset address of the new BPB.
20–21	Segment address of the new BPB.

IOCTL INPUT (Command Code 3)

IOCTL (input/output control) functions allow programs and drivers to communicate by passing i/o control strings to one another through a memory buffer. IOCTL functions may be used with character or block devices that have bit 14 set in their device header's attribute field.

Programs utilize IOCTL functions through the use of MS-DOS function 44H. IOCTL INPUT is used to send control information from the driver to an application program. IOCTL OUTPUT is used to send control information from an application program to the driver.

The following tasks are required for driver commands IOCTL INPUT (command code 3), INPUT (command code 4), OUTPUT (command code 8), OUTPUT WITH VERIFY (command code 9), and IOCTL OUTPUT (command code 12):

1. Perform the requested input or output.
2. Set the number of bytes transferred.
3. Set the status word in the request header.

For the preceding commands, the driver may read the following fields in the request header's data area:

Request Header Offset	Description
13	Media descriptor byte.
14–15	Offset address of transfer buffer.
16–17	Segment address of transfer buffer.
18–19	Size of transfer requested (bytes for character devices, sectors for block devices).
20–21	Starting sector (block devices only).

For the preceding commands, the driver must set the following fields in the request header's data area:

Request Header Offset	Description
18–19	Actual size of transfer (bytes for character devices, sectors for block devices).
22–25	Offset and segment addresses of disk's volume id label. This field is used with command codes 4 and 8 only and only in MS-DOS 3+. If the driver returns error code 0FH (invalid disk change), MS-DOS can use this pointer to retrieve the label and to prompt the user to insert the corresponding disk.

INPUT (Command Code 4)

This command is used to read data from a peripheral device. See IOCTL INPUT (command code 3) for information on this command.

NONDESTRUCTIVE READ (Command Code 5)

This command is used with character devices only. Block drivers should set only bit 8 ("done") in the request header's status word. This command reads a single character from the device's buffer without removing the character from the buffer.

The driver must perform the following tasks:

1. Read a character from the device's buffer.
2. Set the status word in the request header.

The driver must set the following field in the data area:

Request Header Offset   Description
           13   Character read.

INPUT STATUS (Command Code 6)

This command is used with character devices only. Block drivers should set only bit 8 ("done") in the request header's status word. This command tells MS-DOS whether or not there are any characters in the device's buffer ready to be read. If there are no characters to be read, the driver sets the busy bit (bit 9) of the request header's status word field to a value of 1. The busy bit is set to 0 if there is a character to read or if the device does not have a buffer.

The driver must perform the following task:

Set the status word in the request header.

INPUT FLUSH (Command Code 7)

This command is used with character devices only. Block drivers should set only bit 8 ("done") in the request header's status word. This command flushes the device's character buffer by reading characters from the device until the device status indicates that there are no more characters in the buffer.

The driver must perform the following task:

Set the status word in the request header.

OUTPUT (Command Code 8)

This command is used to write data to a peripheral device. See IOCTL IN-PUT (command code 3) for information on this command.

OUTPUT WITH VERIFY (Command Code 9)

This command is used to write data to a peripheral device. Each write is followed by a read to verify that the write was accurate. See IOCTL INPUT (command code 3) for information on this command.

OUTPUT STATUS (Command Code 10)

This command is used with character devices only. Block drivers should set only bit 8 ("done") in the request header's status word. This command checks the status of output-only device buffers (such as print buffers). The driver sets the busy bit (bit 9) of the request header's status word field to 0 if the device is idle or if the buffer is not full. The driver sets the busy bit to 1 if the device is busy or if the buffer is full.

The driver must perform the following task:

Set the status word in the request header.

OUTPUT FLUSH (Command Code 11)

This command is used with character devices only. Block drivers should set only bit 8 ("done") in the request header's status word. This command empties a device's output buffer.

The driver must perform the following task:

Set the status word in the request header.

IOCTL OUTPUT (Command Code 12)

This command is used to send a control string from a program to a device driver. See IOCTL INPUT (command code 3) for information on this command.

DEVICE OPEN (Command Code 13)

This command is implemented in MS-DOS 3.0 and later versions. The command is invoked each time a device is opened if bit 11 of the driver's device header is set to 1. Thus, the command provides the driver with a way of tracking the number of times a device is opened. In conjunction with DEVICE CLOSE (command code 14), this command can be used to limit the number of processes that can access a device at a given time. DEVICE OPEN can also be used to initialize character devices each time that they are used.

The driver must perform the following task:

Set the status word in the request header.

DEVICE CLOSE (Command Code 14)

This command is implemented in MS-DOS 3.0 and later versions. The command is invoked each time a device is closed if bit 11 of the driver's device header is set to 1. Thus, the command provides the driver with a way of tracking the number of times a device is closed. In conjunction with DEVICE OPEN (command code 13), this command can be used to control the number of processes that can access a device at a given time.

The driver must perform the following task:

Set the status word in the request header.

REMOVABLE MEDIA (Command Code 15)

This command is implemented in MS-DOS 3.0 and later versions. It is available only on block devices that have bit 11 of the attribute field in the device header set to 1. The command is invoked by MS-DOS each time that a program issues a call to MS-DOS service function 44H, subfunction 08H (IOCTL removable media). The driver sets the busy bit (bit 9) of the request header's status word to 0 if the media is removable, to 1 if the media is not removable.

The driver must perform the following task:

Set the status word in the request header.

OUTPUT UNTIL BUSY (Command Code 16)

This command is implemented on MS-DOS 3.0 and later versions. It can be used with character devices that have bit 13 of the attribute field in the device header set to 1. This command sends output to the device until it receives a busy signal from the device. Its intended use is for implementing print spoolers.

The driver must perform the following tasks:

1. Report the number of characters written to the device.
2. Set the status word in the request header.

The driver may read the following fields in the data area:

Request Header Offset	Description
13	Media byte descriptor.
14–15	Offset address of memory buffer containing output data.
16–17	Segment address of memory buffer containing output data.
18–19	Number of bytes to be output.

The driver sets the following field in the data area:

Request Header Offset	Description
18–19	Number of bytes actually output.

Command Codes 17 and 18 are undefined.

GENERIC I/O CONTROL (Command Code 19)

This command is implemented in MS-DOS 3.20 and later versions. It can be used on block devices that have bit 0 set in the device header's attribute field. The purpose of this command is to provide a standard IOCTL service for block devices. The command is called when MS-DOS service function 44H, subfunction 0DH is invoked. Refer to the MS-DOS technical manual for details in implementing this command.

The driver must perform the following tasks:

1. Retrieve the major and minor function codes from the request header and verify that they are valid. For MS-DOS 3.20, the only valid major function value is 08H. The valid minor function codes are as follows:

40H	Set device parameters.
41H	Write logical drive track.
42H	Format and verify logical drive track.
60H	Get device parameters.
61H	Read logical drive track.
62H	Verify logical drive track.

2. Set the status word in the request header.

The driver may read the following fields in the data area:

Request Header Offset	Description
13	Major function code.
14	Minor function code.
15–16	Contents of SI register.
17–18	Contents of DI register.
19–20	Offset address of IOCTL request.
21–22	Segment address of IOCTL request.

Command codes 20, 21, and 22 are undefined.

GET LOGICAL DEVICE (Command Code 23)

This command is implemented in MS-DOS 3.20 and later versions. It is used with block devices only. Bit 6 of the attribute field in the device header must be set to 1 if this command is to be used. The command is used to determine the last logical drive letter assigned to a device.

The command must perform the following tasks:

1. Place a value in the unit code field of the request header. If the value is a non-zero number, it represents the last logical drive letter assigned to the device (0 = A, 1 = B, etc.). A zero value indicates that the device is assigned only one logical drive letter.
2. Set the status word in the request header.

SET LOGICAL DEVICE (Command Code 24)

This command is implemented in MS-DOS 3.20 and later versions. It is used with block devices only. Bit 6 of the attribute field in the device header must be set to 1 if this command is to be used. The command is used to assign a logical drive letter to a device.

The command must perform the following tasks:

1. Retrieve the unit code field of the request header. If the value represents a valid logical drive letter (0 = A, 1 = B, etc.), the logical drive letter is assigned to the device. The driver places a value of zero in the unit code field if the value passed does not represent a valid logical drive letter.
2. Set the status word in the request header.

P A R T

3

MS-DOS Commands

- APPEND
- ASSIGN
- ATTRIB
- BACKUP
- BREAK
- BUFFERS
- CHCP
- CHDIR
- CHKDSK
- CLS
- COMMAND
- COMP
- COPY
- COUNTRY
- CTTY
- DATE
- DEL
- DEVICE

- DIR
- DISKCOMP
- DISKCOPY
- ECHO
- ERASE
- EXE2BIN
- FASTOPEN
- FCBS
- FDISK
- FILES
- FIND
- FOR
- FORMAT
- GOTO
- GRAFTABL
- GRAPHICS
- IF
- JOIN

- KEYB
- KEYBxx
- LABEL
- LASTDRIVE
- MKDIR
- MODE
- MORE
- NLSFUNC
- PATH
- PAUSE
- PRINT
- PROMPT
- RECOVER
- REM
- RENAME
- REPLACE
- RESTORE
- RMDIR

- SELECT
- SET
- SHARE
- SHELL
- SHIFT
- SORT
- STACKS
- SUBST
- SWITCHAR
- SYS
- TIME
- TREE
- TYPE
- VER
- VERIFY
- VOL
- XCOPY

MS-DOS Commands

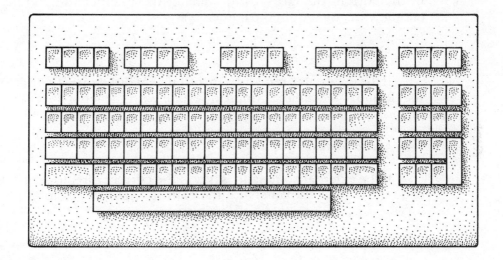

MS-DOS is a *command-driven* operating system. In other words, when you enter a command into your computer, MS-DOS carries it out by performing the appropriate actions. This part of the book will discuss each of the MS-DOS commands, explaining their characteristics, use, and format and giving you examples of each command. The discussion of each command begins with a heading such as the one you see here:

CLS

Internal
MS-DOS 2.X, 3.X

The first line in the heading shows the command in uppercase letters. The second line describes the command as being either an internal or an external command. *Internal* commands are those commands that have been built into MS-DOS. Whenever MS-DOS is booted, these commands are automatically loaded into memory. Internal commands are executed immediately and may be used any time you are operating in MS-DOS, without reinserting the system diskette. Some examples of internal commands are BREAK, CHDIR, COPY, CLS, TIME, and TYPE.

External commands are stored on a disk (usually the system diskette), in the form of a file, until they are needed by MS-DOS. Some examples of external commands are CHKDSK, DISKCOPY, FORMAT, PRINT, and RE-COVER. When you tell MS-DOS to execute an external command, it must load the file containing the command into memory before it can perform the command. Therefore, before you can use an external command, the file containing the command must be in a disk drive. If the external command is in the current directory of the default drive, enter the command name (along with any required parameters):

```
C>chkdsk a:
```

If the external command is in the current directory of a drive other than the default, precede the command name with the letter specifier of the appropriate drive:

```
A>c:chkdsk b:
```

If the external command is not in the current directory of a drive, precede the command name with the path specifier to the appropriate directory:

```
A>c:\dos\chkdsk b:
```

The PATH command can be used to establish a set of path specifiers for MS-DOS to use in looking for external commands. Path specifiers in this set need not be included on the command line when invoking an external command. Current directories, default drives, and path specifiers are discussed in chapters 2 and 3.

The third line in the heading tells you which version(s) of MS-DOS can execute the command. The notation "MS-DOS 2.X" refers to all versions of MS-DOS with a major version number of 2 (e.g., 2.00, 2.10). Similarly, "MS-DOS 3.X" refers to all versions with a major version number of 3. Following the convention used throughout this book, the terms "MS-DOS," "DOS," and "PC-DOS" are used interchangeably, unless otherwise specified.

Command Format

Whenever MS-DOS displays the system prompt (e.g., **A>**, **B>**, **C>**), you may enter a command. However, you must use the proper *format*, or pattern, for that particular command. Let's look at some examples.

The format for the command CLS (CLear Screen) is simply "CLS". This means that to execute the command, you type **cls** and press the Enter key.

Remember that you may use either uppercase or lowercase letters to type the command; MS-DOS will automatically convert all letters to uppercase.

C>*cls*   ←Enter

Many MS-DOS commands require that you include one or more *parameters* when you enter the command. A parameter is an item that gives additional information to MS-DOS. In the command formats used in this book, parameters appear in lowercase italic type. The command's format will tell you which, if any, parameters are used with the command. For example, the format for the command SYS (SYStem files) is "SYS *d:*". The "*d:*" is a parameter indicating that you should specify a drive. If you do not enter a drive letter designator (for example, c: or a:), MS-DOS will use the *d*efault drive. Suppose that you wish to use drive A. Your command statement will look like this:

C>*sys a:*   ←Enter

Some parameters are optional. When the parameter is enclosed in square brackets [like this], the inclusion of that parameter is optional. For example, the format for the command VOL (VOLume) is "VOL [*d:*]". Since the "*d:*" is in brackets, you may enter the command with or without the drive designator. MS-DOS will interpret the command one way if the parameter is present, another way if it is not.

Many MS-DOS 2.X and 3.X command formats include the word "path." *Path* is a parameter telling MS-DOS which path, or course, to take in travelling from one directory to another. In place of the word "path," you must enter the directory names, separated by a backslash (\). The directory names become the "path specifiers." Let's look at the format for the command MKDIR (MaKe DIRectory):

MKDIR [*d*:]*path*

The format tells us that the drive designator is optional, since the "*d:*" is in brackets. However, "*path*" is not in brackets, so you must enter a directory name(s). You can find more information about paths in chapter 3.

Other parameters frequently found in MS-DOS command formats are *filename* and *.ext*. When you see the words "filename" and ".ext" in the format, you must type the name of the file (up to eight characters in length) and its extension (a period and up to three characters), if there is an extension. For example, the format for the command TYPE is:

TYPE [*d*:][*path*]*filename*[*.ext*]

As you can see, this command requires a filename parameter. Optional parameters are the drive designator, path specifier, and filename extension.

Some MS-DOS commands require a *source* and a *target* file. The source contains the data to be used in executing the command. The target contains the data that are the result of command execution. You may specify multiple sources and targets with the use of wildcards, as discussed later in this introduction.

Command Notation

You have probably noticed that several kinds of typefaces and punctuation marks are used in the command formats. Items in **boldface** type are ones that must be entered. You may use either uppercase or lowercase letters in entering them. Items in *italics* are optional variables and are enclosed in square brackets [ ]. Items in ***boldface italics*** are variables that must be entered.

Include all punctuation marks as shown in the format, including commas, colons, semicolons, question marks, slashes, and quotes. Also include any parentheses and plus signs.

Items separated by a vertical bar | are either/or entries. ON|OFF means either ON or OFF. An ellipsis . . . following items means that you may repeat the items as often as needed. As mentioned before, items in square brackets are optional. Do not enter vertical bars, ellipses, or square brackets.

Wildcards

Most MS-DOS commands allow the use of *wildcards* in filenames and filename extensions. Sometimes called "global characters," wildcards replace one or more specific characters in the filename or its extension. When wildcards (? and *) are used, the command is executed once for each matching file that is found. You will find more information about wildcards in chapter 2.

Switches

Another kind of parameter found in some MS-DOS commands is a *switch*. A switch instructs MS-DOS to execute a command in a certain way. To use a switch, type a forward slash (/) followed by a letter or number. The command format will show you which, if any, switches can be used with the command. For example, here is the format for the DIR (DIRectory) command:

DIR [*d*:][*path*][*filename*][.*ext*]][/P][/W]

As you can see, DIR has two switches, /p and /w. Both are optional, since they are enclosed in brackets. Depending on which switch you select, MS-DOS will scroll the directory and pause (/p) when the screen is full, or it will list the directory in wide (/w) columns across the screen. Any switches that may be used with a particular command are explained in the discussion for that command.

Using MS-DOS on a Network

There are now many computer network packages available that will link computers running under MS-DOS. The details of setting up and starting these networks depend on the package used and will not be discussed here. Instead, we will make some general remarks about how MS-DOS commands behave on a network.

Network drives are assigned drive letters, just like drives on your own machine. Suppose that Manny and Joe are using separate computers, but both the computers are on the same network. Manny's computer has drives A, B, and C. Joe's computer also has drives A, B, and C. Manny decides that he wants to use Joe's drive C and that he (Manny) wants to call it drive D. Manny enters a command telling MS-DOS and the network software that, from now on, whenever Manny says drive D, he means Joe's drive C. To Manny, Joe's drive C is network drive D.

Most MS-DOS commands treat network drives like any other drive. For example, if Manny enters the command "dir d:", he sees the contents of Joe's drive C. However, some MS-DOS commands (see box) do not work with network drives. For most of these commands, prohibiting their use with network drives seems reasonable. Network drives are shared resources and must be used respectfully. For example, Joe probably would not appreciate it if Manny entered the command "format d:" and MS-DOS executed it. While some of the restricted commands (such as FASTOPEN and VERIFY) do not appear to pose any danger to the network drives, they may nevertheless be unusable on network drives because of implementation problems.

MS-DOS Commands That Cannot Be Used with Network Drives

FASTOPEN	JOIN	RECOVER	VERIFY
FORMAT	LABEL	SUBST	

APPEND

External
MS-DOS 3.2 and 3.3

Function: Directs MS-DOS to nonexecutable files

Format: **APPEND [/X][/E]**
               APPEND *d:path* [;[*d:*]*path* . . .]

Examples: append /x /e
               append c:\word;c:\turbo

The APPEND command provides a long awaited, much needed enhancement to the PATH command. PATH establishes a list of subdirectories for MS-DOS to search when a file is not located in the current directory. Unfortunately, the information supplied by PATH is useful only in locating files with a filename extension of EXE, COM, or BAT (executable files). The APPEND command corrects this deficiency by allowing the inclusion of nonexecutable files in a directory search path.

Many programs, particularly word processors, consist of an executable file (the "program") plus one or more nonexecutable files. A help facility is an example of a nonexecutable file. Versions of MS-DOS prior to 3.2 have no way of finding such files if the files are not located in the current directory. APPEND overcomes this limitation by providing MS-DOS with path information to all files regardless of filename extension.

The parameters used with APPEND are path specifiers separated by semicolons. APPEND allows up to 128 characters in the complete path specification.

An Example

The word processor used to write this book consists of one executable file ("wp.exe") and four nonexecutable files ("wpmsg.txt", "wpsysd.sys", "wphelp.txt", "wpque.sys"). The five files are stored in the subdirectory \WORD. APPEND is used to let MS-DOS know about the location of these files as follows:

```
C>append c:\word
```

Once the command is entered, any subdirectory can be used as the current directory, since APPEND provides the operating system with the information required to locate all of the files used by the word processor. Notice that the APPEND path specifier included a drive letter. This is a good practice to follow because it allows MS-DOS to locate files regardless of which drive is currently the default.

APPEND is a terminate and stay resident program (see chapter 13). This means that the first time you invoke APPEND, the program is read from the disk and stored in memory. APPEND then remains in memory until the system is turned off or restarted. Once loaded into memory, APPEND can be used to display, modify, or cancel the APPEND path specifier.

Displaying the APPEND Path Specifier

MS-DOS will display the APPEND path specifier in response to APPEND.

```
C>append c:\word

C>append
APPEND=c:\WORD

C>append c:\word;c:\turbo
C>append
APPEND=C:\WORD;C:\TURBO
```

Cancelling APPEND's Path Specifier

APPEND followed by a semicolon cancels the APPEND path specifier.

```
C>append
APPEND=C:\WORD;C:\TURBO

C>append ;

C>append
No Append
```

APPEND remains in memory when the path specifier is cancelled. A new specifier can be set at any time.

The /X Switch

The command "append /x" directs MS-DOS to use (if necessary) the AP-PEND path specifier when it is processing requests for the internal MS-DOS functions SEARCH FIRST, FIND FIRST, and EXEC. The functions SEARCH FIRST and FIND FIRST both direct MS-DOS to search a directory to find the first file that matches the file specifier contained in a command. EXEC is the function used by MS-DOS to load a program into memory for execution. The following examples show how these functions relate to APPEND.

For purposes of these examples, let us say that drive C contains the directory \WORD and that \WORD contains a file named "wp.exe". The command "dir c:\word\wp.exe" tells MS-DOS to use the SEARCH FIRST function to look in directory \WORD for file "wp.exe". In our example, this is what happens:

```
C>dir \word\wp.exe

    Volume in drive C is HARDDISK
    Directory of C:\WORD

WP      EXE  153344  4-14-84  4:19p
    1 File(s)  3313664 bytes free
```

MS-DOS was able to find the entry for "wp.exe" and display information about the file. If the command is changed to "dir wp.exe", the SEARCH FIRST function will be unable to find "wp.exe", since the directory containing the file is not specified. This is where APPEND comes in. In the following listing, the first APPEND command directs MS-DOS to use the APPEND path specifier in processing SEARCH FIRST requests. The second APPEND command then sets the APPEND path specifier.

```
    C>append /x

    C>append \word

    C>dir wp.exe

    Volume in drive C is HARDDISK
    Directory of C:\

WP      EXE  153344  4-14-84  4:19p
    1 File(s)  3313664 bytes free
```

MS-DOS was able to find the file since the APPEND path specifier was available. Notice that MS-DOS seems to think that "wp.exe" is in the root directory (**Directory of C:**) rather than in the directory \WORD. Evidently MS-DOS is confused. Indeed, there are definitely some bugs in APPEND, and we will discuss these in the following text.

Continuing with our discussion of /x, the command "\word\wp" tells MS-DOS to use EXEC to load and execute the file "wp.exe". EXEC is able to locate the program, since the directory is supplied on the command line. If (as in the example) the commands "append /x" and "append \word" had already been entered, MS-DOS could have loaded and executed the program with a command of simply "wp".

The point here is that if "append /x" had not been entered, neither "dir wp.exe" nor "wp" would have worked, regardless of what the APPEND path specifier happened to be.

The /x switch can be used only the first time that APPEND is invoked, that is, when APPEND is loaded into memory. If the /x switch is used, the SEARCH FIRST, FIND FIRST, and EXEC capabilities remain in effect regardless of how many times the APPEND path specifier is modified or cancelled.

The /E Switch

The APPEND path specifier is usually stored as a data structure that can be accessed only by APPEND. The one way to display or modify the specifier is by using the APPEND command. The command "append /e" directs MS-DOS to store the APPEND path specifier as an environment variable (environment variables are discussed in chapter 12). Environment variables may be displayed and modified by using the SET command. However, be certain to read the final section on APPEND before trying to do this.

Like the /x switch, the /e switch can be used only the first time that APPEND is entered. The /x switch and the /e switch may both be used the first time that APPEND is entered.

Problems with APPEND

APPEND is a very useful command. Unfortunately, APPEND is not as well-designed or well-behaved as it should be. The design problem centers around the fact that any file read with the APPEND path specifier is written to the current directory. The directory setup used in writing this book illustrates the problem. The word processor is stored as \WORD\WP.EXE. The contents of this section of the book are stored as \BOOK\COMMANDS\AP-PEND.DOC. One way to set up the system is as follows:

```
C>append /e /x

C>append c:\book\commands

C>cd \word
```

With \WORD as the current directory, the word processor can be started, and, using the APPEND path specifier, the word processor can locate "append.doc" for editing. The problem is that following any changes to the file, the word processor writes "append.doc" to the current directory \WORD. The original file remains unchanged in \BOOK\COMMANDS.

Fortunately, this problem has a simple solution. I can make BOOK \COMMANDS the current directory, and use APPEND to locate "wp.exe":

```
C>append c:\word

C>cd \book\commands
```

Now any changes made to "append.doc" are stored in the original file.

Some other problems with APPEND are not overcome as easily. These problems, which really have to be considered bugs, can be either amusing or annoying, depending on whether they cause you to lose important work.

A previous example in this section showed how the /x switch appears to confuse MS-DOS. The command "append /e" can also confuse MS-DOS. If the APPEND path specifier is stored as an environment variable, and you attempt to display the directory of a blank formatted diskette, MS-DOS will display the contents of the first directory listed in the APPEND path specifier.

I find problems like this somewhat amusing, but obviously the potential for real trouble exists. Even IBM acknowledges that a problem exists. The PC-DOS 3.30 manual states that "APPEND /X may cause problems with some applications. If you experience problems using the /X option, you may want to use the APPEND command without it." The manual goes on to say that the APPEND path specifier must be cancelled prior to using the commands BACKUP and RESTORE. In addition, the manual says that AP-PEND must be used before the ASSIGN command is used. More significantly, there have been published reports of data loss that seems to be related to the use of APPEND.

I have used APPEND while writing this book and have not experienced any serious problems. However, I back up my data frequently and always have my fingers crossed. At this point, the value of APPEND appears to outweigh the apparent risks. If you choose to use APPEND, do so carefully. Let's hope that future implementations of APPEND have these bugs worked out.

ASSIGN

External
MS-DOS 2.X, 3.X

Function: Reassigns the disk operation drive to another drive

Format: ASSIGN [*x*[=]*y*[. . .]]

Examples: assign
               assign a=c
               assign a=c b=c

Note: the commands JOIN and SUBST are more flexible and are safer to use than ASSIGN. Their use is recommended as an alternative to ASSIGN.

Some computer programs will execute only on systems with a particular drive configuration. For example, a program may require that any data used in the program be located on drive A. The ASSIGN command allows you to overcome this limitation by reassigning the specified disk drive to another disk drive.

Suppose you have a program that requires data to be on drive A, but you want to keep the data on your fixed disk, drive C. You can use ASSIGN to tell MS-DOS that all references to drive A are to be redirected to drive C (the fixed disk). Note that you do not have to enter a colon after the drive letter when you are using the ASSIGN command:

```
C>assign a=c
```

Now each time that the program looks for data on drive A, MS-DOS will automatically redirect the program to drive C.

You may make more than one reassignment with each ASSIGN command. The following command tells MS-DOS to redirect all references for drives A and B to drive C:

```
C>assign a=c b=c
```

Entering ASSIGN with no parameters cancels any previous ASSIGN commands and you are returned to the original drive:

```
C>assign
```

ASSIGN is designed primarily for use with MS-DOS 1.X programs that are run on systems without fixed disks. ASSIGN should be used only when necessary and then with caution. Reassigning a floppy disk drive to the fixed disk will redirect all access of the floppy disk to the fixed disk. Unless care is exercised, you can inadvertently erase all or part of the fixed disk.

The makers of MS-DOS recommend that application programs be written so that the user specifies the drive configuration of the system on which the program will be run. Restricting programs to a particular configuration is discouraged.

Note that the MS-DOS commands DISKCOPY and DISKCOMP will ignore any drive reassignments made with ASSIGN. ASSIGN should not be used with BACKUP, RESTORE, LABEL, JOIN, SUBST, or PRINT because drive reassignments can confuse these commands, causing unpredictable results.

ATTRIB

External
MS-DOS 3.X

Function: Modifies read-only and archive file attributes

Format: ATTRIB [+R (or) −R][+A (or)
−A][*d:*][*path*]*filename*[.*ext*][/S]

Example: attrib +r mypro.c

MS-DOS maintains a *file attribute* for each file. The attribute contains information about how the file is stored. Each file's attribute is actually a composite of six individual characteristics that the file may or may not possess. The command ATTRIB allows you to modify two of these attributes: *read-only* and *archive*. See chapter 11 for detailed information about file attributes and for a set of programs allowing you to modify a file's hidden file attribute.

The Read-Only Attribute

MS-DOS files that possess a read-only attribute cannot be written to or erased. ATTRIB can be used to mark files as read-only, thereby protecting the files from accidental modification or erasure. The command "attrib +r *filename*" makes a file read-only. The command "attrib −r *filename*" removes read-only protection, and "attrib *filename*" displays a file's read-only status.

The following commands give the file "mypro.c" read-only status, confirm that the file is read-only, remove the read-only status, and confirm that the read-only status has been removed.

```
C>attrib +r mypro.c   ←set as read-only

C>attrib mypro.c      ←request attribute status

    R C:\MYPRO.C      ←MS-DOS displays (R = read-only)

C>attrib -r mypro.c   ←remove read-only status

C>attrib mypro.c      ←request attribute status

      c:\MYPRO.C      ←read-only removed
```

The Archive Attribute

MS-DOS turns on a file's archive attribute each time that the file is modified. In versions 3.2 and 3.3 of MS-DOS, the archive attribute can also be set by using the command "attrib +a *flename*". A file's archive attribute may be cleared with the command "attrib −a *filename*". The command "attrib *filename*" displays the status of a file's archive attribute. See the discussions of the commands BACKUP and XCOPY for information on how MS-DOS uses a file's archive attribute.

Processing Directories

ATTRIB processes files in the specified (or default) directory which match the file specified in the command line. The /s switch directs ATTRIB to also process all files in the subdirectories of the specified (or default) directory. The following example is executed with \BOOK as the default directory:

```
C>dir                              ←display contents of \BOOK

    Volume in drive C is HARDDISK
    Directory of C:\BOOK

.            <DIR>    3-27-87   3:52p
..           <DIR>    8-11-87   6:10p
NEW          <DIR>    8-11-87   8:10p
OLD          <DIR>    8-11-87   8:11p
MISC    DOC   3210    9-23-87  11:07a
    5 File(s)   3954688 bytes free

C>attrib *.* /s                    ←request attribute status for files in
                                      \BOOK and all subdirectories

A   C:\BOOK\NEW\ATTRIB.DOC         ←MS-DOS displays status for files in
                                      subdirectory \BOOK\NEW
A   C:\BOOK\NEW\ASSIGN.DOC

A   C:\BOOK\NEW\TMP\INTRO.DOC      ←status for files in \BOOK\NEW\TMP

A   C:\BOOK\OLD\DIR.DOC            ←status for files in \BOOK\OLD

A   C:\BOOK\MISC.DOC              ←status for files in \BOOK
```

BACKUP

External
MS-DOS 2.X, 3.X

Function: Creates archival files

Format: BACKUP *d*:[*path*][*filename*[.*ext*]]*d*:[/S][/M][/D:*mm*/*dd*/*yy*][/
T:*hh*:*mm*:*ss*][/F][/L[:[*d*:][*path*]*filename*[.*ext*]]]

Examples: backup c: a:
backup c:*.txt a:
backup c:\book*.txt a:

The BACKUP command allows you to copy files from a fixed disk to a floppy diskette. Enhancements in MS-DOS 3.X allow you to back up files from any disk (or diskette) to any other disk (or diskette). Copies made with BACKUP are stored in *archival* form and are used solely for storage. Archival files can be accessed only with the command RESTORE. BACKUP and RESTORE thus serve as tools for maintaining backup copies of important files.

With BACKUP, you can select files for copying on the basis of the file's path, filename, filename extension, date stamp, or time stamp. You may also back up files that have been changed since the last time a backup was performed.

MS-DOS 3.X uses two strategies in storing files made with BACKUP: (1) files stored on a floppy diskette are placed in the root directory, and (2) files stored on a fixed disk are placed in a subdirectory named \BACKUP. MS-DOS 2.X stores archival files on floppy diskettes only. The files are stored in the root directory using a less-efficient storage method than that used in MS-DOS 3.X.

BACKUP is an external MS-DOS command. This means that BACKUP.COM must be on a disk drive before you can use BACKUP. In the following examples, BACKUP.COM is stored in the root directory of drive C.

Backing Up a File

To create a backup copy of a fixed disk file, first type **backup**, then type the file specification of the file you are copying, next type the drive designator (such as a:) of the target diskette (the floppy diskettte that will store the copy), and finally type any of the four optional switches (see the following discussions).

A *file specification* consists of a letter designating the drive holding the file, followed by the name of the path leading to the directory holding the file, followed by the filename and filename extension of the file. If the BACKUP command does not include a drive letter and path for the file to be copied, BACKUP will assume that the file to be copied is in the current directory of the default drive.

Wildcard characters (see chapter 2) may be used in the filenames and file extensions. When wildcards are used, all of the matching files in the specified (or default) directory will be backed up.

In the first example, we will use BACKUP to make a copy of the fixed disk file "lotsa.dat". The backup will be stored on the target diskette in drive A.

```
C>backup c:lotsa.dat a:
```

MS-DOS beeps and displays this warning:

```
Insert backup diskette 01 in drive A:
Warning! Diskette files will be erased
Strike any key when ready
```

BACKUP will erase any data on the diskette before making the backup copy, unless you use the /a switch. This warning gives you a chance to substitute another diskette if you wish. After double-checking to make sure that you have the right diskette in drive A, go ahead and press any key. BACKUP will copy the fixed disk file onto the diskette in drive A and display the following message on the screen:

```
*** Backing up files to diskette 01 ***
\a:lotsa.dat
```

Keeping Track of Your Backups

BACKUP will prompt you to insert another diskette if the backup process will exceed the capacity of the target diskette. Given the tremendous storage capacity of a fixed disk, it is not uncommon to need several diskettes to finish the job. A good practice is to keep a written record of important BACKUP sessions. You can get a printed copy of the BACKUP screen display by pressing Ctrl-PrtSc before you enter the BACKUP command. All screen display will be echoed (copied) to your printer. Make sure that your printer is turned on before you press Ctrl-PrtSc. At the end of the backup session, press Ctrl-PrtSc again to stop the echoing process.

For a convenient way to automate this record-keeping process with MS-DOS 3.3, see the following discussion of the /l switch in "Other BACKUP Switches."

Backing Up a Directory

All the files in a directory will be backed up if the BACKUP command does not contain a filename. In the following example, all the files in the subdirectory SUBDIR1 will be backed up. Notice that MS-DOS lists each file in the subdirectory as it is being backed up.

```
C>backup c:\subdir1 a:

Insert backup diskette 01 in drive A:
Warning! Diskette files will be erased
Strike any key when ready

*** Backing up files to diskette 01 ***
\SUBDIR1\FILE1
\SUBDIR1\FILE2
\SUBDIR1\FILE3
\SUBDIR1\FILE4
```

Backing Up All Subdirectories

The /s switch is used with BACKUP to copy all the files in a directory and all the files in the directory's subdirectories. The next example backs up all the files in SUBDIR2 as well as all the files in SUBDIR2's subdirectories:

```
C>backup c:\subdir2 a:/s

Insert backup diskette 01 in drive A:
Warning! Diskette files will be erased
Strike any key when ready

*** Backing up files to diskette 01 ***
\SUBDIR2\FILE21
\SUBDIR2\FILE22
\SUBDIR2\FILE23
\SUBDIR2\SUBDIR3\FILE31
\SUBDIR2\SUBDIR3\FILE32
\SUBDIR2\SUBDIR4\FILE41
```

Backing Up Modified Files

The /m switch is used to back up any files that have been modified since the last BACKUP session. This handy option can save you time and diskette space, since it selects only those files that need to be backed up.

Let's say that you use your fixed disk to store your word processing documents. All of the documents have a filename extension of DOC. If you have several hundred document files, it can be difficult to keep track of which files need to be backed up and which files have already been backed up. But you needn't concern yourself with this problem because BACKUP and /m will take care of it for you. All you need to do is enter the following command at the end of each word processing session:

```
C>backup *.doc a:/m
```

Any document file that was modified in the work session will automatically be backed up.

Backing Up Files by Date

The /d switch is used with BACKUP to copy files that were created, or last modified, on or after a specific date. The following command will back up any files in the root directory that were created, or modified, after December 11, 1988.

```
C>backup c:\ a:/d:12-11-88
```

Backing Up Files by Time

The /t switch, implemented in MS-DOS 3.3, allows you to back up files that were created or modified after a specified time of day. The following example creates a backup of all files in the root directory that have a time stamp later than 3:00 pm. The backup copies are stored on drive A.

```
C>backup c:\*.* a:/t:15:00:00
```

Other BACKUP Switches

The /a switch allows you to add BACKUP files to the root directory or to the \BACKUP subdirectory (in MS-DOS 3.X) without erasing pre-existing data.

The /f switch, implemented in MS-DOS 3.3, allows you to use BACKUP to store files on a previously unformatted diskette. MS-DOS must be able to read the file FORMAT.COM from disk in order to execute this option.

The /l switch, implemented in MS-DOS 3.3, directs BACKUP to create a *log file*. The log file consists of a record of all files that have been backed up, along with the date and time of the backup. The log file can be useful in keeping track of files that have been archived. You can specify a drive, path, and filename for the log file. The default is BACKUP.LOG stored in the root of the source drive.

Restrictions with BACKUP

The commands ASSIGN, JOIN, and SUBST instruct MS-DOS to redirect all references for one device to another device. For example, ASSIGN may be used to redirect all references for drive A to drive C. Each of these commands can put MS-DOS in a state that is confusing to BACKUP. The effect is that BACKUP results may be unpredictable if one of these commands has previously been used.

Another restriction in using BACKUP occurs with the APPEND command. BACKUP used in conjunction with APPEND may result in loss of data. See the discussion of APPEND for details.

BACKUP and ERRORLEVEL

ERRORLEVEL is a variable that has special meaning to MS-DOS. The value of ERRORLEVEL is set by the BACKUP command as follows:

0   BACKUP command completed in normal fashion.

1   No files were found on the fixed disk that match the file(s) specified in the BACKUP command.

3   Execution of the BACKUP command was terminated by the user pressing Ctrl-Break.

4   The BACKUP command was terminated due to an error in execution.

Once the value of ERRORLEVEL has been set, ERRORLEVEL may be used in conjunction with the IF command in an MS-DOS batch file. ERRORLEVEL allows you to create batch files that are executed according to the outcome of a BACKUP command. See the discussion of the IF command for further details.

BREAK

Internal
MS-DOS 2.X, 3.X

Function: Controls the frequency with which MS-DOS checks to see if the Ctrl-Break combination has been pressed

Formats: **BREAK ON**
            BREAK OFF
            BREAK

Example: break on

Pressing the Ctrl-Break key combination will halt the execution of a program and return control of the computer to MS-DOS. Normally, MS-DOS will check to see if Ctrl-Break has been pressed only during operations involving the keyboard, the display screen, the printer, and the auxiliary devices. If a program spends most of its time accessing the disk drives and/or manipulating data internally, you may have to wait some time before MS-DOS recognizes that Ctrl-Break has been pressed.

You can use the BREAK command in several ways. The command BREAK=ON will increase the frequency with which MS-DOS checks to see if Ctrl-Break has been pressed. The command BREAK=OFF will limit the occurrence of Ctrl-Break checking to operations involving the keyboard, display screen, printer, and auxiliary devices. Entering BREAK without any parameters causes MS-DOS to display the current BREAK status (BREAK is on, BREAK is off).

When BREAK is on, MS-DOS checks for Ctrl-Break whenever a program requests that an MS-DOS service function be executed (see appendix A). You can automatically turn BREAK on each time that MS-DOS is booted by including a BREAK=ON statement in a CONFIG.SYS file. CONFIG.SYS files are discussed in chapter 14.

BUFFERS

Internal
MS-DOS 2.X, 3.X

Function: Establishes the number of disk buffers that will be set up in memory when MS-DOS is booted

Format: **BUFFERS=*xx***
Note: The value *xx* is a number from 1–99. BUFFERS may be used in a CONFIG.SYS file only.

Example: buffers=5

A *disk buffer* is an area of memory that MS-DOS uses to store data being written to, or read from, a disk. A buffer serves as a way station between the disk and the portion of memory storing a program's data.

MS-DOS transfers data between a disk and a buffer in 512-byte increments. To illustrate how a buffer is used, consider what happens when a program requires a 128-byte record stored on disk. MS-DOS reads a 512-byte portion of the file from the disk. Contained within these 512 bytes are the 128 bytes needed by the program. The 128 bytes are transferred to the program's data area in memory. If the program subsequently requires another 128-byte record, MS-DOS first determines if the record is already stored in a buffer. If it is, no disk access is required.

The BUFFERS command is used to establish the number of disk buffers set up by MS-DOS during booting. Increasing the number of buffers can speed program execution, but only up to a point. The more buffers that exist, the more sectors that can be stored in memory; hence, fewer accesses of the disk are necessary. However, the more buffers, the longer it takes MS-DOS to search all the buffers to see if the needed sector is already in memory. Eventually it becomes faster to access the disk than to search all the buffers.

The amount of memory taken up by the disk buffers is another consideration. Each buffer adds 528 bytes to the amount of memory taken up by MS-DOS. By increasing the amount of memory needed by MS-DOS, the amount of memory available for program data is reduced. Thus, the additional buffers can increase the frequency of disk accesses, causing the program to slow down.

You can use BUFFERS to set up from 1 to 99 disk buffers. The optimal number of buffers varies from program to program. Generally, if a program does little random reading and writing of records, the default setting of 2 buffers will be adequate. If a program performs a large number of random reading and writing, increasing the number of disk buffers will often speed up performance. The best performance can be arrived at only through trial and error.

If CONFIG.SYS does not contain a BUFFERS command, MS-DOS sets up a default number of buffers. In versions of MS-DOS prior to 3.3, the default is 2 buffers. In MS-DOS 3.3, however, BUFFERS has some smarts. On machines with more than 128 Kbytes of RAM, the default is 5 buffers. On machines with more than 256 Kbytes of RAM, the default is 10, and with more than 512 Kbytes of RAM, the default is 15. If a machine has less than 256 Kbytes of RAM, but has a diskette drive with a capacity greater than 360 Kbytes, the default is 3 buffers.

CHCP

Internal
MS-DOS 3.3

Function: Selects a code page for the system
Note: Please refer to appendix D for an overview of code pages and code page switching.

Format: CHCP [*xxxx*]

Examples: chcp
chcp 850

The command CHCP selects a specific code page for each device in the system which supports that code page. Prior to using CHCP, the NLSFUNC command must be invoked. The following two commands assign code page 850 to the system:

```
C>nlsfunc
C>chcp 850
```

Note that the NLSFUNC command need be invoked only one time after the system is booted.

CHCP with no parameters displays the system's currently active code page.

```
C>chcp
```

```
Active code page:  437
```

CHDIR

Internal
MS-DOS 2.X, 3.X

Function: Changes the current directory or displays the current directory's path

Format: CHDIR [[*d*:]*path*]

Examples: chdir \suba1 \suba2
cd b:\subb1
chdir
cd

The *current directory* is the directory in which MS-DOS is currently active. At any given time, there is only one current directory for each drive in the system. You can use the command CHDIR (CHange DIRectory) to instruct MS-DOS to change the drive's current directory. You can also use CHDIR to display the path to a drive's current directory. This command can be entered as "chdir" or abbreviated as "cd".

Changing the Current Directory

To change the current directory, type **chdir** (or **cd**) and then type the path to the new current directory. Suppose that the path from the root directory to the subdirectory SUBA2 is ROOT DIRECTORY, SUBA1, SUBA2 (see Figure 1). MS-DOS represents this path as \SUBA1\SUBA2. Note that the root directory is indicated by the first backward slash.

The following command will make SUBA2 the current directory of drive C:

```
C>chdir \suba1\suba2
```

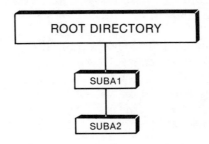

Figure 1. File structure for root directory, SUBA1, SUBA2.

To change the current directory of a drive that is not the default drive, type the drive letter designator and then type the path:

C>*cd a:\subb1*

Displaying the Path to the Current Directory

Entering "chdir" (or "cd") with no parameters directs MS-DOS to display the path to the current directory of the default drive:

C>*chdir*
C:\SUBA1\SUBA2

To display the path to the current directory of a drive other than the default, type **chdir** (or **cd**), followed by the letter designator of the drive:

C>*cd a:*
A:\SUBB1

You can find more detailed information on directories, subdirectories, current directories, and paths in chapter 3.

CHKDSK

External
MS-DOS 1.X, 2.X, 3.X

Functions: Analyzes the file allocation table (FAT), the directory, and any
subdirectories on a disk
Analyzes the status of computer memory

Formats: **CHKDSK** [*d*:]
CHKDSK [*d*:][*filename.ext*][/F][/V] (MS-DOS 2.X and 3.X)

Examples: chkdsk
chkdsk b:
chkdsk/f
chkdsk b:letter.doc /f/v

The CHKDSK (CHecK DiSK) command is an MS-DOS utility that checks the
condition, or status, of a disk's data. MS-DOS stores data in files on a disk. It
keeps track of the files on the disk by consulting the disk's directory and file
allocation table (FAT). CHKDSK analyzes the FAT and the disk directory (and
any subdirectories) for errors and problems. To prevent minor problems
from turning into major ones, it is a good idea to run CHKDSK occasionally
on all your fixed disks and floppy diskettes. You will find more information
about the structure and role of the FAT and the file directory in chapter 11.

Using CHKDSK

Since CHKDSK is an external command, a copy of the file CHKDSK.COM
must be available to the system before you can use the command. This
means that either CHKDSK.COM must be in the current directory of the
default drive or that the location of CHKDSK.COM must have been specified by the PATH command (see the discussion of PATH).

To check a disk, type **chkdsk** and then type the letter designator of the
drive containing the disk to be checked. If you do not enter a drive letter
designator, CHKDSK will examine the disk in the default drive:

```
C>chkdsk

Volume HARDDISK created Jul 6, 1987 2:14p
10592256 bytes total disk space
   57334 bytes in 3 hidden files
  184320 bytes in 42 directories
10264576 bytes in 846 user files
   86016 bytes available on disk
```

```
524288 bytes total memory
320704 bytes free
```

`C>`

Since the preceding command did not include a drive letter designator, CHKDSK examined the disk in the default drive; it did not find any errors. The status report displays information about the disk and the computer memory. The first four lines report the total disk space taken up, the number of files on the diskette, and the remaining available space. The last two lines report on the amount of memory used up and the amount still available.

CHKDSK Features of MS-DOS 2.X and 3.X

The MS-DOS 2.X and 3.X versions of CHKDSK have four additional features:

1. If a filename is included in the command, CHKDSK will display the number of noncontiguous areas (sectors) on the disk that contain the named file. While files that are highly fragmented (having many noncontiguous areas) are acceptable, they can slow down system performance. If you use the wildcard *.* as a filename, CHKDSK will report on each fragmented file on the disk. A fragmented file can be copied into a contiguous area on another disk with the COPY command.

2. By including the /f (fix) switch in the CHKDSK command, you can instruct CHKDSK to correct any errors it finds. If you do not use the /f switch, CHKDSK functions as though it were correcting the errors, but it will not actually write the corrections to the disk.

3. The /b switch will direct CHKDSK to display the name of each subdirectory and file located on the disk and to provide more detailed information about any errors it has found.

4. You can redirect the status report and any messages to a disk file by using the following command:

   `C>chkdsk b:>file`

   Note: Do not use the /f switch in the CHKDSK command if you are redirecting CHKDSK's output.

CHKDSK Error Messages

Allocation error for file, size adjusted

This message will contain the name of a file having an invalid FAT entry. If the /f parameter has been used, the file will be truncated (cut short) at the end of the sector that corresponds to the last valid FAT entry.

Cannot CHDIR to *file specification*
Tree cannot be processed beyond this point

An error exists in the directory entries. CHKDSK cannot follow the directory entries to the path being checked.

Contains invalid cluster, file truncated

This message means the same as the one for allocation error.

Contains noncontiguous blocks

This message is preceded by the name of a file. The message states that the file is not stored in one contiguous area on the disk but rather in *xxx* different areas. Although this message does not indicate a problem with the disk, such a condition may slow down system performance. A badly fragmented file should be copied onto a contiguous block of another disk.

Convert directory to file (Y/N)?

This message is preceded by the name of a directory (or subdirectory) that is no longer functional because of one or more invalid entries. CHKDSK asks if you want this directory converted to a file (which could then be examined with DEBUG). If you enter "Y" (and /f was included in the CHKDSK command), the directory will be converted to a file. If you enter "N", no conversion is made.

Convert lost chains to files (Y/N)?

A *cluster* is a unit of space on a disk. The cluster is said to be "lost" when the FAT entry for the cluster is a nonzero number but the cluster does not belong to any file. A contiguous set of lost clusters is called a *lost chain*. This message asks if you want each lost chain stored in a file. If you reply "Y", MS-DOS creates a separate file for each lost chain. The files are named FILE*nnnn*.CHK, where *nnnn* is a sequential number beginning with 0000. If you reply "N", MS-DOS converts to zero the entries in the FAT that correspond to the lost chains and makes available for new files the areas in the disk occupied by the lost chains. Regardless of your reply, no changes will be written to the disk if you did not include /f in the CHKDSK command.

Disk error writing FAT *x*

CHKDSK was unable to update the FAT. The *x* will either be 1 or 2, depending on which copy of the FAT CHKDSK was trying to update.

Error found, F parameter not specified
Corrections will not be written to disk

The /f switch was not included with the CHKDSK command. The results of the CHKDSK analysis will be displayed, but no changes will be written to the disk.

filename is cross-linked:
On cluster *xx*

Two files are said to be *cross-linked* when the FAT indicates that a cluster belongs to both files. The message will be displayed twice, once for each file that is cross-linked. CHKDSK does not take any action when this situation occurs. Cross-linked files can be salvaged, either partially or entirely, by copying each of the files onto another disk.

First cluster number is invalid,
Entry truncated

This message will be preceded by the name of a file. The file's first cluster, which is located in the file directory, is invalid. The file will be truncated to a length of zero if the /f parameter was included in the CHKDSK command.

Insufficient room in root directory
Erase files from root and repeat CHKDSK

CHKDSK has been instructed to convert lost chains into files. Unfortunately, there is not enough room in the root directory for all the files that CHKDSK wants to create. To solve this problem, copy the files already recovered to another diskette. Then delete the recovered files from the original diskette. Rerun CHKDSK on the original diskette to recover the remaining lost chains.

Invalid subdirectory

CHKDSK has found an invalid entry in the subdirectory that is named. CHKDSK will attempt to correct the error if the /f parameter was included in the CHKDSK command.

Probable non-DOS disk
Continue (Y/N)?

The first byte of the FAT does not contain a valid entry. CHKDSK will indicate the possible corrective measures if you reply with "Y". However, the changes will not be written to the disk if the /f parameter was not included in the CHKDSK command.

xxxxxxx bytes disk space freed

An error in the FAT has been corrected by truncating a file. The portion of the disk previously allocated to the file is now available for data storage.

xxx lost clusters found in *yyy* chains

A cluster is "lost" if the FAT entry for the cluster is a nonzero number but the cluster does not belong to any file. A contiguous group of lost clusters is called a *lost chain*. CHKDSK will ask if you want to convert each lost chain to a file or if you want to free the disk space taken up by the chains.

CLS

Internal
MS-DOS 2.X, 3.X

Function: Clears the screen and moves the cursor to home position

Format: **CLS**

Example: cls

The CLS (CLear Screen) command clears the display screen and moves the cursor to the home position. CLS sends the ASCII character sequence ESC[2J to the console device driver. This is the ANSI command sequence for clearing the screen and moving the cursor to home position.

On some systems, the ANSI.SYS device driver must be installed by the user before the CLS command will operate. See chapter 8 for information on installing the ANSI.SYS device driver.

COMMAND

External
MS-DOS 2.X, 3.X

Function: Invokes a secondary command processor

Formats: **COMMAND [/C *string*][/P]**
        COMMAND [*d*:][*path*][/C *string*][/P][/E:*xxxxx*]   (MS-DOS 3.X)

Examples: command
         command /c dir
         command /c do it.bat

The *command processor* serves as the interface between you and the operating system. It displays the system prompt on the screen, interprets the command you enter, and acts according to the contents of that command. The primary MS-DOS command processor is COMMAND.COM.

You can use COMMAND to invoke a secondary command processor. Invoking the command directs COMMAND to (1) load a copy of the command processor into memory and (2) pass control to the copy (the secondary command processor). MS-DOS uses the path specifier contained in the command to locate the copy of COMMAND.COM that will be loaded. If

COMMAND.COM is not stored in the specified directory, or if no path specifier is included in the command, MS-DOS uses the path stored in the environment to locate COMMAND.COM.

To invoke a secondary command processor, type **command**:

`C>command`

On the surface it appears as though nothing has happened, but you are now operating under the control of a secondary command processor. If you get a "Bad file or command" message, insert your working copy of the system diskette in drive A and try again.

To leave the secondary command processor and return control to the primary command processor, type **exit**:

`C>exit`

Again it appears as though nothing has happened, but you are now back under the control of the primary command processor.

COMMAND Switches

Using the /c switch when you invoke a secondary command processor allows you to enter a command line:

`C>command /c dir`

This command tells MS-DOS to load a secondary command processor and instructs the secondary command processor to execute a DIR command.

The /p switch tells MS-DOS to keep the secondary command processor in memory even if an EXIT command is issued. The /p switch is used when increasing the size of the MS-DOS environment (see chapter 12). If both /p and /c are issued, the /p switch is ignored.

The /e:*xxxxx* switch, implemented in MS-DOS 3.1 but not documented until version 3.2, is used to set the size of the environment that is passed to the secondary command processor. If no environment size is specified, the secondary command processor inherits an environment that is the same size as the environment of the primary command processor.

In version 3.1, *xxxxx* sets the number of paragraphs (16-byte blocks) in the environment. The allowable range is 10 to 2048.

In versions 3.2 and 3.3, *xxxxx* sets the number of bytes in the environment. The allowable range is 160 to 32,768, the environment size being rounded up to the nearest multiple of 16.

The environment variables of the primary processor are inherited by the secondary command processor. Any modifications that the secondary command processor performs on its environment variables are local. The modifications do not affect the environment variables of the primary command processor. The MS-DOS environment and environment variables are discussed in chapter 12.

Purpose of a Secondary Command Processor

A secondary command processor allows a computer program or batch file to utilize other programs, other batch files, or MS-DOS commands. It works something like this: MS-DOS is booted, and the (primary) command processor is loaded into memory and takes control. You enter the name of the file containing a computer program; the command processor loads the program and passes control to it. Your program begins to execute and at some point loads a secondary command processor. The secondary processor receives control, at which point any program, batch file, or MS-DOS command may be executed. At some point, the secondary command processor is exited, and control returns to the original computer program (see figure 2). See chapter 5 for a discussion of the role of a secondary command processor in executing batch files.

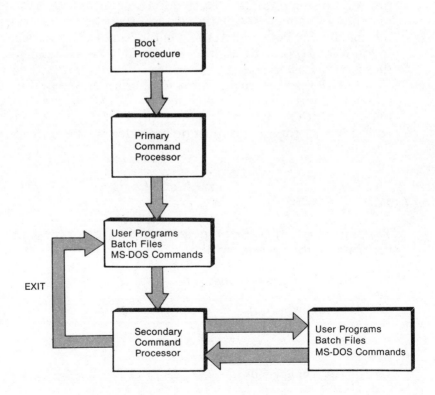

Figure 2. Loading a secondary command processor.

COMP

External
MS-DOS 1.X, 2.X, 3.X

Function: Compares the contents of one file with the contents of another file

Format: COMP [*d:*][*path*][*filename*[.*ext*]][*d:*][*path*][*filename*[.*ext*]]

Examples: comp
comp testfile.txt
comp a:testfile.txt b:testfile.txt

Note: COMP is the file comparison utility that is included with PC-DOS (the version of MS-DOS designed for the IBM personal computer). While many other microcomputers also include a file comparison utility program, the following description and comments relate specifically to COMP, though they can be applied generally to other MS-DOS file comparison utilities.

The COMP (COMPare files) command compares files on a byte-by-byte basis. The first byte of file A is compared with the first byte of file B and so on. Any mismatches are displayed. The comparison is halted if ten mismatches are detected. COMP tells you that the "Files compare ok" if no mismatches are detected. At the completion of a comparison, you are asked if you want to compare another pair of files. No comparison is made if the files are unequal in size.

COMP is an external command; therefore, one of the disks in the system must contain a copy of the file COMP.COM. In the examples presented here, COMP.COM is stored on the C drive. If COMP.COM is not on the default drive, all commands must be preceded by the appropriate drive letter designator.

Using COMP

To compare two files, first type the name of the primary file and then type the name of the secondary file:

```
C>comp one.txt b:one.txt
```

MS-DOS responds:

```
C:ONE        .TXT and B:ONE         .TXT

Files compare ok

Compare more files (Y/N)? _
```

If you enter "Y", COMP will prompt you to enter the names of two other files to be compared. If you enter "N", the MS-DOS prompt will reappear.

COMP can compare files with different names when the files are on the same disk or on different disks. It can compare files with the same name only if they are on different disks or in different directories on the same disk.

COMP may be started without specifying one or both of the files to be compared. COMP will prompt you for the unnamed file(s):

```
C>comp

Enter primary filename
one.txt
Enter 2nd filename or drive id
b:

C:ONE      .TXT and B:ONE      .TXT

Files compare ok

Compare more files (Y/N)? _
```

Notice that only the drive designator was entered for the second file. COMP looks for a file with the same name as the first filename when the second parameter contains only a drive and/or a path.

COMP displays any mismatches between files by listing the hexadecimal offset of the mismatch(es) and the hexadecimal byte value of each file at that offset. *Offset* refers to a byte's position in the file relative to the first byte in the file. The first byte in the file is at offset 0, the second byte at offset 1, and so on.

```
C>comp one.txt two.txt

C:ONE      .TXT and A:TWO      .TXT

Compare error at offset 8
File 1 = 6B
File 2 = 6A

Compare more files (Y/N)? _
```

COMP checks to see if the final byte of each comparison is an end-of-file marker (hexadecimal 1A). If a marker is found, COMP does not take any action. If no marker is found, COMP displays the following message:

```
EOF marker not found
```

COMP determines a file's size from information stored in the file directory. Some computer programs produce directory entries that round a file's size to a multiple of 128. In these cases, COMP may read more data than what actually resides within the file. Failure to find an EOF marker may indicate that mismatches were detected beyond the end of the file.

Wildcard characters can be used to specify files for comparison. The following command tells COMP to compare all files on drive C that have a filename extension of TXT with the file on drive B having the same filename but an extension of ASM:

```
C>comp *.txt b:*.asm
```

A message will be displayed if a matching file cannot be located on drive B.

COPY

Internal
MS-DOS 1.X, 2.X, 3.X

Functions: Copies an existing file
Combines two or more existing files into one file
Transfers data between peripheral devices and files

Format: COPY [/A][/B][*d*:][*path*]*filename*[.*ext*][/A] [/B]
[+[*d*:][*path*]*filename*[.*ext*][/A][/B] . . .] [*d*:][*path*][*filename*
[.*ext*]][/A][/B][/V]

Examples: copy file1
Copy file1+file2 b:file3
copy con: file4.txt

COPY is one of the most important MS-DOS commands. It is used primarily to make copies of existing MS-DOS files. However, COPY can also be used to combine one or more existing files into one file through a process called *concatenation*. Yet another way to use COPY is in the transfer of data between peripheral devices and files.

Copying Files

To copy a file, first type **copy** and then type the file specification of the original file (source file), followed by the file specification of the file that will contain the copy (target file). MS-DOS will make the copy and display a message telling you how many copies it has made:

```
C>copy file.txt b:file.txt
        1 File(s) copied
```

You may omit the filename of the duplicate file if it will have the same name as the original file. In such cases, the copy must be placed on a separate disk or in a separate directory on the same disk as the original file. The following command will copy "file.txt" to drive B:

```
C>copy file.txt b:
        1 File(s) copied
```

Users of MS-DOS 2.X and 3.X may include a path(s) for the original and/or the duplicate file(s). If one or both paths are not specified, MS-DOS will default to the current directory. The following command places a copy of "file.txt" in the subdirectory DATA on drive C. The original copy of "file.txt" is located in the current directory of drive C.

```
C>copy file.txt\data
        1 File(s) copied
```

A file may be copied to the same directory on the same disk only if the copy is given a different name:

```
C>copy file.txt file2.txt
        1 File(s) copied
```

Wildcard characters may be used with the COPY command in filenames and/or extensions. (See chapter 2 for information on MS-DOS wildcards.) The following command copies all files with an extension of DOC that are located on drive C in the subdirectory LETTERS. The copies will be placed in the subdirectory BACKUP of drive B. MS-DOS will display the name of each file as it is copied. Each copied file will have the same name as the original. At the end of the copying process, MS-DOS will display a message stating the number of files that have been copied:

```
C>copy \letters *.doc b:\\backup
COUNTRY.DOC
TICTOCK.DOC
WHATSUP.DOC
ITHURTS.DOC
QUACK.DOC
        5 File(s) copied
```

Combining Files

COPY may be used to concatenate (combine) two or more files. The files to be combined must be specified in the COPY command and separated with a plus (+) sign. The resulting file will be a combination of the specified files, and the files will be in the order in which they were listed in the command.

The next example copies the files "list1.txt" and "list2.txt" into a new file named "biglist.txt". The original files "list1.txt" and "list2.txt" are preserved. At the end of the copying process, MS-DOS states the number of copies created:

```
C>copy list1.txt+list2.txt biglist.txt
      1 File(s) copied
```

Files may be concatenated without specifying a name for the new file. If no name is specified, the new file is given the name of the first file listed for concatenation. The first file is replaced on the disk by the new file.

Wildcard characters may be used in concatenating files. The following command will combine all the files in the current directory of drive C having an extension of TXT. The combined file will be given the filename "combine.dat":

```
C>copy *.txt combine.dat
LETTER1.TXT
INSERT1.TXT
INSERT2.TXT
          1 File(s) copied
```

When concatenating with wildcards, you must specify in the COPY command the filename of the new file. Otherwise, MS-DOS will try to copy the first file listed ("letter1.txt" in the example) onto itself and the copying process will terminate.

The following command will combine each file having the form *.TXT with a matching file having the form *.DAT. If a match exists, the two files will be combined into a file named " *.doc". For example, the files "letter1.txt" and "letter1.dat" will be combined into the file "letter.doc" and so on:

```
C>copy *.txt+*.dat *.doc
LETTER1.TXT
LETTER1.DAT
LETTER2.TXT
LETTER2.DAT
ESSAY1.TXT
ESSAY2.DAT
          3 File(s) copied
```

You should be a little careful when using wildcards in combining files. Let's say that you want to combine all files having an extension of DOC into a filename "big.doc". That should be as simple as:

```
copy *.doc big.doc
```

Right? Unfortunately, it's not so simple.

As soon as the combination process begins, MS-DOS creates the file "big.doc". If there was a previously existing "big.doc", it is lost and the new "big.doc" takes its place. Once the new "big.doc" is on the scene, MS-DOS sees it as a valid "*.doc" file and will entertain thoughts about adding "big.doc" to the combined file. But "big.doc" *is* the combined file. Fortunately, MS-DOS is smart enough to know not to add "big.doc" to itself. The following message is displayed:

```
Content of destination lost before copy
```

MS-DOS then proceeds on its merry way, looking for other "*.doc" files and adding them to "big.doc" in the normal fashion. The preceding message will be displayed whether or not "big.doc" existed before the combining began. The problem is that if "big.doc" previously existed, it will be written over by the new "big.doc" and lost. To compound the problem, the new "big.doc" will not contain the contents of the old "big.doc".

There are two ways to avoid this problem. You can specify "big.doc" as an existing file that is to be appended to the other "*.doc" files:

```
copy big.doc+*.doc
```

Or you can specify a name for the new file that does not match the wildcard filename:

```
copy *.doc big.dat
```

Using COPY to Update the Time/Date Stamp

The COPY command can be used to update the time and date stamp of a file:

```
copy anyfile.ext+,,
```

Unfortunately, if you attempt to update several time/date stamps with a single command (as in **copy *.*+,,**), MS-DOS will update only the stamp of the first file it finds that matches the wildcard.

COPY Switches

There are three optional switches that you may include in a COPY command. Two of the switches (/a and /b) control the way in which COPY reads and writes files. The third switch (/v) is used to verify the accuracy of a COPY operation.

The /a switch tells COPY to treat a file as an ASCII (text) file. If the file is to be copied, this switch tells COPY to copy the file up to, but not including, the first end-of-file marker (hexadecimal 1A). Any data after the marker is not to be copied. If the file is to be a copy, the /a switch tells COPY to add an end-of-file marker to the end of the file.

The /b switch tells COPY to treat a file as a binary file. If a file is to be copied, this switch tells COPY to copy the entire file based on the size stored in the file directory. If a file is to be a copy, the /b switch tells COPY not to place an end-of-file marker at the end of the file.

An /a or a /b switch applies to the preceding file specification and to all succeeding file specifications until another /a or /b switch is encountered. The file status is set to the default when a COPY command does not include an /a or a /b switch. For copying of files, the default file status is binary (/b). For concatenation, the default file status is ASCII (/a).

The /v switch is used to verify the accuracy of the execution of a COPY command. Verification causes the system to run more slowly. The /v parameter provides the same check on COPY as the VERIFY command.

Copying a Peripheral Device

COPY can be used to send files to peripheral devices and to transfer data between devices. The command is used in the same way as described previously, the only difference being that device names are used in place of file specifications. For example, suppose that you want to print a file named "secret.txt". All you have to do is use the COPY command and PRN, the reserved device name for the printer (see table 6-1 in chapter 6 for a list of reserved device names):

```
C>copy secret.txt prn
        1 File(s) copied
```

You can reverse the process and use COPY to send a file from a peripheral device to a file. A useful way to take advantage of this capability, and one that is utilized throughout this book, is to create a text file directly from the keyboard. The keyboard is a peripheral device with the reserved name "CON". The command "copy con filespec" tells MS-DOS to create a file from data input at the keyboard. Type your text in the normal fashion, pressing Enter at the end of each line. When the complete file has been typed, Enter Ctrl-Z and press Enter. The file will be written to the disk:

```
C>copy con: keyboard.txt
This is a sample file that is being created from
the keyboard. Ctrl-Z is typed and the Enter key is
pressed to send the file to the disk. The file can then
be viewed by entering the command TYPE KEYBOARD.TXT.
^Z

        1 File(s) copied
```

Copying between Devices

COPY can be used to send data from one peripheral device to another. The command is used just as described so far, except that one device name is included as the source of the data and a second device name is included as the recipient of the data. In the next example, COPY is used to send data from the keyboard (CON) to the printer (PRN). Press Enter at the end of each line, and press Ctrl-Z and Enter when you have entered the complete file:

```
C>copy con: prn
This is a sample file to demonstrate the use of COPY
in sending data between peripheral devices. At the end
of the input you will press Ctrl-Z and then press Enter.
This text will be sent to the printer.
^Z
        1 File(s) copied
```

Attempts to COPY a device while in binary status will generate this message:

```
Cannot do binary read from a device
```

The problem can be corrected by removing the binary switch or specifying ASCII status with the /a switch.

COUNTRY

External
MS-DOS 3.0

Function: Specifies country-specific information such as date, time, and currency formats
Note: COUNTRY can be used in CONFIG.SYS only

Formats: **COUNTRY=***xxx*   (MS-DOS 3.0 through 3.2)
COUNTRY=*xxx*,[*yyy*][,[*d*:]*filename*[.*ext*]]   (MS-DOS 3.3)

Example: country=001
country=001,437,c:\dos\country.sys

The COUNTRY command, first implemented with MS-DOS 3.0, allows you to specify certain country-specific information such as the date, the time, and currency formats.

Versions 3.0 through 3.2 use this command in a very straightforward manner. A statement of the form "country=*xxx*" is included in the CONFIG.SYS file, with *xxx* being a valid 3-digit country code. See appendix D for a listing of the valid country codes.

Use of the command is more complicated in MS-DOS 3.3. The format is as follows:

COUNTRY=*xxx*,[*yyy*][,[*d:*]*filename*[*.ext*]]

The *xxx* parameter remains a valid 3-digit country code. The *yyy* parameter specifies a code page. A single country has two code pages. COUNTRY determines which code page to use as the system code page. Please refer to appendix D for an overview of code pages and code page switching.

The *filename* parameter refers to the country information file (COUNTRY.SYS).

If there is no "country=" statement in CONFIG.SYS, the default country code is 001, the default code page is 437, and the default country information file is \COUNTRY.SYS.

CTTY

Internal
MS-DOS 2.X, 3.X

Functions: Changes the standard input/output to an auxiliary console
Restores the standard input/output to the keyboard and screen

Format: CTTY *device name*

Examples: ctty com1
ctty con

The keyboard and the display screen form the standard input/output device. This means that unless MS-DOS is instructed otherwise, it will look to the keyboard for input and will send output to the display screen. The CTTY (Change console) command is used to make another peripheral device (such as a modem attached to an asynchronous communications port) the standard input/output device.

To use the CTTY command, type **ctty** and then type the name of the device that will be the new standard input/output device. (See chapter 6 for a list of device names reserved by MS-DOS.) The following command makes the modem attached to the first asynchronous communications port the standard input/output device:

```
C>ctty com1
```

Once this command is entered, MS-DOS will look to the port for input data. It will no longer be possible to enter data from the keyboard in the normal fashion.

The following command will restore the keyboard and display screen as the standard input/output device. The command must be entered at the current input device:

```
C>ctty con
```

CTTY allows you to use any character device as the standard input/ output device. Simply type **ctty** and then type the name of the device that is defined in the device driver. (See chapter 14 for a discussion of devices and device drivers.)

DATE

Internal
MS-DOS 1.X, 2.X, 3.X

Functions: Displays the current date known to MS-DOS
Changes the date known to MS-DOS

Format: DATE [*mm-dd-yy*]

Examples: date
date 12-6-88

The DATE command is used to display and set the current date known to MS-DOS. Each time that you create or modify a file, MS-DOS stores this date as a part of the file's entry in the disk directory.

To display the current date known to MS-DOS, type **date**. MS-DOS will display the date, including the day of the week (Mon, Tue, Wed, etc.). Then MS-DOS will ask if you want to change the current date:

```
C>date
Current date is Fri    12-06-88
Enter new date:
```

To enter a new date, use the form *mm-dd-yy* or *mm/dd/yy* where:

mm is a one- or two-digit number from 1–12,

dd is a one- or two-digit number from 1–31,

yy is a two-digit number from 80–99 or a four-digit number from 1980 to 2099.

```
C>date
Current date is Fri    12-06-88
Enter new date:12/9/88
```

If you want to leave the current date unchanged, just press Enter:

```
C>date
Current date is Mon    12-09-88
Enter new date:       ←Enter
```

You may specify the current date in the DATE command:

```
C>date 12/25/88
```

MS-DOS will prompt for another date if you enter an invalid date.

On machines with permanent clocks, the MS-DOS 3.3 implementation of DATE resets the permanent clock's date. Unfortunately, PC-DOS 3.3 sets only permanent clocks whose memory address is the same as IBM's clock. DATE has no effect on clocks with a different address.

DEL

Internal
MS-DOS 1.X, 2.X, 3.X

Function: Deletes (erases) one or more files from a disk

Format: DEL [*d*:][*path*][*filename*[*.ext*]]

Examples: del badfile.txt
erase badfile.txt

The DEL (DELete) command, also known as the ERASE command, is used to remove a file(s) from a disk. To use DEL, type **del** (or **erase**) and then type the file specification of the unneeded file. (See chapter 2 for a discussion of file specifications.) If you do not include a drive designator and/or a path in the filespec, MS-DOS assumes that the file is located on the default drive and/or in the current directory. In the following example, a file in the current directory of the default drive is deleted:

```
C>del badfile.txt
```

You can delete a group of files with a single command by using wild-card characters. (See chapter 2 for a discussion of wildcards.) Use wildcards with caution, however, since it is easy to inadvertently erase files that you wanted to save. The command in the next example deletes all files in the current directory of drive B that have an extension of DOC:

```
C>del a:*.doc
```

Entering a file specification of *.* tells MS-DOS to delete all the files in the current directory. MS-DOS checks to make sure that you really want to do this:

```
C>del *.*
Are you sure (Y/N)? _
```

Type "N" and press Enter if you are not sure. If you are sure, type "Y", double-check that you really are sure, say goodbye to the files, and press Enter.

Actually, DEL does not remove files from a disk. It only modifies the file directory so that MS-DOS treats the files as if they did not exist. If you ever delete an important file accidentally, you may want to try to recover it with the MS-DOS utility program DEBUG. (See chapters 9 and 11 for some guidance.) There are also commercially available programs that can be used to recover erased files. The important point here is that if you think you may want to recover an erased file, **do not**, **under any circumstances**, **write any data to that disk**. If you do that, the file really does go "bye-bye."

Note that DEL cannot be used to remove a subdirectory. (See the discussion of RMDIR.) Also, DEL cannot be used to delete a file that has its read-only attribute set.

DEL should be used carefully if you use ASSIGN, JOIN, or SUBST. These commands direct MS-DOS to treat one device as if it were another. For example, ASSIGN may be used to direct all references for drive A to drive C. When conditions like this exist, it is easy to inadvertently delete files that you want to keep, so be careful.

DEVICE

Internal
MS-DOS 2.X, 3.X

Function: Instructs MS-DOS to install a device driver
Note: DEVICE can be used in a CONFIG.SYS file only

Format: DEVICE=[*d:*][*path*]***filename***[*.ext*]

Example: device=ansi.sys

The DEVICE command is used to give MS-DOS the filename(s) of any user-specified device drivers that are to be installed in computer memory. (See chapter 14 for a discussion of installable device drivers and their use.)

The DEVICE command can be used only as a statement within a CONFIG.SYS text file. The statements in CONFIG.SYS are read by MS-DOS each time that the system is booted. If any of the statements in CONFIG.SYS are

DEVICE commands, MS-DOS will store (install) in computer memory the device driver named in the command.

To enter a DEVICE command, type **device=** and then type the filename and filename extension of the device driver that is to be installed in memory. A DEVICE command can be added to an existing CONFIG.SYS file with a text editor such as EDLIN (chapter 7). A new CONFIG.SYS file can be created by using the command "Copy con". (See the COPY command, "Copying between Devices.")

CONFIG.SYS must be stored in the root directory of the default drive. In the following example, ANSI.SYS and VDISK.SYS are stored in the sub-directory \DOS of drive C:

```
C>copy con: config.sys
device=c:\dos\ansi.sys
device=c:\dos\vdisk.sys
^Z        ←you press Ctrl-Z
  1 File(s) copied
```

ANSI.SYS (see chapter 8) is a keyboard device driver supplied with MS-DOS 2.X and 3.X. VDISK.SYS is a device driver for a *virtual* (RAM) disk and is discussed next. DRIVER.SYS, an installable device driver for floppy diskette drives, is also discussed.

VDISK.SYS

A virtual disk, also called a RAM disk, is a portion of random access memory (RAM) that the operating system treats as a disk drive. A RAM disk is accessed with a drive specifier as if it were a conventional disk drive. The advantage of a RAM disk is that the data on the disk can be accessed much faster than data on a mechanical disk drive. The disadvantage of a RAM disk is that it is not permanent storage for data. Turning off or rebooting your system destroys the contents of the RAM disk. Any data to be saved must be copied to a mechanical disk.

VDISK.SYS is a RAM disk device driver supplied with MS-DOS 2.X and 3.X. It performs three functions: (1) installs the RAM disk in memory and assigns it a drive letter, (2) formats the RAM disk so that it can store files (you cannot use the FORMAT command on a RAM disk), and (3) acts as an interface between MS-DOS and the RAM disk. The syntax for installing the device driver is:

DEVICE=[*path*]**VDISK.SYS**[*vvv*][*sss*][*ddd*][/E[:*t*]]

The *vvv* parameter sets the size of the virtual disk in kilobytes. The allowable range is from 1 kilobyte up to the size of your system's memory. The default disk size is 64 Kbytes.

If you request too much memory for your RAM disk, VDISK will adjust your request downward to leave 64 Kbytes of memory available after the RAM disk is installed. VDISK will not install the RAM disk if less than 64 Kbytes of memory is available. If the disk size request has been adjusted, VDISK notifies you with the message "Buffer size adjusted".

The *sss* parameter sets the number of bytes per sector on the RAM disk. Acceptable values are 128, 256, and 512. Any other value will default to 128 bytes per sector. Disk sectors are discussed in chapter 11.

The *ddd* parameter sets the number of entries allowed in the disk directory. The allowable range is 2 to 512, with a default of 64. Each directory entry requires 32 bytes. If necessary, VDISK will adjust your request size upward to fill out a complete sector. For example, if your sector size is 512, and you request 12 directory entries, VDISK will adjust upward and give you 16 directory entries (16 × 32 = 512).

Each RAM disk requires 1 boot sector, 1 FAT sector, 1 directory sector, and 1 data sector. VDISK will adjust your directory entry request downward, if need be, to make room for these required sectors. Any adjustment of the number of directory entries is accompanied by the message "Directory entries adjusted".

The /e switch directs MS-DOS to place the RAM disk in extended memory (see chapter 12). The driver itself is still stored in low memory. You may request more than one RAM disk in extended memory by placing multiple "device=vdisk.sys" commands (each with the /e switch) in your CONFIG.SYS file. Each RAM disk in extended memory may be up to 4 megabytes in size.

MS-DOS will display an "Insufficient memory" message if you use the /e switch on a machine that does not have extended memory.

The optional *:t* parameter tells MS-DOS the maximum number of sectors to transfer to extended memory at one time. The range is 1 to 8, with a default of 8. Try adjusting this parameter, as well as the sector size parameter, if you are having trouble getting your RAM disk to work properly in extended memory.

The following example installs a 1000-Kbyte RAM disk:

```
device=vdisk.sys 1000 512 64 /e:4
```

The RAM disk created has a sector size of 512 bytes. The directory may contain up to 64 entries. The RAM disk is placed in extended memory. A maximum of 4 sectors is transferred to extended memory at a time.

DRIVER.SYS

DRIVER.SYS is a diskette device driver supplied with MS-DOS 3.2 and 3.3. It is valuable for two reasons: (1) it can be used to drive all MS-DOS–supported drives (including 1.44-megabyte, 3½-inch drives) and (2) it can be used to drive "logical" as well as "physical" drives. To understand how DRIVER.SYS works, you must first understand how MS-DOS addresses disk drives.

Disk Addressing

When you switch on your computer, one of the actions that MS-DOS takes is to determine which peripheral devices are attached to the computer. After making this determination, MS-DOS reads the CONFIG.SYS file to check for any installable device drivers. During this process, MS-DOS assigns a unique drive letter to each disk drive device on the system. The first internal diskette drive is assigned A; the second, B. The letters from C on are assigned as other system drives are recognized.

On systems with only one internal diskette drive, the single drive is assigned letters A and B. The first fixed disk drive on a MS-DOS computer is always assigned drive letter C.

Disk drives are also given *physical drive numbers*. The first diskette drive is assigned physical drive number 0, the second is assigned physical drive number 1, and so on for the diskette drives.

The first fixed disk on an MS-DOS computer is assigned physical drive number 128, the second is assigned 129, and so on for the fixed disks.

Physical and Logical Drives

A *physical* disk drive is a real disk drive, a piece of hardware. Its existence is totally independent of any computer.

A *logical* disk drive is a product of the logic stored inside a computer. A program (such as the operating system) tells the computer that a logical drive exists at a certain (physical) location, and the computer accepts that information. The logical drive ceases to exist when the computer is turned off.

Drive letters are used to reference logical disk drives. As discussed above, if an MS-DOS computer has one diskette drive, the drive is assigned drive letters A and B. Logical drives A and B both reside on physical drive 0. MS-DOS assigns logical drive letters, in alphabetical order, to disk drives as each logical drive is initialized.

With this background, we can now discuss DRIVER.SYS.

Using DRIVER.SYS

The following discussion requires some knowledge of diskette structure. See chapter 11 if you are unfamiliar with this topic.

The syntax for DRIVER.SYS is:

DEVICE=DRIVER.SYS /D:*ddd*[/T:*ttt*][/S:*ss*][/H:*hh*][/C][/F:*f*]

The /d:*ddd* parameter specifies the physical drive number on which the logical diskette will reside. Allowable values are 0 to 255. As discussed, 0 to 127 refers to diskette drives and 128 to 255 refers to fixed disk drives.

The /t:*ttt* parameter specifies the number of tracks per side of the logical diskettes. Allowable values are 1 to 999. The default is 80 tracks per side.

The /s:*ss* parameter specifies the number of sectors per track of the logical diskette. Allowable values are 1 to 99. The default is 9 sectors per track.

The /h:*bb* parameter specifies the maximum number of heads. Allowable values are 1 to 99. The default is 2 heads.

The /c parameter specifies that the drive detect when the drive door has been opened and closed.

The /n parameter specifies that the physical device on which the logical device will reside be nonremovable (a fixed disk).

The /f:*f* parameter specifies the type of logical device. Allowable values and the corresponding diskette type are given in the following list. The default value is 2.

Value	Diskette Type
/f:0	160 Kbytes/180 Kbytes
	320 Kbytes/360 Kbytes
/f:1	1.2 Mbytes
/f:2	720 Kbytes
/f:7	1.44 Mbytes

Adding a Physical Drive

Let's say that you want to add an external 1.44-megabyte, 3½-inch diskette drive to a system that has one standard internal diskette drive and one fixed disk drive. Physical drive 0 is the internal diskette drive. Physical drive 1 is reserved for a second standard internal diskette. Therefore, the 3½-inch drive will be physical drive 2. The command to install an appropriate device driver is as follows (assume that DRIVER.SYS is in subdirectory C:\DOS):

```
device=c:\dos\driver.sys /d:2 /f:7
```

The **/d:2** parameter specifies physical drive number 2. The **/f:7** parameter specifies a 1.44-Mbyte diskette. Since the DEVICE command is read after drive letters A, B, and C have been assigned, the 3½-disk drive is assigned drive letter D.

Adding a Logical Drive

Sometimes it is useful to create a second logical drive on a physical drive. Assume that you have an IBM AT computer with a 1.2-Mbyte drive as physical drive 0, a 360-Kbyte drive as physical drive 1, and a fixed disk drive as physical drive 128. During system startup, logical drive A is assigned to the 1.2-Mbyte drive, logical drive B is assigned to the 360-Kbyte drive, and logical drive C is assigned to the fixed disk drive. You can assign a second logical drive to the 1.2-Mbyte drive by placing the following command in CONFIG.SYS:

```
device=c:\dos\driver.sys /d:0 /s:15 /c /f:1
```

The /d:0 parameter assigns the logical diskette drive to physical drive 0. Since 80 tracks per side and 2 heads are defaults, no /t:*ttt* or /h:*hh* parameters were needed. The /s:15 parameter specifies 15 sectors per track for the logical drive. The /c parameter specifies that the drive detect when the door has been opened and closed. The /f:1 parameter specifies a logical 1.2-Mbyte drive. The DEVICE command is read after drive letters A, B, and C have been assigned. Therefore, the logical drive is assigned drive letter D.

DISPLAY.SYS

DISPLAY.SYS is a code-page-switching device driver supplied with MS-DOS 3.3. DISPLAY.SYS is used to implement code page switching on a display adapter. For an overview of code pages and code page switching, please refer to appendix D.

DISPLAY.SYS is installed in memory by including a statement having the following format in CONFIG.SYS:

DEVICE=[*d*:][*path*]DISPLAY.SYS CON[:]=(*type*[,[*hwcp*][,(*n,m*)]])

or

DEVICE=[*d*:][*path*]DISPLAY.SYS CON[:]=(*type*[,[*hwcp*][,*n*]])

The *type* parameter specifies the display adapter that will support code page switching. The allowable values are "EGA" and "LCD". EGA refers to both the Enhanced Graphics Adapter and the IBM PS/2 Video Display Adapter. LCD refers to the PC Convertible Liquid Crystal Display Adapter. Code page switching is not currently supported with other types of display adapters.

The *hwcp* parameter specifies the hardware code pages that are to be made available for use. Valid code page numbers are 437 (the default), 850, 860, 863, and 865. Hardware code pages are ready-to-use code pages that are stored in the display device's read-only memory (ROM). Refer to appendix D for further information on hardware code pages, including the meaning of the code page numbers.

The *n* parameter specifies the number of prepared code pages to be supported by the adapter. The allowable range is 1–12. Prepared code pages are discussed in appendix D.

The *m* parameter specifies the number of font sizes to be supported by the adapter. The Enhanced Graphics Adapter can support up to two font sizes (8 × 8 and 8 × 14). The PS/2 Display adapter can also support up to two font sizes (8 × 8 and 8 × 16). The LCD adapter supports only one font size (8 × 8).

The following command illustrates the use of DISPLAY.SYS.

```
device=c:\dos\display.sys con:=(ega,437,2)
```

This command instructs MS-DOS to load the DISPLAY.SYS driver for use with the Enhanced Graphics Adapter. Along with the driver, hardware code page 437 is to be loaded. In addition, the driver is to support two prepared code pages.

PRINTER.SYS

PRINTER.SYS is another code-page-switching device driver supplied with MS-DOS 3.3. As its name implies, PRINTER.SYS supports code page switching on two printers: the IBM Proprinter Model 4201 and the IBM Quietwriter III Model 5202. For an overview of code page switching, please refer to appendix D.

PRINTER.SYS is installed in memory by including a statement of the following format in CONFIG.SYS:

DEVICE=[*d:*][*path*]**PRINTER.SYS***LPT#*[:]=
(*type*[,[(*hwcp1,hwcp2*)][,*n*]])

or

DEVICE=[*d:*][*path*]**PRINTER.SYS***LPT#*[:]=(*type*[,[*hwcp*][,*n*]])

The *LPT#* parameter is used to specify a printer device. The valid parameters are "PRN," "LPT1," "LPT2," and "LPT3."

The *type* parameter refers to the printer that will support code page switching and must equal 4201 or 5202.

The *hwcp* parameter specifies the hardware code pages that are to be made available for use. Valid code page numbers are 437 (the default), 850, 860, 863, and 865. If two or more hardware code pages are specified, they must be enclosed in parentheses. Hardware code pages are ready-to-use code pages that are stored in the printer's read only memory (ROM). Refer to appendix D for further information on hardware code pages, including the meaning of the code page numbers.

The *n* parameter specifies the number of prepared code pages to be supported by the printer. Prepared code pages are discussed in appendix D.

The following command (which must be in CONFIG.SYS) instructs MS-DOS to load the PRINTER.SYS driver for use with the Quietwriter 5202 printer. Along with the driver, hardware code page 850 is to be loaded. In addition, the driver is to support three prepared code pages.

```
device=c:\dos\printer.sys prn:=(5202,850,3)
```

DIR

Internal
MS-DOS 1.X, 2.X, 3.X

Function: Lists directory entries

Formats: DIR [*d*:][*filename*[.*ext*]][/P][/W]
        DIR [*d*:][*path*][*filename*[.*ext*]][/P][/W] (MS-DOS 2.X and 3.X)

Examples: dir
        dir b:
        dir b:\subdir1*.doc /w

The DIR (DIRectory) command is used to display the filename, filename extension, size, and time/date stamp of the files contained on a disk. The MS-DOS 2.X and 3.X versions of DIR also display the disk's volume identification (if one was specified when the disk was formatted) and the amount of free space remaining on the disk.

To use DIR with MS-DOS 1, simply type **dir**. Notice that if you do not enter a drive designator (such as c: or a:), MS-DOS will display the files on the default drive:

```
C>dir
FILE1       BAS       3213      12-02-88   11:42a
PROGRAM1    BAS      12674      10-09-87    9:53a
GWBASIC     EXE      57344       6-21-87   10:44a
COMMAND     COM       4879       3-11-87   11:40a
        4 File(s)
```

The first column of the display gives the name of each file. The second column gives the filename extension. The third column shows the size of the file in bytes. The fourth column shows the date that the file was created or last modified, and the fifth column shows the time that the file was created or last modified.

If you are using the DIR command with MS-DOS 2.X or 3.X, again simply type **dir**. The display will show the same information as the MS-DOS 1 version but will give you additional information about the disk's volume label and the space available for new files. If you do not include a path in the

DIR command, MS-DOS will default to the current directory of the specified (or default) drive:

```
C>dir

Volume in drive C is WAITE_DISK1
Directory of C:\

COMMAND     COM    17664    3-08-87 12:00p
C                  <DIR>    1-01-84 12:07a
WS2PATH     BAT       23   12-07-87  8:18a
CONFIG      SYS      128    9-25-87  7:24p
SETCLOCK    COM      853    9-19-86  4:24p
WS                 <DIR>    9-08-86  4:27p
        6 File(s)   110269 bytes free
```

In the preceding example, notice that the display shows the volume label "WAITE_DISK1" for the disk in the default drive (C:). The volume label is simply the *name* of the disk. The line **Directory of C:** tells you that the files displayed are in the root directory on drive C. Two of the directory entries contain the notation **<DIR>**. These entries represent subdirectories that are contained in the root directory. The final line says that there are 110,269 free bytes remaining on the disk.

To view the contents of a directory other than the current directory, type **dir** and then type the path to the directory:

```
C>dir \ws

Volume in drive A is WAITE_DISK1
Directory of C:\WS

.                  <DIR>    9-08-86  4:27p
..                 <DIR>    9-08-86  4:27a
WS          EXE    60128    6-25-86  7:24p
WS          HLP    45853    6-25-86  7:24p
BATES       DOC     4096    9-17-88  4:27p
GILMORE     DOC     4096    9-18-88  2:15p
        6 File(s)   110269 bytes free
```

Notice the single and double periods that appear in the first two entries. These are shorthand symbols used by MS-DOS in displaying the contents of a subdirectory. The entry in the first column with a single period represents the directory being listed. The entry with two periods represents the listed directory's parent directory. WS is the listed directory. WS's parent directory is the root directory. (See chapter 3 for more information about directories, subdirectories, and parents.)

Using /P and /W with DIR

The DIR command has two optional switches. The /p switch is particularly useful when you wish to view the contents of a large directory. When DIR is directed to display a large number of files, the file information will scroll off the screen faster than you can read it. You can see this by inserting a working copy of your system diskette in drive A and entering the command **dir a:** and pressing Enter. You will be unable to study the information before it's gone from view. By using the /p switch, you can instruct MS-DOS to display one "page" of file information at a time. The display will be suspended each time that the screen is filled. The display will resume when you press any key.

The /w switch is used with DIR to display file information in the "wide" mode. The wide mode displays the filename and filename extension of five files on each line of the display screen. File size and file time/date information are not displayed with the wide mode.

Using DIR to List Selected Files

You can specify a particular file in the DIR command. MS-DOS will look for that filename and, if the file is found, will display the corresponding file information:

```
C>dir ws2path.bat

 Volume in drive C is WAITE_DISK1
 Directory of C:\

WS2PATH    BAT       23   12-07-87     8:18a
        1 File(s)     110269 bytes free
```

This feature can be useful when you are looking for a specific file among a large number of files. Let's say that you want to know if there is a file named "letters.doc" in the subdirectory WS. You could look for the file in two ways. You could enter the command **dir \ws** and scan the display for "letters.doc", or you could enter the command **dir \ws letters.doc**. If you enter the second command, MS-DOS will do the scanning for you. If "letters.doc" exists, MS-DOS will display the file information. If the file does not exist, MS-DOS will let you know.

Wildcards and DIR

Using wildcard characters with DIR allows you to have MS-DOS list a specific group of files. Let's say that you want a listing of the files in the root directory of drive B that have a filename beginning with the letter "Q" and a filename extension of DOC. All you have to do is enter the following command:

```
C>dir b:\q*.doc
```

MS-DOS will pick out the files that you are looking for and display their names on the screen. (For more information on wildcards, see chapter 2.)

By eliminating the filename extension in a DIR command and entering only the filename, you can instruct MS-DOS to list all files with the specified filename. The following command directs MS-DOS to list all files in the root directory of drive B with a filename of "animals":

```
C>dir b:\animals
```

By entering the filename followed by a period and no filename extension, you can instruct MS-DOS to list all files with the specified filename and no filename extension. In the following command, MS-DOS looks for a file having the filename "animals" and no filename extension:

```
C>dir b:animals.
```

DISKCOMP

External
MS-DOS 1.X, 2.X, 3.X

Function: Compares the contents of two floppy diskettes

Formats: **DISKCOMP** [*d*:][*d*:]
DISKCOMP [*d*:][*d*:][/1][/8] (MS-DOS 2.X and 3.X)

Example: diskcomp a: b:

DISKCOMP (COMPare DISKette) is a utility program used to compare the contents of two floppy diskettes. DISKCOMP compares the diskettes on a sector by sector basis. It is most useful in checking the accuracy of copies made with DISKCOPY.

DISKCOMP is used for comparing diskettes only. It cannot be used with fixed disks, RAM disks, or network disks. Nor can it be used in conjunction with SUBST, ASSIGN, or JOIN.

Before using DISKCOMP, you may wish to read the discussion on diskette structure in chapter 11.

Using DISKCOMP

Since DISKCOMP is an external MS-DOS command, a copy of the file DISK-COMP.COM must be available to the system before you can use the command. This means that either DISKCOMP.COM must be in the current directory of the default drive or that the location of DISKCOMP.COM must have been specified by the PATH command (see the discussion of PATH).

If you are using a system with two diskette drives, you will save yourself a lot of diskette swapping by including two drive letter designators in the DISKCOMP command:

```
C>diskcomp c: b:
```

When you press Enter, MS-DOS will prompt you with the statements **Insert the first diskette in drive A:** and **Insert the second diskette in drive B:**. It does not matter which diskette is inserted in which drive. Once the diskettes are in place, the comparison is started by pressing any key.

If you are using a system with only one diskette drive or if you do not enter two drive letter designators in the DISKCOMP start command, MS-DOS will display a prompt telling you when to insert the first diskette and when to insert the second diskette. It is not important which diskette you designate as "first" and which you designate as "second." The important point is to keep the first and second diskettes straight after the comparison begins.

DISKCOMP compares the diskettes on a track-by-track basis. If all tracks match, MS-DOS will display the message **Diskettes compare ok**. If there is a mismatch, MS-DOS will display the track and side where the errors appear.

At the end of a comparison, DISKCOMP asks you if there are any more comparisons to perform. If you reply "Y", DISKCOMP prompts you to insert the next pair of diskettes. If you reply "N", control is returned to MS-DOS.

DISKCOMP Switches

DISKCOMP has two optional switches. The /1 switch tells DISKCOMP to compare only the first side of each diskette. The /8 switch tells DISKCOMP to compare only the first 8 sectors of each track. (See chapter 11 for a detailed discussion of tracks and sectors.)

DISKCOPY

External
MS-DOS 1.X, 2.X, 3.X

Function: Copies the contents of one floppy diskette onto another

Format: DISKCOPY [*d*:][*d*:]
DISKCOPY [*d*:][*d*:][/1] (MS-DOS 2.X and 3.X)

Example: diskcopy a: b:

DISKCOPY is a utility program used to copy the contents of one floppy diskette onto another. It can be used with floppy diskettes only. MS-DOS will display an error message if you try to use DISKCOPY with a fixed disk.

Using DISKCOPY

DISKCOPY is an external MS-DOS command. This means that before you can use DISKCOPY, one of the system drives must contain the file DISK-COPY.COM. In the example used here, DISKCOPY.COM is stored on drive C.

If your system has two diskette drives, you will save yourself a lot of diskette swapping by including two drive letter designators in the DISK-COPY command.

```
C>diskcopy a: b:
```

When the command is entered, MS-DOS will load DISKCOPY.COM into memory and then prompt you to insert the source diskette in the first drive specified in the command and the target diskette in the second drive specified in the command. The *source diskette* is the diskette to be copied; the *target diskette* is the diskette that will contain the copy. Once the source and target diskettes are in place, press any key to begin the DISKCOPY process.

```
Insert source diskette in drive A

Insert target diskette in drive B

Strike any key when ready
```

If your system does not have two diskette drives or if you did not include two drive letter designators in the DISKCOPY command, MS-DOS will prompt you to insert the source and target diskettes. Remember that the source diskette is the original; the target diskette is the copy. If you get them confused, you may inadvertently erase the data stored on the original diskette. To prevent accidental erasure, you can easily write-protect the source diskette by placing a small piece of tape over the notch on the diskette's side. MS-DOS will not send data to a write-protected diskette.

At the end of the copy process, you will be asked if you wish to copy another diskette. If you reply "Y", the DISKCOPY process is repeated. If you reply "N", control is returned to MS-DOS.

The MS-DOS 2.X and 3.X versions of DISKCOPY offer an optional /1 switch. Including the /1 switch tells DISKCOPY to copy only the first side of the source diskette.

Note: Most versions of DISKCOPY will format an unformatted target diskette.

DISKCOPY versus COPY

It is important to recognize the difference between the commands DISK-COPY and COPY. DISKCOPY begins by reading the contents of the first track off the source diskette and writing the contents to the first track of the target diskette. The contents of the second track are then read and written to the second track in the target diskette, and so on. DISKCOPY writes over all preexisting data on the target diskette.

COPY begins by reading the contents of the first sector of a file off the source diskette and writing the contents to the first available sector on the target diskette. The contents of the second sector of the file are then read and written to the next available sector on the target diskette. COPY continues in this manner until the entire file has been copied. The only preexisting data on the target diskette that are written over by COPY are the files named in the COPY command.

A file that does not occupy contiguous sectors on a diskette is called a *fragmented* file. Fragmented files can slow computer performance, since MS-DOS requires more time to read a fragmented file. It is good practice to copy a highly fragmented diskette to an empty diskette by using the command "xcopy *.* /s" (or "copy *.*") rather than using DISKCOPY. The XCOPY or COPY command will copy each of the fragmented files to contiguous sectors on the target diskette, thus improving computer performance.

ECHO

Internal
MS-DOS 2.X, 3.X

Functions: Allows or prevents the screen display of MS-DOS commands during batch file execution
Displays messages during batch file execution

Format: ECHO [ON|OFF|*message*]

Examples: echo on
echo off
echo your message here

A *batch file* is a group of MS-DOS commands that are executed sequentially. ECHO determines whether or not the commands in a batch file are displayed on the screen during execution. ECHO can be used in the following ways:

1. **ECHO ON** tells MS-DOS to display the MS-DOS commands.
2. **ECHO OFF** tells MS-DOS to suppress display of the MS-DOS commands.

3. ECHO [*message*] tells MS-DOS to display [*message*]. The message will be displayed regardless of the current ECHO state.

4. ECHO (with no parameters) tells MS-DOS to display the current ECHO state (ON or OFF).

The use of ECHO in batch files is illustrated in chapter 5.

ERASE

Internal
MS-DOS 1.X, 2.X, 3.X

Function: Erases (deletes) one or more files from a disk

Format: ERASE [*d*:][*path*][*filename*[.*ext*]]

Examples: erase badfile.txt
             del badfile.txt

The ERASE command is identical to the DEL command. Please refer to the DEL command for a description of ERASE.

EXE2BIN

External
MS-DOS 1.X, 2.X, 3.X

Function: Converts EXE files to standard binary files

Format: EXE2BIN [*d*:][*path*]*filename*[.*ext*][*filespec*]

Example: exe2bin testfile

Computer programs that operate under MS-DOS are stored as either COM or EXE files (see chapter 12). EXE2BIN is an MS-DOS utility that is used to convert EXE files to COM files. You need not concern yourself with EXE2BIN unless you are assembling or compiling your own computer programs.

EXE and COM Files

All EXE files contain a *header* (an area at the start of the file) that stores information about the relocatable items within the file. A *relocatable* item is a program variable whose value depends on the location at which MS-DOS loads the program in computer memory. During the loading of an EXE file, MS-DOS refers to the file's header to determine the location of each relocatable item within the file. MS-DOS then modifies the value of each relocatable item according to the memory address of the load.

COM files do not contain any relocatable items; therefore, they do not have a header. A COM file is produced by first creating an EXE file (with either an assembler or a compiler) and then using EXE2BIN to convert the EXE file to a binary file. COM files created with an assembler must begin with the statement ORG 100H. This assembler statement tells MS-DOS to load the file at offset address 100H. A COM file is limited in size to 64 Kbytes.

Since a COM file does not have a header, converting an EXE file to a COM file will conserve computer memory. Thus, it is advantageous to convert to COM files those EXE files that do not contain relocatable items, that begin with an ORG 100H statement, and that are smaller than 64 Kbytes.

Using EXE2BIN

EXE2BIN is an external MS-DOS command. This means that before you can use EXE2BIN, the file EXE2BIN.EXE must be available to the system. Either EXE2BIN.EXE must be in the current directory of the default drive or the location of EXE2.BIN must have been specified by the PATH command (see the discussion of PATH).

To use EXE2BIN, type **exe2bin**, then type the file specification of the file to be converted, and finally type the file specification of the converted file. A filename must be specified for the file to be converted. If no filename extension is specified for the file to be converted, MS-DOS assumes that the file has an extension of EXE. A file specification for the converted file is optional. The default filename is the filename specified for the file to be converted. The default filename extension for the converted file is BIN. The current directory is used if no path is specified for the converted file.

Once you have entered the complete command, press Enter to convert the EXE file. If the EXE file conforms to the requirements of a COM file, the conversion is made and control returns to MS-DOS. The converted file can then be renamed with an extension of COM if you wish.

If the EXE file does not specify where MS-DOS is to load the file (for example, does not contain an ORG statement), EXE2BIN will convert the EXE file to a standard binary file. If such a file contains any relocatable items, MS-DOS will prompt you to enter a "fixup value." The *fixup value* is a hexadecimal number that will be the absolute memory address at which the converted file will be loaded. Such a file can be loaded only by a user application program that specifies where in memory it will be loaded. MS-DOS will be unable to load the file.

If the original EXE file specifies a loading address other than 100H, MS-DOS will display the following message:

```
Files cannot be converted
```

This message will also be displayed if the original file is not a valid EXE file.

FASTOPEN

External
MS-DOS 3.3

Function: Provides rapid access to recently used subdirectories and files

Format: FASTOPEN *d*:[=*nnn*] . . . (use of "=" is optional)

Example: fastopen c:=100

FASTOPEN is used to store in memory the physical disk location of recently accessed subdirectories and files. When MS-DOS needs to access a file, FASTOPEN first checks to see if the file's location is stored in memory. If it is, the file can be located very quickly.

MS-DOS locates a disk file by processing a *linked list*, which points to the file's physical location on the disk. As an example, let's consider what MS-DOS must do in order to execute the following command:

```
C>dir \subdir1\subdir2\subdir3
```

The root directory is always in a specific physical location on the disk. MS-DOS proceeds to this location and scans the root directory for an entry named SUBDIR1. This entry will contain the physical disk location of subdirectory SUBDIR1. MS-DOS proceeds to this location and scans SUBDIR1 for an entry named SUBDIR2. This entry directs the operating system to the physical location of SUBDIR2. Once SUBDIR2 is located, the location of SUBDIR3 can be read, and MS-DOS can proceed to the physical disk location of SUBDIR3. All of these steps must be carried out before the DIR command can be executed. FASTOPEN provides a way to speed up this process.

Using FASTOPEN

FASTOPEN is invoked by including on the command line the letter specifier for each fixed disk on your system, followed by a number from 10 to 999. The number tells FASTOPEN how many subdirectory and file locations to store in memory for that disk. In the following example, FASTOPEN stores 100 locations for drives C and D:

```
C>fastopen c:100 d:100
```

FASTOPEN uses 34 as a default if a drive letter is not followed by a number. Each location requires 35 bytes of system memory.

Each time a file or subdirectory is accessed, FASTOPEN checks to see if the corresponding disk location is stored in memory. If not, the location is determined and stored in memory. This process continues until the number of locations stored in memory matches the number specified on the command line. Thereafter, any location placed in memory displaces the location corresponding to the least recent disk access.

Note: FASTOPEN may be invoked one time only following system startup (you may want to include it in an AUTOEXEC.BAT file). FASTOPEN is used with fixed disks only. It cannot be used with floppy disks or disks defined with the MS-DOS commands ASSIGN, JOIN, or SUBST. Nor can it be used with network drives.

FCBS

Internal
MS-DOS 3.X

Function: Determines the number of file control blocks that may be used when file sharing is implemented
Note: FCBS can be used in CONFIG.SYS only

Format: **FCBS=***m,n*

Example: fcbs=10,5

Recall from chapter 11 that MS-DOS uses two different mechanisms to access disk files. One of these mechanisms utilizes a data structure called a *file control block* (FCB) to store information used by MS-DOS in reading and writing files. If your computer is on a network and you have implemented file sharing (see the SHARE command), MS-DOS limits the number of FCBs that can be open at one time to 4. The FCBS command allows you to increase the number of FCBs that may be open at a time.

FCBS is entered with two parameters. The first parameter determines the number of FCBs that may be open at one time. The allowable range is 1 to 255. The second parameter determines the number of FCBs that MS-DOS must leave open. As an example, suppose that CONFIG.SYS contains the following command:

```
fcbs=10,5
```

This command tells MS-DOS that up to 10 FCBs can be open. In addition, 5 FCBs are protected against automatic closure by MS-DOS. In other words, if 10 FCBs are open, and MS-DOS needs to open more FCBs, the operating system may close up to 5 FCBs but must leave the other 5 open.

If CONFIG.SYS does not contain a "fcbs=" command, a default of m=4, n=0 is set.

If MS-DOS must automatically close an FCB, it looks for the FCB that was least recently used and closes it. If MS-DOS subsequently attempts to use the closed FCB, the following error message is displayed:

```
FCB unavailable
Abort, fail?
```

FDISK

External
MS-DOS 2.X, 3.X

Function: Configures the fixed disk

Format: **FDISK**

Example: fdisk

FDISK is a utility program that is used to partition (configure) a fixed disk assigned to MS-DOS. The use of FDISK is described in chapter 4.

FILES

Internal
MS-DOS 2.X, 3.X

Function: Determines the amount of memory that is set aside for file handles
Note: FILES may be used in a CONFIG.SYS file only

Format: **FILES=**xx

Example: files=25

The FILES command is used to establish the amount of memory for a control block used in managing file handles The amount of memory set aside for this purpose determines the maximum number of file handles that can exist at one time.

A *file handle* is a 16-bit number that is assigned by MS-DOS to a new file when the file is created or to an existing file when the file is opened. File handles are used by MS-DOS to keep track of the files that an application program is using at any one time. The role of file handles is discussed more fully in chapter 11.

Using FILES

A FILES command may be used only as part of a CONFIG.SYS file. CONFIG.SYS is a text file containing one or more commands that are read by MS-DOS during the booting process. Each command in CONFIG.SYS specifies certain parameters under which MS-DOS will operate. In this case, a FILES command establishes the number of file handles that may be used by MS-DOS at one time.

CONFIG.SYS can be created or modified with a text editor such as ED-LIN. CONFIG.SYS can also be created by entering the command "copy con: config.sys" (see the COPY command for details).

```
C>copy con: config.sys
FILES=10
^Z        ←you press Ctrl-Z, Enter
    1 File(s) copied
```

MS-DOS will set aside memory for eight file handles if no FILES command is read during booting. For most application programs, this is sufficient. MS-DOS will display the message "No free file handles" if an application program requires more than eight file handles. MS-DOS will occupy 39 more bytes of memory for each additional file above the default value of 8.

The FILES command does not affect the number of user-specified file control blocks (FCBs) that may be set up and used with MS-DOS service functions 0FH–29H (see appendix A).

FIND

External
MS-DOS 2.X, 3.X

Function: Searches for a specified string of text in a file or files

Format: FIND [/V][/C][/N]*string*[*filespec*][*filespec*] . . .

Examples: find "Bruce" records.txt
find /v "Floyd" records.txt
find /c "Linda" records.txt
find /n "Born" records.txt

FIND is an MS-DOS filter that searches the lines of one or more text files for a specified string. The specified string is enclosed on the command line in double quotes (`"like this"`). Alternatively, output from a program or another MS-DOS command can be piped through FIND. The output from FIND can be sent to the standard output or redirected to a device or a file.

FIND is an external MS-DOS command. This means that before you can use the FIND filter, a copy of the file FIND.EXE must be stored in one of the system drives.

FIND Switches

There are three optional switches for FIND. The /v switch causes FIND to display the lines in a text file that do not contain the specified string. The /c switch instructs FIND to display only a count of the number of lines in a text file that contain the specified string. The /n switch tells FIND to display the lines of a text file that contain the specified string; each line is preceded by its relative line number within the file.

Chapter 6 discusses FIND and describes MS-DOS filters, redirection, and pipes.

FOR

Internal
MS-DOS 2.X, 3.X

Function: Executes a command repeatedly on a set of parameters

Format: FOR %%*variable* IN (*set of parameters*) DO *command*

Examples: for %%a IN (file1 file2 file3) DO del %%a
for %b IN (example.bat program.txt letter) DO copy %b prn

A command can be executed repeatedly on a set of specified parameters by using the command FOR. Each FOR command begins with the word "for", followed by a dummy variable. If a FOR command is located within a batch file, the dummy variable is preceded by two percentage signs (%%). Only one percentage sign is used if the FOR command is not located in a batch file. During the execution of a FOR command, the dummy variable is sequentially replaced by each of the specified parameters.

The dummy variable is followed by the letters "IN". Both letters must be entered in uppercase. "IN" is followed by a set of parameters that must be enclosed in parentheses.

Following the set of parameters are the letters "DO", which must be entered in uppercase. "DO" is followed by the command that will be executed one time for each of the parameters in the set.

In the following example, a FOR command is used to print a copy of the files "example.bat", "program.txt", and "letter":

```
C>for %b IN (example.bat program.txt letter) DO copy %b prn

COPY EXAMPLE.BAT PRN
```

```
          1 File(s) copied

COPY PROGRAM.TXT PRN
          1 File(s) copied

COPY LETTER PRN
          1 File(s) copied
```

The use of FOR in MS-DOS batch files is discussed in chapter 5.

FORMAT

External
MS-DOS 1.X, 2.X, 3.X

Function: Initializes floppy diskettes and fixed disks so that they can be used by MS-DOS

Formats: FORMAT [*d*:][/S]
           FORMAT [*d*:][/S][/1][/8][/V][/B] (MS-DOS 2.X and 3.X)
           FORMAT [*d*:][/S][/1][/8][/V][/B][/4] (MS-DOS 3.X)
           FORMAT [*d*:][/S][/1][/8][/V][/B][/4][/N:*xx* /T:*yy*] (MS-DOS 3.3)

Examples: format b:
           format b:/s
           format c:/s/v

Floppy diskettes and fixed disks must be initialized before they can be used by MS-DOS. This initialization process is called *formatting* and is performed with the command FORMAT.

Formatting divides a floppy diskette or fixed disk into parcels called *sectors*. Sectors are grouped together into tracks. MS-DOS assigns numbers to the sectors and tracks and uses the numbers as references to find its way around the diskette or fixed disk.

Formatting places a *boot record* on each diskette and fixed disk. As you might imagine, MS-DOS uses the boot record whenever it boots up. Formatting also creates a file allocation table and a disk directory on each diskette and fixed disk. MS-DOS uses these structures as a table of contents to the files stored on the diskette or fixed disk.

Chapter 11 contains detailed information on sectors, tracks, the boot record, the file allocation table, and the disk directory.

Using FORMAT

Formatting a diskette destroys any existing data on the diskette. Formatting a fixed disk will destroy any data in the MS-DOS partition of the disk. You will need to format all new, blank diskettes that will be used by MS-DOS. You may occasionally format previously used diskettes. When you do this, make sure that you copy any files that you want to keep onto another (formatted) diskette before using FORMAT. The examples in this section show how to format a floppy diskette. The use of FORMAT to format a fixed disk is nearly identical. Refer to chapter 4 for information on partitioning and formatting a fixed disk.

FORMAT is an external MS-DOS command. This means that before you can begin formatting, a copy of the file FORMAT.COM must be in one of the system drives. FORMAT.COM is one of the files provided on your MS-DOS system diskette. The discussion that follows assumes that FORMAT.COM is located on a diskette in drive A.

If your system has two diskette drives, formatting is most easily accomplished by placing a working copy of your MS-DOS system diskette in drive A and the diskette to be formatted in drive B. If you are using a system with one diskette drive, insert your working copy of the system diskette in drive A. The commands that you will enter will be identical to those used on a two-drive system. MS-DOS will prompt you when it is time to change diskettes.

To begin formatting, enter the following:

```
A>format b:
```

MS-DOS will load FORMAT.COM into memory, display some information about the system manufacturer, and then issue a prompt:

```
Insert new diskette for drive B:
and strike any key when ready
```

Strike any key and formatting will begin. MS-DOS tells you that it is formatting with the following message:

```
Formatting...
```

Formatting a floppy diskette takes about one minute, so sit back and relax. MS-DOS will notify you when formatting has been completed:

```
Formatting...Format complete
```

MS-DOS will also display a status report containing information about the newly formatted diskette:

```
362496 bytes total disk space
362496 bytes available on disk
```

The values in the status report depend on either the type of diskette formatted or the size of the fixed disk partition. After displaying the status report, MS-DOS will ask you if you want to format another diskette:

```
Format another (Y/N)? _
```

Enter "Y" to format another diskette. Enter "N" to return control to MS-DOS.

To format a fixed disk, simply include the drive letter designator in the FORMAT command (for example, **format c:**). Formatting a fixed disk will take several minutes. Once a floppy diskette or fixed disk has been formatted, it is ready for use by MS-DOS.

The System Files

The /s switch is used to add the MS-DOS system files and the file COMMAND.COM to a diskette or fixed disk. The hidden MS-DOS system files have names like IO.SYS and MSDOS.SYS. These two files, along with COMMAND.COM, must be on any diskette or fixed disk that will be used to boot MS-DOS. The order and the location of the system files on a diskette or fixed disk are important. A diskette or fixed disk may not be bootable if you simply use the command COPY to add the system files. The following command will format the diskette in drive B and instruct MS-DOS to add the system files and the COMMAND.COM file.

```
A>format b:/s
```

MS-DOS responds:

```
Insert new diskette for drive B:
and strike any key when ready

Formatting...Format complete
System transferred

    362496 bytes total disk space
     38912 bytes used by the system
   3235684 bytes available on disk

Format another (Y/N)? _
```

Notice that MS-DOS includes the message: "System transferred" and that the status report contains information about the amount of disk space occupied by the system files and COMMAND.COM. If you use the command **dir b:** to examine the newly formatted diskette, the directory entry for

COMMAND.COM will be displayed. No information will be displayed for the hidden system files.

Adding a Volume Label

The MS-DOS 2.X and 3.X versions of FORMAT allows you to assign a *volume label,* or name, to a diskette or fixed disk. A volume label serves only to identify a diskette or fixed disk; it cannot be used as a parameter in any MS-DOS commands. The volume label will be displayed whenever the DIR command is used to examine the contents of a diskette or fixed disk.

To assign a volume label, enter the /v switch in the FORMAT command. At the end of the formatting process, MS-DOS will prompt you to enter a volume label. A volume label can be up to 11 characters long. All characters acceptable in filenames (see chapter 2) are acceptable in volume labels.

```
A>format b:/s/v
```

MS-DOS responds:

```
Insert new diskette for drive B:
and strike any key when ready

Formatting...Format complete
System transferred

Volume label (11 characters, ENTER for none)? WAITE_DISK1

   362496 bytes total disk space
    38912 bytes used by the system
  3235684 bytes available on disk


Format another (Y/N)? _
```

You can use **dir b:** to display the volume label and directory entries of the newly formatted diskette:

```
A>dir b:

 Volume in drive B: is WAITE_DISK1
 Directory of   A:\

COMMAND  COM   15480   3-01-85   2:00a
        1 File(s)     323584 bytes free
```

Formatting 8 Sectors per Track

The MS-DOS 2 version of FORMAT will normally divide each track into 9 sectors. The MS-DOS 3 version of FORMAT will normally divide each track into 9 or 15 sectors, depending on the type of drive holding the target diskette. The /8 switch directs FORMAT to divide each track into 9 or 15 sectors but to use only 8 of the sectors. This feature allows files on diskettes originally formatted with MS-DOS 1.X to be copied onto diskettes formatted under MS-DOS 2.X and 3.X.

Formatting a Single Side

FORMAT determines if the diskette to be formatted is single or double sided and accordingly formats one or two sides. However, if you include the /1 switch in the FORMAT command, only one side will be formatted, regardless of the type of diskette or diskette drive. The /1 switch can be used only with diskettes and is not available with the MS-DOS 1 version of FORMAT.

The /B Switch

Some implementations of MS-DOS 2 and 3 have a /b switch for FORMAT. This switch instructs FORMAT to divide each track on the diskette into 8 sectors and to allocate space on the diskette for the two hidden system files. No files are actually written to the diskette. System files can subsequently be copied to the diskette by using SYS.

The /4 Switch

The /4 switch, implemented in MS-DOS 3, allows you to format a standard diskette on a 1.2-Mbyte drive. (Use the /1 switch and the /4 switch for single-sided diskettes.) Diskettes formatted in this fashion can be used only on 1.2-Mbyte drives.

The /N:*xx* and /T:*yy* Switches

The /n and /t switches are implemented in MS-DOS 3.3. They are used to format a diskette at less than the maximum capacity supported by the diskette drive. The /n switch sets the number of sectors per track. The /t switch sets the number of tracks. The switches must be used together.

The /n and /t switches are implemented primarily to allow the formatting of 720-Mbyte diskettes on 1.44-Mbyte diskette drives. In the following example, it is assumed that drive D is a 3½-inch, 1.44-Mbyte drive that contains an unformatted 720-Kbyte diskette:

```
C>format d: /n:9 /t:80
```

GOTO

Internal
MS-DOS 2.X, 3.X

Function: Transfers control to a specified location within a batch file

Format: GOTO *label*

Example: goto four

A *batch file* is a text file that contains a sequence of MS-DOS commands. Each command is entered as one line in the batch file. Lines in MS-DOS 2.X and 3.X batch files may be labeled. A label simply serves to identify a line. Batch file labels consist of a colon (:) followed by a string of eight or fewer characters.

GOTO directs a batch file to jump to a specific line within the file and to execute the command at that line. In this example, the GOTO command causes execution of the batch file to loop endlessly:

```
:work
rem i am working!
goto work
```

GOTO and the other batch file commands are discussed in chapter 5.

GRAFTABL

External
MS-DOS 3.X

Function: Loads a character table into memory

Formats: GRAFTABL
GRAFTABL [*xxx* or /STATUS] (MS-DOS 3.3)

Examples: graftabl
graftabl 437

Normally, when the color/graphics adapter (CGA) is in graphics mode, the

ASCII characters 128 through 255 cannot be displayed (this group of characters includes the accented letters). The GRAFTABL command is used to load into memory a character table that allows these characters to be displayed when the CGA is in graphics mode.

With the MS-DOS 3.3 version of GRAFTABL, the user can load a table of graphics characters that are specific to a code page. This allows the display of language-specific characters. The code page is selected by including a valid code page number on the command line. The valid numbers are 437, 860, 863, and 865. Please refer to appendix D for an overview of code pages.

The MS-DOS 3.3 version of GRAFTABL returns the ERRORLEVEL codes in the following list. Such codes are returned by MS-DOS commands to communicate information regarding the outcome of the commands. See chapter 5 for ways that ERRORLEVEL codes can be utilized by MS-DOS batch files.

ERRORLEVEL Code	Meaning
0	Code page successfully installed. No code page was previously installed in memory.
1	A code page was previously installed in memory. If a new code page was specified, it was successfully installed.
2	No code page was previously installed in memory. No new code page was installed.
3	Parameter not valid.
4	System is using incorrect version of MS-DOS. Version 3.30 is required.

GRAPHICS

External
MS-DOS 2.X, 3.X

Function: Prints the contents of a graphic screen display

Formats: **GRAPHICS**
GRAPHICS [*printer*][/R][/B] (MS-DOS 3.X)
GRAPHICS [*printer*][/R][/B][/LCD] (MS-DOS 3.3)

Example: graphics color1

One of the more useful features of MS-DOS is its ability to print a full screen of text when the Shift and PrtSc keys are pressed at the same time. The command GRAPHICS expands this capability so that a graphics display can be printed by a dot matrix printer when the Shift PrtSc combination is pressed.

GRAPHICS is another of the MS-DOS terminate and stay resident (TSR) utility programs. When the GRAPHICS command is first entered, MS-DOS reads the program into memory and keeps it there as long as the computer is running. Once GRAPHICS is installed, simply press Shift-PrtSc and GRAPHICS will go to work. Text or graphics will be printed according to the current display mode.

In medium-resolution graphics mode (320 × 200), the screen content is printed in four shades of gray. In high-resolution graphics mode (640 × 200), the image is printed sideways. The upper righthand corner on the screen becomes the upper lefthand corner on the printed image.

GRAPHICS Parameters

There are no parameters for the MS-DOS 1 and 2 versions of GRAPHICS. Starting with MS-DOS 3.0, however, you may specify the type of graphics printer you are using:

Parameter	Description
GRAPHICS	IBM PC graphics printer Epson graphics printer
COLOR1	IBM PC color printer black ribbon
COLOR4	IBM PC color printer red, blue, green ribbon
COLOR8	IBM PC color printer cyan, magenta, yellow, black ribbon
COMPACT	IBM PC compact printer (MS-DOS 3.3)
THERMAL	IBM PC convertible printer (MS-DOS 3.3)

The default printer parameter is GRAPHICS.

With the /r switch, what appears as black on the screen is printed as black and what appears as white is printed as white. The default is to print black as white and white as black.

The /b switch (valid with printer parameters COLOR4 and COLOR8 only) prints the background color of the screen. The default is to not print the background.

The /lcd switch, implemented with MS-DOS 3.3, prints images as they appear on a liquid crystal display.

IF

Internal
MS-DOS 2.X, 3.X

Function: Executes a command if a specified condition is true

Format: IF [NOT] *condition command*

Examples: if exist somefile.dat type somefile.dat
if %1==roses goto roses
if not exist file.bak copy file.txt file.bak

MS-DOS 2.X and 3.X commands can be executed on a conditional basis by including the commands in an IF statement. IF statements are generally used within a batch file. IF can check the following conditions:

IF EXIST *filespec command* IF may be used to determine if a specific file exists in the current directory of a specified (or default) drive. The following statement directs MS-DOS to determine if a file named "somefile.dat" exists in the current directory of drive C (the default drive). If the file does exist, MS-DOS is to display (TYPE) its contents on the screen:

```
C>if exist somefile.dat type somefile.dat
```

IF *string1==string2 command* An IF statement may be used to determine if two character strings are identical. This type of conditional statement is used to compare a string passed to a batch file as a parameter to a string specified within the batch file. The next example checks to see if batch file variable %1 is equal to the character string "roses". Execution of the batch file branches to the line labeled ":roses" if the condition is true:

```
C>if %1==roses goto roses
```

IF ERRORLEVEL *number command* ERRORLEVEL provides a way for batch files to conditionally execute based on the outcome of an MS-DOS command or application program. ERRORLEVEL is a variable that can be set according to the outcome of a program or MS-DOS command.

The value of ERRORLEVEL can be tested with an IF statement. The command specified in the IF statement will be executed if the value of ERRORLEVEL is greater than or equal to "number". The following IF statement checks the value of ERRORLEVEL and directs MS-DOS to display the disk directory (DIR) if ERRORLEVEL is greater than or equal to 2:

```
C>if errorlevel 2 dir
```

Application programmers should refer to MS-DOS functions 31H and

4CH (appendix A) for more information on setting and reading ER-RORLEVEL.

IF NOT   The command contained in an IF NOT statement is executed if the condition tested is false. An IF NOT statement can test the same conditions as an IF statement. The following statement will check the current directory of drive C for a file named "file.bak". If the file does not exist, MS-DOS will copy the file "file.txt" and name the copy "file.bak":

```
C>if not exist file.bak copy file.txt file.bak
```

Please refer to chapter 5 for a discussion of the use of IF and IF NOT.

JOIN

External
MS-DOS 3.X

Function: Creates a logical link between a disk drive and a subdirectory on another disk drive

Format: JOIN *d1*: *d2*:*directory*

Example: join a: c:\adrive

JOIN allows you to reference a disk as though the disk's contents were stored in a subdirectory on another disk. JOIN is useful if you have files located on several disks and you want to avoid changing your current drive.

Say that you have a floppy disk in drive A that contains the files "chapter1.doc", "chapter2.doc", and "chapter3.doc". Drive A can be "linked" to subdirectory ADRIVE on drive C as follows:

```
C>join a: c:\adrive

C>dir \adrive
 Volume in drive C is HARDDISK
 Directory of C:\ADRIVE

CHAPTER1 DOC  7168  6-23-87  10:22a
CHAPTER2 DOC  9259  6-23-87   5:25p
CHAPTER3 DOC  4527  6-27-87   2:20p
    5 File(s)  587760 bytes free
```

JOIN will create a subdirectory if the one specified does not exist. The subdirectory must be empty and must be located exactly one level below the root directory.

A disk drive cannot be accessed directly while it is joined to a subdirectory. In the preceding example, the command "dir a:" will result in an error message.

Displaying and Cancelling JOINs

Using JOIN displays the active links. The /d switch is used to remove a link.

```
C>join
A: => A;\ADRIVE

C>join a: /d

C>join

C>
```

Limits on JOIN

JOIN will not work if a network drive is used as a parameter. Furthermore, JOIN is not reliable when used in conjunction with the commands SUBST and ASSIGN. The commands BACKUP, RESTORE, FORMAT, DISKCOPY, and DISKCOMP should not be used while a JOIN is in effect, since these commands may perform in an unpredictable fashion when confronted with a JOIN.

KEYB

External
MS-DOS 3.3

Function: Loads a keyboard device driver that supports non-U.S. keyboards

Format: KEYB [*xx*[,[*yyy*],[[*d:*][*path*]*filename*[.*ext*]]]]

Example: keyb
keyb fr,850 c:\dos\keyboard.sys

KEYB is a program provided with MS-DOS 3.30 that loads into memory a device driver for non-U.S keyboards. It is important to differentiate KEYB from the KEYB*xx* programs supplied with versions of MS-DOS prior to 3.3. The KEYB*xx* programs are not compatible with MS-DOS 3.3, and KEYB can be used with MS-DOS 3.3 only (a discussion of the KEYB*xx* programs follows this section).

KEYB is used to set the *keyboard code* and the *code page* that are active for the CON device (the combination of the keyboard and the display device).

The keyboard code determines the functional layout of the keyboard, assigning significant foreign language characters to specific keys. For example, if KEYB is used to create a functional French keyboard, pressing the "2" key displays "é" and pressing the "0" key displays "à".

Code pages are *look up* tables that are used to convert into displayable characters the numerical values by which data (including characters) is stored in a computer. Please refer to appendix D for further information on code pages.

The format for using KEYB is:

KEYB[*xx*[,[*yyy*,[[*d:*][*path*]*filename*[*.ext*]]]]]

The *xx* parameter specifies the keyboard code. The *yyy* parameter specifies a code page number. The code page number must correspond to a code page previously prepared with the MODE command (see appendix D for an explanation of the code page numbers). If a code page is not specified, KEYB uses the default code page for the country specified by the keyboard code. The following list shows the allowable combination of keyboard code and code page number parameters. See the discussion of the SELECT command for an explanation of the keyboard codes. Refer to your MS-DOS manual for elaboration on various logical keyboard layouts.

Code Page	Keyboard Code
437	US, UK, FR, GR, IT, SP, LA, SV, SU, NL
850	US, UK, FR, GR, IT, SP, LA, SV, SU, NL, DK, NO, PO, SF, CF, BE, SG
860	PO
863	CF
865	NO, DK

The *filename*[*.ext*] parameter in the KEYB command refers to the system keyboard definition file. If the filename parameter is omitted, KEYB will look in the root directory of the default drive for the file.

The following command illustrates the use of KEYB:

```
keyb fr,850,c:\dos\keyboard.sys
```

This command loads into memory a driver for the French keyboard and activates code page number 850 for the CON device.

Once a driver for a non-U.S. keyboard is loaded, the user may switch to the U.S. keyboard layout by pressing Ctrl-Alt-F1. Pressing Ctrl-Alt-F2 switches to the non-U.S. layout.

Entering **keyb** (with no parameters) directs MS-DOS to display the keyboard code for whichever non-U.S. keyboard driver is currently active in memory.

KEYB returns the following ERRORLEVEL codes. ERRORLEVEL codes are available for processing by batch files (see chapter 5).

ERRORLEVEL Code	Explanation
0	Successful execution.
1	Improper keyboard code number, code page number, or syntax.
2	Bad keyboard definition file or definition file not found.
3	Could not load driver into memory.
4	KEYB is unable to communicate with CON device.
5	Code page requested has not been prepared.
6	Code page selected is not contained in keyboard information file.

KEYB*xx*

External
MS-DOS 3.0–3.2

Function: Installs keyboard device drivers for non-U.S. keyboard layouts

Format: **KEYB*xx***

Example: keybfr

The KEYB*xx*.COM commands supplied with MS-DOS versions 3.0–3.2 serve as installable device drivers for creating keyboards with non-U.S. layouts. As an example, to create a keyboard with a French layout, enter the command **keybfr**. Refer to your MS-DOS manual for further information on the various keyboard layouts available with these commands. Note that the files are external commands; therefore, MS-DOS must be able to locate them on a disk before they can be executed.

The KEYB*xx*.COM files are not compatible with MS-DOS 3.3. The 3.3

command KEYB operates in a different manner than the KEYB*xx* commands (see the preceding KEYB command).

LABEL

External
MS-DOS 3.X

Function: Adds, changes, or inspects a disk's volume label

Format: LABEL [*d*:][*volume label*]

Examples: label c:
              label c:newlabel

A *volume label* is a string of 11 or fewer characters used to identify a diskette or a fixed disk. MS-DOS 2.X allows you to add a volume label using the FORMAT command. Unfortunately, it does not allow you to modify an existing volume label or to add a volume label to a previously formatted disk. The LABEL command provides both of these capabilities.

LABEL, followed by a drive specifier, displays the volume label of the specified disk. The label of the default is displayed if no drive specifier is included. After the label is displayed, a prompt is displayed asking you to enter a new volume label. If you just press Enter, you are asked if you wish to delete the current volume label. The following examples illustrate the use of LABEL:

```
C>label c:

Volume in drive C is HARDDISK

Volume label (11 characters, ENTER for none)?   ←press Enter

Delete current volume label (Y/N)?n             ←enter "n"

C>
```

You can change a volume label by including the label on the command line:

```
C>label a:book back1
```

LABEL should not be used in conjunction with ASSIGN or SUBST, since these commands can cause LABEL to act unpredictably.

LASTDRIVE

Internal
MS-DOS 3.X

Function: Sets the last valid drive letter for the system
                Note: LASTDRIVE may be used in a CONFIG.SYS file only

Format: LASTDRIVE=*drive letter*

Example: lastdrive=z

LASTDRIVE sets the number of drive letters that are valid on a system. The allowable range for *drive letter* is A through Z. The minimum acceptable value is the letter corresponding to the number of physical drives on the system (either locally or on a network). For example, if you have a system with two floppy disk drives and one fixed disk drive, LASTDRIVE must be greater than or equal to C. The default value for LASTDRIVE is E.

LASTDRIVE determines the drive letters that can be assigned to logical drives created with SUBST. See the discussion of SUBST for further information.

MKDIR

Internal
MS-DOS 2.X, 3.X

Function: Creates a subdirectory

Formats: MKDIR [*d*:]*path*
               MD [*d*:]*path*

Examples: mkdir \write
                md b:\programs\business

The MKDIR (MaKe DIRectory) command is used to create a subdirectory. You may enter the command as either **mkdir** or **md**. The MKDIR command may contain a drive letter designator (such as c: or a:) specifying the drive on which the subdirectory will be created. If no drive is specified, the subdirectory will be created on the default drive.

The MKDIR command must specify the path to the subdirectory being created. The first example creates a subdirectory named WRITE:

```
C>mkdir \write
```

No drive was specified in the example, which means that WRITE will be located on the default drive. The path to the new subdirectory is \WRITE. WRITE will be a subdirectory entry contained in the root directory of the default drive.

The next example creates a subdirectory named \BUSINESS:

```
C>md b: \programs\business
```

BUSINESS will be located on drive B. The path to BUSINESS is \PROGRAMS\BUSINESS. This means that BUSINESS is a subdirectory contained in the subdirectory PROGRAMS. PROGRAMS is, in turn, a subdirectory entry contained in the root directory of drive B. See chapter 3 for further examples of the use of MKDIR.

MODE

External
MS-DOS 1.X, 2.X, 3.X

Functions:
1. Sets the mode of operation of a parallel printer
2. Sets the mode of operation of a graphics/color display adapter
3. Sets protocol for an asynchronous communications port
4. Redirects parallel printer output to a serial port
5. Prepares code pages (MS-DOS 3.3)
6. Activates code pages (MS-DOS 3.3)
7. Displays the currently active code page (MS-DOS 3.3)
8. Restores an active code page (MS-DOS 3.3)

Formats:
1. **MODE LPT#**:[*n*][,[*m*][,P]]
2. **MODE *n*** or **MODE** [*n*],*m*[,T]
3. **MODE COM*n*:*baud*[,*parity*[,*databits*[,*stopbits*[,P]]]]
4. **MODE LPT#**:=**COM*n***
5. **MODE *device* CODEPAGE PREPARE**=((*cplist*)[*d*:][*path*]*filename*[.*ext*])
6. **MODE *device* CODEPAGE SELECT**=*cp*
7. **MODE *device* CODEPAGE /STATUS**
8. **MODE *device* CODEPAGE REFRESH**

Examples:
1. mode LPT1:80,6,P
2. mode 40
   mode 80,R,T
3. mode com1:1200,N,7,1

4. mode LPT2:=com1

5. mode con codepage prepare=((805,437)c:\dos\ega.cpi)

6. mode con codepage select=850

7. mode con codepage /status

MODE is an MS-DOS utility program that is used to establish working parameters for the parallel printer and the graphics/color monitor adapter. Beginning with MS-DOS 1.1, MODE is also used to set the parameters of the asynchronous communications port.

MODE is an external command. This means that before you can use MODE, the file MODE.COM must be available to the system. Either MODE.COM must be in the current directory of the default drive or the location of MODE.COM must have been specified by the PATH command (see the discussion of PATH).

Controlling the Printer with MODE

MODE may be used to control the number of characters printed per line and the vertical spacing between lines on the parallel printer. MODE's format is as follows:

MODE LPT#: [*n*][,[*m*][,p]]

where,

    #   is parallel printer number 1, 2, or 3,

    n   is characters per line (80 or 132),

    m   is lines printed per vertical inch (6 or 8),

    p   instructs MS-DOS to try again when it receives a busy signal from the printer (continuous retry on device timeout).

The following command sets parallel printer 1 to print 80 characters per line with 6 lines printed per vertical inch:

```
C>mode LPT1:80,6,p
LPT1: set for 80
Printer lines per inch set
```

The **p** tells MS-DOS to retry continuously to send data to the printer if it receives a busy signal. The retry loop can be halted by pressing Ctrl-Break.

If a parameter is omitted or if an invalid value is specified, the setting for that parameter remains unchanged.

MODE can be used to set the parameters on Epson and Epson compatible printers only. Trying this command with other printers will yield interesting but unpredictable results.

Graphics/Color Display Adapter

If your system is equipped with a graphics/color display adapter, you may use MODE to set the adapter's parameters. There are two formats for MODE when it is used in this fashion:

MODE *n*

MODE [*n*],*m*[,t]

Table 1 contains a complete listing of the parameters used with MODE to control the graphics/color display adapter. The next few examples will show you how some of the parameters can be used. Bear in mind, however, that these examples and the information in table 1 are relevant only to systems having a graphics/color display adapter.

The first example sets the display width to 40 characters per line:

```
C>mode 40
```

The next example switches the active display to the graphics/color display adapter, enables the color, and sets the display width to 80 characters per line:

```
C>mode co80
```

The **m** and **t** parameters are used to adjust the screen display to the right or left. The following command will shift the display one column to the right in 40-column mode and two columns to the right in 80-column mode:

```
C>mode ,r
```

The **t** parameter tells MS-DOS to display a test pattern that can be used as an aid for adjusting the screen display to the right or left. The test pattern consists of the digits 0123456789 repeated four times in the 40-column display and eight times in the 80-column display. After displaying the pattern, MS-DOS asks if you can see the digit to the far right or the far left, depending on whether you specified right or left adjustment. The following example shows the command and the resultant display in 40-column mode:

```
C>mode ,r,t
```

This command requests a right adjustment. The screen will momentarily go blank when the command is entered; then this test pattern and prompt will appear:

```
012345678901234567890123456789012345678901234567890123456789
```

```
Do you see the leftmost 0? (Y/N)
```

Your display needs to be right adjusted if you do not see a 0 at the left side of the screen. If you reply "N", the display will be shifted one column to the right (two columns in 80-column mode). If you reply "Y", control is returned to MS-DOS.

Table 1. Parameters Used with MODE to Control the Graphics/Color Display Adapter

Parameter	Function/Value
n=40	Sets the graphics/color display adapter width to 40 characters per line.
n=80	Sets the graphics/color display adapter width to 80 characters per line.
n=BW40	Switches the active display to the color/graphics display adapter, disables the color, and sets the display width to 40 characters per line.
n=BW80	Switches the active display to the color/graphics display adapter, disables the color, and sets the display width to 80 characters per line.
n=CO40	Switches the active display to the color/graphics display adapter, enables the color, and sets the display width to 40 characters per line.
n=CO80	Switches the active display to the color/graphics display adapter, enables the color, and sets the display width to 80 characters per line.
n=MONO	Switches the active display to the monochrome display adapter. Monochrome always displays 80 characters per line.
m	Is R or L. Shifts the display right or left.
t	Requests a test pattern that is used to align the display.

Communications and MODE

MODE may be used to initialize an asynchronous communications port. The format for the command is:

MODE COM*n:baud*[,*parity*[,*databits*[,*stopbits*[,p]]]]

where,

n is the asynchronous communications port number (1 or 2); MS-DOS 3.3 supports additional port numbers 3 and 4;

baud is the baud rate (110, 150, 300, 600, 1200, 2400, 4800, or 9600); MS-DOS 3.3 supports an additional baud rate of 19200;

parity is either N (none), O (odd), or E (even);

databits are the number of bits per word (7 or 8);

stopbits are the number of stopbits (1 or 2);

p instructs MS-DOS to try again when it receives a busy signal from the port (continuous retry on device timeout).

You must specify the baud rate when using this form of MODE. However, only the first two digits of the baud rate need be entered in the command. All other parameters have defaults that are entered by using a comma in the command. The parity default is even, the databits default is 7, and the stopbits default is 1. The stopbits default is 2 if the baud rate is set at 110.

A **p** tells MS-DOS to continuously retry to send data to the port if it receives a busy signal. The retry loop can be halted by pressing Ctrl-Break. The following example initializes serial port 1 with a baud rate of 1200, no parity, 8 databits, and 1 stopbit. MS-DOS echoes the parameters when the command is entered:

```
C>mode com1:12,,8,,
COM1: 1200,e,8,1,-
```

Redirecting a Parallel Printer with MODE

You can use MODE to redirect parallel printer output to a serial printer that is connected to an asynchronous communications port. The asynchronous port must first be initialized according to the requirements of the serial printer. The format for redirecting is:

MODE LPT#:=COM*n*

where,

\# is the number of the parallel printer,

n is the number of the communications port.

In the following example, communications port 1 is initialized by the first MODE command, and output to parallel printer 1 is redirected to port 1 by the second MODE command. Notice that the port is initialized so that timeout errors are continuously retried:

```
C>mode com1:300,n,8,1,p
COM1; 300,N,8,1,P
C>mode LPT1:=com1
LPT1: redirected to COM1:
```

Code Pages and MODE

As explained in appendix D, MODE is used to generate *prepared code pages* from the code page information files supplied with MS-DOS 3.3. Once a prepared code page is generated, MODE may then be used to select the code page. MODE may also be used to display the set of code pages that are available for a device. Finally, MODE may be used to reestablish an active code page that has been lost. Examples will be presented for each of these applications of MODE.

Generating Prepared Code Pages

The format for generating prepared code pages is:

MODE *device* CODEPAGE PREPARE=
((*cplist*)[*d*:][*path*]*filename*[*.ext*])

The *device* parameter is the character device for which the code pages are being generated. The valid values are CON, PRN, LPT1, LPT2, and LPT3.

The *cplist* is a list of one or more valid code page numbers. These numbers are used to specify the code pages that will be prepared for the character device. Valid code page numbers are 437, 850, 860, 863, and 865. Appendix D discusses the meaning of these code page numbers.

The *filename* parameter specifies the code page information file that will be used to generate code pages. The code page information files supplied with MS-DOS 3.3 and the devices that they support are listed in table 2.

Table 2. MS-DOS 3.3 Code Page Information Files and the Devices That They Support

Device	Code Page Information File
IBM Proprinter Model 4201	4201.CPI
IBM Quietwriter III Printer Model 5202	5202.CPI
Enhanced Graphics Adapter	EGA.CPI
IBM Convertible LCD Adapter	LCD.CPI

Selecting a Code Page

Once a code page has been prepared for use, MODE may be used to select the code page. Selections make the specified code page active for the specified device. The format for code page activation is:

MODE *device* CODEPAGE SELECT=*cp*

The *device* parameter is the device for which the code page is being selected. The *cp* parameter is the code page number being selected. The selected code page number must be either a previously prepared code page or a hardware code page. Hardware code pages are discussed in appendix D.

An Example   Before code page switching can be implemented on a display screen, the device driver DISPLAY.SYS must be loaded into memory. Similarly, before code page switching may be implemented on a printer, the device driver PRINTER.SYS must be loaded into memory.

The following command, when placed in CONFIG.SYS, instructs MS-DOS to install DISPLAY.SYS during the booting procedure:

```
device=c:\dos\display.sys con:=(ega,,2)
```

This command tells MS-DOS to load the DISPLAY.SYS driver for use with the CON device. The parameters **(ega,,2)** instruct MS-DOS: (1) that it should enable code page switching for the Enhanced Graphics Adapter Display, (2) that none of the code pages are hardware code pages, and (3) that two of the pages are prepared code pages.

Using the **device=** statement enables code page switching. The next step is to use the MODE command to generate the prepared code pages for use by the EGA display. The following command generates code pages 437 and 850 using information in the file "ega.cpi". MS-DOS displays a message when the preparation is completed:

```
C>mode con codepage prepare=((437,850)c:\dos\ega.cpi)
Mode Prepare Codepage function completed

C>
```

Once the code pages have been generated, a particular code page may be selected using MODE. The following command selects code page number 850:

```
C>mode con codepage select=850
Mode Select Codepage function completed

C>
```

Code Page Status

The command "mode con codepage /status" directs MS-DOS to display the codepage status for the CON device. In this case the CON device is the EGA display:

```
C>mode con codepage /status
Active codepage for device CON is 850
prepared codepages:
  Codepage 437
  Codepage 850
Mode Status Codepage function completed

C>
```

Code Page Refresh

The command "mode *device* codepage refresh" reestablishes an active code page that has been lost. For example, if you turn off your printer, you may have to use this command to reestablish the active code page.

MORE

External
MS-DOS 2.X, 3.X

Function: Outputs 23 lines of data at a time

Format: MORE

Examples: more < sample.txt
more < sample.txt > prn

MORE is an MS-DOS filter that displays data 23 lines (one full screen) at a time. A text file can be "filtered" through MORE by using the MS-DOS symbol for redirection of input **<**. The output from an application program or another MS-DOS command can also be sent through MORE by using the MS-DOS pipe feature. Output from MORE is sent to the display screen unless it is redirected to some other device (such as a file) or piped as the input to another MS-DOS command or an application program. The symbol for redirection of output is **>**.

Data filtered through MORE is sent out to the display screen (or some other device) 23 lines at a time. After each 23 lines of output, the message **-More-** appears at the bottom of the screen. Pressing any key outputs another 23 lines of data.

MORE is an external MS-DOS command. This means that before you can use the MORE filter, a copy of the file MORE.EXE must be contained in a system drive. The use of MORE is discussed in chapter 6.

NLSFUNC

External
MS-DOS 3.3

Functions: Specifies the country information file
Provides support for code page switching using the MS-DOS command CHCP

Format: NLSFUNC [[*d*:][*path*]*filename*[.*ext*]]

Example: nlsfunc
nlsfunc c:\dos\country.sys

The NLSFUNC command is used to specify the system's country information file. The country information file contains country-specific information such as the date, time, and currency formats.

The NLSFUNC must be invoked before code pages can be set using the CHCP command. Please refer to appendix D for an overview of code pages and code page switching.

NLSFUNC remains resident in memory once it is invoked. Therefore, one invocation of NLSFUNC will support all subsequent invocations of CHCP.

If NLSFUNC is entered without specifying a country information file, the file defined by the COUNTRY command is used as the system's country information file.

The format for using NLSFUNC is:

NLSFUNC [[*d*:][*path*]*filename*[.*ext*]]

PATH

Internal
MS-DOS 2.X, 3.X

Function: Specifies directories to be searched by MS-DOS

Format: PATH [[*d*:]path[[;[*d*:]*path*] . . .]]

Examples: path \program1\business
path b:\program2\write1;b:\program2\write2

PATH tells MS-DOS which subdirectories are to be searched if an external command or a batch file is not found in the current directory. The parameters entered in PATH are the paths to the subdirectories to be searched. (Subdirectories and paths are discussed in chapter 3.)

Consider the following situation. Suppose that you have a diskette in drive A that contains several files and a subdirectory named PROGRAM1. PROGRAM1 contains a batch file named "business.bat". Let's say that the current directory on drive C is the root directory and that you want to execute "business.bat".

To start a batch file, you simply enter the filename of the batch file. Let's see what happens when you do that:

```
C>business
Bad command or file name
```

What happened is that MS-DOS searched the current directory of drive C for "business.bat". Since the root directory is the current directory, and "business.bat" is in the subdirectory PROGRAM1, MS-DOS was unable to find the batch file. MS-DOS assumed that "business.bat" did not exist and the "Bad command or file name" message was displayed.

There are two solutions to this problem. You could change the current directory on drive C. Then MS-DOS would be able to find "business.bat" when "business" was entered. The drawback to this solution is that changing the current directory on drive C may be inconvenient. It would be to your advantage to keep the root directory as the current directory if most of the files and programs that you are using are in the root directory.

The second solution is to use PATH to tell MS-DOS where to look for "business". All you have to do is type **path** followed by the path to the directory containing "business.bat":

```
C>path \program1
```

Once PATH has been used, MS-DOS knows where to look for a command or batch file that is not in the current directory. The last PATH command entered sets the current path. MS-DOS will display the current path if you enter PATH without any parameters:

```
C>path
PATH=\PROGRAM1
```

The current path remains in effect until it is changed by another PATH command.

A PATH command may contain more than one path. Multiple paths are separated by semicolons. MS-DOS searches the paths in the order in which they are listed. In the next example, the PATH command contains two paths on drive B. Once the command has been entered, MS-DOS will look in the subdirectory WRITE1 (which is a subdirectory entry in the subdirectory

PROGRAM2) if a command or batch file is not located in the current directory. MS-DOS will then look in the subdirectory WRITE2 (another subdirectory entry in the subdirectory PROGRAM2) if the command or batch file is not contained in WRITE1.

```
C>path b:\program2\write1;b:\program2\write2
```

The current path is cancelled if you enter PATH followed by a semicolon:

```
C>path
PATH=B:\PROGRAM2\WRITE1;B:PROGRAM2\WRITE2

C>path;

C>path
No Path
```

PAUSE

Internal
MS-DOS 1.X, 2.X, 3.X

Function: Suspends execution of a batch file

Format: PAUSE [*comment*]

Example: pause

PAUSE is used to temporarily suspend the execution of a batch file. PAUSE may also be used to display a message up to 21 characters in length. The following message is displayed when MS-DOS encounters a PAUSE:

```
Strike a key when ready . . .
```

Execution of the batch file halts until you strike a key. Note that you can strike any key except Ctrl-Break. Pressing Ctrl-Break stops the process.

PAUSE is generally used in a batch file to allow you time to perform a specific task, such as inserting a diskette. You will find more information on PAUSE in chapter 5.

PRINT

External
MS-DOS 2.X, 3.X

Function: Prints a list of files in the "background" while MS-DOS is
being used to perform other tasks

Formats: PRINT [[*d*:][*filename*[.*ext*]][/T][/C][/P] . . .]
PRINT [/D:*device*][/B:*buffersize*]
       [/U:*busyticks*][/M:*maxticks*]
       [/S:*timeslice*][/Q:*queuesize*]
       [*d*:][*filename*[.*ext*]]
       [/T][/C][/P] . . .] (MS-DOS 3.X)

Examples: print file1.txt
print file?.txt
print file1.txt file2.txt/c file3.txt file4.txt

The PRINT command is a utility program that allows you to print a set of
files while simultaneously using MS-DOS to perform other tasks. The printing is said to occur in the "background" while the other work that you are
doing is performed in the "foreground." The MS-DOS 3.X implementation
of PRINT has several enhancements that are discussed at the end of this
section.

     PRINT is an external MS-DOS command. The first time you invoke the
command, PRINT.COM is read from disk and installed in memory. PRINT
remains resident in memory until the power is shut off.

Using PRINT

To use PRINT, simply type **print** and then type the file specifications of the
files that you want to print. Each file that you enter is placed in a *queue* (list).
The files in the queue are printed one at a time, according to their order in
the queue. The queue may contain up to ten files at a time. A file is deleted
from the queue after it has been printed.

     The first time that you use PRINT in a working session, MS-DOS dis-
plays the prompt `Name of list device [PRN]:`. MS-DOS is asking you
for the device name of the printer. "PRN" is the default device name that
MS-DOS assigns to the parallel printer. If you want to use the default, simply
press Enter. Otherwise, type the device name and press Enter. (Devices and
device names are discussed in chapter 6.)

     The first PRINT example instructs MS-DOS to print the files "file1.txt",
"file2.txt", and "file3.txt". These files are all located in the current directory
of drive C.

```
C>print file1.txt file2.txt file3.txt
Name of list device [PRN]:      ←Enter
Resident part of print installed

      C:FILE1.TXT is currently being printed
      C:FILE2.TXT is in queue
      C:FILE3.TXT is in queue


C>
```

As you can see, MS-DOS has displayed a queue status report stating the file currently being printed. The remaining files in the queue are listed in the order in which they will be printed.

MS-DOS displays its system prompt to tell you that another command may be entered. Even though the PRINT command is executing, you may enter another command while printing continues in the background. Any MS-DOS command or program can be executed while PRINT is operating in the background as long as the command or program does not use the printer being used by PRINT.

Additional PRINT commands can be entered while PRINT is executing. The effect of these subsequent commands is to either add or delete files from the queue (see the following discussion of the /c, /p, and /t switches).

You can use the wildcard characters * and ? to specify a group of files in the PRINT command. The preceding example could have been entered as:

```
C>print file?.txt
```

If there are any files in the current directory of drive C that match the wildcard, other than "file1.txt", "file2.txt", and "file3.txt", those files will also be printed by the preceding command. (Wildcards are discussed in chapter 2.)

A PRINT command may specify for printing only files that are located in the current directory of each system drive. After you have issued a PRINT command, you can change the current directory on a drive. You can then issue a subsequent PRINT command that will add files contained in the new current directory to the queue. (Directories and current directories are discussed in chapter 3.)

MS-DOS will display a queue status report if you enter PRINT with no parameters:

```
C>print
```

```
C:FILE2.TXT is currently being printed
C:FILE3.TXT is in queue
```

The /C Switch

The /c switch may be used in a PRINT command to delete one or more files from the queue. The /c switch is inserted in a PRINT command immediately after a file specification. That file and all subsequent files specified in the PRINT command are then deleted from the queue.

If a command to delete a file from the queue is issued while that file is being printed, printing of the file is halted and the message `<filespec>` `Canceled by operator` is sent to the printer. The printer paper then advances to the next page, and printing continues with the next file in the queue.

The following command adds "file4.txt" to the queue and deletes "file2.txt" and "file3.txt". Remember that /c affects the immediately preceding file and all subsequent files in the PRINT command.

```
C>print file4.txt file2.txt/c file3.txt
```

The /P Switch

Most MS-DOS manuals say that the /p switch is used in the PRINT command to "set the print mode." This is a little confusing. It's simpler to think of /p as turning off a previous /c switch. The /p switch is inserted in a PRINT command immediately after a file specification. That file and all subsequent files specified in the PRINT command are added to the queue.

The following command deletes "file4.txt" from the queue and adds "file5.txt" and "file6.txt" to the queue:

```
C>print file4.txt/c file5.txt/p file6.txt
```

You can see how the /p switch turns off the /c switch. If a PRINT command does not contain a /c switch, there is no need to use the /p switch.

A PRINT command can contain a second /c switch that will turn off a previous /p switch. A second /p switch can be used to turn off the second /c switch and so on.

The /T Switch

The /t switch is used with PRINT to delete all files from the queue and terminate execution of the PRINT command. The command **print** /t halts the printing process, deletes all files from the queue, sends the message "All files canceled by operator" to the printer, and returns control of the computer to MS-DOS:

```
C>print /t
```

```
PRINT queue is empty

C>
```

MS-DOS 3.X Enhancements

There are six PRINT switches implemented in MS-DOS 3.X. These switches can be set only when PRINT is loaded into memory. Their use is therefore restricted to the first time the PRINT command is invoked.

The /d:*device* switch allows you to specify a valid printing device. If you do not use this switch, MS-DOS will ask you to specify a printer (as is done with the MS-DOS 2 version of PRINT).

The /b:*buffersize* switch sets the size of the print buffer. The print buffer is the area of memory that stores the file's contents prior to sending the contents to the printer. The larger the buffer, the fewer disk accesses that are necessary, and the faster the printing is completed. The default size for the print buffer is 512 bytes.

The /q:*queuesize* switch controls the number of files that may be in the printing queue at any one time. The allowable range is 1 to 32. The default is 10.

The three remaining switches control the way in which the computer's resources are shared between PRINT (the background process) and MS-DOS (the foreground process). When you are using PRINT, it may appear that the computer is doing two things at one time. Actually the computer can execute only one task (or process) at a time, but it switches between processes so rapidly that the two processes seem to execute simultaneously.

Each process is allocated a certain number of system clock ticks to perform its work. The /s:*timeslice* switch determines how many clock ticks the MS-DOS foreground process can run before giving control to the PRINT background process. The allowable range is 1 to 255 clock ticks. The default is 8.

The /m:*maxticks* switch determines how many clock ticks the PRINT process can run before giving control back to the foreground MS-DOS process. The allowable range is 1 to 255 clock ticks. The default is 2.

The /u:*busyticks* switch determines the maximum number of clock ticks that PRINT can wait if the printer is unavailable. If this amount of time elapses and PRINT is still waiting, control is returned to the foreground MS-DOS process. The allowable range for busyticks is 1 to 255 clock ticks. The default is 1.

PROMPT

Internal
MS-DOS 2.X, 3.X

Function: Sets the MS-DOS system prompt

Format: PROMPT [*text*]

Example: prompt Enter Command:

A *system prompt* is a signal from MS-DOS to you that all systems are operating and that MS-DOS is ready to receive your command. The standard MS-DOS system prompt consists of an uppercase "A," "B," or "C" followed by the greater than symbol, >. The letter used in the prompt tells you which system drive is the current default. For example, the C> prompt indicates that the current default drive is drive C.

You can use the PROMPT command to change the system prompt. Simply type **prompt** followed by the character string that you want MS-DOS to use as the new system prompt. Once you have entered the PROMPT command, the new system prompt will be displayed each time that MS-DOS is ready to accept a command. The PROMPT command will remain in effect until you issue another PROMPT or until you reboot MS-DOS. For example, if you wanted the system prompt to be "Enter Command:" instead of "C>", you would enter the following command:

```
C>prompt Enter Command:

Enter Command:
```

The new system prompt is now "Enter Command:". To return to the original prompt C>, enter **prompt** without any other text:

```
Enter Command:prompt

C>
```

MS-DOS provides a set of *meta-strings* that can be used with PROMPT to create system prompts containing special characters. A meta-string is a dollar sign ($) followed by one of eleven ASCII characters. Table 3 lists the meta-strings and the resultant characters.

Meta-strings may be combined with each other and with other character strings to form system prompts. In the following example, four meta-strings are used in a PROMPT command. The PROMPT command will set the system prompt to perform the following: (1) display the message "The current time is:" followed by the current time stored by MS-DOS, (2) perform a carriage return and line feed so that the cursor is at the beginning

**Table 3. Meta-strings and the Resultant Character(s)
in the System Prompt**

Meta-string	Character(s)
$t	The current time stored by MS-DOS.
$d	The current date stored by MS-DOS.
$p	The current directory of the default drive; if drive C is the default and the root directory is the current directory on drive C, $p in the PROMPT command would place "C:\" in the system prompt.
$v	The version of MS-DOS being used (e.g., 3.3).
$n	The default drive.
$g	The > character.
$l	The < character.
$b	The | character.
$q	The = character.
$$	The $ character.
$h	A backspace and erasure of the previous character.
$e	The ESCape character; PROMPT and $e can be used to send an ESCape character to the ANSI.SYS device driver (see chapter 8).
$	Carriage return plus line feed.

of the next line, (3) display the drive letter designator of the default drive, and (4) display a "$>$" character.

```
C>prompt $t$ $n$g

The current time is:    9:27:45.35

C>
```

MS-DOS now displays the current time whenever the system prompt is displayed. Initially, you must set MS-DOS's internal clock if you want the time displayed to be the current time. (See booting MS-DOS in chapter 1 or the TIME command for details.)

The nice feature of this system prompt is that, besides displaying the current time, the prompt automatically changes when the default drive is changed:

```
C>prompt $t$ $n$g

The current time is:    9:27:45.35
```

```
C>b:

The current time is:    9:28:00.39

B>
```

If you use any character in a meta-string other than those listed in the preceding table, MS-DOS will treat that character as a null character. A null character can be used to start a system prompt with one of the MS-DOS delimiters (space, comma, semicolon, or tab). For example, if you want a blank system prompt, you cannot enter PROMPT followed by one or more blanks. MS-DOS will interpret this as PROMPT followed by no text, and the prompt will revert to the standard system prompt:

```
The current time is:    9:28:00.39

B>prompt    <followed by a string of blanks>

B>
```

The preceding command simply changed the prompt back to the standard prompt (with drive B as the default). For a blank prompt (no prompt displayed), type **prompt** followed by a null character. MS-DOS will recognize the null character as the start of the system prompt. The prompt in the following example is a blank line:

```
B>prompt $j
```

←no prompt is displayed.

RECOVER

External
MS-DOS 2.X, 3.X

Functions: Recovers data from files that have bad sectors
Recovers data from an entire disk that has a damaged file directory
Note: RECOVER cannot be used with network drives

Formats: **RECOVER** [*d*:][*path*]filename[*.ext*]
RECOVER *d*

Examples: recover badfile.txt
recover b:

Floppy diskettes and fixed disks used by MS-DOS are divided into storage units called *sectors*. Sectors are created during the formatting process. Each sector stores 512 bytes of data. The larger the file, the more sectors required to store it.

Floppy diskettes and fixed disks each contain a *file directory*. The file directory serves as MS-DOS's table of contents to the files that are contained on the floppy diskette or fixed disk. The directory, which is created during formatting, is modified each time that a file is added, deleted, or modified. (For further information on sectors, file directories, and related topics, please refer to chapters 3 and 11. You should be familiar with this material before using RECOVER.)

Occasionally one or more sectors on a floppy diskette or fixed disk become damaged. When this happens, MS-DOS may not be able to read the data stored in those sectors. MS-DOS will then display the following message when it comes across a sector that it cannot read:

```
Data error reading C:
Abort, Retry, Ignore?
```

The command RECOVER is used to recover data that MS-DOS is unable to read because of damaged sectors. RECOVER can be used to recover an individual file or an entire disk that is unreadable because of damaged sectors in the file directory.

When RECOVER is used on an individual file, only the data in the undamaged sectors of a file are recovered. The data in the damaged sectors are lost. The damaged sectors are labeled so that MS-DOS will not use them in the future.

Once a file has been recovered, MS-DOS will be able to read it. A recovered file will have the same filename and filename extension as the unreadable file. A recovered file will usually have some extraneous data attached at the end, since RECOVER produces files that are multiples of 512 bytes (one sector) in size.

Recovering a File

Since RECOVER is an external command, a copy of the file RECOVER.COM must be available to the system before you can use the command. This means that either RECOVER.COM must be in the current directory of the default drive or that the location of RECOVER.COM must have been specified by the PATH command (see the discussion of PATH).

To use RECOVER, type **recover** and then type the file specification of the file to be recovered. MS-DOS will load RECOVER.COM into memory and then pause to allow you to change diskettes if necessary. Make any necessary swaps and then press any key. The specified file will be recovered.

MS-DOS will display a message that tells you how many bytes from the original file have been recovered. The following is an example:

```
C>recover b:badfile.txt

Press any key to begin recovery of the
file(s) on drive B:


x        ←you press the "x" key
900 of 1412 bytes recovered


C>
```

If you use wildcard characters to specify the file, MS-DOS will recover only the first file that matches the wildcard.

Recovering a Disk

Using RECOVER to recover all the files on a disk is a drastic measure. RE-COVER looks at the file allocation table to determine where each file is located on the floppy diskette or fixed disk. RECOVER cannot distinguish a damaged directory entry from an undamaged entry; therefore, all files on the disk are recovered.

To recover a disk, type **recover** and then type the letter designator of the drive containing the floppy diskette or fixed disk to be recovered. MS-DOS will load RECOVER.COM into memory and then pause for any necessary disk swapping. Press a key and all files on the disk will be recovered. The following is an example:

```
C>recover b:
Press any key to begin recovery of the
file(s) on drive B:



x
22 file(s) recovered
```

The first recovered file is given the name "file0001.rec", the second "file0002.rec", and so on. Any subdirectories are treated as files. All recovered files are placed in the root directory. MS-DOS will display a message if there is not enough room in the root directory for all of the recovered files. If this should happen, copy the recovered files onto another diskette and then delete them from the partially recovered disk. Run RECOVER again and there should be enough room in the root directory for the remaining unrecovered files.

Once an entire disk has been recovered, you can use the command DIR to see that all of the files have names like "file0001.rec," "file0002.rec", and so on.

REM

Internal
MS-DOS 1.X, 2.X, 3.X

Function: Displays a message during the execution of a batch file

Format: REM [*message*]

Example: rem The Message is Love

The REM (REMark) command is used to display a message or to insert comments during the execution of a batch file. At the appropriate line in the batch file, type **rem** and then type the text of the message. When the batch file is executed and the REM command is read by MS-DOS, the message contained in that line will be displayed on the screen. The message in a REM command may be up to 123 characters long. (See chapter 5 for a discussion of batch files.)

RENAME

Internal
MS-DOS 1.X, 2.X, 3.X

Function: Renames a file

Formats: RENAME [*d:*][*path*]*filename*[*.ext*]*filename*[*.ext*]
REN [*d:*][*path*]*filename*[*.ext*]*filename*[*.ext*]

Examples: rename file1 file2
ren newfile.txt oldfile.txt

RENAME (or REN) is used to change the filename and/or filename extension of an MS-DOS file. It is one of the most frequently used, and most useful, MS-DOS commands.

To change a file's name, type **rename** and then type the file specification of the file, followed by the new filename and filename extension. For example, an existing file on drive A named "newfile.txt" would be renamed to "oldfile.txt" as follows:

```
C>rename a:newfile.txt oldfile.txt
```

MS-DOS will ignore any drive letter specifier preceding the new filename and extension. MS-DOS will display an error message if a path specifier precedes the new filename and extension.

Wildcard characters may be used with RENAME (see chapter 2).

REPLACE

External
MS-DOS 3.2, 3.3

Function: Selectively replaces or adds files

Format: REPLACE [*d*:][*path*]*filename*[.*ext*][*d*:][*path*] [/A][/P][/S][/W]

Example: replace ch1.doc c:\ /s

REPLACE is an external MS-DOS command that allows you to selectively replace or add files to a target directory. When files are being replaced, *filename*[.*ext*] in the command line specifies the files in the target directory that are to be replaced by matching files in the source directory. Only matches are replaced. When files are being added, *filename*[.*ext*] specifies the files in the source directory that are to be added to the target. Files are added only if the target does not already contain a match. The following examples demonstrate the use of the REPLACE command.

Using REPLACE

The examples given here use two directories, TMP1 and TMP2. The contents of the directories are as follows:

```
C>dir tmp1 /w

 Volume in drive C is UCSFMIS
 Directory of C:\TMP1

 .           ..        TERRY  LET  BRUCE   LET  PAPER  TXT
        5 File(s)   491520 bytes free

C>dir tmp2 /w

 Volume in drive C is UCSFMIS
 Directory of C:\TMP2

 .           ..        BRUCE   LET
```

    3 File(s) 491520 bytes free

First we will replace TMP2\BRUCE.LET with TMP1\BRUCE.LET:

C>*replace tmp1\bruce.let tmp2*

Replacing C:\TMP2\BRUCE.LET

1 file(s) replaced

Let's see what happens if we try to replace TMP2\TERRY.LET:

C>*replace tmp1\terry.let tmp2*

No files replaced

No files are replaced since TMP2 does not already contain a file named "terry.let".

The /A Switch

The /a switch is used to add new files to a target directory (as opposed to replacing existing files).

  C>*replace tmp1\terry.let tmp2 /a*

  Adding C:\TMP2\TERRY.LET

  1 file(s) added

Files are added only if the target directory does not contain a match:

  C>*replace tmp1\bruce.let tmp2 /a*

  No files added

The /S Switch

The following command goes through all of the directories on drive A, replacing any copies of the file "sample.txt" that it finds.

  C>*replace sample.txt a:\ /s*

The /s switch is used to replace all occurrences of a file in a target directory and all subdirectories contained in the target. If the root directory is the target, all occurrences of the file on the disk are replaced. The /a and /s switches cannot be used together.

Other Switches

The /p switch prompts you with `Replace <file name> (Y/N)?` for each *filename* specified as a source file.

The /r switch replaces files that have their read-only attribute set. (See ATTRIB for a discussion of the read-only attribute.)

The /w switch instructs REPLACE to wait for you to insert a diskette prior to executing the command.

REPLACE and ERRORLEVEL

The following list gives the ERRORLEVEL values returned by REPLACE. These values may then be used by batch files or programs running under MS-DOS. See chapter 5 for a demonstration of the use of ERRORLEVEL values.

ERRORLEVEL Value	Meaning
2	No source files were found.
3	Invalid source or target path.
5	An attempt was made to access a read-only file without the /r switch.
8	Insufficient memory.
11	Invalid parameters or invalid number of parameters entered on the command line.
15	Invalid drive specified.
22	Incorrect version of MS-DOS.

RESTORE

External
MS-DOS 2.X, 3.X

Function: Restores one or more files from one disk to another disk

Formats: RESTORE *d:* [*d:*][*path*][*filename*[.*ext*]][/S][/P]
RESTORE *d:*[*d:*][*path*[*filename*[.*ext*]][/S][/P][/B:*mm-dd-yy*]
[/A:*mm-dd-yy*][/M][/N][/L:*time*][/E:*time*] (MS-DOS 3.3)

Examples: restore a: \subdir1 \file.doc
restore a: \subdir2

restore a: \subdir3 /s
restore a: \subdir4*.doc /p

The RESTORE command is used to retrieve files that were stored using BACKUP. RESTORE cannot be used on any other types of files.

Since RESTORE is an external MS-DOS command, one of the system drives must contain the file RESTORE.COM before you can use RESTORE. In the following examples, it is assumed that RESTORE.COM is stored on the fixed disk drive (drive C).

Restoring a File

To restore a file to the fixed disk, type **restore** and then type the letter designation of the drive containing the copy of the files to be restored. You may specify the directory path on the fixed disk that will contain the restored files. If you do not specify a path, the default is the current directory on the default disk. You may also specify the name of a file to be restored. If no filename is specified, all files in the specified (or default) directory are restored. When you enter a RESTORE command, MS-DOS prompts you to insert the diskette containing the files to be restored and then instructs you to press any key to restore the files to the fixed disk.

In the first example, the file "file1.doc" is located in the directory SUBDIR1. The backup copy of "file1.doc", which is stored on the diskette in drive A, is restored to the fixed disk:

```
C>restore a: \subdir1\file1.doc

Insert backup diskette 01 in drive A:
Strike any key when ready

*** Files were backed up 12/11/1988 ***

*** Restoring files from diskette 01 ***
\SUBDIR1\FILE1.DOC

C>
```

Wildcard characters may be used in filenames and extensions specified in a RESTORE command. All matching files in the specified (or default) directory will be restored.

Note: MS-DOS 3.3 allows you to restore from a fixed disk, provided, of course, that the fixed disk was the target of a BACKUP command.

Restoring a Directory

In the next example, all the files stored on the backup diskette that have a path of \SUBDIR1\SUBDIR2 are restored:

```
C>restore a: \subdir1\subdir2
```

Restoring All Subdirectories

The /s switch is used with RESTORE to restore all files in a directory and all files in the directory's subdirectories. In the following example, all files in SUBDIR3 and all files in SUBDIR3's subdirectories are restored:

```
C>restore a: \subdir3 /s

Insert backup diskette 01 in drive A:
Strike any key when ready

*** Files were backed up 12/11/1988 ***

*** Restoring files from diskette 01 ***
\SUBDIR3\FILE1.DOC
\SUBDIR3\FILE2.DOC
\SUBDIR3\SUBDIR4\FILE3.DOC
\SUBDIR3\SUBDIR4\SUBDIR5\FILE3.DOC

C>
```

Selective Restoring with /P Switch

You may not want to restore a file that has been modified since the last time it was backed up. Such a restoration would destroy any modifications in the file. Using the /p switch at the end of your command will cause MS-DOS to check to see if any of the files being restored have been modified since they were last backed up. If so, MS-DOS will warn you that a file is about to be overwritten. A prompt will appear asking you if the (modified) file should be replaced (by the unmodified version). If you respond "N", the file is not restored and processing continues in the normal fashion. If you respond "Y", the file is restored with the unmodified copy, and processing continues in the normal fashion.

The MS-DOS 3.X version of the /p switch also prompts you before restoring any read-only files. See the ATTRIB command for information about read-only files.

Other Switches

MS-DOS 3.3 contains six additional switches that allow further selectivity in the restore process.

The /n switch restores files that have been deleted. The /m switch restores files that have been deleted or modified since they were backed up.

The /b:*mm-dd-yy* switch restores all files modified on or before the specified date. The /a:*mm-dd-yy* switch restores all files modified on or after the specified date.

The l:*time* switch restores files that were modified at or later than the specified time. The /e:*time* switch restores files that were modified at or earlier than the specified time.

Some Restrictions with RESTORE

RESTORE cannot be used with JOIN, ASSIGN, SUBST, and APPEND. These commands contain bugs that cause RESTORE to act in an unpredictable fashion.

RESTORE and ERRORLEVEL

ERRORLEVEL is a variable that has special meaning to MS-DOS. RESTORE will set the value of ERRORLEVEL as follows:

0   RESTORE command completed in normal fashion.

1   The backup diskette did not contain any files matching the file(s) specified in the RESTORE command.

2   Some files were not restored due to sharing conflicts.

3   Execution of the RESTORE command was terminated by the user pressing Esc or Ctrl-Break.

4   The RESTORE command was terminated because of an error in execution.

Once the value of ERRORLEVEL has been set, it may be used in conjunction with the IF command in MS-DOS batch files. ERRORLEVEL allows you to write batch files that are executed according to the outcome of a RESTORE command. (See the discussion of the IF command for further details.)

RMDIR

Internal
MS-DOS 2.X, 3.X

Function: Deletes a subdirectory

Formats: **RMDIR** [*d:*]*path*
              RD [*d:*]*path*

Examples: rmdir \write
              rd b:\programs\business

The RMDIR (ReMove DIRectory) command is used to delete a subdirectory from a disk. You may enter the command as either **rmdir** or **rd**. However, before MS-DOS can carry out your command, all the files in the subdirectory must be deleted. This is a safety feature that prevents accidental loss of files.

Your RMDIR command may include a drive letter designator (such as c: or a:) that specifies the drive containing the subdirectory to be deleted. MS-DOS assumes that the subdirectory is located on the default drive if no drive is specified.

The RMDIR command must specify the path to the subdirectory that is to be deleted. In the first example, the command is used to delete the subdirectory WRITE:

```
C>rmdir \write
```

No drive is specified, so MS-DOS assumes that WRITE is located on the default drive. The path `\write` tells MS-DOS that WRITE is a subdirectory contained in the root directory of drive C.

The next example deletes a subdirectory named BUSINESS:

```
C>rd b:\programs\business
```

The command specifies that BUSINESS is located on drive B. The path `\programs\business` tells MS-DOS that BUSINESS is a subdirectory contained in PROGRAMS. PROGRAMS is a subdirectory contained in the root directory of drive B.

The current directory and the root directory of each drive cannot be deleted with RMDIR. (For more information on subdirectories, root directories, current directories, and paths and for more examples of the use of RMDIR, please refer to chapter 3.)

SELECT

External
MS-DOS 3.X

Function: Creates a language-specific system disk

Formats: **SELECT *aaa bbb*** (MS-DOS 3.0–3.2)
   SELECT [[A: or B:][*d:*][*path*]] *xxx yy* (MS-DOS 3.3)

Examples: select 033 fr
   select a: c:\dos 033 fr

SELECT is used to create a country-specific system disk. At boot time, the new system disk will: (1) automatically load country-specific information such as the time, date, and currency formats and (2) automatically configure the keyboard according to a country-specific layout. Country-specific information and country-specific keyboard configuration are discussed under the commands COUNTRY, KEYB, and KEYB*xx*.

Versions 3.0–3.2 of MS-DOS implement SELECT in a different fashion than version 3.3 does. The following paragraphs discuss each implementation separately.

The format for SELECT in versions 3.0–3.2 is:

SELECT *aaa yy*

The *aaa* parameter is a 3-digit country code. The *yy* parameter is a valid keyboard code. The valid combinations of country code and keyboard codes are listed in table 4 at the end of this section.

This implementation of SELECT requires that a system diskette be placed in drive A to serve as the *source* in creating the new system diskette. The *target* must be another diskette that will be swapped with the source in drive A. MS-DOS executes the command by first using DISKCOPY to copy the source to the target. MS-DOS automatically formats the target if necessary. It then prompts the user to change diskettes in drive A as required. When the copy is completed, MS-DOS uses DISKCOMP to compare the target to the source. Next, a new CONFIG.SYS file is created in the root directory of the target that contains the command "country=*aaa*" where *aaa* is the country code entered on the command line. Finally, a new AUTOEXEC.BAT file is created in the root of the target. This file will load the country-specific keyboard driver when the new diskette is used to reboot the system.

The format for the MS-DOS 3.3 version of SELECT is:

SELECT [[A: or B:][*d:*][*path specifier*]] *xxx yy*

The *xxx* and *yy* parameters are the country and keyboard codes. The

"A: or B:" is used to specify the drive containing the source system diskette. If no source drive is specified, SELECT uses drive A as the source. The *d:path* parameter is used to specify the destination for the MS-DOS command files on the target. If no drive for the target is specified, drive B is assumed to hold the target diskette. If no path is specified for the target system files, the files are copied to the root of the target. This implementation allows a fixed disk to be the target.

The 3.3 implementation of SELECT formats the target, then uses XCOPY to copy the system files to the target. A CONFIG.SYS file is created containing the statement "country=*xxx*", and an AUTOEXEC.BAT file is created with the following commands:

```
path \;[\path specifier]
keyb yy xxx
echo off
date
time
ver
```

The [\path] parameter refers to the optional path parameter that may have been included in the SELECT command line. This is useful if you want to have your system files in a subdirectory (such as \DOS).

Table 4. Valid Combinations of Country and Keyboard Codes

Country	Country Code	Keyboard Code
Arabic	785	
Australia	061	US
Belgium	032	BE
Canada (Eng.)	001	US
Canada (Fr.)	002	CF
Denmark	045	DK
Finland	358	SU
France	033	FR
Germany	049	GR
Israel	972	
Italy	039	IT
Latin America	003	LA
Netherlands	031	NL
Norway	047	NO
Portugal	351	PO
Spain	034	SP

Table 4. (cont'd)

Country	Country Code	Keyboard Code
Sweden	046	SV
Swiss (Fr.)	041	SF
Swiss (Ger.)	041	SG
United Kingdom	044	UK
United States	001	US

SET

Internal
MS-DOS 2.X, 3.X

Function: Places a string in the MS-DOS environment

Format: SET [*name*=[*parameter*]]

Example: set xyz=abc

The *environment* is an area of computer memory set aside by MS-DOS to store a series of ASCII strings. Each string in the environment consists of two sets of ASCII characters separated by an equals sign. The characters to the left of the equals sign are referred to as the *name,* those to the right as the *parameter.* The strings are grouped in this area so that they may be easily referenced by MS-DOS as well as by any programs that are running under MS-DOS. MS-DOS stores the segment address of the environment at offset 2CH in the program segment prefix (see appendix A).

Each string in the environment is terminated by a byte of zero. The final string is terminated by 2 bytes of zero. The first string in the environment has the name COMSPEC. The right side of the string contains the path to the file COMMAND.COM (for example, COMSPEC=\COMMAND.COM). MS-DOS also stores the last PROMPT and PATH commands issued in the environment.

The SET command is available to programmers who want to place their own strings in MS-DOS's environment. An application program could then search the environment for the string by first looking up the environment's address in the program segment prefix.

To place a string in the environment, type **set** and then type the string:

```
C>set d1=\subdir1\subdir2
```

The current set of environment strings will be displayed if SET is entered with no other parameters:

```
C>set
COMSPEC=\COMMAND.COM
PATH=\SUBDIR1
D1=\SUBDIR1\SUBDIR2
```

To delete a string from the environment, type **set** followed by the string's name followed by an equals sign:

```
C>set path=
C>set
COMSPEC=\COMMAND.COM
D1=\SUBDIR1\SUBDIR2
```

See chapter 11 for more information on the MS-DOS environment.

SHARE

External
MS-DOS 3.X

Function: Provides support for file sharing and file locking

Format: **SHARE** [/F:*xxx*][/L:*yyy*]

Example: share /f:1024 /l:20

The SHARE command is used to provide support for *file sharing* on a computer network. Computer programs that use MS-DOS function 3DH to open a computer file will store in memory a *sharing code*. The sharing code is used by the operating system to determine the type of access other programs (on the network) have to the opened file.

Once a program has gained access to a file, it may use MS-DOS function 5CH to place a "lock" on a portion of the file. A lock gives the program exclusive access to that portion of the file.

SHARE sets aside computer memory for sharing codes and locks. The **/f:*xxx*** flag sets aside *xxx* bytes for sharing codes. The default is 2048 bytes. Each file opened by function 3DH requires storage for its filename plus 11 bytes.

The **/l:*yyy*** flag sets aside memory for *yyy* file locks. The default is 20 locks.

See appendix A for more information on MS-DOS functions 3DH and 5CH.

SHELL

Internal
MS-DOS 2.X, 3.X

Function: Instructs MS-DOS to load a command processor
Note: SHELL can be used in a CONFIG.SYS file only

Format: SHELL=[*d*:][*path*]*filename*[.*ext*]

Example: shell=custom.com

The SHELL command is a high-level command generally used only by advanced MS-DOS programmers. SHELL is used when you wish to use a command processor other than COMMAND.COM, the standard MS-DOS command processor. COMMAND.COM, which is loaded into memory during booting, serves as the link between MS-DOS and you. (See chapter 12 for details.)

The SHELL command can be used only as a statement in the CONFIG.SYS file. A SHELL command in CONFIG.SYS alerts MS-DOS that a new command processor will be used.

In the following example, the CONFIG.SYS file is created. The SHELL command that makes up the file tells MS-DOS to load the command processor CUSTOM.COM into memory:

```
C>copy con: config.sys
shell=custom.com
^Z        ←you press Ctrl-Z
       1 file(s) copied
```

Using SHELL to Increase the MS-DOS Environment

The MS-DOS environment has a default size of 160 bytes. With MS-DOS 3.1 and subsequent versions, you can use SHELL to increase the environment's size.

The format for the SHELL statement is:

SHELL=c:\COMMAND.COM /P /E:*xxxx*

In MS-DOS 3.1, *xxxx* is the number of paragraphs (16-byte blocks) in the environment. The allowable range is 10 to 2048. In MS-DOS 3.2 and 3.3, *xxxx* is the actual number of bytes in the environment. The allowable range is 160 to 32,768.

Note: chapter 12 describes a way to modify the environment's size for MS-DOS versions prior to 3.1.

SHIFT

Internal
MS-DOS 2.X, 3.X

Function: Allows you to specify more than ten batch file parameters

Format: SHIFT

Example: shift

A batch file can contain up to ten dummy variables (%0 through %9). These dummy variables may be sequentially replaced by a list of character strings included in a batch file start command. For example, %0 is replaced by the filename of the batch file, %1 is replaced by the first character string included in the start command, %2 is replaced by the second character string, and so on.

The SHIFT command "shifts" each character string one position to the left, allowing you to pass more than ten character strings to a batch file. After one SHIFT, %0 is replaced by the first character string in the start command, %1 is replaced by the second string, and so on. Each successive SHIFT moves the parameters one position to the left. The use of SHIFT is demonstrated in chapter 5.

SORT

External
MS-DOS 2.X, 3.X

Function: Sorts data

Format: SORT [/R][/+*n*]

Examples: sort < records.txt
sort /+17 < records.txt
sort /r+52 < records.txt

SORT is an MS-DOS filter that reads data from an input device, sorts the data, and then writes the data to an output device. Data are sorted using the ASCII sequence (appendix F), according to the character in a specified column of each line. If no column is specified, the data are sorted according to the first character in each line.

A text file can be input to SORT by using the MS-DOS redirection symbol <. The output from an application program or another MS-DOS command can be sent to SORT as input by using the pipe feature. Output from SORT can be redirected or piped using these same features.

SORT is an external MS-DOS command. This means that a system drive must contain a copy of the file SORT.EXE before you can use the SORT filter.

SORT has two optional switches. The /r switch sorts data in reverse order. The /+n switch sorts data according to the character located in column *n* of each line.

Chapter 6 describes the use of SORT and discusses MS-DOS filters, redirection, and pipes.

STACKS

Internal
MS-DOS 3.2–3.3

Function: Allocates stack frames to handle hardware interrupts
Note: STACKS can be used in CONFIG.SYS only

Format: STACKS=*n,s*

Example: stacks=12,256

STACKS is used to set the number and size of *stack frames* allocated by MS-DOS to handle hardware interrupts (refer to appendix A for a discussion of interrupts and the role that stacks play in the processing of interrupts).

The format for STACKS is:

STACKS=*n,s*

where *n* equals the number of stack frames allocated and *s* equals the size of each stack frame in bytes. The allowable range for *n* is 8–64. The allowable range for *s* is 32–512.

If a "stacks=" command is not included in CONFIG.SYS, MS-DOS defaults to n=0 and s=0 for PC- and XT-type machines; n=9 and s=128 for AT- and PS/2-type machines.

You should use the STACKS command in CONFIG.SYS if you are getting an "Internal Stack Error" message.

SUBST

External
MS-DOS 3.X

Function: Assigns a path specifier to a drive letter

Format: SUBST *d*: *d*:*path*

Example: subst e: c:\subdir1\subdir2\subdir3

The SUBST command allows you to assign a path specifier to a drive letter. Once the assignment is made, the drive letter may be used as a substitute for the specifier. SUBST was implemented for use by programs (such as Word-Star) that cannot process path specifiers. SUBST can also save you some typing if you are using files located at the end of a long path.

```
A>dir \tmp\tmp1\tmp2

    Volume in drive A is UCSFMIS
    Directory of A:\TMP\TMP1\TMP2

    .          <DIR>     6-26-88   12:02p
    ..         <DIR>     6-26-88   12:02p
    FOO  .        16     6-26-88    5:00p
        3 File(s)    308224 bytes free

A>subst e: \tmp\tmp1\tmp2

A>dir e:

    Volume in drive E is UCSFMIS
    Directory of E:

    .          <DIR>     6-26-88   12:02p
    ..         <DIR>     6-26-88   12:02p
    FOO           16     6-26-88    5:00p
        3 File(s)    308224 bytes free
```

The drive receiving the assignment cannot be the current drive or the drive of the path specifier. The receiving drive letter may be any letter up to the value specified by LASTDRIVE in the CONFIG.SYS file (see the discussion of the LASTDRIVE command in this section). The default for LAST-DRIVE is E. SUBST cannot be used with network drives.

Displaying and Cancelling Substitutions

SUBST displays the active substitutions. The /d switch deletes them.

```
A>subst
E: => A:TMP\TMP1\TMP2

A>subst e: /d

A>subst

A>
```

Problems with SUBST

IBM admonishes users of PC-DOS 3.3 that SUBST should not be used with ASSIGN, BACKUP, DISKCOMP, DISKCOPY, FDISK, FORMAT, JOIN, LABEL, or RESTORE. Big Blue makes no elaborations, but the obvious implication is that SUBST confuses these other commands. Any system command that interferes with at least nine other commands is to be avoided. Consider staying away from SUBST until IBM and Microsoft rid it of its bugs.

SWITCHAR

Internal
MS-DOS 2.0–2.1

Function: Changes the switch character
             Note: SWITCHAR can be used in CONFIG.SYS only

Format: SWITCHAR=*character*

Example: switchar=–

The character used to separate an operating system command from an optional switch is called the *switch character*. The forward slash (/) is the standard MS-DOS switch character. Users of other operating system (most notably UNIX) often prefer to be able to use the same switch character regardless of which operating system they are using. MS-DOS 2.0 and 2.1 implement SWITCHAR, a convenient way to change the switch character. The format for the command (which must be used in CONFIG.SYS) is:

SWITCHAR=*character*

where *character* is the new switch character.

Changing the Switch Character in MS-DOS 3.X

SWITCHAR is not implemented in versions of MS-DOS after 2.10. However, changing the switch character is possible in post-2.10 versions. In the following listing, DEBUG is used to create an assembly language program called `switchar.com`. Refer to chapter 9 for details on using DEBUG. The program uses the undocumented MS-DOS function 37H to set the switch character to the character whose ASCII value is stored in the DL register.

```
C>debug
-n switchar.com
-a

3A3D:0100 MOV    DL,2F                    ;default switchar
3A3D:0102 CMP    BYTE PTR [0080],00       ;length of command tail
3A3D:0107 JZ     010D                     ;no tail entered
3A3D:0109 MOV    DL,[0082]                ;tail entered, dl gets ASCII
3A3D:010D MOV    [012E],DL                ;copy to message string
3A3D:0111 MOV    AX,3701                  ;set switchar
3A3D:0114 INT    21                       ;call MS-DOS
3A3D:0116 MOV    DX,0122                  ;point to message
3A3D:0119 MOV    AH,09                    ;output string function
3A3D:011B INT    21                       ;call MS-DOS
3A3D:011D MOV    AX,4C00                  ;exit function
3A3D:0120 INT    21                       ;call MS-DOS
3A3D:0122 DB     'switchar= ',AF,' / ',AE,0D,0A,'$'
3A3D:0134
-rcx
:0000
34
-w
Writing 0034 bytes
-q

C>
```

Once the program is created, the switch character is changed by entering "switchar *character*". Entering "switchar" with no parameters sets "/" as the switch character.

SYS

External
MS-DOS 1X, 2.X, 3.X

Function: Transfers the system files to a specified disk

Format: SYS *d*:

Example: sys b:

The MS-DOS system files are two "hidden" files that form an integral part of MS-DOS. The files are described as hidden because you cannot list them with the DIR command. The system files must be contained at a specific location and in a specific order on a disk if you are to use the disk for booting. (You will find more information on the system files in chapter 11.)

The SYS (SYStem) command is used to transfer the system files to a disk. The disk receiving the files must be either a blank formatted disk, a disk that has been formatted using the command **format** *d*:/s, or a disk formatted with the command **format** *d*:/b. If the disk is a blank formatted one, SYS will be able to place the system files at the required location on the disk. If the disk has been formatted using either the /s or the /b switch, the required location will have been allocated for the system files. Otherwise, SYS would be unable to correctly place the files.

When transferring files with SYS, you should use your working copy of the system diskette. In the following example, a working copy of the system diskette is in drive A. With your diskette in place, type **sys** and then type the letter designator of the drive containing the disk that will receive the system files:

```
A>sys c:

System transferred
```

TIME

Internal
MS-DOS 1.X, 2.X, 3.X

Functions: Displays the current time known to MS-DOS
Changes the time known to MS-DOS

Format: TIME [*hh:mm:ss.xx*]

Examples: time
time 11:30

The TIME command is used to display and set the current time known to MS-DOS. When a file is created or modified, the current time known to the system is stored in the file directory. This information, along with the current date, forms the file's time-date stamp.

To display the time, type **time**. MS-DOS will display the time and ask if you want to change it:

```
C>time
Current time is 11:42:23.07
Enter new time:
```

To enter a new time, use the form *hh:mm:ss.xx*, where:

hh is a one- or two-digit number from 0–23 (hours),

mm is a one- or two-digit number from 0–59 (minutes),

ss is a one- or two-digit number from 0–59 (seconds),

xx is a one- or two-digit number from 0–99 (hundredths of a second).

To leave the current time unchanged, simply press Enter:

```
C>time
Current time is 11:42:23.07
Enter new time:        ←you press Enter
```

The current time may be specified in the TIME command:

```
C>time 11:59
```

MS-DOS will prompt for another time if an invalid time is entered. Any fields not specified are set to zero. For example, if the time entered is 2:00, the current time is set to 2:00:00.00.

On machines with permanent clocks, the MS-DOS 3.3 implementation of TIME resets the permanent clock's time. Unfortunately, PC-DOS 3.3 sets only permanent clocks whose memory address is the same as IBM's clock. TIME has no effect on clocks with a different address.

TREE

External
MS-DOS 2.X, 3.X

Function: Displays the directory paths on the specified drive

Format: TREE [*d*:][/F]

Examples: tree
tree b: /f

The TREE command is used to produce a list of the directories on a disk. Each directory on the floppy diskette or fixed disk is listed by its full path name. Subdirectories are grouped and listed according to the directory in which they exist.

TREE is an external MS-DOS command. This means that a copy of the file TREE.COM must be in a system drive before you can use the TREE command. To use TREE, type **tree** and then type the letter designator of the drive containing the disk to be analyzed. The default drive is assumed if no drive is specified. MS-DOS will list the files in each directory if you include the /f switch in the command.

TYPE

Internal
MS-DOS 1.X, 2.X, 3.X

Function: Displays the contents of a file

Format: TYPE [*d*:][*path*]*filename*[.*ext*]

Example: type b:letter.txt

The TYPE command is used to display the contents of a file on the screen. TYPE is generally used only with text (ASCII) files. Attempts at displaying binary files can give unexpected results.

To display a file, enter **type** followed by the filespec of the desired file. MS-DOS will read the file into memory and then display it on the screen:

```
C>type b:letter.txt
```

The display will scroll off the screen if the file contains more than 23 lines. To suspend the display, press Ctrl-NumLock. Press any key to resume the display.

To obtain a printout of a file, press Ctrl-PrtSc before entering the TYPE command. This key combination tells MS-DOS to "echo" the screen display to the printer.

Wildcard characters cannot be used with TYPE.

VER

Internal
MS-DOS 2.X, 3.X

Function: Displays the MS-DOS version number

Format: VER

Example: ver

The VER command tells you the version of MS-DOS that you are currently using. Simply type **ver** if you want MS-DOS to display the version number of MS-DOS that you are working with:

```
C>ver
MS-DOS Version   3.30
```

VERIFY

Internal
MS-DOS 2.X, 3.X

Function: Turns the write-verify switch on or off

Format: VERIFY [ON|OFF]

Examples: verify
verify on
verify off

The VERIFY command is used to turn MS-DOS's write-VERIFY operation on or off. When VERIFY is on, MS-DOS performs a series of checks following each disk-write operation to verify that the data just written can be read without error. During verification, the system will run more slowly. This command serves the same purpose as the /v switch in the COPY command.

To turn VERIFY on, type **verify on**. To turn VERIFY off, type **verify off**. The current VERIFY state is displayed when you enter VERIFY with no parameters:

```
C>verify
VERIFY is on
```

VOL

Internal
MS-DOS 2.X, 3.X

Function: Displays the volume label of the disk in the specified drive

Format: VOL [*d*:]

Examples: vol
vol b:

The VOL (VOLume) command is used to display the volume label of the disk in the specified drive. Simply type **vol** followed by the letter designator of the desired drive. The default is assumed if you do not specify a drive.

```
C>vol

Volume in drive C is MS-DOS_BIBLE
```

XCOPY

External
MS-DOS 3.2, 3.3

Function: Provides enhanced file copying capability

Format: XCOPY[*d*:][*path*]*filename*[.*ext*][*d*:][*path*][*filename*][.*ext*][/A]
[/D:*mm-dd-yy*][/E][/M][/P][/S][/V][/W]

Example: xcopy *.* a: /e /s /a

XCOPY is a greatly enhanced version of the COPY command. It allows you to (1) selectively copy files that have their archive attributes set (see ATTRIB), (2) selectively copy files according to their date stamp, and (3) copy files located in the subdirectories of the specified directory. The following examples will demonstrate that XCOPY can also be much faster than COPY. Figure 3 shows the file structure used in the examples.

XCOPYing Subdirectories

Assume that \BOOK is the current directory on drive C and that \COMMANDS is a subdirectory in \BOOK. A major limitation of COPY is that the contents of \BOOK and the contents of \COMMANDS cannot be copied

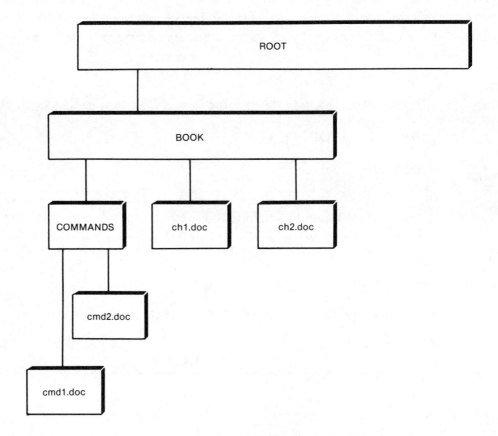

Figure 3. File structure for XCOPY examples.

with a single invocation of COPY. The /s switch provides XCOPY with the ability to copy all files in all subdirectories below the specified source directory. The specified source directory in this example is the default BOOK. Remember that since XCOPY is an external command, MS-DOS must be able to read the command from disk before execution. (Internal and external commands are discussed in the beginning of Part 3.)

```
C>xcopy *.* a: /s

Reading source file(s)...
CH1.DOC
CH2.DOC
COMMANDS\CMD1.DOC
COMMANDS\CMD2.DOC
        4 File(s) copied

C>
```

The nice feature of the /s switch is that it directs XCOPY to create the subdirectories on the target if they do not already exist. This capability makes XCOPY very useful in copying large multilevel directory structures.

Another feature of XCOPY is that it copies groups of files faster than COPY does. XCOPY reads as many source files into memory as is possible before making any copies. This minimizes disk access time and greatly speeds up the process.

XCOPY by Date

The /d switch allows you to selectively copy files that have a date stamp on or after a specified date. The date is specified in the format determined by the SELECT or COUNTRY command.

```
C>xcopy *.* a: /s /d:6-29-88

Reading source file(s)...
COMMANDS\CMD2.DOC
        1 File(s) copied
```

XCOPYing Archived Files

XCOPY can be used to selectively copy files that have their archive attributes set (see ATTRIB for a discussion of archive attributes). The /a switch directs XCOPY to copy a file if the archive attribute is set, leaving the attribute unchanged. The /m switch directs XCOPY to copy a file if the archive attribute is set, clearing the attribute in the process. The batch file "write.bat", discussed in chapter 5, uses the command "xcopy /m".

The /m switch was used daily in the writing of this book. At the end of each day, I would enter the following command:

```
xcopy *.doc a: /m
```

Since all of the files I worked on that day had their archive attribute set, this one command let me copy an entire day's work. Equally neat is that files not worked on were not copied. Also, since the /m flag cleared the archive bit, the files wouldn't be copied until I worked on them again.

Other Switches

The /e switch directs XCOPY to create a copy of any empty subdirectories specified in the command.

The /p switch produces the prompt:

```
path\filename.ext (Y/N)?
```

prior to each copy.

The /v switch directs MS-DOS to verify that each copy is performed accurately.

The /w switch tells XCOPY to wait for you to insert diskettes before searching for source files.

XCOPY versus BACKUP

Although there are strong similarities between XCOPY and BACKUP (e.g., subdirectories are copyable, archive attributes and dates are selectable), it is important to bear in mind the differences. BACKUP is used specifically to create backup copies of files. Files generated by BACKUP can be used with RESTORE only. No other MS-DOS commands can utilize these files. On the other hand, the files generated with XCOPY are conventional MS-DOS files.

P A R T

4

Appendixes

A

MS-DOS Interrupts and Function Calls

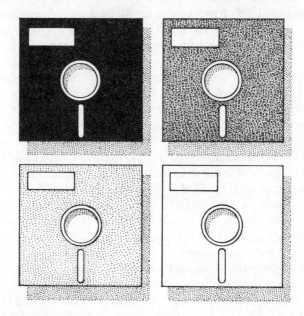

What Is an Interrupt?

An *interrupt* (int) is a signal, generated by either hardware or software, that alerts the central processing unit (CPU) that some function needs to be carried out. For example, each time a key is struck, the keyboard hardware generates an interrupt that tells the CPU that data were entered from the keyboard.

Each interrupt is assigned a unique number (e.g., the keyboard interrupt is "9") that the CPU uses to determine which *interrupt handler* must be used to process the interrupt. By convention, interrupt numbers are expressed in hexadecimal format. See chapter 13 for more information on interrupts, interrupt handlers, and CPU registers.

MS-DOS reserves for its own use interrupts 20H through 2FH. This means that programs designed to be portable across different implementations of MS-DOS should use interrupts 20H through 2FH only to perform specific tasks defined by the operating system. The most frequently used MS-DOS interrupt is interrupt 21H, the MS-DOS function dispatcher.

The MS-DOS Function Dispatcher

Interrupt 21H is the *MS-DOS function dispatcher*. The function dispatcher is responsible for carrying out most of the work done by MS-DOS. It does this by providing access to the *MS-DOS functions*. Each function performs a specific task, such as opening a file, sending a string to the display screen, allocating a block of memory, or determining which version of MS-DOS is running. Each function is identified by a function number.

In order to use the MS-DOS functions, a program must perform three tasks: (1) place the appropriate function number in the CPU's AH register; (2) place any parameters required by the function in other CPU registers, the register(s) used being determined by the particular function; and (3) issue a 21H interrupt. When the interrupt is issued, control passes from the program to MS-DOS. The operating system determines which function is to be executed by the number stored in the AH register. Any parameters are read from other CPU registers, after which the requested function is carried out. MS-DOS places any return parameters in specific CPU registers and returns control to the calling program. The program may then inspect the registers to determine the results of the function call.

Each of the MS-DOS functions is discussed in this appendix. For each function, there is a description of: (1) what the function does, (2) which parameters must be sent to the function and which registers must be used, and (3) which parameters are returned from the function to the calling program and which registers are used.

As an example of using functions, let us consider how an assembly language programmer might set up a program so that it could determine which version of MS-DOS was currently running. MS-DOS function 30H is used to obtain the MS-DOS version number. The description of function 30H in this appendix says that the function returns the minor MS-DOS version in the AH register and the major MS-DOS version in the AL register. In other words, if MS-DOS 3.30 is running, 30 is returned in AH and 3 is returned in AL.

```
                    ;Determines the version of MS-DOS running

                              ;Set up to issue interrupt
            mov     ah,30h    ;Requested service
            int     21h       ;call MS-DOS function dispatcher
                              ;
                              ;Read parameters returned
            mov     minor_num,ah    ;Save minor version number
            mov     major_num,al    ;Save major version number
```

Note: Those readers with little or no assembly language experience are referred to appendix E.

Interrupts and High-Level Programming Languages

Programs writtten in assembly language use explicit instructions (such as "int 21H") when issuing interrupts. Programs written in high-level languages (such as BASIC, Pascal, and C) do not use explicit interrupt instructions. Rather, high-level language commands (such as opening a file) are processed by the language's interpreter or compiler to generate the appropriate "int" instructions. In most cases, this arrangement is satisfactory for the high-level language programmer. The loss of "total machine control" provided by assembly language is offset by the ease of programming provided by the natural language structure of high-level programming languages.

In certain cases, though, it is desirable for the high-level language programmer to be able to issue explicit interrupts. The programs contained in this appendix are written in Turbo Pascal and Microsoft C. Both programs utilize explicit interrupts to illustrate how the MS-DOS functions can be accessed from high-level languages. Before getting to the programs, however, we need to discuss the use of interrupts to access the ROM BIOS.

Accessing the ROM BIOS

The ROM BIOS (read-only memory, basic input-output system) forms the interface between MS-DOS and the hardware. Programs also access the ROM BIOS through interrupts. For example, when a program needs to send a character to the display screen, the program may issue a call to the MS-DOS function dispatcher by using interrupt 21H. The dispatcher then accesses the ROM BIOS using interrupt 10H, and the BIOS goes on to display the character. In some cases (generally, increased speed of execution), it is desirable for the program to access the ROM BIOS directly. Program `BREAK_OFF.C` (listing A-2) shows how this is done.

Since the ROM BIOS directly interfaces with the hardware, programs that access the BIOS directly tend to be not as portable as those that access the ROM through MS-DOS. You should refer to your computer system's technical manual for detailed ROM BIOS information.

ENVSIZE.PAS

`ENVSIZE.PAS` (listing A-1) is a program written in Turbo Pascal. The program counts the number of bytes actually stored in the DOS environment. You may find it useful in measuring how efficiently you are using the space reserved for the environment. The MS-DOS environment is discussed in chapter 12. The discussion of the SHELL command in Part 3 describes how to adjust the environment's size.

ENVSIZE.PAS uses the function MsDos(), a predefined Turbo Pascal function that can be used to access the MS-DOS function dispatcher. MsDos() takes as a parameter a Pascal record of type registers, which contains 10 integers. When MsDos() is called by the program, the function takes the first integer from the parameter record and places it in the AX register. The function then takes the second integer from the parameter record and places it in the BX register, and so on for each of the 10 integers (see listing A-1, lines 8–10). MsDos() then goes on to call the appropriate function. Upon return from the function, MsDos() takes the value stored in the AX register and places it in the first integer of the parameter record. The BX value is placed in the second integer of the parameter record, and so on. In this program, dosreg is declared as a variable of type registers.

The program begins (line 73) by calling procedure vernum, which will return the major number of the version of MS-DOS being used. Line 19 sets the AX field of dosregs to $3000 (Turbo Pascal denotes hexadecimal numbers by a leading "$" rather than a trailing "H"). The effect of line 19 is to place a value of 30H in the AH register and a value of 00H in the AL register. This establishes the conditions for a call to function 30H.

Line 20 is a call to the MS-DOS function dispatcher (interrupt 21H) with parameters passed in dosreg. On return from the function dispatcher, the major MS-DOS version number is stored in the AL register. Line 21 uses the Turbo function Lo() to assign the value in AL (the low byte in dosreg.ax) to vernum. The major version number is then returned to the main program module, which displays a message and terminates if vernum is less than 3.

The procedure get_envaddr uses MS-DOS function 62H to obtain the segment address of the program segment prefix and assigns the address to the variable psp_seg (lines 32–34). Procedure vernum must be called prior to calling get_envaddr since service function 62H is not implemented in versions of MS-DOS prior to 3.00.

Listing A-1. ENVSIZE.PAS

```
1 program EnvSize;
2
3 {This program determines the size of its MS-DOS environment.
4 The program uses service function 62H. Therefore, MS-DOS 3.0 or
5 later is required.}
6
7 type
8      registers = record
9                   ax,bx,cx,dx,bp,si,di,ds,es,flags: integer;
10                  end;
11 var
12    dosreg:     registers;
13    env_seg:         integer; {Segment address of environment}
```

```
14
15
16  {Returns the version of MS-DOS being used.}
17  function vernum : integer;
18  begin
19      dosreg.ax:= $3000;       {Set AH to 30H.}
20      MsDos(dosreg);           {Call MS-DOS}
21      vernum:= Lo(dosreg.ax); {Major version number in AL}
22  end;
23
24
25  {Obtains segment address of psp using service function 62H.
26  Reads segment address of environment at psp:002CH.}
27
28  procedure get_envaddr;
29  var
30      psp_seg : integer;
31  begin
32      dosreg.ax := $6200;
33      MsDos(dosreg);
34      psp_seg := dosreg.bx;
35      env_seg := MemW[psp_seg:$002C];
36  end;
37
38
39  {Returns the number of byte characters stored in the MS-DOS
40  environment. env_seg is global and contains environment's
41  segment address}
42
43  function get_size : integer;
44  var
45      count : integer;    {Counts characters in environment}
46      firstZero,secondZero : boolean;{Flag records if last byte = 00}
47      env_ptr : ^Byte;               {Environment pointer}
48  begin
49      env_ptr := Ptr(env_seg,$0);    {Start of environment}
50      count := 0;
51      firstZero := false;
52      secondZero := false;
53
54      while secondZero = false do     {Read environment}
55      begin
56      env_ptr := Ptr(env_seg,count); {Point to next byte}
57      count := count + 1;
58
59      if env_ptr^ = 0 then            {Byte of 00 read}
60      begin
61          if firstZero = true then    {2 consecutive 00's}
62          secondZero := true
63          else firstZero := true      {only 1 byte of 00 read}
64      end
```

```
65        else firstZero := false;        {00 byte not read}
66     end;
67
68     get_size := count;
69  end;
70
71
72
73  begin
74     if vernum < 3 then
75            writeln('MS-DOS 3.0 or later required.')
76     else begin
77            get_envaddr;
78            writeln('Environment Size: ',get_size,' bytes');
79     end;
80  end.
```

> **ENVSIZE.PAS** will run under MS-DOS 2.1, and subsequent versions, with a few minor modifications. Change line 32 to:
>
> ```
> dosreg.ax := $5100
> ```
>
> The result is that MS-DOS now calls undocumented function 51H, which also returns the psp's segment address in BX. The other change (which is left to the reader) is to have the program check to make sure that MS-DOS version 2.1 or greater is running prior to calling the procedure **get_envaddr**.
>
> MS-DOS function 51H is used in the program **PSPEEP.PAS**, which is presented in chapter 12.

Line 35 uses the predefined array **MemW** to assign the segment address of the MS-DOS environment to the variable **env_seg**. The value of **MemW[psp_seg:$002C]** is the value of the word stored at segment address **psp_seg**, offset address 2CH. As discussed in chapter 12, this is the memory location that stores the segment address of the MS-DOS environment.

The function **get_size** initializes a counter and two boolean flags (lines 50—52) before entering a loop (lines 54—65). On entering the loop, **env_ptr** points to the first byte in the MS-DOS environment. Each traversal of the loop increments the variable count and moves **env_ptr** to the next byte in the environment. The loop is exited when two consecutive bytes of zero are read. Two consecutive bytes of zero indicate that the end of the environment's character strings has been reached. Upon exiting the loop, the variable **count** stores the number of bytes stored in the environment. Note that this is not the storage capacity of the environment, but a count of the number of character bytes actually stored there. The value of count is assigned to `get_size`, returned to the program's main module, and displayed on the screen (line 78).

BRK_OFF.C

`BRK_OFF.C` (listing A-2), which is written in Microsoft C, uses the MS-DOS functions to capture any Ctrl-C or Ctrl-Break entered on the keyboard. The program also accesses the ROM BIOS to position the cursor on the screen.

Listing A-2. BRK_OFF.C

```
 1  /*This program illustrates how the MS-DOS service functions are
 2  *accessed using Microsoft C, version 4.0. The program implements
 3  *a keyboard routine that captures Ctrl-C.
 4  */
 5
 6  #include  <stdio.h>
 7  #include  <dos.h>
 8  #define        TRUE            1
 9
10  union   REGS    Regs;                   /*General registers*/
11  struct  SREGS   Sregs;                  /*Segment registers*/
12
13  char    message[] = "Ctrl-C disabled, press X to quit";
14
15  int     x_cur, y_cur;
16
17
18  /*Call to ROM BIOS which returns cursor's x coordinate in the Regs.h.dh
19  *register, the y coordinate in the Regs.h.dl register. These values
20  *are saved in global variables x_cur and y_cur. Prior to call,
21  *current page number is stored in Regs.h.bh.
22  */
23
24  void get_cursor_pos()
25  {
26    Regs.h.ah = 0x03;          /*Read cursor function*/
27    int86(0x10,&Regs,&Regs); /*Call BIOS*/
28    x_cur = Regs.h.dl;
29    y_cur = Regs.h.dh;
30    return;
31  }
32
33
34  /*Calls ROM BIOS to restore cursor position which has been saved in
35  *global variables x_cur and y_cur. Prior to call, Regs.h.bh
36  *contains active page number.
```

```
37  */
38
39  void reset_cursor()
40  {
41    Regs.h.ah = 0x02;           /*Set cursor function*/
42    Regs.h.dl = x_cur;          /*DL stores x value*/
43    Regs.h.dh = y_cur;          /*DH stores y value*/
44    int86(0x10,&Regs,&Regs);
45    return;
46  }
47
48
49  /*Calls ROM BIOS to display message at bottom of screen. Current
50   *position of cursor is saved prior to displaying message. Cursor
51   *position is restored after message is displayed.
52   */
53
54  void display_message()
55  {
56    Regs.h.ah = 0x0f;           /*Get active page*/
57    int86(0x10,&Regs,&Regs);    /*Call BIOS*/
58    get_cursor_pos();           /*Save cursor position*/
59
60    Regs.h.ah 0x02;             /*Set cursor function*/
61    Regs.h.dh = 0x18;           /*Row position*/
62    Regs.h.dl = 0x14;           /*Column position*/
63    int86(0x10,&Regs,&Regs);    /*Call BIOS*/
64    printf("%s",message);
65
66    reset_cursor();             /*To current position*/
67    return;
68  }
69
70
71  /*Calls DOS service function 02h to display a character on screen
72   *at current position of cursor. Prior to call, Regs.h.al contains
73   *byte data for character to be displayed.
74   */
75
76  void echo()
77  {
78    Regs.h.dl = Regs.h.al;
79    Regs.h.ah = 0x02;
80    intdos(&Regs,&Regs);
81    return;
82  }
83
84
85  /*Calls ROM BIOS, first to get the active page number in Regs.h.bh
86   *then to position cursor at 0,0. Then endless loop captures Ctrl-C.
87   *Loop is broken when "X" typed at keyboard. Other characters are
```

```
 88  *echoed to screen.
 ?9  */
 90
 91  break_off()
 92  {
 93     Regs.h.ah = 0x0f;                      /*Get active page*/
 94     int86(0x10,&Regs,&Regs);               /*Call BIOS*/
 95
 96     Regs.h.ah = 0x02;                      /*Position cursor*/
 97     Regs.h.dl = 0x00;                      /*  to 0,0 */
 98     Regs.h.dh = 0x00;
 99     int86(0x10,&Regs,&Regs);               /*Call BIOS*/
100
101     while (TRUE)                           /*Loop forever*/
102     }
103            Regs.h.ah = 0x07;               /*Input, no echo*/
104            intdos(&Regs,&Regs);            /*Call MS-DOS*/
105
106            if (Regs.h.al = '^C')
107                    display_message();
108            else if (Regs.h.al != 'X')
109            echo();
110            else break;                     /*Break from loop*/
111     }
112     return;
113  }
114
115  main()
116  {
117     break_off();
118     exit(0);
119  }
```

The program declares **Regs** and **Sregs** (listing A-1, lines 10–11) to be variables of types **REGS** and **SREGS**, respectively. **REGS** is a predefined Microsoft C data type that contains eight integer fields, each of which corresponds to one of the CPU's general registers. **SREGS** is a predefined Microsoft C data type that contains four integer fields, each of which corresponds to one of the CPU's segment registers. As will be seen, these data structures perform the same role as the **register** variable used in the preceding Turbo Pascal program.

BRK_OFF.C begins (line 117) by calling **break_off()** (line 91). The first portion of **break_off()** positions the cursor at position 0,0 (the upper left corner) on the screen. In order to do this, the program accesses the ROM BIOS two times.

In Microsoft C, ROM BIOS accesses are carried out using the predefined function **int86()**. This function takes three parameters: (1) an integer that specifies an interrupt number, (2) a **REGS**-type data structure that contains parameters to be passed to the ROM BIOS, and (3) a second **REGS**-type data structure that will store parameters returned from the ROM BIOS to the calling program. The ROM BIOS video services are accessed using interrupt 10H. The number of the video function requested is passed in the AH register.

The first ROM BIOS call (line 94) is performed to determine the active display page. Since the ROM BIOS maintains a cursor position for each display page, the program needs to know which page is active before the ROM BIOS can be instructed to position the cursor. The active display page is returned in the BH register by video function 0FH. Accordingly, line 96 sets the AH field of **Regs** to 0902 (02H). Line 94 is a call to the ROM BIOS service using **int86()**. On return, **Regs.h.bh** contains the active display page number. Note that Microsoft C allows a program to access: (1) the high-order byte stored in a general register, for example **Regs.h.ah**; (2) the low-order byte stored in a general register, for example **Regs.h.al**; and (3) the two-byte word stored in a general register, for example **Regs.x.ax**.

Lines 96–99 position the cursor at 0,0. This is accomplished by calling video function 02H. Prior to the call, the *x* coordinate for the cursor is placed in the DL register, the *y* coordinate in the DH register. Function 02H also requires that the BH register contain the active display page number. This was accomplished by the previous ROM BIOS call.

Once the cursor is positioned, the program enters an infinite loop, which begins at line 101. The first part of the loop (lines 103–104) uses MS-DOS function 07H to read a character from the keyboard without echoing it to the screen. The MS-DOS functions are accessed using the predefined function **intdos()**, which does not take an interrupt parameter because all of the MS-DOS service functions are accessed via interrupt 21H.

Line 103 places 07H in **Regs.h.ah**. This will tell MS-DOS that function 07H is requested. Once MS-DOS is called (line 104), the operating system will wait until a character is entered at the keyboard. When a character is entered, MS-DOS returns control to the program and the byte value of the entered character is stored in **Regs.h.al**.

When control returns from MS-DOS to the program (line 106), **BRK_OFF.C** first checks to see if Ctrl-C was entered. Note that the **^C** in line 106 is a single control character. Most word processors allow you to enter a literal control code character into text.

If Ctrl-C was entered, line 106 is evaluated as true and control is passed to **display_message()**. This function starts by repeating the call to ROM BIOS video function 0FH to determine the active display page. With the display page number back in **Regs.h.bh**, **display_message()** calls **get_cursor_pos()**, which uses ROM BIOS video function 03H to determine the position of the cursor. The cursor's coordinates are saved in the global variables **x_cur** and **y_cur** (lines 28–29), and control is returned to **display_message()**.

The function **display_message()** then uses ROM BIOS video service function 02H to position the cursor at row 18H, column 14H (lines 60–63). The C function **printf** is used to display a message saying that Ctrl-C has been disabled. Line 66 then issues a call to **reset_cursor()**, which uses video service function 02H to restore the cursor to the coordinates saved in x_cur and y_cur. Control is returned to break_off(), which repeats the infinite loop and waits for another character to be entered.

All of this happens (very quickly!) if Ctrl-C is pressed. We need to return to the infinite loop to see what happens if some other character is pressed. If, on return from MS-DOS function 07H, line 106 evaluates as false, the program checks to see if "X" was entered. If not, the program issues a call to echo(). If "X" was entered, the program breaks out of the infinite loop and returns to main(), where program execution terminates.

If neither Ctrl-C nor "X" was entered, break_off() issues a call to echo(). This function uses MS-DOS function 02H to display the character entered. Line 78 copies to Regs.h.dl the character returned by the previous call to MS-DOS. Function 02H is then called to display this character, after which control returns to break_off(), and the infinite loop is repeated.

The MS-DOS Interrupts

Interrupt	Description
Int 20H	***General program termination.*** This interrupt is one of several ways in which a program running under MS-DOS may terminate. The interrupt restores the terminate, Ctrl-Break, and critical error addresses, which are stored in the program's program segment prefix. This interrupt is a carryover from the early days of MS-DOS. Before issuing int 20H, CS must contain the psp's segment address. Most programmers use MS-DOS function 4CH to terminate because the function can be used to return an ERRORLEVEL value.
Int 21H	***MS-DOS function request.*** This interrupt is used to access the MS-DOS function calls, which are discussed in the next section.
Int 22H	***Program termination address.*** This interrupt points to the address in memory to which control is passed when a program is terminated. The address is stored in the program segment prefix of the program.
Int 23H	***Ctrl-Break address.*** This interrupt points to the address in memory of the routine that takes control when the user presses Ctrl-Break. The address is stored in the program segment prefix of the program.
Int 24H	***Critical error handler.*** This interrupt points to the address in memory of the routine that takes control when MS-DOS encounters a critical error. The address is stored in the program segment prefix. Prior to

Interrupt	Description
Int 24H (cont'd)	executing this interrupt, MS-DOS places an error code in the lower half of the DI register:

Error Code	Description of Error
0	Write-protected diskette.
1	Unknown unit.
2	Drive not ready.
3	Unknown command.
4	Data error.
5	Bad request structure length.
6	Seek error.
7	Unknown media type.
8	Sector not found.
9	Printer out of paper.
A	Write fault.
B	Read fault.
C	General failure.

BP:SI will contain the segment: offset address of the device header control block (see chapter 14) that was involved in the critical error.

Int 25H	***Absolute disk read.*** This interrupt is used to read logical disk sectors into memory. Prior to calling the interrupt, the following registers must be initialized:

AL	Drive number containing the disk to be read (0=A, 1=B, etc.).
CX	Number of sectors to be read.
DX	Number of first logical sector to be read.
DS:BX	Segment: offset address of memory location that will receive the data to be read.

This interrupt destroys the contents of all registers except for the segment registers. If the read is successful, the carry flag will be zero on return. The carry flag will equal one on return if the read was not successful. If there is an error, the AL register will contain the MS-DOS error code. Refer to the discussion of int 24H for an interpretation of MS-DOS error codes. This interrupt does not pop the status flags on return.

Int 26H	***Absolute disk write.*** This interrupt is used to write data to logical disk sectors. Except for the fact that this is a write operation, its description is identical to that for the preceding interrupt 25H.

Interrupt	Description
Int 27H	***Terminate but stay resident.*** This interrupt is used to terminate the execution of a program while keeping the program resident in memory. Prior to executing the interrupt, the DX register must be set to the offset address of the program's end plus 1 byte. This offset is taken relative to the program's program segment prefix. Int 27H restores terminate, Ctrl-C, and critical error vectors. Therefore, it cannot be used to install critical error handlers. Programs that use int 27H are limited in size to 64 Kbytes. The preferred method for terminate and stay resident (under MS-DOS 2.X and 3.X) is MS-DOS service function 31H.
Int 28H	Used internally by MS-DOS (see appendix B).
Int 29H–2EH	Reserved for MS-DOS (see appendix B).
Int 2FH	***Multiplex interrupt.*** This interrupt, implemented in MS-DOS 3.0 and later versions, is used to establish a multiplexing interface between two processes. A *process* is any program or command that is running. In *multiplexing*, the CPU runs one process for a period of time, halts the execution of that process and starts a second, halts the second and restarts the first, and so on, until both processes have finished executing. Int 2FH is used in the implementation of the command PRINT, which allows printing to occur in the background while another program is executing in the foreground (see PRINT in Part 3).
	Each program that runs under multiplexing (such as PRINT) is given a specific *multiplex number*. MS-DOS has reserved multiplex numbers 00–7FH for its own use. PRINT has been given multiplex number 1. Multiplex numbers 80H–FFH are available for use by application programmers. There is no method for assigning a multiplex number to an application and, as is explained subsequently, each application must have a unique multiplex number. Therefore, IBM and Microsoft recommend that programs be written so that multiplex numbers are changeable.
	As if to emphasize the importance of changeability, MS-DOS 3.3 assigns multiplex number B7H to a subfunction that determines if APPEND has been installed. IBM recommends that programs written to run under 3.3 should use multiplex numbers in the range C0H through FFH.
	Each multiplexing program installs in memory an

Interrupt	Description
Int 2FH (cont'd)	int 2FH handler. These handlers form a chain, similar to that formed by installable device drivers (see chapter 14). Prior to calling interrupt 2FH, a program places in the AH register the multiplex number of the handler that the program wishes to access. When MS-DOS receives control, the operating system scans the chain of int 2FH handlers until it locates one with a number matching the value stored in AH. MS-DOS passes control to that handler, which is then responsible for servicing the interrupt.
	Programs issuing int 2FH also place a *function code* in the AL register. The function code communicates to the handler the type of service requested by the caller. All int 2FH handlers are required to service a *get installed state* request (AL=00) from the caller. In response to this request, a return code is to be placed in AL:
	AL = 0 Handler not installed; okay to install.
	AL = 1 Handler not installed; not okay to install.
	AL = FF Handler installed.
Int 30H–3FH	Reserved for use by MS-DOS.

The MS-DOS Functions

The MS-DOS functions form the heart of the operating system. All of the functions are accessed by placing their function number in the AH register and issuing an interrupt 21H. See chapter 12 for examples of how functions are used in assembly language programming. The programs presented earlier in this apppendix demonstrate accessing the functions using Turbo Pascal and Microsoft C.

The "Reserved" Functions

Several of the functions are described as "reserved for use by MS-DOS." These functions are used by the operating system, but Microsoft and IBM refuse to officially document what the functions do. Thanks to the combined efforts of many determined hackers, the purpose of some of these functions is known. People who use these functions generally refer to them as "undocumented" rather than "reserved." Several of the undocumented functions are used in programs contained in this book. Appendix B describes some undocumented MS-DOS functions.

Error Codes

Many of the functions implemented in MS-DOS 2.X and 3.X set the CPU's carry flag and return an error code in the AX register if an error occurs during the call. These same functions clear the carry flag if no error occurs.

Error Code	Meaning
01H	Invalid function number.
02H	File not found.
03H	Path not found.
04H	Too many files opened (no handles left).
05H	Access denied.
06H	Invalid handle.
07H	Memory control block destroyed.
08H	Insufficent memory.
09H	Invalid memory block address.
0AH	Invalid environment.
0BH	Invalid format.
0CH	Invalid access code.
0DH	Invalid data.
0EH	Reserved for use by MS-DOS.
0FH	Invalid drive specification.
10H	Attempted to remove current directory.
11H	Not same device.
12H	No more files.

The following error codes are implemented in MS-DOS 3.00 and subsequent versions:

Error Code	Meaning
20H	Sharing violation.
21H	Lock violation.
22H	Invalid disk change.
23H	FCB unavailable.
24H	Sharing buffer overflow.
25H–31H	Reserved.
32H	Network request not supported.
33H	Remote computer not listening.
34H	Duplicate name on network.

Error Code	Meaning
35H	Network name not found.
36H	Network busy.
37H	Network device does not exist.
38H	Network BIOS command limit exceeded.
39H	Network adapter hardware error.
3AH	Incorrect response from network.
3BH	Unexpected network error.
3CH	Incompatible remote adapter.
3DH	Print queue full.
3EH	Print queue not full.
3FH	Print file deleted (not enough space).
40H	Network name deleted.
41H	Access denied.
42H	Network device type incorrect.
43H	Network name not found.
44H	Network name limit exceeded.
45H	Network BIOS session limit exceeded.
46H	Temporarily paused.
47H	Network request not accepted.
48H	Print or disk redirection paused.
49H–4FH	Reserved by MS-DOS.
50H	File already exists.
51H	Reserved.
52H	Cannot make directory entry.
53H	Failure on int 24H.
54H	Too many redirections.
55H	Duplicate redirection.
56H	Invalid password.
57H	Invalid parameter.
58H	Network device fault.

MS-DOS Function	Description	Implemented in Versions
00H	***Program terminate.*** Used to terminate program execution. Restores the terminate, Ctrl-Break, and critical error addresses that were stored in the program's program	1, 2, 3

MS-DOS Function	Description	Implemented in Versions
00H (cont'd)	segment prefix. This function is identical to int 20H. Any files that were opened with FCBs should be closed before using function 00H. Prior to the call, the CS register must contain the psp's segment address. Therefore, it is generally used in COM programs only.	1, 2, 3
01H	***Read input with echo.*** When this function is called, MS-DOS waits for a character to be entered at the standard input device. The character is then echoed to the standard output device, and the ASCII code for the character is returned in the AL register. The function must be called twice to read extended ASCII codes (as generated by the function keys).	1, 2, 3
02H	***Display output.*** Prior to executing this function, an ASCII value is placed in the DL register. When the function is called, the value in DL is sent to the standard output device.	1, 2, 3
03H	***Auxiliary input.*** When this function is invoked, MS-DOS waits for a character to be input from the standard auxiliary device. The ASCII value for the character is returned in the AL register.	1, 2, 3
04H	***Auxiliary output.*** An ASCII value is placed in the DL register prior to invoking this function. The function then sends the value in DL to the standard auxiliary device.	1, 2, 3
05H	***Printer output.*** An ASCII value is placed in the DL register prior to invoking this function. The function then sends the value in DL to the standard printer device.	1, 2, 3
06H	***Direct console I/O.*** The role of this function depends on the value stored in the DL register when the function is invoked:

If DL has a value of FFH, invoking function 06H directs MS-DOS to see if a character has been entered at the standard input device. If a character has been entered, the zero flag is set to 0 (cleared) and the ASCII value of the character entered is placed in the AL register. If a character has not been entered, the zero flag is set to 1 and a value of 00H is placed in the AL register. | 1, 2, 3 |

MS-DOS Function	Description	Implemented in Versions
06H (cont'd)	If DL has a value other than FFH, the value in DL is sent to the standard output device. This function does not check for Ctrl-Break.	
07H	***Console input without echo.*** This function directs MS-DOS to wait for a character to be entered at the standard input device. The ASCII value of the character is returned in the AL register. This function does not echo the character to the display screen or check for Ctrl-Break.	1, 2, 3
08H	***Read keyboard.*** This function is identical to function 07H except that it checks for Ctrl-Break.	1, 2, 3
09H	***Print string.*** Prior to invoking this function, DS:DX is set to point to the segment: offset address of an ASCII string. The string must end with "$" (ASCII value 24H). Each character in the string (except the "$") is sent to the standard output device when the function is called.	1, 2, 3
0AH	***Buffered keyboard input.*** This function is used to set up and utilize an area of memory as a buffer for input from the standard input device. Prior to invoking the function, you must do the following:	1, 2, 3

    1. Set DS:DX to point to the segment: offset address of the first byte in the buffer.

    2. Specify the length of the buffer by placing a value in the buffer's first byte.

When the function is called, MS-DOS places characters in the buffer as they are entered at the standard input device. The characters are stored beginning at the third byte of the buffer. Characters are stored in the buffer until carriage return (ASCII 0DH) is entered. If the buffer is filled to one less than the maximum, any remaining characters are ignored and the bell sounds until carriage return is entered. MS-DOS sets the second byte of the buffer to the number of characters entered (not counting carriage return). The buffer can be edited using the MS-DOS editing keys (see chapter 7).

MS-DOS Function	Description	Implemented in Versions
0BH	***Check standard input status.*** This function returns a value of FFH in the AL register if there are characters available from the standard input device. AL returns with a value of 00H if no characters are available.	1, 2, 3
0CH	***Flush buffer, read standard input device.*** Prior to invoking this function, a value of 01H, 06H, 08H, or 0AH is placed in the AL register. When the function is called, the standard input device buffer is cleared and the MS-DOS function corresponding to the value in the AL register is invoked.	1, 2, 3
0DH	***Disk reset.*** This function flushes all file buffers. Files that have been modified in size should be closed (functions 10H and 3EH). It is not necessary to flush a file that has been closed.	1, 2, 3
0EH	***Select disk.*** This function selects the drive specified in the DL register (0=A, 1=B, etc.) as the default. The number of drives in the system is returned in the AL register. If a system has one diskette drive, the one drive is counted as two, since MS-DOS considers the system to have two logical diskette drives.	1, 2, 3
0FH	***Open file.*** Prior to invoking this function, DS:DX must be set to point to the segment: offset address of an unopened file control block (FCB). When the function is called, the disk directory is searched for the file named in the FCB. If a match is found in the directory, the function returns a value of 00H in the AL register and the FCB is filled as follows:	1, 2, 3

If the drive code of the FCB (offset 0) was set to default (00H), MS-DOS changes the code to match the actual drive used (1=A, 2=B, 3=C, etc.).

The current block field of the FCB (offset 0CH) is set to zero.

The record size field of the FCB (offset 0EH) is set to the default value of 80H.

The file size (offset 10H), date (offset 14H), and time (offset 16H) fields of the FCB are set according to information stored in the disk directory.

MS-DOS Function	Description	Implemented in Versions
0FH (cont'd)	You must set the current record field of the FCB (offset 20H) before performing any sequential disk operations.	
	You must set the relative record field of the FCB (offset 21H) before performing any random disk operations.	
	You may modify the record size field if a file size of 80H bytes is not appropriate.	
	Function 0FH returns a value of FFH in the AL register if no match is made between the file named in the FCB and the entries in the disk directory. (The file control block is discussed in chapter 11.)	
10H	***Close file.*** This function must be used to update the disk directory whenever a file has been modified. Prior to invoking this function, DS:DX must point to the segment: offset address of an opened file control block. When the function is called, the current directory on the disk specified in the FCB is searched for the file named in the FCB. If a match is found, the file's entry in the directory is updated according to the information in the FCB and a value of 00H is returned in the AL register. A value of FFH is returned in AL if no match is found.	1, 2, 3
11H	***Search for first match.*** Prior to invoking this function, DS:DX points to an unopened file control block (FCB). When the function is called, MS-DOS searches the current directory of the disk specified in the FCB for the first filename matching the filename specified in the FCB. The name in FCB may contain the wildcard characters "*" and "?". A value of FFH is returned in the AL register if no match is found. Otherwise:	1, 2, 3
	A value of 00H is returned in the AL register.	
	An unopened FCB is created for the matching file at the disk transfer address (DTA). You may use MS-DOS function 2FH to obtain the current DTA.	
	DS:DX may point to a standard or an extended FCB (see chapter 11). The FCB created at the DTA will be of the same type.	

MS-DOS Function	Description	Implemented in Versions
11H (cont'd)	If the attribute byte of an extended FCB is set to zero, only normal files that match will be found. If the attribute byte of an extended FCB specifies hidden, system, and/ or directory entries, the search will find the specified types of entries that match, plus all normal files that match. If the attribute specifies volume label, only the volume label entry is returned. (See chapter 11 for a discussion of file attributes.)	
12H	***Search for next match.*** After function 11H has been used, this function is used to find additional directory entries matching the filename in the FCB at DS:DX. This function is used when the filename in the FCB contains wildcards. Prior to invoking this function, DS:DX must point to the segment: offset address of the FCB previously used by function 11H. If an additional match is found, function 12H creates an unopened file control block at the disk transfer area and a value of 00H is returned in the AL register. A value of FFH is returned in AL if no further match is found.	1, 2, 3
13H	***Delete file.*** Prior to invoking this function, DS:DX points to the segment: offset address of an unopened file control block. When the function is called, MS-DOS searches the current directory of the disk specified in the FCB for an entry with a filename matching the one specified in the FCB. If a match is found, the file is deleted from the directory. If the filename in the FCB contains wildcards, all matching files are deleted. A value of 00H is returned in the AL register if any files are deleted. A value of FFH is returned in AL if no match is found.	1, 2, 3
14H	***Sequential read.*** Prior to invoking this function, DS:DX must point to an opened file control block (FCB). The current block (offset 0CH) and current record (offset 20H) fields of the FCB determine a record within the file that is named in the FCB. The size of the record is determined by the record size field (offset 0EH) in the FCB. When the function is called: The specified record is read into memory at the disk transfer address (DTA).	1, 2, 3

MS-DOS Function	Description	Implemented in Versions
14H (cont'd)	The current block and current record fields are incremented to point to the next record.	

The AL register returns a value of:

00H	If the read was successful.
01H	If an end-of-file mark is read, indicating no more data in the file.
02H	If there is not enough room at the DTA to read a record.
03H	If an end-of-file mark is read, indicating that a partial record was read and padded with zeros.

The DTA is set with MS-DOS function 1AH. The current DTA is returned with MS-DOS function 2FH.

MS-DOS Function	Description	Implemented in Versions
15H	***Sequential write.*** Prior to invoking this function, DS:DX must point to an opened file control block (FCB). The data to be written begin at the disk transfer address (DTA). The current block (offset 0CH) and current record (offset 20H) fields of the FCB determine a record within the file that is named in the FCB. The size of the record is determined by the record size field (offset 0EH) in the FCB. When the function is called:	1, 2, 3

The specified record is written to the disk.

The current block and current record fields are incremented to point to the next record.

The AL register returns a value of:

00H	If the write was successful.
01H	If the disk is full and the write has been cancelled.
02H	If there is not enough room at the DTA for one record; therefore, the write has been cancelled.

MS-DOS Function	Description	Implemented in Versions
16H	***Create file.*** Prior to invoking this function, DS:DX must point to an unopened file control block (FCB). When the function is called, MS-DOS checks the current directory of the drive specified in the FCB for an entry	1, 2, 3

MS-DOS Function	Description	Implemented in Versions
16H (cont'd)	matching the file specified in the FCB. If a matching entry is found:	
	The data in the existing file are released, making a file of zero length. The open file function (function 0FH) is then called.	
	If no match is found:	
	MS-DOS looks for an empty entry in the current directory. If an empty entry is available, MS-DOS initializes the file to have a length of zero and calls the open file function (function 0FH). A value of 00H is returned in the AL register. A value of FFH is returned in AL if there are no empty entries in the current directory.	
	A hidden file is created by using an extended FCB with the attribute byte set to a value of 02H (see chapter 11).	
17H	***Rename file.*** Prior to invoking this function, DS:DX must point to the segment: offset address of a "modified" FCB. The FCB contains a drive number and filename beginning at offset 00H. The FCB contains a second filename beginning at offset 11H. When the function is called, MS-DOS searches the current directory of the drive specified in the FCB for an entry matching the first filename in the FCB. If a match is found:	1, 2, 3
	The filename in the directory is changed to the second filename in the FCB. If "?" characters are used in the second filename, the corresponding positions in the original filename are not changed. A value of 00H is returned in the AL register.	
	If no match is found or if an entry is found matching the second filename:	
	A value of FFH is returned in the AL register.	
18H	Reserved for use by MS-DOS.	
19H	***Current disk.*** This function returns the number of the current default drive in the AL register (0=A, 1=B, etc.).	1, 2, 3
1AH	***Set disk transfer address.*** This function is used to set the disk transfer address (DTA). Prior to invoking this function, DS:DX must point to the segment: offset address of the first	1, 2, 3

MS-DOS Function	Description	Implemented in Versions
1AH (cont'd)	byte in the DTA. MS-DOS establishes a default DTA at offset 80H in the program segment prefix if function 1AH is not invoked.	
1BH	***Allocation table information.*** This function returns information about the default drive's file allocation table (FAT). On return:	1, 2, 3

DS:BX points to the segment: offset address of a memory location that stores the first byte in the FAT.

DX contains the number of allocation units on the disk in the default drive.

AL stores the number of sectors per allocation unit.

CX stores the number of bytes in each sector.

In MS-DOS 2.0 and subsequent versions, this function does not return the address of the complete FAT, since the entire FAT is not stored in memory.

MS-DOS Function	Description	Implemented in Versions
1CH	***Allocation information for specific drive.*** This function is identical to function 1BH except that prior to invoking the function, the DL register contains the number of the drive from which the FAT information will be obtained (0=A, 1=B, etc.).	1, 2, 3
1DH–20H	Reserved for use by MS-DOS (see appendix B).	
21H	***Random read.*** Prior to invoking this function, DS:DX must point to the segment: offset address of an opened file control block (FCB). The current block (offset 0CH) and current record (offset 20H) fields of the FCB must be set to agree with the relative record field (offset 21H). When the function is called, the record addressed by these fields is read into memory at the disk transfer address. A value is returned in the AL register as follows:	1, 2, 3

00H	Read completed successfully.
01H	No data available in file.
02H	Not enough room in DTA to read one record; read cancelled.
03H	End-of-file mark encountered. A partial record was read and padded with zeros.

MS-DOS Function	Description	Implemented in Versions
22H	***Random write.*** Prior to invoking this function, DS:DX must point to the segment: offset address of an opened file control block (FCB). The current block (offset 0CH) and current record (offset 20H) fields of the FCB must be set to agree with the relative record field (offset 21H).	1, 2, 3
	When the function is called, the record addressed by these fields is written from the disk transfer address to the file specified in the FCB. A value is returned in the AL register as follows:	
	00H Write completed successfully.	
	01H Disk full.	
	02H Not enough room in DTA to write one record; write cancelled.	
23H	***File size.*** Prior to invoking this function, DS:DX is set to point to the segment: offset address of an unopened file control block (FCB). The record size field (offset 0EH) of the FCB must also be set prior to calling this function. When the function is called, MS-DOS searches the current directory of the drive specified in the FCB for a file that matches the filename in the FCB. If a match is found, the relative record size field (offset 21H) is set to the number of records in the file, and a value of 00H is returned in the AL register. A value of FFH is returned in AL if no match is found.	1, 2, 3
24H	***Set random record field.*** Prior to invoking this function, DS:DX must point to the segment: offset address of an opened file control block (FCB). This function sets the relative record field (offset 21H) of the FCB to point to the record indicated by the combination of the current block (offset 0CH) and current record (offset 20H) fields.	1, 2, 3
25H	***Set interrupt vector.*** This function is used to set the memory location that receives control when a specific interrupt is invoked. Prior to invoking this function, DS:DX is set to point to the segment: offset address of the first byte in the interrupt handling routine, and AL contains the number of the specified interrupt.	1, 2, 3

MS-DOS Function	Description	Implemented in Versions
26H	***Create a new program segment prefix.*** Prior to invoking this function, DX contains the segment address of what will be a new program segment. When the function is called, the first 100H bytes of the current program segment are copied into the first 100H memory locations of the new program segment. Offset 06H in the new segment is updated to contain the size of the new program segment. The addresses for the termination, Ctrl-Break, and critical error routines are stored in the new program segment beginning at offset 0AH. Programs written to run under MS-DOS 2.0 and subsequent versions should use function 4BH instead of this function.	1, 2, 3
27H	***Random block read.*** This function is used to read a block of records from a file. Prior to invoking the function, DS:DX must point to the segment: offset address of an opened file control block (FCB). CX must contain the number of records to be read. The size of each record must be stored in the record size field (offset 0EH) of the FCB. The read starts with the record specified in the relative record field (offset 21H) of the FCB. The records are read into memory at the disk transfer address (DTA). A value is returned in the AL register as follows:	1, 2, 3

    00H   Read completed successfully.
    01H   End-of-file mark encountered; no data in record.
    02H   Not enough room in DTA to read one record; read cancelled.
    03H   End-of-file mark encountered. A partial record was read and padded with zeros.

MS-DOS function 1AH is used to set the DTA. MS-DOS function 2FH returns the current DTA.

MS-DOS Function	Description	Implemented in Versions
28H	***Random block write.*** This function is used to write a block of records to a file. Prior to invoking the function, DS:DX must point to the segment: offset address of an opened file control block (FCB). CX must contain the	1, 2, 3

MS-DOS Function	Description	Implemented in Versions
28H (cont'd)	number of records to be written. The size of each record must be stored in the record size field (offset 0EH) of the FCB. The write starts with the record specified in the relative record field (offset 21H) of the FCB. The data written is located at the disk transfer address (DTA). If CX equals zero on entry, no records are written, but the file size stored in the disk directory is adjusted according to the number of records specified by the relative record field. A value is returned in the AL register as follows:	

00H   Write completed successfully.
01H   Disk full. No records written.
02H   Not enough room in DTA to hold one record; write cancelled.
03H   End-of-file mark encountered. A partial record was read and padded with zeros.

MS-DOS function 1AH is used to set the DTA. MS-DOS function 2FH returns the current DTA.

MS-DOS Function	Description	Implemented in Versions
29H	***Parse filename.*** This function is used to parse the information contained in a command line of the form "*d*: filename.ext" so that the information can be stored in a file control block (FCB). Prior to invoking this function, DS:SI points to the segment: offset address of the command line, and ES:DI points to the segment: offset address of what will be an unopened FCB. Parsing is controlled by the status of the first four bits in the AL register:	1, 2, 3

If bit 0=1, then any leading separator characters (see following text) are ignored.

If bit 0=0, then parsing stops if a leading separator character is encountered.

If bit 1=1, then the drive number in the FCB is not changed if the command line does not contain a drive number.

If bit 1=0, then the drive number in the FCB is set to 00H if the command line does not contain a drive number.

MS-DOS Function	Description	Implemented in Versions
29H (cont'd)	If bit 2=1, then the filename in the FCB is not changed if the command line does not contain a filename.	
	If bit 2=0, then the filename in the FCB is set to eight blank characters if the command line does not contain a filename.	
	If bit 3=1, then the extension in the FCB is not changed if the command line does not contain an extension.	
	If bit 3=0, then the extension in the FCB is set to three blank characters if the command line does not contain an extension.	
	Filename separators are: . ; : = + SPACE and TAB. AL returns a value of 01H if either ? or * appears in the filename or extension. AL returns FFH if the drive number is invalid. ES:DI returns the address of the first byte of the FCB. DS:DI points to the first character following the command line that was parsed.	
2AH	***Get date.*** This function returns the current date stored by MS-DOS. The CX register returns the year. DH returns the month (1=January, 2=February, etc.). DL returns the day of the month. AL returns the day of the week (0=Sunday, 1=Monday, etc.).	1, 2, 3
2BH	***Set date.*** This function sets the current date stored by MS-DOS. Prior to invoking the function, the CX register stores the year, DH stores the month (1=January, 2=February, etc.), and DL stores the day of the month. When the function is called, AL returns a value of 00H if the date entered was valid. AL returns a value of FFH and the function is cancelled if an invalid date is entered.	1, 2, 3
	On machines with permanent clocks, the MS-DOS 3.3 implementation of function 2BH resets the permanent clock's date. Unfortunately, PC-DOS 3.3 sets only permanent clocks whose memory address is the same as IBM's clock. 2BH has no effect on clocks with a different address.	
2CH	***Get time.*** This function returns the current time stored by MS-DOS. On return, the CH register stores the hours, CL has the minutes,	1, 2, 3

MS-DOS Function	Description	Implemented in Versions
2CH (cont'd)	DH has the seconds, and DL has the hundredths of a second.	
2DH	***Set time.*** This function sets the current time stored by MS-DOS. Prior to invoking this function, the CH, CL, DH, and DL registers are set, using the format described for function 2CH. AL returns a value of 00H if the time entered was valid; otherwise, the function is cancelled and AL returns FFH. On machines with permanent clocks, the MS-DOS 3.3 implementation of function 2DH resets the permanent clock's time. Unfortunately, PC-DOS 3.3 sets only permanent clocks whose memory address is the same as IBM's clock. 2DH has no effect on clocks with a different address.	1, 2, 3
2EH	***Set/reset verify switch.*** Prior to invoking this function, the AL register must contain either 00H (verify off) or 01H (verify on). Each disk write is checked for accuracy when verify is on. The current state of the verify switch can be determined by using MS-DOS function 54H.	1, 2, 3
2FH	***Get DTA.*** This function returns the segment: offset address of the current disk transfer address (DTA) in ES:BX.	2, 3
30H	***Get DOS version number.*** On return, this function stores the major MS-DOS version number in the AL register and the minor version number in the AH register. It can be assumed that a pre-2.00 version of MS-DOS is being used if AL returns a value of zero.	2, 3
31H	***Terminate and stay resident (Keep process).*** This function terminates execution of a program and keeps the program resident in memory. Prior to invoking the function, the AL register contains an exit code, and the DX register stores the number of paragraphs (16-byte blocks) of memory to be kept by the program. MS-DOS allocates this memory to the program; it will not be used for other purposes unless it is deallocated. There is no 64-Kbyte limit on the amount of memory that may be kept by the terminating program (compare with int 27H). The exit code passed in AL is retrievable with MS-DOS function 4DH.	2, 3

MS-DOS Function	Description	Implemented in Versions
32H	Reserved for use by MS-DOS (see appendix B).	
33H	***Ctrl-Break check or set.*** MS-DOS maintains a Ctrl-Break flag that determines when the operating system checks to see if Ctrl-Break has been pressed. If the flag is set, checking occurs each time an MS-DOS function is called. If the flag is not set, checking occurs only when input or output is requested. The AL and DL registers control this function. On entry:	2, 3

AL=00H   The function checks the current Ctrl-Break state.
AL=01H   The function sets the Ctrl-Break state. If DL=0, state is set off. If DL=1, state is set on.

On return:

DL=00H   Ctrl-Break state is off.
DL=01H   Ctrl-Break state is on.
AL=FFH   Invalid value in AL on entry.

MS-DOS Function	Description	Implemented in Versions
34H	Reserved for use by MS-DOS (see appendix B).	
35H	***Get interrupt vector.*** This function is used to obtain the memory address of an interrupt handling routine. Prior to invoking this function, the interrupt number is placed in the AL register. The function returns the interrupt's segment: offset address in ES:BX.	2, 3
36H	***Get disk free space.*** This function is used to obtain disk information. A drive number (0=default, 1=A, etc.) is placed in DL prior to invoking the function. Information is returned as follows:	2, 3

BX   The number of available clusters on the drive.
DX   The total number of clusters on the drive.
CX   The number of bytes per sector.
AX   The number of sectors per cluster. AX will store FFFFH on return if an invalid drive was specified on entry.

MS-DOS Function	Description	Implemented in Versions
37H	Reserved for use by MS-DOS (see appendix B).	
38H	***Retrieve or set country dependent information.*** Country dependent	2, 3

MS-DOS Function	Description	Implemented in Versions
38H (cont'd)	information includes specifications for a date format, a currency symbol, and a decimal separator. Countries are specified by a country code, which is typically the international telephone prefix for the country. Country dependent information may be retrieved with the MS-DOS 2.X implementation of this function. Country dependent information may be retrieved or set with the MS-DOS 3.X implementation.	

Information is retrieved as follows: The AL register contains the code of the desired country. If AL is set to zero, the information for the current country is retrieved. The MS-DOS 2.X implementation of this function can specify country codes only in the range 0–255. In MS-DOS 3.X, if a value of FFH is placed in AL, a 16-bit country code can be specified in BX. DS:DX is set to point to a memory buffer that will store the returned information. The format of the returned information in MS-DOS 2.X is as follows:

Offset	Value
0–01	Date/time format. A value of 00 specifies the USA standard (*hh:mm:ss mm/dd/yy*). A value of 01 specifies the European standard (*hh:mm:ss dd/mm/yy*). A value of 02 specifies the Japanese standard (*hh:mm:ss dd/mm/yy*).
2	ASCII code for currency symbol.
3	Byte of zero.
4	ASCII code for thousands separator.
5	Byte of zero.
6	ASCII code for decimal separator.
7	Byte of zero.
8–31	Reserved by MS-DOS.

The format for the information returned in the MS-DOS 3.X implementation is as follows:

Offset	Value
0–1	Date format. A value of 00 specifies the USA standard (*mm/dd/yy*), 01 specifies the European standard (*dd/*

MS-DOS Function	Description	Implemented in Versions
38H (cont'd)	*mm/yy*), and 02 specifies the Japanese standard (*yy/mm/dd*).	
	2–5 Null terminated currency symbol string.	
	7 ASCII code for thousands separator.	
	8 Byte of 00.	
	9 ASCII code for decimal separator.	
	10 Byte of 00.	
	11 ASCII code for date separator.	
	12 Byte of 00.	
	13 ASCII code for time separator.	
	14 Byte of 00.	
	15 Currency format. Bit 1 equals the number of spaces between the currency symbol and the value. Bit 0 equals zero if the currency precedes the value. Bit 1 equals 1 if the symbol follows the value.	
	16 Number of digits after decimal in currency.	
	17 Time format. Bit 1 equals zero if 12-hour format. Bit 1 equals 1 if a 24-hour format.	
	18–21 Case map call address (see following text).	
	22 ASCII code for data list separator.	
	23 Byte of 00.	
	24–33 Reserved by MS-DOS.	

The case map call address is the segment: offset address of a procedure that converts lowercase characters to uppercase. The function is used to set country information by placing a value of FFFFH in DX prior to the call. The function sets the carry flag and returns a value of 02 in AX if the country code is not valid.

MS-DOS Function	Description	Implemented in Versions
39H	***Create a subdirectory.*** Prior to invoking this function, DS:DX points to the segment: offset address of an ASCII string that will be the path specifier of the new subdirectory. The string is terminated with a byte of zero. The function sets the carry flag upon return if an error occurs. The AX register contains information about any errors:	2, 3

MS-DOS Function	Description	Implemented in Versions
39H (cont'd)	AX=03H The path specifier was not valid or was not terminated with a byte of zero.	
	AX=05H No room in parent directory for new subdirectory, the subdirectory already exists, or a reserved device name was used in the path specifier.	
3AH	***Remove a subdirectory.*** Prior to invoking this function, DS:DX points to the segment: offset address of an ASCII string that is the path specifier of the subdirectory to be deleted. The string must be terminated by a byte of zero. A subdirectory must be empty before it can be deleted. This function cannot be used to remove the current directory. The function sets the carry flag if an error occurs. The AX register contains information about any errors:	2, 3
	AX=03H The path specifier was not valid, was not found, or was not terminated with a byte of zero.	
	AX=05H The specified subdirectory was not empty, was not a directory, or was the root directory.	
	AX=16H The specified subdirectory is the current directory.	
3BH	***Change current directory.*** Prior to invoking this function, DS:DX points to the segment: offset address of an ASCII string that is the path specifier of a subdirectory. The string must be terminated with a byte of zero. The function makes the specified subdirectory the current directory. The function returns a value of 03H in the AX register if the ASCII string is not a valid path specifier or if the string is not terminated with a byte of zero.	2, 3
	MS-DOS functions 3CH through 46H allow you to utilize disk files without the necessity of a file control block. When these functions are used, MS-DOS uses a *file handle* to keep	

MS-DOS Function	Description	Implemented in Versions
3BH (cont'd)	track of files. A file handle is a hexadecimal number that MS-DOS places in the AX register when a file is created (function 3CH) or opened (function 3DH). The following handles are predefined by MS-DOS for peripheral devices. Devices do not have to be opened before reading or writing:	

00H   Standard input device.
01H   Standard output device.
02H   Standard error device.
03H   Standard auxiliary device.
04H   Standard printer device.

MS-DOS Function	Description	Implemented in Versions
3CH	***Create a file.*** Prior to invoking this function, DS:DX points to the segment: offset of an ASCII string that specifies a drive, path, and filename for a file to be created. The string must be terminated with a byte of zero. The attribute code for the file to be created is placed in the CX register (see function 43H). If the carry flag is not set on return from this function, the AX register contains the file handle. If the specified file did not previously exist, it is created in the appropriate directory. If the file did previously exist, it is truncated to a length of zero. The carry flag is set on return if an error occurred in execution of the function. AX contains information about any errors:	2, 3

AX=03H   The path specified was not valid.
AX=04H   The file was created, but there are no file handles available.
AX=05H   CX specified a directory or volume id attribute, or a directory previously existed with the same name.

MS-DOS Function	Description	Implemented in Versions
3DH	***Open a file.*** Prior to invoking this function, DS:DX points to the segment: offset of an ASCII string that specifies a drive, path, and filename of the file to be opened. The string must be terminated with a byte of zero. AL	2, 3

MS-DOS Function	Description	Implemented in Versions
3DH (cont'd)	contains an access code that determines the manner in which the file is opened.	

In MS-DOS 2.X, only the first two bits of AL are significant; the other bits should be set to zero.

Bit Setting	Access Mode
00	read only
01	write only
02	read and write

In MS-DOS 3.X, other bits are used to determine the type of access to the file that other processes and other network users will have:

bit 7   = 0 if file is to be inherited by any child processes.

       = 1 if file is private to parent.

bits 4–6 = 000 if network processes are denied access.

       = 001 if read/write access is denied to network processes.

       = 010 if write access is denied to network processes.

       = 011 if read access is denied to network users.

       = 100 if full access is allowed to network users

bit 3   Reserved (should equal 0).

bits 0–2 = 000 if read access for owner process.

       = 001 if write access for owner process.

       = 010 if read/write access for owner process.

If the carry flag is clear on return, then AX contains the file handle. Any subsequent reference to the file is through the 16-bit file handle. On return, the file's read/write pointer is set to the file's first byte and the file's record size is set to 1 byte.

MS-DOS Function	Description	Implemented in Versions
3DH (cont'd)	If an error occurs in execution of the function, on return the carry flag will be set and the AX register will contain one of the following error codes:	

01	Function number invalid (file-sharing required).	
02	File not found.	
03	Path not found.	
04	Too many files open; no handle available.	
05	Access denied.	
0CH	Access code invalid.	

MS-DOS Function	Description	Implemented in Versions
3EH	***Close a file handle.*** Prior to invoking this function, the BX register contains a file handle that was returned from functions 3CH, 3DH, or 45H. The corresponding file is closed upon return if the carry flag is not set. The function flushes all internal buffers. If an invalid file handle was specified, the carry flag is set and a value of 06H is placed in the AX register on return.	2, 3
3FH	***Read from a file or device.*** Prior to invoking this function, BX contains a file handle and DS:DX contains the segment: offset address of a buffer in memory. The number of bytes to be read are stored in the CX register. When the function is called, the specified number of bytes are read into the memory buffer. If the carry flag is not set on return, the AX register contains the number of bytes read. If the carry flag has been set, AX stores an error code:	2, 3

AX=05H	The file handle passed in BX was opened in a mode that does not allow reading.	
AX=06H	The file handle passed is not open.	

MS-DOS Function	Description	Implemented in Versions
40H	***Write to a file or device.*** Prior to invoking this function, BX contains a file handle and DS:DX contains the segment: offset address	2, 3

MS-DOS Function	Description	Implemented in Versions
40H (cont'd)	of a buffer in memory. The number of bytes to be written are stored in the CX register. When the function is called, the specified number of bytes are written from the memory buffer. If the carry flag is not set on return, the AX register contains the number of bytes actually written. If the carry flag has been set, AX stores an error code:	

AX=05H   The file handle passed in BX was opened in a mode that does not allow writing.

AX=06H   The file handle passed is not open.

Note: If on entry CX stores a value of 00H, function 40H will set the file's size to correspond to the current position of the file's read/write pointer.

41H	***Delete a directory entry.*** Prior to invoking this function, DS:DX points to the segment: offset of an ASCII string that specifies a drive, path, and filename of a directory entry to be deleted. The string must be terminated with a byte of zero. The entry has been deleted if the carry flag is not set on return. The AX register stores an error code if the carry flag has been set:	2, 3

AX=02H   File not found.

AX=05H   Access denied.

42H	***Move file pointer.*** MS-DOS establishes a "read/write pointer" for each created or opened file by using functions 3CH and 3DH. When a file is created (or opened), the file pointer is set to the first byte in the file. Each time a read or write is made to the file, the file pointer advances according to the number of bytes in the read or write. Function 42H is used to move a file's read/write pointer without making a read or write. Prior to invoking this function, the distance the pointer will be moved is stored as a 4-byte number in the CX and DX registers. The	2, 3

MS-DOS Function	Description	Implemented in Versions
42H (cont'd)	most-significant bytes are stored in CX. The file handle is stored in the BX register. The AL register is set to a value that determines the way in which the pointer is moved:	

AL=00H	The pointer is moved CX:DX bytes from the beginning of the file.
AL=01H	The pointer is moved to its current location plus CX:DX.
AL=02H	The pointer is moved to the end of the file plus CX:DX.

If the carry flag is not set on return, the new pointer location is stored as a 4-byte number in the DX and AX registers. The most-significant bytes are in DX. If the carry flag is set on return, AX contains an error code:

AL=01H	The number passed in AL on entry is not valid.
AL=06H	The handle passed in BX is not open.

MS-DOS Function	Description	Implemented in Versions
43H	***Change file's attribute.*** A file's attribute is determined by the bit pattern stored in the eleventh byte of the file's directory entry:	2, 3

Bit	File Attribute If Bit Set (Equals 1)
0	Read-only file. Any attempt to write to such a file will generate an error.
1	Hidden file. Such a file is not listed during a standard directory search.
2	System file. These files are used to boot MS-DOS and perform many other system operations.
3	Volume label. The filename and filename extension in this directory entry form the disk's volume id label. Each disk may have only one file with this attribute, and the file must be located in the disk's root directory.
4	Subdirectory. Files with this attribute are subdirectories.

MS-DOS Function	Description	Implemented in Versions
43H (cont'd)	5 Archive. This bit is set if a file has been modified but not copied by BACKUP.	

Function 43H is used to change a file's attribute. Prior to invoking this function, DS:DX is set to point to the segment: offset address of an ASCII string that forms a file's path and filename. The string must be terminated by a byte of zero. AL must be set to 00H or 01H:

AL=01H   Prior to entry, CX is set to the byte value of the desired attribute. Calling the function changes the attribute of the file specified by the string at DS:DX.

AL=00H   Calling the function returns the byte value of the current attribute.

An error condition exists if the carry flag is set on return. Error information is returned in the AL register:

AL=01H   The entry value of AL was not 00H or 01H.

AL=03H   The file specified was not valid, or the ASCII string was not terminated with a byte of zero.

AL=05H   An attempt was made to modify the attribute of a directory or volume id label.

MS-DOS Function	Description	Implemented in Versions
44H	***I/O control for devices (IOCTL).*** This function is used to send information to, and receive information from, input/output control channels. The function is also used to determine the input/output status of peripheral devices. A device (or file) is specified by placing a file handle in the BX register. File handles 0000H through 0004H are reserved by MS-DOS for specific peripheral devices (see the list in function 3BH).	2, 3

Function 44H is divided into 16 subfunctions.

MS-DOS Function	Description	Implemented in Versions
44H (cont'd)	A subfunction is selected by placing a value of 00H–0FH in AL prior to calling the function.	

If an error is encountered, upon return the carry flag will be set and AL will contain one of the following error codes:

AL=01H	Invalid subfunction number, or Ctrl bit was set to zero.
AL=04H	No handle available.
AL=05H	Access denied.
AL=06H	Invalid handle.
AL=0DH	Invalid data.
AL=0FH	Invalid drive number.

Device Information Subfunctions (00H and 01H)

AL=00H	Get device channel information. This subfunction returns information in the DX register that describes a device control channel. The device channel is specified by the file handle placed in BX. The interpretation of the value returned in DX is described in figure A-1.
AL=01H	Set device information. This subfunction is used to set the device information of a control channel. The channel is determined by the file handle placed in BX. The information set is determined by a value placed in DX prior to calling the function.

Control String Subfunctions (02H through 05H)

These four subfunctions are used to receive command strings from, or send command strings to, a device.

AL=02H	Read string from device. Prior to invoking this subfunction, AL

```
        Bit
        15  14  13  12  11  10   9   8   7   6   5   4   3   2   1   0
      ┌───┬───┬───────────────────────┬───┬───┬───┬───┬───┬───┬───┬───┐
      │ R │ C │                       │ I │ E │ R │ R │ I │ I │ I │ I │
      │ E │ T │                       │ S │ O │ A │ E │ S │ S │ S │ S │
      │ S │ R │        Reserved       │ D │ F │ W │ S │ C │ N │ C │ C │
      │   │ L │                       │ E │   │   │   │ L │ U │ O │ I │
      │   │   │                       │ V │   │   │   │ K │ L │ T │ N │
      └───┴───┴───────────────────────┴───┴───┴───┴───┴───┴───┴───┴───┘
```

ISDEV=1 if channel is a device. ISDEV=0 if channel is a disk file.

If ISDEV = 1, then:

  EOF   = 1 if end of file on input.

  RAW   = 1 if operating in binary mode (no check for Ctrl-Z).

  RAW   = 0 if operating in ASCII mode (checks for Ctrl-Z as end-of-file mark).

  ISCLK = 1 if the device is the clock device.

  ISNUL = 1 if the device is the null device.

  ISCOT = 1 if the device is the console output.

  ISCIN = 1 if the device is the console input.

  CTRL   = 1 if the device can process command strings. This bit cannot be set with function 44H.

  CTRL   = 0 if the device cannot process command strings.

If ISDEV = 0, then:

  EOF   = 0 if the channel has been written.

Bits 0–5 represent the channel's block device number (0=A, 1=B, etc.).

Figure A-1. Channel information sent (when AL=00H) and received (when AL=1H) is determined by the bit pattern of the 2 bytes in the DX register.

MS-DOS Function	Description	Implemented in Versions
44H (cont'd)	is set to 02H, a file handle is placed in BX, DS:DX points to a buffer that will receive the read, and CX stores the number of bytes to be read.	
	AL=03H Write string to a device. Prior to invoking this subfunction, AL is set to 03H, a file handle is placed in BX, DS:DX points to a buffer that contains the string to be written, and CX stores the number of bytes to be written.	
	AL=04H Read string from a disk drive. This subfunction is identical to 02H except that a disk drive number (00H=default, 01H=A, etc.) is placed in BL prior to calling the subfunction.	
	AL=05H Write string to a disk drive. This subfunction is identical to 03H except that a disk drive number (00H=default, 01H=A, etc.) is placed in BL prior to calling the subfunction.	

Input/Output Status Subfunctions (06H and 07H)

These two subfunctions allow you to see if a device or a file is ready for input or output.

AL=06H Get input status. Prior to invoking this subfunction, 06H is placed in AL and a file handle is placed in BX. When the file handle represents a device, the subfunction will return FFH in the AL register if the device is ready for input; 00H is returned if the device is not ready. When the handle in BX represents a file, the subfunction will return FFH in AL until the end of the file has been reached, at which point 00H is returned.

AL=07H Get output status.

MS-DOS Function	Description	Implemented in Versions
44H (cont'd)	This subfunction is identical to 06H except that it checks output status instead of input status.	

Other Subfunctions

MS-DOS Function	Description	Implemented in Versions
AL=08H	Test to see if block device has changeable media. The function returns zero in AX if the media is removable, one if the media is fixed. This subfunction is implemented in MS-DOS 3.0 and subsequent versions.	
AL=09H	Test to see if a drive is local or is remotely located on a network. For local drives, the attribute word from the drive's device header is returned in DX. For remote drives, bit 12 in DX is set on return. This subfunction is implemented in MS-DOS 3.1 and subsequent versions.	
AL=0AH	Test to see if a file handle is local or remote. For local handles, the device header's attribute word is returned in DX. For remote handles, bit 15 in DX is set upon return. This subfunction is implemented in MS-DOS 3.1 and subsequent versions.	
AL=0BH	Change sharing retry count. This subfunction is used to reset the length of delay between retries and to set the number of retries that can be attempted in carrying out file-sharing operations. Prior to calling this subfunction, CX contains the number of delay loops (the length of the pause), and DX contains the number of retries. The default is delay loops = 1, retries = 3. This subfunction is implemented in MS-DOS 3.0 and subsequent versions.	

MS-DOS Function	Description		Implemented in Versions
44H (cont'd)	AL=0CH	Change code page used by device. This subfunction is used to assign a different code page to a peripheral device. This subfunction is implemented in MS-DOS 3.3.	
	AL=0DH	Generic IOCTL request. This subfunction is used to perform the following tasks:	
		Get peripheral device parameters.	
		Set peripheral device parameters.	
		Read a track on a logical device.	
		Write a track to a logical device.	
		Format a logical device.	
		For details on the use of this subfunction, refer to the MS-DOS 3.2 or 3.3 technical reference manual.	
	AL=0EH	Get last logical drive used. This subfunction is used to determine if a block device has more than one logical device assigned to it. On call, BL contains the block devices drive number (0 = default, 1 = A, etc.). On return, AL contains 0 if there is only one logical device assigned to the block device; otherwise AL contains the drive number of the last logical drive letter that used the block device. This subfunction is implemented in MS-DOS 3.2 and subsequent versions. The discussion of subfunction 0FH illustrates how subfunction 0EH might be used.	
	AL=0FH	Assign logical device. This function is used to assign a logical device to a block device that is supporting more than one logical device. Prior to calling, BL contains the drive	

MS-DOS Function	Description	Implemented in Versions
44H (cont'd)	number of the logical drive to be assigned (1 = A, 2 = B, etc.).	
	As an example, consider a system with one floppy disk drive. The single drive will be supporting logical drives A and B. Only one logical drive is assigned to the disk drive at a time. If A is assigned to the drive, and MS-DOS needs to access B, MS-DOS will display the prompt: `Insert diskette for drive B:` and `strike any key when ready.`	
	An application program can use subfunction 0FH, in conjunction with subfunction 0EH, to suppress this prompt. The following assembly language code illustrates this:	

```
;insert this code prior to accessing drive B

                      ;Get logical drive
        mov   ah,44h  ;MS-DOS function 44h
        mov   al,0eh  ;Subfunction 0eh
        mov   bl,1    ;Drive A
        int   21h     ;Call MS-DOS
        cmp   al,2    ;B already assigned?
        je    exit    ;If yes, exit

                      ;Set logical drive
        mov   ah,44h  ;MS-DOS function 44h
        mov   al,0fh  ;Subfunction 0fh
        mov   bl,2    ;Logical drive B
        int   21     ;Call MS-DOS

exit:
```

MS-DOS Function	Description	Implemented in Versions
	Both subfunctions 0EH and 0FH set the carry flag and place an error code in AL if an error is encountered.	
45H	***Duplicate a file handle.*** Prior to invoking this function, BX contains a file handle. On	2, 3

MS-DOS Function	Description	Implemented in Versions
45H (cont'd)	return, AX contains a second file handle for the same file. Both file handles use the original file pointer; moving the pointer using one handle will move the pointer for the other handle. The carry flag is set on return if an error was encountered. AX contains information about any errors:	
	AX=04H No free file handles available. AX=06H The handle passed in BX is not currently open.	
46H	***Force a duplicate of a handle.*** This function is used to assign a specific file handle to an open file. Prior to invoking this function, BX contains a file handle and CX contains a second file handle. On return, the CX file handle will refer to the same file as the BX handle. If the CX handle initially referenced another file, that file is first closed. On return, both file handles use the original file pointer; moving the pointer using one handle will move the pointer for the other handle. The carry flag is set on return if an error was encountered. AX contains information about any errors:	2, 3
	AX=04H No free file handles available. AX=06H The handle passed in BX is not currently open.	
47H	***Get current directory.*** Prior to invoking this function, DS:SI is set to point to the segment: offset address of a 64-byte block of memory and DL contains a drive number (00H=default, 01H=A, etc.). On return, the memory block will contain an ASCII string that is the path specifier of the drive designated by DL. The string will not contain the drive letter and will not begin with a backslash. The string will terminate with a byte of zero. The carry flag is set on return if an invalid drive was specified.	2, 3
48H	***Allocate memory.*** This function is used to allocate a block of memory to a process. On entry, BX contains the number of paragraphs (a paragraph is 16 contiguous bytes of memory) to be allocated. On return, AX	2, 3

MS-DOS Function	Description	Implemented in Versions
48H (cont'd)	contains the segment address of the allocated memory block. The carry flag is set on return if an error was encountered. AX contains information about any errors:	

AX=07H   Memory control blocks destroyed.

AX=08H   Allocation failed due to insufficent memory. BX contains the largest block of memory available for allocation.

MS-DOS Function	Description	Implemented in Versions
49H	***Free allocated memory.*** On entry, ES contains the segment address of a memory block that has been allocated with function 48H. Function 49H returns the memory block to the system pool. The carry flag is set on return if an error was encountered. AX contains information about any errors:	2, 3

AX=07H   Memory control blocks destroyed.

AX=09H   The block passed in ES was not allocated with function 48H.

MS-DOS Function	Description	Implemented in Versions
4AH	***Modify allocated memory blocks.*** On entry, ES contains the segment address of an allocated block of memory and BX contains the number of paragraphs of memory to be contained in the modified block (a paragraph is 16 contiguous bytes). When the function is called, the specified block is adjusted to the size specified in BX. The carry flag is set on return if an error was encountered. AX contains information about any errors:	2, 3

AX=07H   Memory control blocks destroyed.

AX=08H   Modification failed due to insufficent memory. BX contains the largest block of memory available for allocation.

AX=09H   The block passed in ES was not allocated with function 48H.

MS-DOS Function	Description	Implemented in Versions
4BH	***Load and execute a program.*** Through the use of this function, a program can load and execute another program. The original	2, 3

MS-DOS Function	Description	Implemented in Versions
4BH (cont'd)	program is called the *parent*; the program that is loaded and executed is called the *child*. MS-DOS commands can be executed from within a program by calling function 4BH and specifying COMMAND.COM (the MS-DOS command processor) as the child.	

Prior to invoking this function, a "function value" is placed in the AL register:

AL=00H   Load and execute a program. MS-DOS will construct a program segment prefix for the child, load the program, and execute it. MS-DOS sets the child's terminate and Ctrl-Break addresses to the instruction in the parent that follows the function 4BH call. Register contents are not preserved by this function.

AL=03H   Load overlay. MS-DOS does not construct a program segment prefix. The child is loaded at a specified memory location but not executed. Control returns immediately to the parent.

Prior to invoking this function, DS:DX points to the segment: offset address of an ASCII string that contains the drive, path, and filename of the file to be loaded (the child). The string must terminate with a byte of zero.

The third and final requirement prior to calling this function is that ES:BX must point to the segment: offset address of a memory block that contains information required by the function. There is one format for the block used with the execute function (AL=00H) and another format for the block used with the overlay function (AL=03H). In either case, the block must be set up prior to calling the function. The memory block formats are presented in tables A-1 and A-2.

When the parent first receives control, MS-DOS allocates all available memory to it.

MS-DOS Function	Description	Implemented in Versions
4BH (cont'd)	Before a child can be loaded with function 4BH, some memory must be deallocated with MS-DOS function 4AH. When this function is invoked, MS-DOS uses the loader portion of COMMAND.COM to load the child. The loader is located in the transient portion of the command processor, which is stored in the high end of memory.	
	The carry flag is set by this function if an error is encountered. The AX register contains information about any errors:	

AX=01H	The number passed in AL was not 01H or 03H.
AX=02H	The file specified by DS:DX was invalid or not found.
AX=05H	Access denied.
AX=08H	There is not enough memory available to load the child process.
AX=0AH	The environment passed was larger than 32K bytes.
AX=0BH	The file pointed to by DS:DX contains inconsistent information.

Table A-1. Load and Execute Memory Block (AL=00H)

Address	Parameter
ES:BX	A 2-byte word that forms the segment address of the "environment" passed to the child. The address is stored with the least-significant byte first. The child will inherit the parent's environment if a value of zero is stored at this address.
	The *environment* is a series of ASCII strings that are referenced by MS-DOS. The environment always contains a string that begins "COMSPEC=" followed by the path to COMMAND.COM. MS-DOS references the COMSPEC string when it needs to locate the command processor. Other strings located in the environment include any statements entered with the MS-DOS commands PATH and PROMPT. Each string in the environment is terminated with a byte of zero. The final string in the environment is

Table A-1. (cont'd)

Address	Parameter
	terminated with 2 bytes of zero. The environment is limited to 32K bytes in size. MS-DOS stores the segment address of a program's environment at offset 2CH in the program segment prefix.
ES:BX+2	A 4-byte double-word pointer to the segment: offset address of a command line. The offset address is stored at ES:BX+2 (least-significant byte) and ES:BX+3 (most-significant byte). The segment address is stored at ES:BX+4 (least-significant byte) and ES:BX+5 (most-significant byte). The command line will be copied to offset 80H in the child's program segment prefix (psp).
	The 128 bytes beginning at offset 80H in the psp form the "unformatted parameter area." This is the location that MS-DOS commands examine for any information on a command line following the command's name. If the command **edlin sample.txt** is entered, MS-DOS loads EDLIN. EDLIN would then find the string "0B 20 53 41 4D 50 4C 45 2E 54 58 54 0D" beginning at offset 80H in the psp. The first byte in this string tells MS-DOS the number of characters in the command line. The first character in the command line is a blank (20H). The remaining bytes are the ASCII values of the characters in the string "sample.txt". The string terminates with a carriage return (0DH).
ES:BX+6	A 4-byte double-word pointer to the segment: offset address of a file control block. The offset address is stored at ES:BX+6 (least-significant byte) and ES:BX+7 (most-significant byte). The segment address is stored at ES:BX+8 (least-significant byte) and ES:BX+9 (most-significant byte). The file control block will be copied to offset 5CH in the child's psp.
ES:BX+10	A 4-byte double-word pointer to the segment: offset address of a file control block. The offset address is stored at ES:BX+10 (least-significant byte) and ES:BX+11 (most-significant byte). The segment address is stored at ES:BX+12 (least-significant byte) and ES:BX+13 (most-significant byte). The file control block will be copied to offset 6CH in the child's psp.
	Offsets 5CH and 6CH in a program's psp are the starting addresses of 12-byte "formatted parameter areas." File specifiers contained in the command line at offset 80H are "parsed" and placed in the formatted parameter areas. (Refer to the discussion of MS-DOS function 29H for information on parsing.)

Table A-2. Overlay Memory Block (AL=03H)

Address	Parameter
ES:BX	A 2-byte word that contains the segment address at which the child will be loaded. The address is stored with the least-significant byte first.
ES:BX+2	A 2-byte word that stores the factor used to modify the memory addresses of any relocatable items in the child. The factor is stored with the least-significant byte first.

MS-DOS Function	Description	Implemented in Versions
4CH	***Terminate a process.*** This function is used to terminate a process passing a return code in the AL register. The return code can be read with an IF ERRORLEVEL within a batch file or by MS-DOS function 4DH. All files are closed by this function.	2, 3
4DH	***Retrieve the return code of a child process.*** This function retrieves a return code previously set by a child process. (See the function 4BH for a discussion of parent and child processes.) The function returns the return code set by the child in the AL register. The AH register is set according to the manner in which the child process was terminated:	2, 3

AH=00H   Normal termination.
AH=01H   Terminated by Ctrl-Break.
AH=02H   Terminated by a critical error.
AH=03H   Terminate and stay resident.

MS-DOS Function	Description	Implemented in Versions
4EH	***Find first matching file.*** This function is used to search a directory for a filename matching one that is specified. The specified filename may contain the wildcard characters "?" and "*". Prior to invoking this function, DS:DX is set to point to the segment: offset address of an ASCII string containing the drive specifier, path specifier, and filename of the specified file. The string must terminate with a byte of zero. An attribute for the file is specified in the CX register (see function 43H). If the function finds a matching file, the current disk transfer address (DTA) is filled as follows:	2, 3

MS-DOS Function	Description		Implemented in Versions
4EH (cont'd)	Offset	Value	
	00H–14H	Reserved by MS-DOS for use by MS-DOS function 4FH.	
	15H	Attribute of file found.	
	16H–17H	File's time stamp.	
	18H–19H	File's date stamp.	
	1AH–1BH	File's size (low word).	
	1CH–1DH	File's size (high word).	
	1EH–2AH	Name and extension of file found, followed by a byte of zero.	

The carry flag is set upon return if any errors are encountered. AX contains information about any errors:

AX=02H	The string specified by DS:DX was not valid or was not terminated with a byte of zero.
AX=12H	No matching files found.

MS-DOS Function	Description	Implemented in Versions
4FH	***Find next matching file.*** This function is used to find subsequent matching files after function 4EH has been used to find the first match. Prior to invoking the function, the current DTA must contain the information returned by function 4EH. Function 4FH returns any matching files in the manner described for function 4EH. The carry flag is set on return if no subsequent matches are found.	2, 3
50H–53H	Reserved for use by MS-DOS (see appendix B).	
54H	***Get verify state.*** This function returns 00H in the AL register if the verify state is off, 01H in AL if the verify state is on. The verify state can be set with MS-DOS function 2EH.	2, 3
55H	Reserved for use by MS-DOS.	
56H	***Rename a file.*** Prior to invoking this function, DS:DX points to the segment: offset address of an ASCII string that contains the drive specifier, path specifier, and name of a file to be renamed. ES:DI points to an ASCII string that contains the new path specifier and filename. Both strings must terminate	2, 3

MS-DOS Function	Description	Implemented in Versions
56H (cont'd)	with a byte of zero. This function cannot be used to change the drive specifier. The carry flag is set if an error occurs on execution. The error code is returned in the AX register:	

AX=02H   File not found.
AX=03H   Path not found.
AX=05H   Access denied.
AX=11H   Not same device.

57H	***Get/set a file's time and date stamp.*** Prior to invoking this function, BX contains a valid file handle. If AL=00H on entry, then the file's date stamp is returned in DX and the file's time stamp is returned in CX. If AL=01H on entry, the file's date stamp is set to the value in DX and the file's time stamp is set to the value in CX. A file must be closed before a new time/date stamp can be stored.	2, 3

The time and date stamps are passed using the format described in function 38H. The high-order byte is stored in DL (or CL), and the low-order byte is stored in DH (or CH).

The carry flag is set if an error occurs. The error code is passed in AX:

AX=01H   The entry value of AL was not 00H or 01H.
AX=06H   The file handle passed in BX is not open.

58H	***Get or set allocation strategy.*** When a program requests that a block of memory be allocated to it (via function 48H), MS-DOS must search memory to find a block to allocate. There are three "strategies" that MS-DOS can use in selecting a memory block to allocate:	3

1. *First fit*—beginning at the low end of memory, search until a large enough block is found. Allocate that block.

2. *Best fit*—beginning at the low end of memory, search all of memory, keeping track of each block that is large enough. Allocate the block that is closest in size to the allocation request.

3. *Last fit*—beginning at the high end of

MS-DOS Function	Description	Implemented in Versions
58H (cont'd)	memory, search until a large enough block is found. Allocate that block.	
	Function 58H allows a program to determine what the current allocation startegy is and to set the allocation strategy. To get the allocation strategy, place 00H in AL. The strategy code is returned in AX. To set the allocation strategy, place 01H in AL and one of the strategy codes in BX.	

Strategy Codes

00H	First fit
01H	Best fit
02H	Last fit

The function sets the carry flag if an error occurs. An error code of 01H is returned in AX if the function code sent is not valid.

MS-DOS Function	Description	Implemented in Versions
59H	***Get extended error information.***	3

Function 59H is used to obtain extended information on an error. The error must have occurred on an immediately preceding call to int 24H or to one of MS-DOS functions 2FH–62H. The BX register must be set to 00H prior to calling function 59H.

On return, function 59H places in AX the MS-DOS error code for the preceding error (the int 24H error codes and the MS-DOS function error codes are listed at the beginning of this appendix). Function 59H also returns three types of information: (1) An *error class* is returned in BH. The error class contains some descriptive information about the nature of the error (see the following list). (2) A *recommended action* is returned in BL. The recommended action (see the following list) can be used by the program in attempting to recover from the error. (3) An *error locus* is returned in CH. The error locus (see the following list) describes the type of hardware that may have been involved in the error.

BH = Error Class

01H	Out of resource (such as storage).
02H	Temporary situation (such as locked

MS-DOS Function	Description	Implemented in Versions
59H (cont'd)	file), which should be expected to end.	
	03H Authorization problem.	
	04H Internal software error.	
	05H Hardware failure.	
	06H System software problem.	
	07H Application program error.	
	08H File not found.	
	09H Invalid file type.	
	0AH File interlocked.	
	0BH Wrong disk in drive or bad disk.	
	0CH Other error.	

BL = Recommended Action

01H	Retry; then prompt user to select ignore or abort.
02H	Retry with delay between tries; then prompt user to ignore or abort.
03H	Get correct information from user.
04H	Abort program in as timely a manner as possible (close files, release locks, etc.).
05H	Abort immediately; system is probably corrupted.
06H	Ignore error.
07H	Retry after user intervention.

CH = Error Locus

01H	Unknown.
02H	Block device.
03H	Network related.
04H	Serial device.
05H	Memory related.

MS-DOS Function	Description	Implemented in Versions
5AH	***Create a temporary file.*** This function will create a file with a unique name in a specified directory. The function is useful for word processors and other programs that use temporary scratch files.	3

Prior to calling this function, DS:DX points to the segment: offset address of a path specifier string. The string must end with a backslash (\) followed by a byte of zero. On return from the function, DS:DX points to the file specifier for the new file. The file specifier will end with a byte of zero. The carry flag is

MS-DOS Function	Description	Implemented in Versions
5AH (cont'd)	set if an error occurs. AX holds any error code.	

AX	Error
03H	Path not found.
05H	Access denied.

5BH	***Create new file.*** Prior to calling this function, DS:DX contains a pointer to an ASCII file specifier and CX contains a file attribute code. On return, AX contains a file handle that is used to access the new file. This function is identical to function 3CH, with the exception that the function call will fail if the named file already exists. The carry flag is set and AX contains an error code if an error occurs.	3

AX	Error
03H	Path not found.
04H	No handle available.
05H	Access denied.
50H	File exists.

5CH	***Lock/Unlock file access.*** This function is used to temporarily gain exclusive access to a portion of a file. In a network environment, data may be unreliable if simultaneous access to files is not controlled, thus the need for file *locking*.	3

A file is locked by placing 00H in Al prior to the call. Also prior to the call, the handle for the file to be locked is placed in BX, the high-order offset of the region to lock in CX, the low-order offset of the lock region in DX, the high-order of the length of the region to be locked in SI, and the low-order of the length to be locked in DI. On return, the carry flag is set and AX contains an error code if an error occurred. IBM and Microsoft recommend a call to function 59H if an error occurs.

AX	Error
01H	Function code not valid.
06H	Handle not valid.

MS-DOS Function	Description	Implemented in Versions
5CH (cont'd)	AX Error 21H All or part of region already locked. A locked portion of a file is unlocked with the same procedure as that described for locking, with the exception that AH is set to 01H prior to the call. Any region that is locked must be unlocked, or unpredictable results will ensue.	
5DH	Reserved for use by MS-DOS (see appendix B).	
5E00H	***Get machine name.*** This function is used only on computers running IBM PC Net or Microsoft Networks. Prior to the call, AX is set to 5E00H and DS:DX points to a memory buffer that will store the computer's network name. On return from the call: DS:DX points to a character string that stores the computer's name; the string is terminated with a byte of zero; CH is set to zero if the computer's name is not defined; and CL returns the NETBIOS name number if CH is nonzero. The carry flag is set and AX contains an error code if an error occurs. AX Error 01H Function code not valid.	3
5E02H	***Set printer setup.*** This function is used only on computers running IBM PC Net or Microsoft Networks. It is used to send a control string to a network printer. Once a network user invokes this command for a particular printer on the network, each file that the user subsequently sends to the printer is preceded by the same control string. This allows different users on the network, using the same printer, to each have their own control strings. Prior to calling this function: AX is set to 5E02H, BX is set to the index number in the redirection list of the desired printer (see function 5F03), CX is set to the length of the control string, and DS:SI points to the control string.	3

MS-DOS Function	Description	Implemented in Versions
5E02H (cont'd)	On return, the carry flag is set and AX contains an error code if an error occurred.	

AX   Error

01H   Function code not valid.

5E03H	***Get printer setup.*** This function is used only on computers running IBM PC Net or Microsoft Networks. It returns the printer control string sent with function 5302H. Prior to issuing the call, AX is set to 5E03H, BX is set to the index number in the redirection list (see function 5F03) of the desired printer, and ES:DI points to a buffer that will store the control string. Maximum length of the control string is 64 bytes. On return, CX contains the length of the control string and ES:DI points to the control string.	3

On return, the carry flag is set and AX contains an error code if an error occurred.

AX   Error

01H   Function code not valid.

5F02H	***Get redirection list.*** This function is used only on computers running IBM PC Net or Microsoft Networks. It provides access to the network's system redirection list (see function 5F03H). Each entry in the list is indexed; the first entry is index entry zero.	3

Prior to calling this function, AX is set to 5F02H, BX is set to a redirection list index number, DS:SI points to a 128-byte buffer that will store the local device name, and ES:DI points to a 128-byte buffer that will store the device's network name.

On return, the following conditions exist:

The zero bit in BH is set to zero if the device is valid. The zero bit is set to 1 if the device is not valid.

BL is set to 03H if the device is a printer, to 04H if the device is a disk drive.

CX contains the parameter value that was stored using function 5F03.

MS-DOS Function	Description	Implemented in Versions
5F02H (cont'd)	The contents of DX and BP are destroyed.	
	DS:SI points to a string that is the device's local name. The string ends with a byte of zero.	
	ES:DI points to a string that is the device's network name. The string ends with a byte of zero.	
	On return, the carry flag is set and AX contains an error code if an error occurred.	

AX	Error
01H	Function code not valid.
12H	No more files.

5F03H	***Redirect device.*** This function is used only on computers running IBM PC Net or Microsoft Networks. It establishes an association between a local device name and a network name. The list of associations is called the *redirection list*. The redirection list is indexed. The first local name/network name pair on the redirection list is at index value zero. The redirection list is used by functions 5E02H, 5E03H, 5F02H, and 5F04H.	3

Prior to calling this function, the following holds:

AX is set to 5F03H.

BL is set to 03H if the device is a printer, to 04H if the device is a disk drive.

CX is set to a parameter that will also be stored in the redirection list.

DS:SI points to a string containing the device's local name. The string ends in a byte of zero.

ES:DI points to three strings, each separated by a byte of zero. The first string contains the device's network name. The second string contains a network path specifier. Network path specifiers must start with two backslashes (\\). The third string is a network password that must be followed by a byte of zero.

MS-DOS Function	Description	Implemented in Versions
5F03H (cont'd)	On return, the carry flag is clear if the function has executed successfully. The carry flag is set and AX contains an error code if an error occurred.	

AX	Error
01H	Function code not valid, string in wrong format, or device already redirected.
03H	Path not found.
05H	Access denied.
08H	Insufficient memory.

MS-DOS Function	Description	Implemented in Versions
5F04H	***Cancel redirection.*** This function is used only on computers running IBM PC Net or Microsoft Networks. It removes an entry from the redirection list (see function 5F03H).	3
	Prior to calling this function, AX contains 5F04H and DS:SI points to a string that contains either a local device name or a network path specifier (which must begin with "\\"). The string must be followed with a byte of zero. If a network path specifier is used, this function will close the connection between the local machine and the network.	
	On return, the carry flag is set and AX contains an error code if an error occurred.	

AX	Error
01H	Function code not valid or string not valid.
0FH	Redirection paused on server.

MS-DOS Function	Description	Implemented in Versions
62H	***Get program segment prefix.*** This function allows a program to locate its program segment prefix (psp). Prior to calling the function, AH stores 62H. On return, BX contains the segment address of the program's psp.	3
63H	***Get lead byte table.*** This function obtains the system table of valid byte ranges for extended characters, sets the interim console flag, and gets the interim console flag. This function is implemented in MS-DOS 2.25	2.25

MS-DOS Function	Description	Implemented in Versions
63H (cont'd)	only. It is not supported by any other versions of MS-DOS.	
	Prior to issuing a call, AH contains 63H, AL is set to:	
	00H If getting address of lead byte table.	
	01H If setting or clearing interim console flag.	
	02H If getting value of interim console flag.	
	If AL = 01H, then DL = 01H if setting the flag, DL = 00H if clearing the flag.	
	On return, if getting the address of the lead byte table, DS:SI points to the table. If getting the value of the interim console flag, DL is set to the value of the flag.	
65H	***Get global code page.***	3.3
66H	***Set global code page.***	3.3
67H	***Set handle count.*** As described in chapter 12, 20 bytes in the psp are used to store file handles. This sets a limit of 20 on the number of files a process can have open at a time. This function can be used to override this limit.	3.3
	Prior to calling the function, BX contains the desired number of file handles. On return, the carry flag is clear if the function succeeded. The carry flag is set and AX contains an error code if an error was encountered. This function is implemented in MS-DOS 3.3. DOS allocates a block of memory to store the new file handle table. The amount of memory allocated is rounded up to the nearest paragraph boundary. In addition, one paragraph of memory (16 bytes) is allocated to serve as a memory control block (see chapter 12).	
	Two bugs have been reported with the PC-DOS implementation of function 67H:	
	1. When an even number of file handles is requested, MS-DOS allocates an additional 64 Kbytes for the handle table.	
	2. When the value set in BX approaches FFFFH, MS-DOS attempts to allocate more	

MS-DOS Function	Description	Implemented in Versions
67H (cont'd)	memory than exists. This can cause the system to hang.	
	IBM is aware of these bugs, but Big Blue has announced no correction will be implemented until the next release of MS-DOS.	
68H	***Commit file.*** This function flushes all buffers associated with a file handle and updates the file's directory information. Prior to calling the function, BX contains the file handle. On return, the carry flag is cleared if the function succeeded. The carry flag is set and AX contains an error code if an error was encountered. This function is implemented in MS-DOS 3.3.	3.3

B

Some Undocumented
Features of MS-DOS

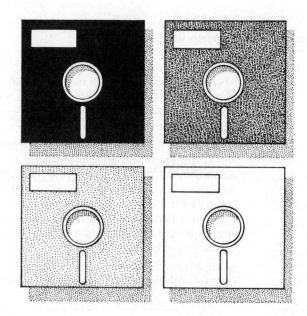

The term "undocumented feature" is applied to those interrupts and function calls that are utilized by MS-DOS, but whose use is not publicly sanctioned by Microsoft or IBM. Undocumented features are usually discovered by programmers scrutinizing the unassembled machine code that makes up MS-DOS.

There are two potential risks when using undocumented features. First, since there is no official description of what the feature does or how it does it, unpleasant surprises are always a possibility. Fortunately, the features presented here have been used by enough programmers for a long enough time that their behavior *seems* to be reasonably well understood.

The second potential risk is that Microsoft and IBM are not compelled to support the undocumented features in future versions of MS-DOS. In fact, for precisely this reason, the two companies have repeatedly warned programmers about using undocumented features.

Programmers must consider these risks whenever the use of undocumented features is being considered. It is hoped that Microsoft and IBM will someday officially describe the features listed here. In the meantime, programmers will have to rely on each other in understanding this shady area within MS-DOS.

Undocumented Interrupts

Interrupt	Description
28H	***The MS-DOS scheduler.*** Interrupt 28H is generated by MS-DOS to signal that DOS may be carefully reentered. (See chapter 13 for details.) The default handler for int 28H is simply an `iret` instruction. The interrupt appears to exist solely to provide TSRs with a safe access to MS-DOS.
29H	***Character output.*** This interrupt sends a character to the display device. The character is sent through ANSI.SYS if ANSI.SYS is installed. int 29H is much faster than MS-DOS functions 2 and 9. Like these two functions, int 29H advances the cursor after a character is displayed. This makes it easier to use than int 10H. It would be interesting to see if int 29H can be used safely within a TSR. Best guess is that it could be used safely.
	If int 29H is used to sound the speaker (AL = 7), additional output with int 29H is suppressed while the speaker is sounding.

Undocumented Functions

Undocumented functions are called just like documented functions are. The function number is placed in AH, other registers are set as required, and interrupt 21H is called. Function 1FH is implemented in MS-DOS 1.X, 2.X, and 3.X. Functions 32H through 53H are implemented in versions 2.X and 3.X. Function 5DH is implemented in version 3.X.

MS-DOS Function	Description
1FH	This function is almost the same as function 32H, described next. The difference is that the table is accessed for the default drive. The format of the table is slightly different under MS-DOS 1.X.
32H	***Get pointer to drive parameter table.*** On the call, DL contains a drive number (0=default, 1=A, etc.). On return,
32H	if AL is set to 00, the drive exists, and DS:BX points to the drive's parameter table. AL returns a value of FFh if the drive does not exist.

The format of the drive parameter table is as follows (offsets are in hexadecimal):

Offset	Function
00	Drive (0 = A, 1 = B, etc.).
01	Unit within drive (0, 1, 2, etc.).
02–03	Bytes per sector.
04	Sectors per cluster minus 1.
05	Number of times to left-shift (multiply by 2) bytes per sector to obtain bytes per cluster.
06–07	Number of boot sectors.
08	Number of FAT copies.
09–0A	Number of root directory entries.
0B–0C	Number of first sector containing data.
0D–0E	Total number of clusters minus 1.
0F	Number of sectors used by FAT.
10–11	Number of first sector in directory.
12–15	Offset and segment address of device driver's header.
16	Media descriptor byte (see chapter 14).
17	00 if the disk has been accessed.
18–1B	Offset and segment address of the next drive parameter table; set to FFFF FFFFH if last block in the chain.

34H	***Get address to INDOS flag.*** On return, the flag's address is stored in ES:BX. Refer to chapter 13 for details.
37H	***Get/set switchar.*** The switch character separates a command flag from the rest of the command. The default switch character is "/". To get the current switch character, set AL to 00. On return, the ASCII byte value for the current switch character will be in DL. To set the

MS-DOS Function	Description
37H (cont'd)	switch character, place a value of 01 in AL, and the byte value for the desired switch character in DL.
	In MS-DOS 2.X, function 37H can also be used to set or get the "forced \DEV\ flag". If the flag is set, device names must be preceded by "\DEV\". If the flag is clear, \DEV\ is optional. The flag is read with a value of 02 in AL. On return, DL equals 00 (flag set) or 01 (flag clear). The flag is set by calling the function with AL equal to 03 and DL equal to 00. Clear the flag with AL equal to 3 and DL equal to 1.
4BH	***Load program; do not execute.*** This undocumented subfunction of function 4B is used by DEBUG when it loads a program. On the call, AL contains a value of 01 and ES:BX points to a parameter block with the same format as that used by function 4BH, subfunction 0 (see appendix A). On return, the loaded program SS, SP, CS, and IP values are stored at ES:[BX+0EH].
50H	***Set current process id.*** Prior to the call, BX stores a process id number. The function designates that process to be current.
	A program's *id* is the segment address of the program's psp. MS-DOS stores the id of the currently executing program in an internal variable called the current process id.
	This function is important in TSRs that use file handles (see chapter 13).
51H	***Get current process id.*** On return, BX stores the current process id. This function is used, in conjunction with function 50H, in TSRs that use file handles. Function 51H is almost identical to function 62H. The only differences are that 51H is implemented in MS-DOS 2.X and function 62H is documented.
52H	***Return pointer to "invars".*** On return, ES:BX points to invars. Invars is a table of pointers used by MS-DOS. The name "invars" is a wholly unofficial one that is widely used (just like "INDOS").
	The value at ES:BX is a pointer to the drive parameter block for drive A. The value at ES:[BX−2] is the location of MS-DOS' first memory control block (mcb). Chapter 12 presents a discussion in which function 52H is used to locate the mcb chain.
	The device drive header for the NULL device is located at ES:[BX+22H]. This is the first header in the system's chain of device driver headers. The first 4 bytes of the

MS-DOS Function	Description
52H (cont'd)	header form a pointer to the next header in the chain. Refer to chapter 14 for details on the structure of device driver headers.
53H	***Generate drive parameter table.*** On the call, DS:SI contains the address of a bios parameter block (BPB) and ES:BP points to the area that will hold the drive parameter table (see function 32H). Refer to chapter 14 for a discussion of BPBs.
5DH	***Critical error information.*** This function has several subfunctions. Subfunctions are selected by placing a subfunction number in AL prior to the call.
	Subfunction 06H returns the address of the critical flag in DS:SI. The use of this subfunction is demonstrated in chapter 13. Subfunction 0AH sets extended error information. Prior to the call, DS:DX points to three words of error data. Extended error information is retrieved with function 59H. Subfunction 0AH can be used in TSRs that need to preserve and then restore the error information that existed when the TSR was called. Refer to the description of function 59H in appendix A for further discussion of extended error information.

C

Practical Batch Files

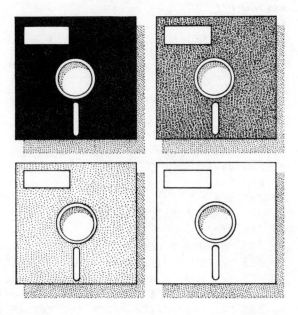

This appendix will show you how to create a menu and five batch files that combine many of the principles discussed in this book. The material presented here will provide you with ideas for customizing MS-DOS to suit your own needs. It also will demonstrate to you the convenience and flexibility offered by MS-DOS batch files.

The batch files given here require MS-DOS 2.00 or later versions. Since these batch files will be used during booting, you will need to store them on a diskette that has been formatted with the MS-DOS system files. The diskette must also contain the MS-DOS files SORT.EXE, MORE.COM,

TREE.COM, and CHKDSK.COM because these files will be utilized by the batch files. The menu and batch files will require approximately 3,000 bytes of disk storage space. (Please refer to chapter 5 for a discussion of MS-DOS batch files and to chapters 3 and 6 for a discussion of the commands used in these batch files.)

Before creating the batch files, we will use DEBUG to create a menu for controlling the batch files. Enter the DEBUG commands as they appear in the program listings. (DEBUG is discussed in chapter 9.) Note that the program listings assume that the root directory of drive C is used to boot MS-DOS.

```
C>debug
-e 100 ba
-e 14f ba
-f 101 14e 20
-m 100 14f 150
-m 100 19f 1A0
-m 100 23f 240
-m 100 37f 380
-m 100 32f 600
-e 100 c9
-e 14f bb
-f 101 14e cd
-e 240 cc
-e 28f b9
-f 241 28e cd
-e 7e0 c8
-e 82f bc
-f 7e1 82e cd
-e 16f "SAMPLE BATCH FILES"
-e 1c6 "from"
-e 210 "MS-DOS BIBLE"
-e 383 "1. SORT DIRECTORY ALPHABETICALLY (specify drive)"
-e 423 "2. SORT DIRECTORY BY DATE (specify drive)"
-e 4c3 "3. REPORT STATUS OF DISK (specify drive)"
-e 563 "4. EXIT BATCH FILES AND RETURN TO MS-DOS"
-rcx
cx 0000
:730
-n batmenu.txt
-w
Writing 0730 bytes
-q
```

You have just used DEBUG to create a file named "batmenu.txt". This file will serve as a menu for the batch files you are about to create. You can see what the menu looks like by entering the command **type batmenu.txt**.

Now you are ready to create the batch files themselves by using the command "copy con: [*filename*]". (See the discussion of COPY in Part 3 for details.) The first batch file is named AUTOEXEC.BAT and will be used to set the date and time and then display the menu when MS-DOS is booted:

```
C>copy con: autoexec.bat
echo off
cls
date
time
cls
type batmenu.txt
prompt ENTER A NUMBER (follow 1, 2, or 3 with a drive letter) $g
^Z       ←you enter Ctrl-Z
        1 File(s) copied
```

The next batch file is called "1.bat" and uses the MS-DOS filter SORT to alphabetically sort a disk's directory entries according to filenames. The batch file then uses the filter MORE to display one full screen of the sorted directory at a time:

```
C>copy con:1.bat
echo off
cls
prompt $n$g
echo SORTING DIRECTORY ALPHABETICALLY...STANDBY
dir %1: ¦sort ¦more
pause
echo off
cls
type batmenu.txt
prompt ENTER A NUMBER (follow 1, 2, or 3 with a drive letter) $g
^Z
        1 File(s) copied
```

Batch file "2.bat" sorts directory entries by their date stamp. This is accomplished by sorting the directory entries according to the character in column 24 of each entry. The sorted directory is then displayed one screen at a time. This technique requires that all of the date stamps be for the same year. It will not work with different years; for example, 6-12-88 would be listed ahead of 12-14-86.

```
C>copy con: 2.bat
echo off
cls
prompt $n$g
echo SORTING DIRECTORY BY DATE...STANDBY
```

```
dir %1: |sort/+24| more
pause
echo off
cls
type batmenu.txt
prompt ENTER A NUMBER (follow 1, 2, or 3 with a drive letter) $g
^Z
        1 File(s) copied
```

Batch file "3.bat" uses the MS-DOS command CHKDSK to check a disk's status. This batch file also uses the command TREE, along with the filter MORE, to display information about the disk's directory and file structure. The information is listed one screen at a time:

```
C>copy con: 3.bat
echo off
cls
prompt $n$g
echo STATUS OF DISK IN DRIVE %1
echo **************************
vol %1:
chkdsk %1:
pause
cls
echo STRUCTURE OF DIRECTORIES AND FILES OF DISK IN DRIVE %1
echo ******************************************************
tree %1: |more
echo off
pause
cls
type batmenu.txt
prompt ENTER A NUMBER (follow 1, 2 or 3 with a drive letter) $g
^Z
        1 File(s) copied
```

Batch file "4.bat" removes the menu from the screen and displays the standard MS-DOS system prompt. Any MS-DOS command may be entered once the standard prompt has been displayed:

```
C>copy con: 4.bat
echo off
prompt $n$g
cls
^Z
        1 File(s) copied
```

Our final batch file will display the menu whenever we enter the word "menu":

```
C>copy con: menu.bat
echo off
cls
type batmenu.txt
prompt ENTER A NUMBER (follow 1, 2 or 3 with a drive letter) $g
^Z
        1 File(s) copied
```

Having created the menu and the five batch files, you are ready to go. Type **menu** (or reboot your system) to display the menu. Now simply enter a number to select a batch file for execution. You may specify a drive for selections 1 through 3. For example, you might enter 1 B to get an alphabetical listing of the directory in drive B. The batch file selected will be executed on the default drive if you do not specify a drive letter.

D

Code Pages and Code Page Switching

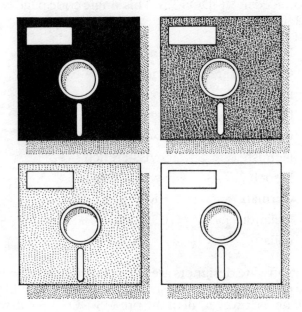

This appendix looks at code pages and the principles and techniques involved in activating, or switching, the code pages. Display devices that support code page switching are listed, and important guidelines from IBM for using code pages are given.

Overview

A *code page* is a table that is used to convert stored numerical data into displayable characters. Designing a single code page that is appropriate for all languages is not possible, since languages differ in the character sets that they require.

Prior to MS-DOS 3.3, there were four different code pages used by MS-DOS. Each copy of MS-DOS had a single fixed code page. Copies of MS-DOS sold in the United States came with a code page appropriate for American English (code page 437). Similarly, copies sold in French Canada or Portugal came with the appropriate code pages (code pages 863 and 860, respectively). Given this situation, problems arose when software written to run with one code page was used with a copy of MS-DOS that had another code page.

To remedy this problem, a multilingual code page (code page 850) was introduced in MS-DOS 3.3. This single code page is designed to transfer data written in the following languages:

Belgian French	Norwegian
Canadian French	Portugese
Danish	Spanish
Dutch	Latin-American Spanish
Finnish	Swedish
Flemish	Swiss French
French	Swiss German
German	UK English
Icelandic	US English
Italian	

Software designers are encouraged now, and in the future, to use code page 850 as the standard, so that their software will have the widest possible audience. However, all of the pre-MS-DOS 3.3 software was written for code pages other than 850. Obviously this software is not going to disappear. To accommodate this base of existing software, *code page switching* was implemented in MS-DOS 3.3.

What Is Code Page Switching?

Many printers and video display adapters support the use of downloadable fonts. This means that users may select character sets to be used with these devices. Code page switching basically allows the user, or the application programmer, to activate a particular code page for use with the display adapter, keyboard, and printer. The remainder of this appendix discusses the principles and the various MS-DOS commands involved in code page switching.

Code Page Switching Must Be Supported

Code page switching can be implemented only on devices that specifically support it. Support is provided in the form of code page information (cpi) files. Currently, there are two display adapters and two printers that support code page switching (table D-1). The code page information files for these devices are supplied with MS-DOS 3.3. The role of the cpi files is discussed in the next section.

Table D-1. Display Devices That Support Code Page Switching

Display Device	CPI File
IBM Proprinter Model 4201	4201.CPI
IBM Quietwriter III Printer Model 5202	5202.CPI
Enhanced Graphics Adapter	EGA.CPI
IBM Convertible LCD Adapter	LCD.CPI

Code page switching also requires support on the device driver level. MS-DOS 3.3 supplies a printer device driver (PRINTER.SYS) and a display driver (DISPLAY.SYS) that support code page switching. The device drivers must be installed in memory prior to implementing code page switching on printer or display devices. Refer to the discussion of DEVICE, in part 3, for details on installing these drivers.

Hardware and Prepared Code Pages

A device that supports code page switching may have one or more code pages built into its hardware. These *hardware code pages* are prepared for use when the device's driver is installed in memory.

Code pages are also generated by the MODE command, using information contained in the cpi files. Code pages generated in this fashion are called *prepared code pages*. As an example, the following command generates code pages 437 and 850 for use by the display device (con). The code pages are generated using the file "ega.cpi":

```
mode con codepage prepare=((437,850) c:\dos\ega.cpi)
```

Refer to part 3 of this book for details on using MODE to generate prepared code pages.

Switching Code Pages

There are three ways in which code page switching is actually carried out: (1) the CHCP command, (2) the MODE command, and (3) MS-DOS function 44H.

The CHCP command is used to select a specific code page for as many devices as possible. For example, the following command selects code page 850 for each device that has a code page 850 available to it:

```
chcp 850
```

Recall from the previous section that code pages are made available to a device in two ways: (1) during installation of the device's driver or (2) through use of the MODE command. The MODE command can also be used to select a specific code page for a particular device. The code page must have previously been made available for the device. The following command selects code page 850 for the display (con) device:

```
mode con codepage select=850
```

The use of CHCP and MODE to select code pages is discussed more thoroughly in part 3 of this book.

Code pages can be selected from an application program by the use of MS-DOS function 44H, subfunction 0CH.

Some Code Page Programming Guidelines

IBM has published a list of guidelines for the applications programmer who uses code pages. Some of the more important guidelines are listed here. For a complete listing, refer to *IBM Personal System/2 Seminar Proceedings* (vol 5, no 6, May 1987).

1. Make sure that application programs will run on machines that do not support code page switching. One way to do this is to limit the characters used in displaying messages to a set of common characters.
2. Restrict the use of graphics characters to those in the common set.
3. If you must use a code page element for a control character, choose one that is not an alphabetic element in any of the code pages.
4. Construct a table of word delimiters that is not code page specific.

A P P E N D I X

E

An Assembly Language Primer

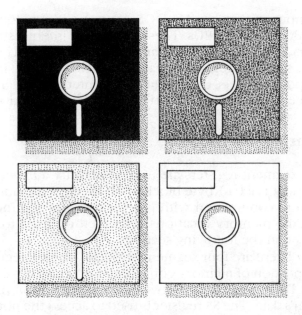

This appendix is provided for those readers with little or no experience with assembly language programming. The information presented here is sufficient to follow chapter 13's presentation of terminate and stay resident programs and chapter 14's presentation of device drivers. You may also wish to consult any of the excellent books available on assembly language programming for PC/XT/AT-type computers.

What Is Assembly Language Programming?

Assembly language programming provides the programmer with direct access to, and control of, memory, the central processing unit (CPU), and the peripheral devices. Assembly language programmers like to say that they are "closer" to the computer than are programmers who use a high-level language (such as BASIC or Pascal). This increased intimacy with the computer allows assembly language programmers to write programs that execute faster and require less memory. In addition, programs that are closely linked to MS-DOS (such as device drivers and TSRs) are generally written in assembly language, since MS-DOS itself is written in assembly language.

The MS-DOS Hardware

Computers that run MS-DOS contain CPUs belonging to the 8088/8086/80x86 family of CPUs. These CPUs have internal storage devices called *registers*. Each register has a name that identifies it. There are six types of registers: segment registers, stack pointer registers, index registers, general-purpose registers, the instruction pointer register, and the flags register. Each of the registers is discussed in the following sections.

Segment Registers

The segment registers are used to identify a *memory segment*. A memory segment is a 64-Kbyte block of contiguous memory. Segment registers are used in conjunction with pointer registers and index registers to identify specific memory locations. The method used to accomplish this is discussed in the following sections.

There are four segment registers. The **CS** register is used to reference the portion of memory containing the program's code (the program itself). The **DS** register is used to access the portion of memory storing the program's data. The **SS** register is used to access the portion of memory known as the *stack*. The stack serves as a temporary storage area for information needed by MS-DOS or the program. The **ES** register is the extra segment register. It has various functions, some of which are discussed here.

Stack Pointer Registers

There are two stack pointer registers. These registers are used, in conjunction with the SS registers, to define the stack. The **SP** register, also called the *stack pointer*, is used, in conjunction with the SS register, to identify the *top of the stack*. Similarly, the **BP** register, also called the *base pointer,* is used, in conjunction with SS, to identify the base (bottom) of the stack.

Index Registers

There are two index registers. The **SI** and **DI** registers (source index and destination index) are used, in conjunction with one of the segment registers, to identify a memory location. SI is generally used with DS, and DI is generally used with ES.

General-Purpose Registers

There are four general-purpose registers: **AX**, **BX**, **CX**, and **DX**. As their class name implies, these registers perform many different functions.

The Instruction Pointer Register

The **IP** register is used, in conjunction with the CS register, to identify the memory location of the next machine instruction to be executed. The manner in which this is accomplished is discussed in the following text.

The Flags Register

The flags register contains nine 1-bit *flags*. These flags are used to record the status of certain machine operations.

Register Storage Capacity

Each of the registers stores 2 bytes, or 16 bits, of data. The general-purpose registers are actually composites of single-byte registers. Thus, AX is composed of AH, which holds AX's high-order byte, and of AL, which holds AX's low-order byte. Similarly, BH, BL, CH, CL, DH, and DL are each 1-byte registers.

Accessing Memory

Memory is accessed by combining the contents of one of the segment registers with one of the other registers. The value stored in the segment register is called the *segment address*. The value stored in the other register is called the *offset address*. The actual physical memory location is computed by multiplying the segment address by 16 and adding the offset.

For example, if CS stores a value of 22BH and IP stores a value of 100H, 22BH is the segment address and 100H is the offset. The physical address referenced by the two registers is computed as follows:

segment * 16 + offset = physical address
22BH * 16 + 100H = 22B0H + 100H = 23B0H

The physical address is usually written as the segment followed by a colon followed by the offset. Thus, in the example this would be:

physical address = segment:offset = cs:ip = 22B:100

Note that numbers in assembly language programs are decimal unless they are followed by an *H* or *h*, in which case they are hexadecimal (base 16).

Assembly Language Statements

Assembly language statements are stored in memory as *machine instructions*. Programs are executed as follows: (1) the instruction at address CS:IP is read and executed, (2) IP is incremented so that CS:IP points to the next instruction, and (3) steps 1 and 2 are repeated until the program terminates.

There are many types of assembly language statements. We will discuss the most common ones here. A *move* (written *mov*) copies data from a register or memory location to another register or memory location. Moves directly from one memory location to another memory location are not allowed. A "mov" is actually a copy, since the original data are unchanged. The following statements illustrate the use of mov.

Statement	Comment
mov ax,bc	;copy contents of register BX into register AX.
mov ax,temp	;copy contents of memory location "temp" in AX.
mov ax,00A2h	;copy a value of A2H into AX.

Compares (written *cmp*) are used to compare the value stored in a register or memory location against a value stored in another register or memory location. The following statements illustrate the use of cmp.

Statement	Comment
cmp ax,bx	;compare the contents of AX to that in register BX.
cmp dx,0060h	;compare the contents of register DX to 60H.

The results of a compare are recorded in the CPU status flags. Compares are used in conjunction with conditional "jumps," which are discussed next.

A *jump* (written *jmp*) is used to direct the computer to a memory location that contains the next instruction to be executed. Generally, instructions are executed in a sequential fashion: after a statement is executed, the statement at the next highest memory location is executed. Jumps provide a mechanism for program execution to branch to nonneighboring memory locations. Jumps are either conditional or unconditional. A conditional jump first checks the settings of the status flags. If they are set in a particular pattern, the jump is executed; otherwise, the jump is not executed. Unconditional jumps are executed without checking the status flags. The following statements illustrate the use of unconditional and conditional jumps.

Statement	Comments
jmp Init	;jump to memory address "Init".
	;this jump is unconditional.
cmp ax,bx	;compare AX contents to BX contents.
je exit	;if the contents are equal, jump to
	;memory address "exit".
cmp cx,0000h	;compare contents of CX to 0000H.
jg loop	;if contents of CX are greater than 0000H,
	;jump to memory address "loop".

A *call* (written *call*) is used to excute a set of instructions called a *procedure*. The first instruction in the procedure will generally have a label that is used as an access device. When a call is executed, MS-DOS places the contents of the IP register on the stack. Placing items on the stack is called a *push*. MS-DOS then places the offset address of the procedure being called in IP, and control is passed to the instruction at CS:IP.

The final statement in any procedure is a *return* (*ret*). This instruction directs MS-DOS to remove the IP value that was stored on the stack. Removing an item from the stack is called a *pop*. When the IP value is popped, execution continues with the instruction immediately following the original call.

A long call is identical to a regular (or short) call with one exception. With a long call, the called procedure lies outside the current code segment. When the long call is executed, MS-DOS pushes both the CS and IP values onto the stack and replaces them with the segment and offset addresses of the called procedure. When the called procedure terminates (with a far return), the old CS and IP values are popped and execution continues at the instruction following the long call.

Invoking an interrupt is similar to a long call, with one exception. Before the CS and IP values are pushed, the value stored in the flags register is pushed onto the stack. When the interrupt handler terminates (with an "iret" statement), CS, IP, and the flags register are popped, and execution continues with the instruction following the interrupt call. Interrupts are discussed further in appendix A.

A P P E N D I X

F

ASCII Cross-Reference Tables

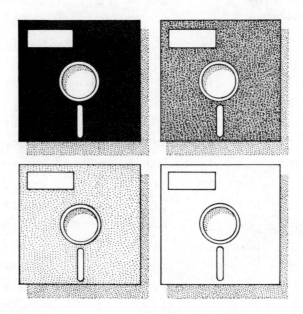

In addition to ASCII (see table F-1) and IBM ASCII extended cross-reference tables (see table F-2), this appendix explains how to convert from decimal to hexadecimal and vice versa. Table F-3 shows the extended ASCII code.

Table F-1. ASCII Cross-Reference

DEC X_{10}	HEX X_{16}	OCT X_8	ASCII	IBM GRA. CHAR.	Terminal Key *
0	00	00	NUL	(null)	< Ctrl-@ >
1	01	01	SOH	☺	< Ctrl-A >
2	02	02	STX	☻	< Ctrl-B >
3	03	03	ETX	♥	< Ctrl-C >
4	04	04	EOT	♦	< Ctrl-D >
5	05	05	ENQ	♣	< Ctrl-E >
6	06	06	ACK	♠	< Ctrl-F >
7	07	07	BEL	●	< Ctrl-G >
8	08	10	BS	▫	< Ctrl-H >
9	09	11	HT	○	< Ctrl-I >
10	0A	12	LF	■	< Ctrl-J >
11	0B	13	VT	♂	< Ctrl-K >
12	0C	14	FF	♀	< Ctrl-L >
13	0D	15	CR	♪	< Ctrl-M >
14	0E	16	SO	♫	< Ctrl-N >
15	0F	17	SI	☼	< Ctrl-O >
16	10	20	DLE	►	< Ctrl-P >
17	11	21	DC1	◄	< Ctrl-Q >
18	12	22	DC2	↕	< Ctrl-R >
19	13	23	DC3	‼	< Ctrl-S >
20	14	24	DC4	¶	< Ctrl-T >
21	15	25	NAK	§	< Ctrl-U >
22	16	26	SYN	—	< Ctrl-V >
23	17	27	ETB	↨	< Ctrl-W >
24	18	30	CAN	↑	< Ctrl-X >
25	19	31	EM	↓	< Ctrl-Y >
26	1A	32	SUB	→	< Ctrl-Z >
27	1B	33	ESC	←	< Esc >
28	1C	34	FS	∟	< Ctrl-\ >
29	1D	35	GS	↔	< Ctrl-` >
30	1E	36	RS	▲	< Ctrl-= >
31	1F	37	US	▼	< Ctrl- ->
32	20	40	SP	(Space)	< SPACE BAR >

Table F-1. (cont.)

DEC X_{10}	HEX X_{16}	OCT X_8	ASCII	IBM GRA. CHAR.	Terminal Key *
33	21	41	!	!	! (Exclamation mark)
34	22	42	"	"	" (Quotation mark)
35	23	43	#	#	# (Number sign or octothorpe)
36	24	44	$	$	$ (Dollar sign)
37	25	45	%	%	% (Percent)
38	26	46	&	&	& (Ampersand)
39	27	47	'	'	' (Apostrophe or acute accent)
40	28	50	(	(	((Opening parenthesis)
41	29	51	)	)	) (Closing parenthesis)
42	2A	52	*	*	* (Asterisk)
43	2B	53	+	+	+ (Plus)
44	2C	54	,	,	, (Comma)
45	2D	55	-	-	- (Hyphen, dash, or minus)
46	2E	56	.	.	. (Period)
47	2F	57	/	/	/ (Forward slant)
48	30	60	0	0	0
49	31	61	1	1	1
50	32	62	2	2	2
51	33	63	3	3	3
52	34	64	4	4	4
53	35	65	5	5	5
54	36	66	6	6	6
55	37	67	7	7	7
56	38	70	8	8	8
57	39	71	9	9	9
58	3A	72	:	:	: (Colon)
59	3B	73	;	;	; (Semicolon)
60	3C	74	<	<	< (Less than)
61	3D	75	=	=	= (Equals)
62	3E	76	>	>	> (Greater than)
63	3F	77	?	?	? (Question mark)
64	40	100	@	@	@ (Commercial at)
65	41	101	A	A	A

Table F-1. (cont.)

DEC X_{10}	HEX X_{16}	OCT X_8	ASCII	IBM GRA. CHAR.	Terminal Key *
66	42	102	B	B	B
67	43	103	C	C	C
68	44	104	D	D	D
69	45	105	E	E	E
70	46	106	F	F	F
71	47	107	G	G	G
72	48	110	H	H	H
73	49	111	I	I	I
74	4A	112	J	J	J
75	4B	113	K	K	K
76	4C	114	L	L	L
77	4D	115	M	M	M
78	4E	116	N	N	N
79	4F	117	O	O	O
80	50	120	P	P	P
81	51	121	Q	Q	Q
82	52	122	R	R	R
83	53	123	S	S	S
84	54	124	T	T	T
85	55	125	U	U	U
86	56	126	V	V	V
87	57	127	W	W	W
88	58	130	X	X	X
89	59	131	Y	Y	Y
90	5A	132	Z	Z	Z
91	5B	133	[	[	[(Opening bracket)
92	5C	134	\	\	\ (Reverse slant)
93	5D	135	]	]	] (Closing bracket)
94	5E	136	^	^	^ (Caret or circumflex)
95	5F	137	_	_	_ (Underscore or underline)
96	60	140	`	`	` (Grave accent)
97	61	141	a	a	a
98	62	142	b	b	b

Table F-1. (cont.)

DEC X_{10}	HEX X_{16}	OCT X_8	ASCII	IBM GRA. CHAR.		Terminal Key *
99	63	143	c	c	c	
100	64	144	d	d	d	
101	65	145	e	e	e	
102	66	146	f	f	f	
103	67	147	g	g	g	
104	68	150	h	h	h	
105	69	151	i	i	i	
106	6A	152	j	j	j	
107	6B	153	k	k	k	
108	6C	154	l	l	l	
109	6D	155	m	m	m	
110	6E	156	n	n	n	
111	6F	157	o	o	o	
112	70	160	p	p	p	
113	71	161	q	q	q	
114	72	162	r	r	r	
115	73	163	s	s	s	
116	74	164	t	t	t	
117	75	165	u	u	u	
118	76	166	v	v	v	
119	77	167	w	w	w	
120	78	170	x	x	x	
121	79	171	y	y	y	
122	7A	172	z	z	z	
123	7B	173	{	{	{ (Opening brace)	
124	7C	174	¦	¦	¦ (Vertical bar; logical OR)	
125	7D	175	}	}	} (Closing brace)	
126	7E	176	~	~	~ (Tilde)	
127	7F	177	DEL	DEL	< Del >	

Table F-2. IBM ASCII Extended Cross-Reference

BINARY X_2	OCT X_8	DEC X_{10}	HEX X_{16}	Ext. ASCII
1000 0000	200	128	80	Ç
1000 0001	201	129	81	ü
1000 0010	202	130	82	é
1000 0011	203	131	83	â
1000 0100	204	132	84	ä
1000 0101	205	133	85	à
1000 0110	206	134	86	å
1000 0111	207	135	87	ç
1000 1000	210	136	88	ê
1000 1001	211	137	89	ë
1000 1010	212	138	8A	è
1000 1011	213	139	8B	ï
1000 1100	214	140	8C	î
1000 1101	215	141	8D	ì
1000 1110	216	142	8E	Ä
1000 1111	217	143	8F	Å
1001 0000	220	144	90	É
1001 0001	221	145	91	æ
1001 0010	222	146	92	Æ
1001 0011	223	147	93	ô
1001 0100	224	148	94	ö
1001 0101	225	149	95	ò
1001 0110	226	150	96	û
1001 0111	227	151	97	ù
1001 1000	230	152	98	ÿ
1001 1001	231	153	99	Ö
1001 1010	232	154	9A	Ü
1001 1011	233	155	9B	¢
1001 1100	234	156	9C	£
1001 1101	235	157	9D	¥
1001 1110	236	158	9E	P_t
1001 1111	237	159	9F	ƒ
1010 0000	240	160	A0	á

Table F-2. (cont.)

BINARY X_2	OCT X_8	DEC X_{10}	HEX X_{16}	Ext. ASCII
1010 0001	241	161	A1	í
1010 0010	242	162	A2	ó
1010 0011	243	163	A3	ú
1010 0100	244	164	A4	ñ
1010 0101	245	165	A5	Ñ
1010 0110	246	166	A6	a̲
1010 0111	247	167	A7	o̲
1010 1000	250	168	A8	¿
1010 1001	251	169	A9	⌐
1010 1010	252	170	AA	¬
1010 1011	253	171	AB	½
1010 1100	254	172	AC	¼
1010 1101	255	173	AD	¡
1010 1110	256	174	AE	«
1010 1111	257	175	AF	»
1011 0000	260	176	B0	░
1011 0001	261	177	B1	▒
1011 0010	262	178	B2	▓
1011 0011	263	179	B3	│
1011 0100	264	180	B4	┤
1011 0101	265	181	B5	╡
1011 0110	266	182	B6	╢
1011 0111	267	183	B7	╖
1011 1000	270	184	B8	╕
1011 1001	271	185	B9	╣
1011 1010	272	186	BA	║
1011 1011	273	187	BB	╗
1011 1100	274	188	BC	╝
1011 1101	275	189	BD	╜
1011 1110	276	190	BE	╛
1011 1111	277	191	BF	┐
1100 0000	300	192	C0	└
1100 0001	301	193	C1	┴

Table F-2. (cont.)

BINARY X_2	OCT X_8	DEC X_{10}	HEX X_{16}	Ext. ASCII
1100 0010	302	194	C2	⊤
1100 0011	303	195	C3	⊦
1100 0100	304	196	C4	—
1100 0101	305	197	C5	+
1100 0110	306	198	C6	⊨
1100 0111	307	199	C7	⊩
1100 1000	310	200	C8	⊾
1100 1001	311	201	C9	⌐
1100 1010	312	202	CA	⊥
1100 1011	313	203	CB	⊤
1100 1100	314	204	CC	⊩
1100 1101	315	205	CD	=
1100 1110	316	206	CE	⊹
1100 1111	317	207	CF	⊥
1101 0000	320	208	D0	⊥
1101 0001	321	209	D1	⊤
1101 0010	322	210	D2	⊤
1101 0011	323	211	D3	⌊
1101 0100	324	212	D4	⊢
1101 0101	325	213	D5	⌐
1101 0110	326	214	D6	⊓
1101 0111	327	215	D7	╫
1101 1000	330	216	D8	╪
1101 1001	331	217	D9	⌐
1101 1010	332	218	DA	⌐
1101 1011	333	219	DB	■
1101 1100	334	220	DC	▬
1101 1101	335	221	DD	▮
1101 1110	336	222	DE	▮
1101 1111	337	223	DF	▬
1110 0000	340	224	E0	α
1110 0001	341	225	E1	β
1110 0010	342	226	E2	Γ

Table F-2. (cont.)

BINARY X_2	OCT X_8	DEC X_{10}	HEX X_{16}	Ext. ASCII
1110 0011	343	227	E3	π
1110 0100	344	228	E4	Σ
1110 0101	345	229	E5	σ
1110 0110	346	230	E6	μ
1110 0111	347	231	E7	τ
1110 1000	350	232	E8	Φ
1110 1001	351	233	E9	Θ
1110 1010	352	234	EA	Ω
1110 1011	353	235	EB	δ
1110 1100	354	236	EC	∞
1110 1101	355	237	ED	ϕ
1110 1110	356	238	EE	ϵ
1110 1111	357	239	EF	$\cap$
1111 0000	360	240	F0	$\equiv$
1111 0001	361	241	F1	$\pm$
1111 0010	362	242	F2	$\geq$
1111 0011	363	243	F3	$\leq$
1111 0100	364	244	F4	$\lceil$
1111 0101	365	245	F5	$\rfloor$
1111 0110	366	246	F6	$\div$
1111 0111	367	247	F7	$\approx$
1111 1000	370	248	F8	$\circ$
1111 1001	371	249	F9	$\cdot$
1111 1010	372	250	FA	$\cdot$
1111 1011	373	251	FB	$\sqrt{}$
1111 1100	374	252	FC	η
1111 1101	375	253	FD	^{2}
1111 1110	376	254	FE	$\blacksquare$
1111 1111	377	255	FF	(blank 'F')

* Those key sequences consisting of "< Ctrl– >" are typed in by pressing the CTRL key and, while it is being held down, by pressing the key indicated. These sequences are based on those defined for the IBM Personal Computer series keyboards. The key sequences may be defined differently on other keyboards. IBM Extended ASCII characters can be displayed by pressing the <Alt> key and then typing the decimal code of the character on the keypad.

Abbreviations:
        DEC = Decimal (Base 10)
        HEX = Hexadecimal (Base 16)
        OCT = Octal (Base 8)
        ASCII = American Standard Code for Information Interchange

Table F-3. Extended ASCII Code

Key(s) Pressed	Extended ASCII Code Generated	Key(s) Pressed	Extended ASCII Code Generated
F1	0,59	Ctrl-F1	0,94
F2	0,60	Ctrl-F2	0,95
F3	0,61	Ctrl-F3	0,96
F4	0,62	Ctrl-F4	0,97
F5	0.63	Ctrl-F5	0,98
F6	0,64	Ctrl-F6	0,99
F7	0,65	Ctrl-F7	0,100
F8	0,66	Ctrl-F8	0,101
F9	0,67	Ctrl-F9	0,102
F10	0,68	Ctrl-F10	0,103
Shift-F1	0,84	Alt-F1	0,104
Shift-F2	0,85	Alt-F2	0,105
Shift-F3	0,86	Alt-F3	0,106
Shift-F4	0,87	Alt-F4	0,107
Shift-F5	0,88	Alt-F5	0,108
Shift-F6	0,89	Alt-F6	0,109
Shift-F7	0,90	Alt-F7	0,110
Shift-F8	0,91	Alt-F8	0,111
Shift-F9	0,92	Alt-F9	0,112
Shift-F10	0,93	Alt-F10	0,113

Hexadecimal to Decimal Conversion

Figure F-1 shows how the hexadecimal number 7D2F is converted to its decimal equivalent:

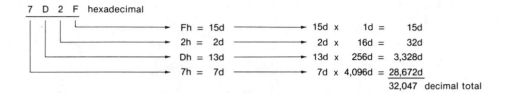

Figure F-1. Converting a hexadecimal number to decimal.

Each hexadecimal digit is always 16 times greater than the digit immediately to the right.

Decimal to Hexadecimal Conversion

The process is reversed when you convert decimal numbers to hexadecimal. Start by selecting the leftmost digit and determine its significance in the number (thousands, hundreds, etc.). Then the decimal is divided by the hexadecimal value of the first digit's relative position. That is, if the first digit is in the thousands position, divide by 4,096 (hexadecimal equivalent of 1,000 decimal). The result is the first hexadecimal digit. Then the remainder is divided by the hexadecimal value of the next digit's relative position (for example, divide the hundreds digit by 256 because 256 is the hexadecimal equivalent of 100 decimal). Figure F-2 shows how the decimal number derived in the previous example is converted back to hexadecimal.

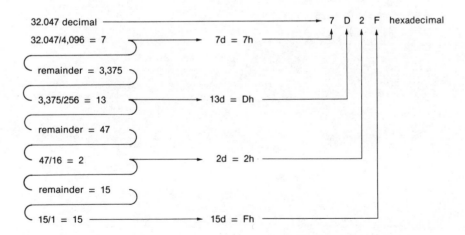

Figure F-2. Converting a decimal number to hexadecimal.

Index

The Waite Group's MS-DOS Developer's Guide, Second Edition

John Angermeyer, Kevin Jaeger, The Waite Group

Expanding upon the first edition, *MS-DOS Developer's Guide* covers the MS and PC DOS operating systems, concentrating on techniques for developing applications programs. Ideally suited for programmers, developers, and "power users," the book highlights the specifics of the operating system's internal behavior which is so essential to system integration and software development.

This revised guide includes special emphasis on undocumented DOS functions as well as coverage of MS-DOS file structures and their differences.

Topics covered include:

- Tools for Structured Coding
- The Design and Implementation of Modular Programs
- Program and Memory Management
- Real-Time Programming
- Installable Device Drivers
- Writing Programs for the Intel 8087/80287 Math Coprocessor
- LANs and MS-DOS
- Disk Layout and File Recovery Information
- Recovering Data Lost in Memory
- Differences Between MS-DOS Versions
- High-Level Languages
- Debugging Techniques
- Microsoft Windows
- Appendices: Development Tools, Bibliography, ASCII Cross-Reference and Number Conversions, Product Enhancements

550 Pages, 7½ x 9¾, Softbound
ISBN: 0-672-22630-8
No. 22630, $24.95

The Waite Group's Understanding MS-DOS®

Kate O'Day and John Angermeyer, The Waite Group

MS-DOS is a very powerful and intricate operating system with millions of users. This operating system can be explored by beginning programmers in a hands-on approach, at the keyboard.

Understanding MS-DOS introduces the use and operation of this popular operating system for those with little previous experience in computer hardware or software. The fundamentals of the operating system such as EDLIN, tree-structured directories and pathnames, and such advanced features as redirection and filtering are presented in a way that is easy-to-understand and use.

Topics covered include:

- Organizing Data into Files
- Redirecting Input and Output
- Using the Text Editor EDLIN to Create and Edit Files
- Using Commands to Manage Files
- Special Function Keys and Key Combinations
- Creating Batch Files of Often Repeated Commands
- Create and Use Tree Structured Directories

300 Pages, 7 x 9, Softbound
ISBN: 0-672-27067-6
No. 27067, $17.95

The Waite Group's Tricks of the MS-DOS® Masters

John Angermeyer, Rich Fahringer, Kevin Jaeger, and Dan Shafer, The Waite Group

This title provides the personal user (not necessarily the programmer or software developer) with a wealth of advanced tips about the operating system and tricks for using it most successfully.

Also included are advanced tips on using popular software packages such as WordStar.®

Topics covered include:

- Secrets of the Batch File Command Language
- Secrets of Pipes, Filters, and Redirection
- Secrets of Tree-Structured Directories
- Discovering Secrets: A Debugger Tutorial
- Secrets of DOS Commands
- Secrets of Files
- Secrets of Free and Low-Cost Software
- Secrets of Add-on Software, Boards, and Mass Storage
- Secrets of System Configuration
- Secrets of Data Encryption

568 Pages, 7½ x 9¾, Softbound
ISBN: 0-672-22525-5
No. 22525, $24.95

The Waite Group's Discovering MS-DOS®

Kate O'Day, The Waite Group

This comprehensive study of MS-DOS commands such as DEBUG, LINK, and EDLIN begins with general information about operating systems. It then shows how to use MS-DOS to produce letters and documents; create, name, and manipulate files; use the keyboard and function keys to perform jobs faster; and direct, sort, and find data quickly.

It features a command summary card for quick reference.

Topics covered include:

- Introduction to MS-DOS
- What is a Computer System?
- What is an Operating System?
- Getting MS-DOS off the Ground
- System Insurance
- Editing
- Filing
- Batch Files
- Paths
- Input/Output
- Hard Disks
- Appendices: Error Messages, Reference Card

296 Pages, 7½ x 9¾, Softbound
ISBN: 0-672-22407-0
No. 22407, $19.95

Visit your local book retailer, use the order form provided, or call 800-428-SAMS.

MS-DOS® Papers
Edited by The Waite Group

A collection of tutorials written by a diverse selection of experts, *MS-DOS Papers* presents some of the lesser-known features of MS-DOS. It provides additional insight into the operating system for programmers, developers, and "power-users" in an interesting and easy-to-read format.

The book includes such topics as inside BIOS, terminate and stay resident programming, and advanced MASM. The material has been compiled by recognized experts and "gurus" in the computer industry. Although tutorial in nature, the book is an excellent reference on each of the various aspects of the MS-DOS operating system.

Topics covered include:

- A Fast File Search Utility
- PCnix: A UNIX-like Shell
- Adding Power with Batch Language and MS-DOS Programming
- Advanced MASM Techniques
- Undocumented DOS Functions
- Terminate and Stay Resident Programming
- Data and File Security Techniques
- The Spy Utility: Investigating Windows
- DOS Services for Device Drivers
- Sounder: A Musical Device Drive
- Programming the EGA
- C Serial Port Programming
- Enhanced Memory System (EMS)

400 Pages, 7½ x 9¾, Softbound
ISBN: 0-672-22594-8
No. 22594, $26.95

Hard Disk Management Techniques for the IBM®
Joseph-David Carrabis

This is a resource book of in-depth techniques on how to set up and manage a hard disk environment directed to the everyday "power user," not necessarily the DOS expert or programmer.

Each fundamental technique, based on the author's consulting experience with Fortune 500 companies, is emphasized to help the reader become a "power user." This tutorial highlights installation of utilities, hardware, software, and software applications for the experienced business professional working with a hard disk drive.

Topics covered include:

- Introduction to Hard Disks
- Hard Disks and DOS
- Backup and What You Need to Know
- Service and Maintenance
- Setting Up a Hard Disk
- Organizing a Hard Disk
- Hard Disk Managers
- Utilities to Find Files, Get Overlays, unERAse Files, Recover Damaged Files, Speed Up Disk Access, and Restore and Backup Disks
- Maintenance Utilities
- File Security Utilities
- Security Utilities

250 Pages, 7½ x 9¾, Softbound
ISBN: 0-672-22580-8
No. 22580, $22.95

IBM® PC AT User's Reference Manual
Gilbert Held

Includes everything you need to know about operating your IBM PC AT—how to set the system up, write programs that fully use the AT's power, organize fixed-disk directories, and use IBM's multitasking TopView.

Includes a BASIC tutorial for beginners and includes several fixed disk organizer programs—all clearly described, explained, and illustrated.

Topics covered include:

- Hardware Overview
- System Setup
- Storage Media and Keyboard Operation
- The Disk Operating System
- Fixed Disk Organization
- BASIC Overview
- Basic BASIC
- BASIC Commands
- Advanced BASIC
- Data File Operation
- Text and Graphics Display Control
- Batch and Shell Processing
- Introduction to TopView
- Appendices: ASCII Code Representation, Extended Character Codes, BASIC Error Messages, Programming Tips and Techniques

453 Pages, 7 x 9¼, Softbound
ISBN: 0-8104-6394-6
No. 46394, $29.95

IBM® PC & PC XT User's Reference Manual, Second Edition
Gilbert Held

Expanded to include the more powerful PC XT, this second edition contains the most up-to-date information available on the IBM PC. From setup through applying and modifying the system, this book continues to provide users with clear, step-by-step explanations of IBM PC hardware and software—complete with numerous illustrations and examples.

Highlights of the second edition include instructions for using DOS 3.1 and upgrading a PC to an XT; information on the customized hardware configuration of the PC and XT; explanations on how to load programs on a fixed disk and how to organize directories; and material on available software, including compilers.

Topics covered include:

- Hardware Overview
- System Setup
- Storage Media and Keyboard Operation
- The Disk Operating System
- Fixed Disk Organization
- BASIC Overview
- BASIC Commands
- Data File Operations
- Text and Graphics Display Control
- Batch Processing and Fixed Disk Operations
- Audio and Data Communications
- Introduction to TopView
- Appendices: ASCII Code Representation, Extended Character Codes, BASIC Error Messages, and Programming Tips and Techniques

496 Pages, 7 x 9¼, Softbound
ISBN: 0-672-46427-6
No. 46427, $26.95

Visit your local book retailer, use the order form provided, or call 800-428-SAMS.

The Waite Group's Desktop Publishing Bible
James Stockford, Editor

Publish high-quality documents right on your desktop with this "bible" that tells you what you need to know— everything from print production, typography, and high-end typesetters, to copyright information, equipment, and software.

In this collection of essays, experts from virtually every field of desktop publishing share their tips, tricks, and techniques while explaining both traditional publishing concepts and the new desktop publishing hardware and software.

Topics covered include:

- Publishing Basics: Traditional Print Production, Conventional Typography, Case Studies in Selecting a Publishing System, and a Comparison of Costs for Desktop and Conventional Systems
- Systems: The Macintosh, PC, MS-DOS, An Overview of Microsoft Windows, Graphics Cards and Standards, Monitors, Dot and Laser Printers, UNIX, and High-End Work Stations
- Software: Graphics Software, Page Layout Software, Type Encoding Programs, PostScript, and JustText
- Applications: Newsletters, Magazines, Forms, Comics and Cartooning, and Music

480 Pages, 7½ x 9¾, Softbound
ISBN: 0-672-22524-7
No. 22524, $24.95

Personal Publishing with PC PageMaker®
Terry M. Ulick

Here is everything you need to know about PC PageMaker to design publications. It shows you how to select and use type, work in multicolumn and multipage layouts, create graphs, and merge text with graphic elements.

Hands-on instruction at the terminal, numerous visual examples, and a detailed explanation of typesetting terms provide the information necessary to help the beginning to intermediate PC user produce attractive copy.

Topics covered include:

- Assembling a Personal Publishing System
- Selecting the Right Hardware and Software
- Pages on the IBM®
- Electronic Page Assembly
- Working with Type
- PostScript™ and LaserJet Plus™ TypeStyles
- Formatting Type
- Working with PageMaker
- Building Master Pages
- Placing Elements on a Page
- Adding Graphic Elements
- Linking PageMaker Files
- Printing Page Files
- High-Volume Printing
- Multicolored Pages
- Grids and Sample Pages

304 Pages, 7½ x 9¾, Softbound
ISBN: 0-672-22593-X
No. 22593, $18.95

Micro-Mainframe Connection
Thomas Wm. Madron

Focusing on the organizational environment, this book explores the opportunities, technologies, and problems involved in implementing the transfer of data between the mainframe and the micro workstation—more comprehensively than any other book on the market.

Designed to help managers and technical support people design and implement micro-mainframe networks, it gives complete information about features, facilities, and requirements, including cost considerations.

Topics covered include:

- The Micro-Mainframe Link
- Features, Facilities, and Problems in the Micro-Mainframe Connection
- Local Area Networks in the Micro-Mainframe Connection
- Micros as Mainframe Peripherals: Mainframes as Micro Peripherals
- Micros and IBM® Mainframes in a Synchronous Network
- Asynchronous Devices in a Synchronous Network: Protocol Conversion
- File Transfer
- Data Extraction, Data Format, and Application Specific File Transfers
- Making the Micro-Mainframe Connection

256 Pages, 7½ x 9¾, Hardbound
ISBN: 0-672-46583-3
No. 46583, $29.95

The Waite Group's Modem Connections Bible
Curtis and Majhor

This book describes modems, how they work, and how to hook ten well-known modems to nine name-brand computers. A handy Jump Table shows where to find the appropriate connection diagram and applies the illustrations to eleven more computers and seven additional modems. It also features an overview of communications software, an explanation of the RS-232C interface, and a section on troubleshooting.

Topics covered include:

- Types of Modems
- How Modems Work
- Connecting Equipment
- The RS-232 Connector
- The Progress of a Call
- Full Duplex and Half Duplex Mode
- Types of Communications Programs
- Features and Uses
- Voice/Data Switching
- How to Read the Charts
- Jump Table
- Appendices: Types of Online Services and Costs, The RS-232C Interface, Further Reading, Glossary, Troubleshooting, Communications Software for Microcomputers

192 Pages, 7½ x 9¾, Softbound
ISBN: 0-672-22446-X
No. 22446, $16.95

Visit your local book retailer, use the order form provided, or call 800-428-SAMS.